GOSUB WITHOUT RETURN

Between the Lines of the
BASIC Programming Language
(Beginner's All-purpose Symbolic Instruction Code)

Mark Jones Lorenzo

SE BOOKS
Philadelphia | Pittsburgh

Ψ

SE BOOKS
5307 West Tyson Street
Philadelphia, Pennsylvania 19107
www.sebooks.com

Library cataloging information is as follows:

Lorenzo, Mark Jones
  GOSUB without RETURN : between the lines of the BASIC programming language (Beginner's All-purpose Symbolic Instruction Code)/ Mark Jones Lorenzo.
  p. ; cm.
  Includes bibliographical references.
  I. Title
1. Basic (computer programming language). 2. History (computers). 3. Programming (computers).
  QA76.19 C22 2022
  005.1331'53718—js22

ISBN: 979-8-843-01704-0

10 9 8 7 6 5 4 3 2 1

GOSUB WITHOUT RETURN

$$\nrightarrow$$

BASIC programmers never die, they GOSUB and don't RETURN.

—UNKNOWN

CONTENTS

INTRODUCTION

Imagine a visit to the BASIC Museum. Not one that's virtual, but an actual, physical, real-life museum. Granted, such a brick-and-mortar structure doesn't exist (yet), but put that inconvenient fact out of your mind for this thought experiment.

On a brisk fall morning, the golden and brown leaves falling gently off the trees, you arrive at the doorstep of a four-story brick building, situated at the periphery of the Dartmouth College campus in bucolic New England. The BASIC Museum beckons.

You swing open the door and are greeted at the front desk with a floor map detailing the exhibits. On the ground level, the birth of the language is the focus; perhaps the first floor's theme is "BASIC in the 1960s" or "BASIC and the DTSS (Dartmouth Time-Sharing System) on Mainframes." On the second level, you can explore how BASIC spread outside of Dartmouth; the theme might be "BASIC in the Early 1970s" or "BASIC on Minicomputers." Travel up to the third floor, and you'll learn how BASIC became a centerpiece of the microcomputer revolution; "BASIC in the Late 1970s and the 1980s" or "BASIC on Microcomputers" will probably be the theme. Finally, on the top level, you can peruse exhibits documenting the rise of Visual BASIC and other GUI BASICs; the likely theme is "BASIC in the 1990s and Beyond" or "BASIC in an Interconnected World." But the fourth floor devotes a fair amount of space to the decline of the language as well, featuring educational offerings like COMAL, FOCAL, Logo, Pascal, Scratch, Python, the Raspberry Pi, and the micro:bit, all nipping away at BASIC's heels, ever-eager to replace it.

In the book *Endless Loop*, you took a guided tour of the BASIC Museum, starting on the ground level and finishing on the fourth floor with BASIC celebrating its fiftieth birthday. Spending only a couple of hours inside the museum, you saw all the major exhibits, heard a few short lectures, shuttled between collections of artifacts, but didn't linger for long in any one area. Effectively, you took a survey course on BASIC. Stopping by the gift shop on the way out, you were back at the hotel in time for some sightseeing around Hanover, capped off by an early dinner.

A year passed. Then two years. Then three. You kept meaning to get back to New England, and back to the museum, but there was always something that came up preventing your return. Some responsibility you had to take care of, some obligation you needed to fulfill. A pandemic hit, further delaying another visit. But finally, your calendar is free, the weather is clear, and the time is right. So you make the trip once again.

As you drive due north on the interstates and highways, you review a mental list of ten questions you've had about BASIC. Questions that either weren't addressed, or were not fully answered, when visiting the museum five years ago. Questions that seemed to, at first, percolate up from the dark depths of your subconscious like little dust bunnies but then grew over time into monstrously thick cobwebs littering your mind—so thick, in fact, that it became painful to think about BASIC knowing that the answers to these questions might be secreted in a museum hundreds of miles away and workaday obligations impeded another visit. But no longer.

You arrive at your hotel, drop off your belongings, and then make a beeline to the BASIC Museum, only several blocks away. Though it's offered, you don't want the guided tour this time. No, you want to explore on your own, at a leisurely pace. Even if you don't see every exhibit or hear every lecture, you'll trade that for the opportunity to investigate the answers to your ten all-consuming questions, to pore over the details and focus intently even on the ephemera, to see where the journey might lead—even if that journey isn't linear but is instead circuitous, a path filled with tangents and potholes and cul-de-sacs. As you explore, you'll devote the needed time to unlocking BASIC's best-kept secrets. It won't be a survey course this time around. No, during this visit to the museum, you will specialize to your heart's content. You'll pull out all the stops, venturing between the lines of BASIC to answer these ten critical questions:

1. Why did BASIC arise at Dartmouth but not elsewhere?
2. What led to the design decisions for BASIC and the DTSS (Dartmouth Time-Sharing System)?
3. Did computing pioneer Sister Mary Kenneth Keller help create Dartmouth BASIC?
4. Why did the formal standardization of BASIC fail?
5. Did Microsoft develop TI BASIC for the Texas Instruments 99/4 home computer?
6. How did the emergence of "computer literacy" spell the end of BASIC?
7. Why did BASIC explode in popularity in the United Kingdom in the 1980s?
8. What can we learn from the 1980s Usborne BASIC books?
9. How does GW-BASIC generate pseudorandom numbers?
10. Can a BASIC interpreter be written using a BASIC interpreter?

In short, you are ready to **GOSUB** without **RETURN**ing to your hotel until you learn the elusive answers to these questions and, in the process, clear the cobwebs from your mind.

Endless Loop traced BASIC's rise, fall, and central role in the history of computing. This book offers a complementary but very different reading experience by narrowing the scope and sharpening the focus, revealing the story of a language in unprecedented detail; expect to tread over new ground as we mine the deepest recesses and map the outermost reaches of BASIC territory. In addition, though BASIC's center of gravity has always been firmly planted in the United States, BASIC resonated with users in many other countries as well; therefore, anticipate an international flavor to the proceedings.

Each chapter in GOSUB WITHOUT RETURN investigates a single question—except for the first and third chapters, which both deal with two.

Chapter 1, "When BASIC Ruled Campus," explores why only Dartmouth College had the right set of ingredients for BASIC's birth, while also tracing the reasoning behind a number of language and time-sharing design decisions. Chapter 2, "BASIC Sainthood," centers on the disputed account of Sister Mary Kenneth Keller's ostensible participation in the development of Dartmouth BASIC. Chapter 3, "Fiddling While BASIC Burned," documents the causes leading up to the failure of BASIC's formal language standardization while simultaneously describing even more of those fateful early language-design decisions. Chapter 4, "Lone Star Mystery," attempts to pin down Microsoft's involvement, if any, with TI BASIC for Texas Instrument's TI-99/4 home computer. Chapter 5, "Computer Literacy and Its Discontents," examines how BASIC was displaced in the educational arena. Chapter 6, "The UK Connection, Part I," takes a deep dive into the spread of BASIC in the United Kingdom, while Chapter 7, "The UK Connection, Part II," follows up with a thorough survey of the 1980s Usborne BASIC Books. Chapter 8, "Open Source," peels back the layers of several GW-BASIC source files in an effort to understand the language's method of pseudorandom number generation. Finally, Chapter 9, "Calisthenics and Orthodontia Redux," builds a new BASIC interpreter using an old BASIC interpreter.

All nine chapters are a blend of historical, biographical, and technical elements, with the last three chapters in particular more heavily weighted toward technical explorations. (Full programs and snippets of code, which make frequent appearances throughout the text, are displayed in one of two fonts: `Consolas` for BASIC as well as time-sharing commands, and `Courier New` for everything else.)

Although they can be read in any order, it is probably best to start with the first chapter in order to learn about the origins of BASIC and the DTSS, especially if you are unfamiliar with the history. Otherwise, feel free to jump—or rather GOSUB—around the book, without any obligation to RE...well, you know.

GOSUB WITHOUT RETURN

$$\rightleftharpoons$$

CHAPTER 1

WHEN BASIC RULED CAMPUS
<u>The Birth and Rise of the Language</u>

Why did BASIC arise at Dartmouth but not elsewhere?
What led to the design decisions for BASIC and the DTSS?

The story of BASIC—the Beginner's All-purpose Symbolic Instruction Code—has become the stuff of legend, a grand technology creation myth originating not in Silicon Valley but at modest Dartmouth College in Hanover, New Hampshire, in the early 1960s. The brainchild of two Dartmouth mathematics professors, John G. Kemeny and Thomas E. Kurtz, BASIC was taught to millions of students in the second half of the twentieth century—and, in the process, eventually satisfied a democratic vision of computing for all.

At first, though, Kemeny and Kurtz's vision was highly circumscribed: open-access computing only for students at Dartmouth, who happened to be all male and mostly white at the time. That lack of diversity was not entirely by design. The college's history stretched back centuries, prior to the founding of the Republic, when comprehensive educational opportunities were offered by the institution not only to "English Youth and Others" but also to "Youth of the Indian Tribes" in New England.

In the twentieth century, the paths that brought both Kemeny and Kurtz to the storied Dartmouth campus were circuitous. Kemeny arrived at Hanover by way of Princeton, where he had earned a doctorate in mathematics under the logician Alonzo Church. (Kemeny also audited a number of courses in philosophy, nearly earning a master's in the discipline.) Years before, however, at only eighteen years old, and not having yet completed his undergraduate degree at Princeton, Kemeny was drafted and shipped to Los Alamos. While there, he worked grueling shifts on the Manhattan Project with physicist Richard Feynman, helping to build the first atomic bomb. Working six days a week, Kemeny frequently used IBM bookkeeping calculators as mechanical aids for his computations.

After the war, Kemeny traveled back to his alma mater to pursue a doctorate. While writing his dissertation, he served as a research assistant to Albert Einstein at the Institute for Advanced Study (IAS) for three or four days per week; at the time, Einstein's energies were consumed by unified field theory: unifying the general theory of relativity with electromagnetism. The young doctoral student checked many of Einstein's calculations—"many long calculations, deriving one formula from another to solve a differential equation," recalled Kemeny—later claiming that the greatest scientist of the twentieth century simply "wasn't very good at math." (This quotation has been widely misunderstood. It wasn't that Einstein struggled with mathematics, it was just that "he was not an up-to-date research level mathematician," Kemeny explained.)

Kemeny also had frequent run-ins at the IAS with John von Neumann, a mathematician who helped develop the earliest computers. They were simpatico, partly because of their common backgrounds: both from Hungary, both of Jewish descent, and both transplants to the United States, arriving prior to the outbreak of World War II. And like von Neumann, Kemeny would later work at the RAND Corporation in Santa Monica, California, but only for a short time.

Kemeny, while walking with Einstein at the IAS one day, encountered von Neumann. Einstein was disappointed with the elder Hungarian mathematician, accusing him of "[making] the wrong kind of computer. Why don't you invent a computer that would help me in my work? I don't need a numerical computer." Einstein wanted a machine that could do more than arithmetical calculations at lightning speed; rather, he envisioned a computer that could perform symbolic manipulation, such as finding derivatives and integrals at the press of a button. Von Neumann assured him that computers would one day be able to accomplish those feats—and much more.

Before his formative experiences at the Institute for Advanced Study, Kemeny was worried that mathematicians and physicists had to become peculiar—in terms of personality and disposition—in order to become great. But together, Einstein and von Neumann disabused Kemeny of that notion. Both men were quite normal. In fact, "Einstein was the kindest, nicest human being I ever met in my life," Kemeny remembered.

Kemeny refused to intellectually pin himself down to just one discipline, teaching both mathematics and philosophy for several years at Princeton until finally decamping to Hanover. When Kemeny arrived at Dartmouth in 1953—he was lured there by the dean of faculty, Donald Morrison, who worried that too many professors were near retirement age—there were no computers on campus. Despite this, Dartmouth's history with computing was storied. In 1940, Bell Telephone Laboratories researcher George Stibitz successfully demonstrated remote computing using a Teletype Model 26. In 1956, the computer scientist John McCarthy ran an extended summer conference on artificial intelligence at the college. (McCarthy's definition of AI: "machines that can perform tasks that are characteristic of human intelligence.") That same year, the New England Regional Computer Center (also referred to as the New England Computation Center) opened at MIT, fully stocked with IBM equipment—including Big Blue's state-of-the-art mainframe, an IBM 704.

After taking a sabbatical his first year, Kemeny quickly acquired a fair share of institutional power at Dartmouth, rising to chairmanship of the mathematics department within two years of his hire date. Von Neumann and Einstein, speaking highly of the young upstart, were influential in helping Kemeny land the position; a recommendation from Princeton mathematician Albert W. Tucker helped as well.

As chairman, Kemeny shifted the focus of the mathematics department toward research. He also cleaned house, hiring a number of new faculty members, among them Thomas Kurtz. Born on February 22, 1928, in Oak Park, Illinois, Kurtz remained in the state to earn an undergraduate degree in mathematics from Knox College in Galesburg. Then he traveled to Princeton University to study under the renowned statistician John W. Tukey.

Tukey was an iconoclastic thinker, prodigious writer, and certainly the person most responsible for the full flowering of the subdiscipline of statistics called data analysis. He brought to bear more than just intellect and logic; Tukey examined data with unparalleled mathematical instincts. But he was also a great teacher. A thesis advisor to fifty-six students, he went out of his way to help his charges carry out their own independent research. One of those students was Frederick Mosteller, who would go on to a successful career as a statistician in his own right. Tukey's interactions with Mosteller, unlike those with Kurtz, are well documented. When Mosteller was writing his dissertation, he would seek out Tukey for suggestions; Tukey would take measure of the problem at hand, and then suggest "something entirely different to work on," recalled Mosteller. He prodded his pupil to move forward and discover fresh approaches, even if they resulted in whole new sets of questions to answer. "Boundaries between disciplines, organizations, and people never lasted long in his mind, for he thought in terms of bridges, entrances, and opportunities," remembered Mosteller.

In the early-to-middle 1950s, when Kurtz studied under Tukey, the Princeton professor was consumed with the so-called *problem of multiple comparisons*. Simply stated: If we have multiple hypotheses for a single data set that we wish to test simultaneously, we cannot simply perform the significance tests separately without controlling for the fact that these tests will find significant results by chance alone at a higher rate than anticipated. For example, if the probability of observing a significant result due to chance alone is five percent (i.e., the significance level $\alpha = 0.05$), then the probability of observing at least one significant result due to chance alone among ten hypothesis tests (that are all not significant) on the same data grows to about forty percent (which is calculated as $1 - 0.95^{10} = 0.401$). More compactly, we can term this problem one of *multiplicity* which, early in the decade, Tukey was at the forefront of addressing; to that end, he wrote a three-hundred-page manuscript called "The Problem of Multiple Comparisons" that treated the topic of simultaneous inference in substantial depth, and his approach continues to guide applications and research in the field in the twenty-first century. Thomas Kurtz's dissertation under Tukey, completed in 1956, was titled "An Extension of Multiple Comparisons Procedure."

Like John Kemeny, John Tukey was a true generalist who stitched together ideas from numerous disciplines, including computing. He also had a proclivity for fashioning neologisms. New concepts often required new words with which to speak about them, after all. As Charles Petzold writes in *Code: The Hidden Language of Computer Hardware and Software* (2000),

Sometime around 1948, the American mathematician John Wilder Tukey (born 1915) realized that the words *binary digit* were likely to assume a much greater importance in the years ahead as computers became more prevalent. He decided to coin a new, shorter word to replace the unwieldy five syllables of *binary digit*. He considered *bigit* and *binit* but settled instead on the short, simple, elegant, and perfectly lovely word *bit*.

With a love of language also came an affinity for mystery paperbacks and especially science fiction, with Tukey losing himself in stories like "Incommunicado" (1950) by Katherine MacLean. Set on a space station near Pluto, the plot hinges on the uniquely musical means of communication between resident workers and the station's computer. "Incommunicado" resonated with scientists at places like Bell Labs—Tukey split his time between Princeton University and Bell—not only because of the story's exploration of advanced computing technology but also because it emphasized the importance of intuition when uncovering scientific truth, including in the realm of data analysis. "As a scientist and investigator you can never give over your responsibilities as a thinking, judging, noticing, feeling person," Tukey warned. He believed scientific knowledge was "not reducible to mechanical mathematical procedure," explained Alexander Campolo in an article about the statistician published in the University of Chicago Press Journal *KNOW: A Journal on the Formation of Knowledge*. Instead, "Tukey emphasized the empirical, provisional character of scientific knowledge…."

We can infer that even though Tom Kurtz likely worked on his dissertation mostly independently, he was almost certainly influenced not only by Tukey's mathematical, statistical, and other interdisciplinary interests (e.g., on issues related to the problem of multiple comparisons), but also by Tukey's instinctual behaviors toward technical matters—relying on subjective, idiosyncratic judgments colored by deep experience rather than leaning on checklists and pat algorithms operating under the guise of objectivity. "Again and again [Tukey] warned against the dangers of optimization and the powerful but ultimately illusory attraction of quantitative precision in the computerized Cold War sciences," Campolo added. "Better, in his words, 'to be approximately right' than 'exactly wrong.'"

Though Kurtz had been a student at Princeton while Kemeny taught there, they never crossed paths. "[In 1956] I was recruited [to Dartmouth] to teach statistics, among other things," Kurtz told interviewer John Szczepaniak in 2012, "and it turned out that IBM, MIT, and UCLA were establishing regional computer centers in the East and the West." To earn him some extra money, the new professor was designated a "research associate" in this computation project, requiring Kurtz to take a course on SAP, the low-level Symbolic/SHARE Assembly Program for the IBM 704, at MIT before teaching his first class at Dartmouth. He took naturally to computing, later admitting that if computer science had been an option while he was a student, he would have pursued the discipline.

Kemeny and Kurtz were simpatico almost immediately. Toiling away on the top floor of Dartmouth Hall, they wrote computer programs by hand for the IBM 704 installation at MIT's New England Regional Computer Center, one of several thousand computer installations in the United States in the late 1950s that were found mostly at university, military, and business sites. Their programs were coded in SAP and format-ted onto punched cards to be fed into the hopper of the machine. Although Kurtz gained experience writing programs while still a student at Princeton, Kurtz and Keme-ny more or less learned SAP together. (Kurtz was first exposed to computing at a 1951 summer program at the National Bureau of Standards Institute for Numerical Analysis located at UCLA, an institution then in the midst of building the vacuum-and-William tubes hybrid machine called SWAC—the Standards Western Automatic Computer. Kurtz wrote a program on SWAC that calculated the tail probabilities of statistical dis-tributions. Ken Iverson, also a student at the summer program, later developed the programming language APL.)

Every two weeks, Kurtz took a steel box filled to the brim with SAP punched cards on a train to MIT. (Kurtz and others on campus didn't have to submit their handwrit-ten programs to keypunch operators; rather, they could punch their own cards, since Dartmouth had IBM keypunch equipment available.) Living in a world of batch pro-cessing, where only one program ran to completion (or premature termination) at a time, Kurtz had to wait his turn: after handing off the punched cards to the machine operator, he would then be forced to whittle away the daylight hours—Kurtz would pass the time by connecting with fellow professors at MIT or Harvard, or wandering leisurely through Cambridge—before the IBM 704 generated printouts, which he took back to Dartmouth. Kurtz would make the trip several times a month, hoping against hope that the programs were error-free.

Thanks to the long turnaround time, a month passed before Kurtz realized that one particular SAP program he wrote didn't work as intended. The young Dartmouth pro-fessor had done everything to optimize the code, including excising repeat calculations and even employing the 704's sense lights found on the front panel of the machine, which were typically used as program flags.

Though SAP was a product of a brilliant computer engineer named Roy Nutt, Ke-meny in particular was dissatisfied with the assembly language's lack of user friendli-ness. One of computer scientist Alan J. Perlis's famous "epigrams on programming" effectively captured the difficulties of using SAP: "A programming language is low level when its programs require attention to the irrelevant." If SAP's complexity made it dif-ficult even for fellow academics to understand, then students didn't stand a chance of learning it, Kemeny believed.

So, Kemeny set out to design a simpler version of SAP, calling it DARSIMCO, for DARtmouth SIMplified COde. DARSIMCO grouped SAP operations, like loops and arithmetic calculations, into *templates*, or sequences of three instructions at a time. To add quantities stored in A and B and then place the result into C, a programmer would key in the following:

```
LDA  A
FAD  B
STO  C
```

But DARSIMCO faded from the scene quickly for two reasons. First, the Dart-mouth faculty failed to make much use of it. And second, FORTRAN (FORmula

TRANslation) was released less than a year after DARSIMCO—and the language up-ended the nascent computing industry.

Developed at IBM over a three-year period in the mid-1950s, FORTRAN was the first high-level computer language to attain significant widespread usage. High-level lan-guages (HLLs) hide, automate, or otherwise abstract away the gory details involving the underlying operations of processors, offering natural- and algebraic-language forms as alternatives to coding in a low-level fashion with zeros and ones or the mnemonics of assembly languages. FORTRAN made it relatively straightforward and intuitive for en-gineers, scientists, and mathematicians—namely, those familiar with algebraic equa-tions—to program a computer; specifically, FORTRAN was designed for the IBM 704, but platform-independent implementations followed. The HLL leveled the playing field: if you knew mathematics, you could learn to program in FORTRAN. There was no need to understand the mechanics of how, precisely, the computer managed memory or otherwise operated.

Programming in FORTRAN was much, much easier than squeezing out code in SAP. It was also significantly more user friendly than DARSIMCO, bringing "compu-ting to a wider audience," admitted Kurtz. Indeed, mathematician John Backus, who led the IBM team that developed FORTRAN, realized that the language, which spread quickly to Dartmouth as well, was antithetical to the designs of the computing gate-keepers. "Just as freewheeling westerners developed a chauvinistic pride in their fron-tiersmanship and a corresponding conservatism," he later wrote, "so many program-mers of the freewheeling 1950s began to regard themselves as members of a priesthood guarding skills and mysteries far too complex for ordinary mortals." FORTRAN was the equivalent of nailing Ninety-five Theses to the church door: the priesthood was put on notice.

But it would be Kemeny and Kurtz who ultimately triggered a Reformation, liberat-ing programming from an oppressive authority of experts—but it wouldn't be with FORTRAN. The Dartmouth duo were wary of FORTRAN and held it at arm's length, at least for a while. "[A]cceptance [of FORTRAN] was tempered by its alleged ineffi-ciency in comparison to assembly language," Kurtz said. But his opinion of FORTRAN changed once he used it. Kurtz needed to program a challenging statistical problem on the 704; by force of habit, he coded it in assembly since he, too, was swayed by the conventional wisdom: that FORTRAN was woefully inefficient and therefore not a suitable replacement for low-level coding. Kurtz tried for months on end, tinkering with the problem, trying to coax the program into running properly—all to no avail. In a fit of desperation, he rewrote the program in FORTRAN, not paying any particular attention to issues of efficiency or optimization. And all it took was about five minutes of computer time until the 704 spit out a printout of the statistical prob-lem's answer. Reflecting on the experience years later, Kemeny said that "[t]his lesson that programming in higher level languages could save computer time as well as person time—impressed me deeply…. For klutzes like me, one had to use higher level lan-guages."

Nineteen fifty-nine would mark the installation of a permanent computer at Dartmouth. That year, Kemeny and Kurtz shopped around for suitable hardware before settling on the LGP-30 (Librascope General Precision). The eight-hundred-pound air-cooled desk computer was a binary (base 2), magnetic drum-based (rotating at 3700 RPM), 32-bit word (including *sign bit* and *spacer bit*, the latter demarcating words on the drum and treated as zero in memory; therefore, only thirty-one bits were available for programs), 4K memory (on the drum, there were sixty-four tracks each containing sixty-four sectors for a total of $64 \times 64 = 4096$, or 2^{12}, 31-bit words), fixed-point, single-address machine.

Developed by Stanley Frankel at Caltech as the MINAC, Frankel's design was purchased by Librascope and put into production in 1956 by Librascope's parent company, General Precision Equipment Corporation (GPE), partnering with the Royal McBee Corporation, a major typewriter manufacturer. The LGP-30, requiring little more than one hundred vacuum tubes—with only twenty-four tubes dedicated to the CPU, or central processing unit—interfaced with an electric typewriter for input/output, plugged into a standard wall socket, and featured sixteen instructions.

The *instruction set* is enumerated below, including the *code letters* for each command (i.e., the *mnemonics*, or short English abbreviations for the low-level instructions; on the electric typewriter, keys for these code letters were color-coded in white, while the remaining keys were painted brown). (Note: In the following description, an *accumulator* refers to a special type of register that temporarily holds the intermediate results of calculations, while the letter *m* designates an arbitrary memory location. The LGP-30 boasted three registers: an accumulator, a control counter register, and an instruction register. Since there was no index register or indexing capabilities to speak of, implementing *self-modifying code*—code that rewrote itself during execution—was necessary.)

- BRING (b): replace the accumulator's contents with those in *m*.
- ADD (a): sum the contents of the accumulator with the value held in *m*, storing that result in the accumulator.
- SUBTRACT (s): compute the difference between the contents of the accumulator and the value held in *m*, storing that result in the accumulator.
- MULTIPLY (m for fractional, n for integral): obtain the product of the contents in the accumulator and the value held in *m*; if fractional multiplication, then terminate the product at thirty binary places and store the most significant half of the result in the accumulator; if integral multiplication, then store the least significant half of the product in the accumulator.
- DIVIDE (d): compute the quotient of the contents of the accumulator and the value held in *m*, storing the result in the accumulator; round to thirty bits.
- HOLD (h): store the accumulator's contents in *m* but do not clear the accumulator's contents.
- CLEAR (c): store the accumulator's contents in *m* and then clear the accumulator's contents.

- STORE ADDRESS (y): capture the address portion of the word in the accumulator and store it in *m*, but do not touch the remainder of the word in *m*.
- RETURN ADDRESS (r): Add 1 to the contents of the control counter register, and then replace the address in *m* with the contents of the control counter register.
- EXTRACT (e): change any digits in the accumulator to zero to match the positions of existing zeros in *m* (the word stored in *m* is called the *extract mask*), leaving the remainder of the contents of the accumulator unaffected.
- TRANSFER CONTROL (u): transfer control to *m* unconditionally, obtaining the next instruction from *m*.
- TEST (t): transfer control to *m* conditionally—only if the contents of the accumulator are negative.
- INPUT (i): gather data from the electric typewriter and store it in the accumulator.
- PRINT (p): output a symbol on the electric typewriter.
- STOP (z): either terminate the program unconditionally or terminate it conditionally based on five *break point switches* found on the machine's control panel.

Notice that instead of instructions to directly perform *bit shifts*, which transposed binary representations of numbers left or right—the effective equivalent of multiplying or dividing the binary values by a factor of two—the LGP-30 offered instructions for multiplication and division.

The *Electronic Computer LGP-30 Programming Manual* (1957) offered an example program illustrating how the LGP-30's single-operand instructions—particularly, the bring, multiply, add, and hold instructions—could be strung together to evaluate the expression $(((a_0 x + a_1)x + a_2)x + a_3)x + a_4$.

addr	instr	operand	result (notes)
1000	b 2002	a 2005	initial add instruction
1001	c 1005	.	
1002	h 2000	zero	initialize working storage
1003	b 2000	working storage	
1004	m 2004	x	
1005	a (2005)	a_n	
1006	h 2000	working storage	intermediate and final results
1007	b 1005	a (2005 + n)	
1008	a 2001	1 at 29	
1009	h 1005	a (2005 + n+1)	
1010	s 2003	a 2010	flag
1011	t 1003	.	
1012	h 2000	final result	
1013	r 3050	.	
1014	u 3000	print routine	
1015	z 000	.	

```
2000      working storage
2001      1 at 29
2002      a 2005
2003      a 2010
2004      x
2005      a0
2006      a1
2007      a2
2008      a3
2009      a4
```

The output subroutine, beginning at address 3000, is not shown.

A 1960 advertisement for the LGP-30, printed in the periodical *Datamation*, boasted that its

> [i]nternal components have been greatly reduced to insure highest operating reliability. The logic circuit and few etched circuit cards are easily removed for checkout and maintenance. *and*…The LGP-30 operates from any wall outlet, [and] requires no site preparation. With its simplified command structure, the LGP-30 is the easiest computer to program and operate. It is delivered complete with tape typewriter for alpha-numeric input-output. An extensive library of programs and sub-routines is available.

Money to purchase the computer, which cost around thirty-seven thousand dollars, was creatively reallocated from funds earmarked for the construction of Dartmouth's Bradley Hall, the future home of the mathematics department and one of the two Shower Towers north of Elm Street on campus (Gerry Hall was the other "tower"). The LGP-30 purchase was classified as part of "Furniture and Decorations," an existing provision of the Bradley Hall budget.

That summer, Kemeny and Kurtz invited a handful of undergrads to test out what Kurtz playfully dubbed "the new toy." The students took to it like ducks to water, with some even joining a users' group for the machine. In only a few weeks, physics major Robert Hargraves programmed DART, a FORTRAN-like compiler for the LGP-30. A *compiler* translated *source code*, human-readable instructions written by a programmer, into *object code*, machine language instructions generated by the compilation. Although limited—simplified arithmetic expressions, replete with parentheses, was about all it could handle—DART caught the attention of both Kemeny and Kurtz, who noted that a "good undergraduate student could achieve what at the time was a professional-level accomplishment, namely, the design and writing of a compiler. The observation was not overlooked."

The LGP-30 even attracted students from nearby universities. Edgar T. Irons, a Princeton student, wrote a syntax-directed compiler on the machine—thereby inspiring Kemeny, Kurtz, and the Dartmouth undergraduates to investigate ALGOL 58, an influential high-level language jointly developed by American and European computer scientists (including, among them, John Backus). ALGOL (ALGOrithmic Language), which offered support for structured programming, was developed in part as a response to the deficiencies of FORTRAN, but it was never widely adopted in the United States. Mathematician Richard "Dick" Hamming, best known for developing error-correcting codes, explained why FORTRAN survived and flourished while ALGOL withered on the vine and died. FORTRAN, he said in a 1995 talk on the history of computer software, was a "psychological language. They [John Backus and his team at IBM] designed it to fit *people*," while ALGOL was, by contrast, "designed logically"—a surefire recipe for failure.

A team of four Dartmouth undergrads—Hargraves, Steve Garland, Jorge Llacer, and Anthony Knapp—led by Kurtz began writing an ALGOL 58 compiler for the LGP-30. But then they shifted course when the ALGOL 60 specifications were released, preferring to model their compiler on the newer version of the language instead. Kurtz and company simplified ALGOL 60, eliminating recursion, strings, variable array bounds, and arrays called by value. Strict limits had to be placed on for loops as well, with their compiler only able to employ around a third of the LGP-30's word memory. Parameters, however, could be called by name using something they termed "thunks." The team christened their creation ALGOL 30.

Though ALGOL 30 was only a subset of ALGOL 60, its biggest limitation involved compilation speed: the compiler required two passes through the source code, and the relocatable binary code equivalent had to be punched on paper tape. Because the compilation time was interminable, a load-and-go system—which would compile and then execute a program—was needed. Enter SCALP, the Self Contained ALgol Processor designed by Kurtz, Garland, and Knapp. Using it, at least five student jobs could be run in around fifteen minutes, which was many times faster than FORTRAN on the IBM 704. (Although, in fairness, by this point FORTRAN was typically used on more advanced hardware than the 704.)

Meanwhile, Kemeny was busy at work on his own language project for the LGP-30. Called DOPE (Dartmouth Oversimplified Programming Experiment), he employed the help of undergraduate Sidney Marshall, who was enrolled in a calculus course at the time. DOPE foreshadowed BASIC in several key ways. For one thing, DOPE appropriated certain elements of FORTRAN, such as built-in mathematical functions, the unconditional jump, and the three-way conditional statement. In addition, DOPE's input formats, line numbers for jumps, and variable-naming conventions—involving a single alphabetic letter or a letter followed by a single digit—were later adopted for BASIC.

DOPE automatically numbered lines of code sequentially, from 1 to 99; the DOPE programmer wasn't permitted to number lines by 5s or 10s, for instance. As they would in BASIC, line numbers functioned as statement labels, with the T operation serving as the pre-**GOTO** unconditional jump. And loops were available to use as well, although they were more limited than BASIC's, with the counter incrementing by one unit per iteration being the only option.

In a recent article for *Vice*, software developer, podcaster, and author Sean Haas describes how he managed to track down DOPE, becoming "one of the few people to run a DOPE program in nearly 60 years. The language is strange," he writes, "but undeniably shows the skeleton of BASIC starting to form." Haas discovered a file folder containing a paper on DOPE dated 1962. "The paper describing DOPE was also never published," he notes. "Partly, because it wasn't really a formal language description. Instead it was part primer, part lesson plan. Students were being used as guinea pigs on the path to a better programming language."

Realizing he had to find a way to use the language in order to understand it, Haas set out to write his own DOPE interpreter—by using the "DOPE paper [which] laid bare all the details of the language, example problems, logical diagrams, and every idiosyncrasy." Lines of DOPE had the same structure as BASIC lines: they started with a line number, continued by featuring an operation, and then ended with arguments; Haas separated each line of his interpreter into tokens based off this simple, and predictable, structure. However, BASIC would offer more flexibility than DOPE; for example, as Haas discovered, while mathematical expressions could be coded directly in BASIC—such as LET A=1+1—because the expressions were classified as arguments, in DOPE

> that same BASIC statement, just adding 1 and 1, comes out to "+'1'1'A". That's not very pretty, is it? Superficially, DOPE looks a lot more like assembly language than anything else. Most operations are a single character, each line can only perform a simple operation, argument lists are all of a fixed length. All the usual operations for math, assignment, loops, and printing are present, just in a consolidated form.

Note the single quotation marks, rather than spaces, serving as the delimiter. (In his 2012 article for *Game Developer* magazine celebrating the forty-eighth anniversary of BASIC, John Szczepaniak offered the DOPE code example 5 + A B C, which added the quantities stored in A and B and placed the result into C. But as Haas explains, "The other fun complication is the matter of single quotes. DOPE doesn't separate things with spaces, as near as I can tell this is due to its host hardware.")

What's more, DOPE couldn't handle strings, and only floating-point variables were available. The variables named E, F, G, and H served as arrays that could each store a maximum of sixteen numbers. Not finding much rhyme or reason behind why these particular four letters were set aside, Haas makes an educated guess as good as any: "E, F, G, and H were hardcoded as arrays since those are common names for vectors in physics, but that's just a shot in the dark. For a newcomer it's just an arbitrary rule. Kemeny and Kurtz were right to ditch this one [when writing BASIC]."

Clearly, neither DOPE—nor ALGOL 30, for that matter—was user friendly enough to roll out to undergraduates without technical expertise. The Kurtz Papers (dated 1962) reveal, however, that DOPE purposely served as an experiment in teaching freshman the basics of programming "in a course of three one-hour lectures," paving the way for a larger-scale approach to educating students that was just over the horizon.

In the early 1960s, only around a quarter of Dartmouth undergrads majored in engineering or science. Yet, as Kemeny and Kurtz realized, "the nonscience group produce[d] most of the decision makers of business and government." Meaning that future U.S. leaders likely wouldn't recognize the importance of computers, not having been exposed to the machines while in college. "How can sensible decisions about computing and its use be made by persons essentially ignorant of it?" they wondered.

As noted by technology writer Steve Lohr, Kemeny and Kurtz's perspectives on the divide between the sciences and the humanities was influenced by a famous Rede Lecture delivered in 1959 at Cambridge University by chemist C. P. Snow. Called "The Two Cultures," Snow described a "gulf of mutual incomprehension" between scientific thinkers on the one hand, and literary intellectuals—those "natural luddites"—on the other; since he frequented both worlds, Snow found himself uniquely qualified to describe the cultural split.

> For constantly I felt I was moving among two groups—comparable in intelligence, identical in race, not grossly different in social origin, earning about the same incomes, who had almost ceased to communicate at all, who in intellectual, moral and psychological climate had so little in common that instead of going from Burlington House or South Kensington to Chelsea, one might have crossed an ocean.

He fingered the intellectual miscommunication between these "two polar groups" as a "problem of the entire West," not just the United Kingdom. "It is the traditional culture, to an extent remarkably little diminished by the emergence of the scientific one, which manages the Western world," noted Snow. He then refined the point:

> A good many times I have been present at gatherings of people who, by the standards of the traditional culture, are thought highly educated and who have with considerable gusto been expressing their incredulity at the illiteracy of scientists. Once or twice I have been provoked and have asked the company how many of them could describe the Second Law of Thermodynamics. The response was cold: it was also negative. Yet I was asking something which is the scientific equivalent of: *Have you read a work of Shakespeare's?*

Snow urged schools to offer a corrective: less specialization and more preparation for a world remade by the scientific revolution. He also praised the American and Russian educational systems, with both superpowers taking radical steps to adjust to the new state of affairs—at least as compared to Britain's inertia. The upshot of Snow's analysis was simple: "politicians, administrators, an entire community, [need to] know enough science to have a sense of what the scientists are talking about."

Thanks to literary critic F.R. Leavis's (partly ad hominem) critique of "The Two Cultures," which was also delivered as a lecture and published in *The Spectator*, Snow's argument became well known. "The Two Cultures" was symptomatic of a widespread existential crisis that had befallen the humanities in the face of the dominance of *positivism*, the notion that the truth of the world derived from the natural sciences.

Especially concerned with scientific literacy, John Kemeny referenced "The Two Cultures" in his 1983 article "The Case for Computer Literacy," published in *Daedalus*—"not because I think his [Snow's] essay is that great," Kemeny told an interviewer, "but [because] his basic point is fundamental."

> It is not just that we are split into humanistic and scientific cultures—this is more applicable to the United States than to the England for whom he wrote it—but the terribly dangerous thing is that most scientists admit that a well-educated person should know literature, or music or whatever, while the humanistic culture is not willing to concede that understanding science is part of being a cultured individual. I think that is where the great danger comes.

Of course, there are so many internal, external, and indirect influences baked into the authorship of any programming language that to try to disentangle them all is a fool's errand, since even the language's creators themselves might not know precisely why they made particular decisions. To claim otherwise is to profess a kind of auteur theory, albeit for computer language developers rather than film directors.

Regardless of what influenced them, by the early 1960s, Kemeny and Kurtz had arrived at a decision: Every Dartmouth undergraduate must be taught computing, one way or another. A lecture format, with an instructor at the front of the classroom, wouldn't suffice. Instead, students had to be made to *use* a computer—and that meant writing programs, with all the attendant joys, frustrations, and technical training therein. "Lecturing about computing doesn't make any sense, any more than lecturing on how to drive a car makes sense," explained Kurtz.

But which programming language should be taught to Dartmouth students? Assembly language was too arcane, too complicated, for the non-mathematically inclined, which left ALGOL and FORTRAN as the only viable alternatives. Yet Kemeny and Kurtz had significant reservations about both these high-level languages. "The majority [of students]," Kurtz realized, "would balk at the seemingly pointless detail" of these HLLs, the pickiness of FORTRAN's variable typing (i.e., variables specially designated as either integer or floating point) being a prime example. Kurtz warned that "[n]o nonobvious punctuation, like the ALGOL semicolon to terminate statements, or the mysterious FORTRAN IF [A] 100, 200, 300," could be part of any teaching language at the college.

"Kemeny and Kurtz had no intention of making Dartmouth a training group for professional programmers," Steve Lohr explains in his book *Data-ism: Inside the Big Data Revolution* (2015). Training the undergraduates to be generalists was their goal.

> They wanted to give their students a feel for interacting with these digital machines and for computational thinking, which involves analyzing and logically organizing data in ways so that computers can help solve problems. The Dartmouth professors weren't really teaching programming. They were trying to change minds, to encourage their students to see things differently.

By the early 1960s, Kemeny and Kurtz had developed a four-part plan to change those minds. First, they would dispense with punched cards in exchange for time-sharing terminals. *Time-sharing*, which permitted multiple users to share a computer's resources simultaneously, was relatively new. John McCarthy, who in 1961 delivered an MIT centennial lecture called "Time-Sharing Computer Systems"—publicly arguing for a time-sharing system that could simulate each user having his own "large private computer" on demand—demonstrated the cutting-edge technology to Kurtz at MIT using a Digital Equipment Corporation PDP-1 computer. "Why don't you guys do time sharing?" John McCarthy suggested to Kurtz. Excited by the prospect, Kurtz parroted McCarthy by telling Kemeny, "I think we ought to do time sharing." The mathematics department chairman simply replied, "OK."

Kemeny was amenable to the time-sharing concept because he realized that teaching students programming on a batch-processing system was a nonstarter. When Kemeny consulted for RAND, "some of the world's most famous scientists [would] stand in line for an hour to get five seconds of computing time." Maybe these famous scientists could tolerate such abuse, but Dartmouth students would never stand for it (quite literally). "[O]nly the most hardy student could persevere through the actual experience of running programs on the typical batch-processing system then in vogue," Kemeny and Kurtz argued in a 1968 article appearing in *Science* magazine titled "Dartmouth Time-Sharing." "The debugging (error-correcting) process usually requires a large number of tries before the problem is successfully solved. If it takes on the order of 1 day for one try, the student will either lose interest or forget what the problem was."

Time-sharing didn't originate with John McCarthy, who worked at MIT with computer scientist Fernando José Corbató to build one of the first time-sharing systems: the Compatible Time-Sharing System (CTSS). (In fact, when studying potential time-sharing designs, Kurtz would communicate with Corbató in late 1961.)

Rather, IBM employee Robert "Bob" William Bemer, often called the "Father of ASCII," wrote a paper in 1957 on the feasibility of time-sharing after seeing the term in a paper on the MIT Lincoln Laboratory TX-2 computer. (Originating in the 1960s, ASCII, which stands for American Standard Code for Information Interchange, is a character set designed to facilitate the exchange of data between electronic machines.) Management at Big Blue, though, was not pleased with Bemer's proposed time-sharing system, considering it not "in line with their policy," and he was nearly fired for writing the paper.

But time-sharing was an idea whose time had come. In a January 1, 1959, five-page memorandum written to MIT physicist Philip M. Morse about a proposed time-sharing system for the IBM 709 (the mainframe was due to arrive at the MIT Computation Center within a year), McCarthy noted that he had "not seen any <u>comprehensive</u> written treatment of the time-sharing problem and [had] not discussed the problem with anyone who had a complete idea of the problem." However, McCarthy also made clear that "the equipment required for time-sharing is well understood, [and] is being developed for various advanced computers e.g. Stretch TX2, Metrovich 1010, Edsac 3." The memo sketched out, in some detail, the problems that needed solving in order to make time-sharing function efficiently on the 709, including obtaining "[i]nterrogation and display devices" like Flexowriters (teleprinters) as well as "[a]n exchange to mediate between the computer and the external devices. This is the most substantial engineering problem, but IBM may have solved it." There were also issues with programming the system, such as memory allocation and "[r]ecovery from stops and loops."

Despite initial opposition to Bemer's concept, IBM brass reversed course and developed its own time-sharing system called Quiktran (sometimes spelled "QUIKTRAN" or even "QUICKTRAN" in the literature), supporting forty users simultaneously by employing IBM 7040/44 scientific computers using the IBM 1050 Data Communications System terminal. Development of Quiktran began in 1961, led by the long-time IBMer John Morrissey. By 1963, the time-sharing system was up and running. Users interacted with Quiktran via a FORTRAN interpreter, which offered debugging features and terminal control.

It is with Quiktran that we likely see the first "command mode" (or "desk calculator" mode), in which each statement entered by the user is run with results immediately displayed on the terminal, and a "program mode," in which statements are stored and only executed once the user keys in a separate command. (The JOSS programming language, running off the JOHNNIAC computer built by the RAND Corporation, had a similar two-mode environment, but probably did not predate Quiktran.)

Executable statements were stored as Polish strings (in Polish notation), which were "created by using a bi-directional 'forcing table,' which was also used to recreate the source," explained computer scientist Frances Allen in "The History of Language Processor Technology in IBM." "Because of this capability and because the language was standard FORTRAN, a program could be debugged using this system, and then recreated for compilation by a standard FORTRAN compiler."

IBM conducted a demonstration of Quiktran at Dartmouth one afternoon, temporarily installing a single terminal in the Teletype room. But much to the company's embarrassment, even after two hours of work Big Blue employees couldn't manage to convince their "little program" to run, recalled Dartmouth time-sharing operator Nancy Broadhead.

Besides Quiktran, a number of other time-sharing systems arose in the 1960s, some which used traditional mainframe computers while others employed minicomputers from Digital Equipment Corporation's PDP line.

Minicomputers were compact, general-purpose machines significantly smaller and less expense than large-scale mainframes, although they still cost thousands of dollars. The 1970s brought about the microcomputer revolution. As early as 1973, proto-micros like the Intel 8008-based SCELBI (which ran a version of BASIC called SCELBAL), the MCM/70, and the Micral appeared; some micros were available in fully-assembled form, while others came only as do-it-yourself kits. While a minicomputer could be thought of as a scaled-down mainframe, a microcomputer was a small, inexpensive machine housing a CPU contained on a single semiconductor chip. Microcomputers were fully realized personal computers: standalone machines designed for one person.

In their 1968 *Science* article, Kemeny and Kurtz briefly relayed the history of time-sharing systems. "The concept of time-sharing was first realized around 1960 on a small [mini]computer, the Digital Equipment Corporation PDP-1, and was developed jointly by personnel from M.I.T. and from Bolt Beranek and Newman Inc."

Around 1964, a research project at the Massachusetts Institute of Technology led individuals from MIT, General Electric, and Bell Labs to cooperatively build an early mainframe general-purpose time-sharing operating system called Multics, or Multiplexed Information and Computing Service. Multics was written in PL/I (Programming Language One), an HLL that struck a balance between the scientific functionality of FORTRAN and the business data-processing capabilities of COBOL (COmmon Business-Oriented Language).

Multics was successful in part due to programmer Harold W. "Bud" Lawson, who helped write the first COBOL compiler at Remington Rand Univac. Lawson, who left

Univac for IBM in the 1960s, later developed high-level language pointer variables and integrated them into PL/I; they would soon appear in C, C++, and Pascal, among other languages. *Pointers*, which stored the memory addresses of other variables, offered programmers the power to leverage complex data structures. Multics used a number of pointers to great effect.

By the end of the decade, Bell Labs withdrew from the project, while Honeywell took it over. Multics inspired the UNIX operating system, implemented by Dennis Ritchie and Ken Thompson on a DEC PDP-7 minicomputer.

Also in the early 1960s, the electrical engineering company Ferranti supplied their Atlas processing units to the University of Cambridge, whereby an effort headed by computer scientist David Wheeler led to pared down (and marketable) Atlas computers for Ferranti and a prototype called Titan, installed at the university in 1963. By mid-decade, a time-sharing operating system for the university was running on the Titan. Like Multics, Cambridge's time-sharing system was geared toward researchers.

Commercial time-sharing systems were being built by Bolt, Beranek and Newman (BBN), Keydata Corporation, and RAND. But time-sharing at Dartmouth would be focused on the needs of undergraduate students and not be for profit. At the college, punched cards could be avoided courtesy of Teletype Model 33 and 35 terminals interfacing with the computer; ASCII codes would be used to communicate between machines. Programs would be shared by the central computer, each one given a dedicated *time slice*; before a time slice concluded, the program could be interrupted to wait for input. (By the time they penned their 1968 article for *Science* magazine, Kemeny and Kurtz had realized "that any response time which averages more than 10 seconds destroys the illusion of having one's own computer," so they made sure the total number of users on the system would never increase the maximum wait time for any individual user beyond ten seconds, except in rare circumstances.)

Besides the punched cards' fragility, Kemeny and Kurtz were also concerned that students would be "prejudiced against" the cards in part because radical leftist student groups had coopted the infamous warning printed on them: "Do not fold, spindle, or mutilate."

The second part of Kemeny and Kurtz's plan involved developing a programming language. Unlike Kemeny, Kurtz was initially opposed to writing a language from scratch; he believed that a subset of ALGOL (like ALGOL 30) or FORTRAN would be sufficient.

"It was my idea then to say, while we are at it, can't we design a language better than FORTRAN?" Kemeny asked Kurtz. Kemeny was not one to ever play it safe, he admitted later on.

"Yes, but what's the use of teaching a language to Dartmouth students that they will never be able to use anywhere else except at Dartmouth?" Kurtz replied.

"This belief proved wrong," Kurtz later conceded. "Tom was normally farsighted," Kemeny added, "but that was his famous incorrect prediction." To support Kemeny's perspective, consider that FORTRAN's variable typing would be challenging for students not particularly technically adept to understand. What's more, the syntax of loops and conditional statements in FORTRAN was peculiar and tricky to master.

Kemeny and Kurtz needed a true user-oriented language that could, first and foremost, ease in inexperienced users while also offering valuable tools for more advanced ones. The Dartmouth duo certainly did not conceive of this language exploding in popularity, not only on campus but far outside it; never did they consciously intend to create a language that would attain worldwide domination. But they did, early on, realize that their language had to be directed toward more than just beginners—it had to appeal to more experienced programmers as well.

"Very early, then, I agreed with Kemeny that a new language was needed to meet our requirements," he said. BASIC was consciously patterned after FORTRAN; Purdue University computer scientist Saul Rosen tellingly labeled BASIC "like a beginners [*sic*] subset of FORTRAN." (Not everyone agreed with this assessment. In a September 1971 *Datamation* article critiquing BASIC, author Jerry L. Ogdin argued that "BASIC probably more closely resembles ALGOL than FORTRAN.") Though FORTRAN produced highly efficient object code, efficiency wasn't Kemeny and Kurtz's primary goal. A 1963 memorandum by the pair describing the design goals of the new language underscored that point: "In all cases where there is a choice between simplicity and efficiency, simplicity is chosen."

To that end, there were limits to what BASIC would be able to do. In the first Dartmouth BASIC manual, the maximum length of a program was specified imprecisely: "...in general about two feet of teletype paper filled with BASIC statements is about it."

Reflecting on the creation of BASIC decades later in an interview for the book *Masterminds of Programming: Conversations with the Creators of Major Programming Languages* (2009), Kurtz pointed to several "considerations" when designing the language, including:

- "All arithmetic is floating point": Protecting the beginner from the complexities of numeric typing (integer versus float) was part and parcel of the larger project of simplicity.

- "Line numbers are **GOTO** targets": Dartmouth BASIC predated WYSIWYG (What You See Is What You Get) editors, so, functionally, assigning statements line numbers solved a number of logistical issues. "Inventing a new concept of 'statement label' didn't seem like a good idea to use," Kurtz said. Plus, FORTRAN had a GO TO statement, and "the thing [an unconditional jump] was important at the time because that was how people wrote programs for computers in machine language and assembly language."

- "One line, one statement": Having one, and only one, statement per line was paramount. That way, punctuation denoting the end of a line—such as the period in the JOSS programming language, or the semicolon in ALGOL—could be avoided. In addition, conventions like the continuation character in FORTRAN, which extended a single statement over more than one punched card, were deemed nonstarters.

In addition to the considerations listed above, Kurtz added that BASIC was, from the beginning, intended to be hardware independent, and also had to be easy to remember so users could recall the basics after long periods of nonuse.

Like FORTRAN, however, BASIC was designed to be a compiled language. By the late 1970s, however, most people programming in BASIC were using an *interpreter*, where a source program was translated, one line at a time, while it was running. Interpreters had a certain cachet: they were considered "interactive." But Kemeny and Kurtz wanted their new language to boast quick compile-to-execution times, while also not bogging down resources of the time-sharing computer by offering real-time identification of syntax errors. Indeed, Dartmouth BASIC would only relay user feedback once a program was run in its entirety, not before—and even that feedback was limited to at most five error messages after each compilation, appearing on a terminal within seconds. (This five-error limit was influenced by Kurtz's difficulties with programming in FORTRAN. "I can recall FORTRAN error printouts many pages in length," he said in *Masterminds of Programming*, "detailing *all* syntax errors in a program, usually from omitting but one key punctuation at the beginning.")

Kurtz hypothesized that BASIC interpreters became popular as the language spread beyond Dartmouth because of an inherent bias against compilers: they were, in general, slow, since most compilers performed multiple passes on source code. But Dartmouth BASIC would perform just a single pass.

Part three of the Dartmouth duo's plan involved the creation of a computing course centered on BASIC. A standalone class was ruled out; there were enough required courses at the college already. Instead, second-term calculus and Finite Mathematics would now have a mandatory lab class featuring application problems that students would have to solve by writing BASIC code. This proved a remarkably successful approach; around eighty-five percent of Dartmouth students would take at least one of the two courses (more detail on the computer-related content of these courses is presented later in the chapter).

The faculty, however, were not uniformly positive about the encroaching technology. Michael Busch, one of the undergraduates who would help program the time-sharing system, recalled that some professors pushed back at the new emphasis on computing as a central feature of the educational experience on campus. "For some years after the system became operational there was a certain level of hostility among certain factions of the faculty," he explained. Busch and fellow undergrad Kevin O'Gorman took a music class; at some point during the term, they were assigned a composition to write. After arranging it, they coded a program to check musical compositions for technical errors (e.g., involving the proper construction of triads). Even if a composition was unpleasing aesthetically, the program would ensure that technically, at least, it was competent. Once the professor realized what Busch and O'Gorman had done, he nearly kicked them out of the class. By the end of the term, though, they had convinced the professor of the benefits of the technological approach. By the 1970s, Dartmouth was leading the way in the study of electronic music, specifically with Professor Jon Appleton's work—which was supported by none other than John Kemeny, who had risen to the post of college president.

Other intrepid students, employing computers to complete homework assignments in a variety of courses, were often met with pushback from their professors. It took several years before the use of computers became an accepted feature of campus life, remembered Busch. Steven Hobbs was a freshman when was Busch was a senior; as a sophomore, Hobbs took a physics class. In the required physics lab, he decided to complete one of the assignments by using a computer. The lab assistant, a graduate student, rebuked him. "Computer? No. You're supposed to be doing this by hand. I don't want to see it." The lab assistant then told the lecturer. Instead of agreeing with the assessment, the lecturer not only told him to *encourage* students to make use of the computer, he instructed the lab assistant to take the two-hour course on how to use the machine offered to faculty members. The culture at Dartmouth had changed.

The fourth and final part of Kemeny and Kurtz's plan involved open access. Modeled after Dartmouth's Baker Library open-stack concept—which offered free, democratized access to knowledge—the pair envisioned a world in which computing was free and accessible to all, no permission necessary and no strings attached. Kemeny was never shy about giving his colleague Tom Kurtz the credit for what was, in those days, a "terribly radical idea," Kemeny later said. Kemeny explained the concept to the public in a mid-1960s brochure titled "The Kiewit Computation Center & The Dartmouth Time-Sharing System" that served as an advertisement for the newly established Kiewit Computation Center (named for millionaire donor Peter Kiewit, who attended Dartmouth for a year):

> We think of our computer as an educational facility comparable to the Baker Library with its open stacks of books. Any student can walk into the library, browse among the books, or take some back to his room. No one asks him why he wants the book, and he does not need anyone's permission. Similarly, any student may walk into the Kiewit Computation Center, sit down at a console, and use the time-sharing system. No one will ask whether he is solving a serious research problem, doing his homework the easy way, playing a game of football, or writing a letter to his girlfriend.

In the brochure, Kemeny unpacks the acronym for BASIC as "Beginner's All-purpose Simplified Instruction Code," rather than "Symbolic." Interestingly, in a chapter he penned for the *Encyclopedia of Physical Science and Technology [3rd ed.]* published in 2001, Kurtz also uses the word "Simplified" in place of "Symbolic." Yet in the pair's definitive book on the development of the language, 1985's *Back to BASIC*, the "S" in BASIC is denoted as "Symbolic." In addition, in one of the many interviews Kurtz would give about BASIC in the years to come, he told freelance gaming journalist John Szczepaniak, "I had already used the word BASIC for a statistics text I wrote several years earlier [i.e., *Basic Statistics*, 1963]. John Kemeny liked acronyms, so we settled on BASIC, for which he devised the expansion…. By the way, it has always been 'Symbolic' and never 'Simplified.'" (Also observe that the apostrophe in the word "Beginner's" in the early days and beyond has sometimes appeared after the letter s, as in "Beginners'" denoting the plural form of the term. In *Back to BASIC*, Kemeny and Kurtz use "Beginner's" rather than the alternative. That is also the convention used here.)

Around this time, Kemeny, a man with wide-ranging interests, was also reimagining libraries. In a talk entitled "A Library for 2000 A.D." delivered at the MIT centennial (and reprinted in the 1962 book *Computers and the World of the Future*, edited by Martin Greenberger), Kemeny predicted how "our university libraries will be obsolete by 2000 A.D." With present (1960s) libraries growing exponentially in size, "unless one knows the exact name of an author (including initials) or unless one knows the exact title of a book," for example, "it may become hopeless to locate it." Kemeny underscored the point by presenting a timeline of his recent search to locate a single book, which consumed well over two hours, required hundreds of steps of walking, and necessitated interacting with a "Professor S" who finally retrieved it. It had become cheaper to repurchase a book misplaced on a shelf than to conduct a thorough search for the item.

In the future, research and reference at libraries would have to be both computerized and digitized, thus permitting electronic search of article abstracts. "I look forward with delight," he told the attendees, which included panel discussants Robert M. Fano, a professor of electrical communications at MIT, and Gilbert W. King, the director of research at IBM, "to being able to find in 10 minutes everything relevant that has been written on a given subject, or to find that nothing relevant has been written." Though, it should be noted, Kemeny couldn't imagine that anyone would ever want to read Shakespeare or an entire history book on a screen.

Since Dartmouth faculty and administration typically didn't seek out government grants for research, students and faculty didn't have the pressure of competition for scarce resources—i.e., computing time—hanging over them. Therefore, Dartmouth had no need to charge for computer access. The pair foresaw students flocking to computing terminals like moths to a flame, with democratic access to computing a reality. Most intriguingly, as the dean of engineering explained in a letter, "There would be complete privacy [when using the terminals]. No one would know what the students were doing." This veil of privacy, though, would have consequences, which are discussed in the next chapter.

Kemeny and Kurtz realized that the LGP-30 wasn't powerful enough to host the time-sharing system, so Kemeny greased the wheels of institutional power to sell the idea of user-centered computing. With help from a sympathetic administration headed by Dartmouth president John S. Dickey as well as two National Science Foundation grants (which focused on hardware, the logistics of time-sharing, and curriculum development) and educational discounts offered by General Electric, new hardware was budgeted and ordered. (Kemeny and Kurtz had considered purchasing computers manufactured by Bendix, Burroughs, and IBM before finally settling on General Electric machines.)

GE was a relatively new player in the computing business. The company's first venture came in the mid-1950s, when Bank of America commissioned GE to build a system automating check processing. The result was ERMA (the Electronic Recording Machine—Accounting), developed by the Stanford Research Institute (SRI), that employed MICR (magnetic ink character recognition) for encoding and decoding the checks.

Approval of the two NSF grants in January 1964 set off a "hectic month or two," recalled Kemeny and Kurtz, as "emergency alterations were made in the basement of an old college building—the only available site for the computer." The cramped 1700-square-foot space required revamped electrical power lines and an air conditioning unit, the latter of which would fail to pull its weight. In the last week of February, a GE-225 (typically priced at a quarter million dollars in the early 1960s), along with a DATANET-30 communications computer—which would serve as an intermediary between the GE-225 and time-sharing users—arrived on campus. By mid-March, the system had been installed and connected to the power line. Then the student programmers—around a dozen or so undergraduates, mostly mathematics majors together with a handful of undeclared sophomores—got to work, day and night. They often put in fifty-hour weeks with the machines despite carrying a full course load (three courses during each ten-week term; each academic year had three terms), and oftentimes their grades suffered as a consequence of that divided attention, though no student flunked out.

Kemeny and Kurtz had high expectations of their young charges. Reflecting on these seminal events in a speech he gave at Class Officers Weekend in May 1974, Kemeny said,

> Tom and I sort of laid down the general framework…and we told them they had three months to complete this project. If we had not been so terribly ignorant, we would have known that we should have had a team of twenty professionals working three years on the project. Instead, we picked an undergraduate and said, "You have three months," and when that student took three months and a week, we got terribly angry at him for not working hard enough.

Roughly two years before General Electric's hardware arrived on campus, Tom Kurtz and Anthony Knapp traveled to the GE computer department, based in Phoenix, Arizona, to take their first look at the GE-225 and the DATANET-930 (an earlier model of what was ultimately delivered to Dartmouth). When they returned to campus, Knapp drew up plans for a time-sharing system integrating these GE components, despite not having any of the equipment on hand. These "MESS" plans were sent to GE; Kurtz and Knapp believed that MESS would excite company engineers so much that they would make haste and send Dartmouth the equipment. But GE was silent. Regardless, in April 1963, Dartmouth reached out to General Electric, formally notifying the company of its desire to purchase the hardware. (As documented in the National Science Foundation application, Kurtz was intent on obtaining the GE-235, not the 225 model, but the 235 was not released until the fall of 1964.)

Design of the GE-225 mainframe began in the late 1950s, as Arnold Spielberg—father of film director Steven—and Charles Propster, working in GE's Industrial Computer Department in Phoenix, put forward proposals to company brass describing a potential business computer. But CEO Ralph Cordiner was dead set against computers for anything other than industrial use. "Every time a plan was sent to him that mentioned going into business computers," Spielberg recalled, "he would write 'No' across it and send it back." Nonetheless, the 20-bit GE-225, with its one thousand circuit boards, ten thousand transistors, twenty thousand diodes, and multiple storage options, was finalized in 1959 and ready for public consumption by the early 1960s, with a high-profile customer set to take delivery: Bank of America. Cordiner got wind of the project at some point after the contract with BofA was signed, and he waited patiently to mete out punishment. After the CEO attended the computer's dedication ceremony, he unceremoniously fired Barney Oldfield, head of the Industrial Computer Department. "[Cordiner] gave the company 18 months to get out of the business," Spielberg said, but demand for the two-thousand-pound, room-sized machine quickly outpaced supply and GE found themselves knee-deep in the computer business.

By the mid-1960s, the GE-225 had predicted a U.S. presidential election to within five percentage points and coordinated the ticket sales of the Cleveland Browns football team. Art Modell, president of the Browns, wondered if, one day, "there might come a time when computers will help call the next play."

In the summer of 1963, Kemeny began sketching out a compiler, leveraging several GE-225 computers residing in New England. He assigned two undergrads, Michael Busch and John McGeachie, the work of programming the time-sharing operating system for the DTSS (Dartmouth Time-Sharing System) on paper, aided by sets of printed manuals for the GE-225, the GE-235, and the DATANET-30.

The Dartmouth time-sharing design was cutting edge, with the intrepid students creating novel means of communication and control between machines. The GE computer would be connected to tape drives, a printer, a card reader, a card punch, and a master computer: the DATANET-30. From the master computer were dozens of phone lines connecting to the phone system, which the teletypewriters directly tapped into. All user computing took place within the GE computer, but the executive program was stored in the DATANET-30—that way, no user program could affect the executive program, potentially causing the time-sharing system to grind to a halt. The executive program would periodically check to ensure that all operations were proceeding smoothly on the GE, and could intervene if the machine entered troubled waters. The D-30, brandishing a clock, could not only interrupt the GE at any time but also enter control commands into its memory; two-way communication between the computers was facilitated by specially designated memory cells in the GE called "mailboxes." When an interrupt came from the master computer, the GE would save what it was working on and then scan the mailboxes for instructions on how to proceed. If any instructions were found, the GE would acknowledge their receipt by entering a code into a specific mailbox; then, the machine would carry out the task(s) and insert a "task-completed" code into another mailbox. With the task(s) (if any) dispensed with, the GE would continue on its way, resuming its current work, spending only several seconds processing one problem at a time.

Recalling the events years later, Busch said he was "involved in writing the first master executive for the DATANET-30," adding that he was the "principal adversary" of John McGeachie, who was tasked with programming the GE computer. Indeed, Kemeny recalled years later, it wasn't the computers (the DATANET-30 and the GE-225) that weren't communicating well, it was the two undergraduates themselves, who would "stand at opposite ends of the room and yell at each other," in effect standing in for the computers they were responsible for programming. To settle a particular argument, McGeachie inserted two messages into the two-part executive program, one of which declared, "Busch did it," the other of which read, "I did it." McGeachie was sure that the "I did it" message—implying he lost the argument—would not arise. Much to McGeachie's embarrassment, "I did it" popped up on the console the next day.

Their arguments were often fueled by a key assumption: that the DATANET-30— with its internal clock interrupting the CPU's execution of a program at various intervals, allowing the system to check for other programs or user requests and also cycle between the execution of programs based on priority—could never be wrong. But this assumption neglected the fact that the executive program in the D-30 was checked with a dummy routine in the GE computer; thus, the set up simulated real-time processing but didn't actually engage in any of it. As the days turned into months, Busch and McGeachie found it progressively more difficult to load new versions of the executive program, while the ever-increasing contingent of users came to expect smooth operation of the system. So, Busch and McGeachie would arrive at their stations at two o'clock in the morning, load in the new binary decks and throw away the old ones— therefore ensuring that there was no way to back up data the next day. It was an "interesting" approach to "system reliability," McGeachie said, which led to some trouble. "Unfortunately," he recalled, "we did this once when…Kemeny had a demonstration scheduled."

General Electric wasn't merely on the sidelines during BASIC's gestation period; the company was providing support, both "moral and material," remembered Kurtz. The relationship proved mutually beneficial, at least for a time. GE sent the college a FORTRAN compiler; they also shipped Dartmouth spare magnetic tape drives. Later that fall, when Dartmouth had an opportunity to present the fruits of its labors at the Fall Joint Computer Conference (FJCC) held in San Francisco, GE even footed most of the bill. At the FJCC, the DTSS was available for a trial run at a Dartmouth booth, which housed three working teletypewriters. Kurtz was at the conference, as were two Dartmouth students, Ken Lochner and Bill Zani, who distributed paraphernalia to attendees.

By early 1965, partly thanks to visits by two Dartmouth students to Phoenix that winter, GE had a DTSS clone (with BASIC) set up and running in their computer department. By that fall, GE was operating commercial time-sharing services in both Phoenix and New York, despite a contemporaneous survey the company conducted among its programming managers which found only lukewarm support for BASIC; after all, FORTRAN could do everything BASIC could do, albeit more efficiently. But Jerry Weiner, a GE project manager and among the first in the company to openly support the efforts of Kemeny and Kurtz, pushed back. "[Y]ou missed the point completely," he told GE brass. "It's a simple system for the *users*."

Lukewarm support for BASIC was one thing, but GE Phoenix seemed to want to stamp out any mention of "Dartmouth" in the technical package and complicated set up that the college had provided them, which included more than just BASIC. It also encompassed an ALGOL compiler that had a unique fingerprint: whenever it generated output from a program run, the words "Dartmouth ALGOL" appeared at the top of the printout. GE Phoenix went to considerable lengths to remove that text, poring through the compiler listing line by line and searching for "Dartmouth," but to no avail.

When GE initially repackaged the DTSS as its own commercial time-sharing system, their manual was titled "Dartmouth/GE BASIC." In the next iteration, it became "GE/Dartmouth." Finally, it simply read as "GE," with the vestiges of its birth in a university setting cast away.

Due to the high cost of long-distance communications, when GE pushed out their time-sharing services and expertise (including on the MIT Multics project) nationwide, the company employed dozens of regionally located centers both in the United States and internationally. "It was in one of these centers in Seattle that Bill Gates was first introduced to computing and BASIC," Kurtz said. "My best guess is that he was about 13 years old at the time."

All the preparation and support during BASIC's gestation ultimately paid off. Though Kemeny joked at the May 8, 1974, Pioneer Day session—held at the National Computer Conference to celebrate the ten-year anniversary of the college's time-sharing system—that both he and Kurtz were "quite ignorant about computing," not realizing that "what we were about to attempt to do was impossible," a BASIC program successfully ran on the DTSS on May 1, 1964, at around 4:00 AM. That first program *may* have been the following, but perhaps not; the program below, however, is one of the earliest BASIC programs preserved for posterity.

```
10 LET X=(7+8)/3
20 PRINT X
30 END
```

Note that, unlike many later non-Dartmouth BASICs, the **END** statement was required. Also, as Kurtz explained in a chapter for the *Encyclopedia of Physical Science and Technology (3rd ed.)*, "Note that, in 1964, long before personal computers or display terminals, one entered a program by typing (as now) and the computer responded by typing back onto yellow paper (rather than displaying the results on the screen)."

For his part, Kemeny half-heartedly suggested at the Pioneer Day event that "it [the first BASIC program] probably was adding two plus two...." But Mike Busch cut him off: "...it had to be prime numbers by the sieve method." Busch is referring to the sieve of Eratosthenes, an iterative process for identifying prime numbers that is thousands of years old. But in the article "GOTO 1964," published on the fiftieth birthday of BASIC in the German language magazine *Telepolis*, author Stefan Holtgen explicitly claims that "this program [was used] to test their completed BASIC compiler on the night of April 30th to May 1st, 1964":

```
10  READ A1,A2,A3,A4
15  LET D=A1*A4-A3*A2
20  IF D=0 THEN 65
30  READ B1, B2
37  LET X1=(B1*A4-B2*A2)/D
42  LET X2 =(A1*B2-A3*B1)/D
55  PRINT X2,X2
60  GO TO 30
65  PRINT "NO UNIQUE SOLUTION"
70  DATA 1,2,4
80  DATA 2,-7,5
85  DATA 1,3,4 ,-7
90  END
```

"The compiler worked," added Holtgen, "but the program itself produced an error ('NO DATA') after a short time."

Elusive first program aside, it is unclear who was actually there to witness history that night. Perhaps only Busch and McGeachie, as asserted in the 2014 documentary *The Birth of BASIC* (interestingly, watch the documentary and, the way several shots are cut together, the implication is that the three-line program shown on the previous page was indeed the first one); other sources place "John Kemeny and a student programmer" at the scene. In *Telepolis*, Holtgen writes that Kemeny, Kurtz, and "some of their students" were there that night. And in the article "BASIC Necessities: How GE Helped Launch the Computing Language That Changed the World," found on the GE website, we read, "In the wee hours on May 1, 1964, in the basement of Dartmouth's College Hall, something extraordinary happened. Professor John Kemeny and a student typed a single-word command, 'RUN,' from two separate computer terminals at the same time, and the program executed flawlessly." The attendees at the birth of BASIC on the DTSS will likely forever remain unknown.

Which brings us to another mystery. Was BASIC really born on May 1, 1964?

In a 1968 article for *Science* magazine, Kemeny and Kurtz wrote, "On 1 May 1964, at 4 AM, the Dartmouth time-sharing system was born as it successfully executed its first problem, one that had been supplied to it from a teletype, in Basic, with the answers being returned to the same teletypewriter." By 1989, in an article penned by Bill Gates for *Byte* magazine titled "The 25th Birthday of BASIC," the famous birthdate is stated as fact, matter-of-factly: "On May 1, 1964, Dartmouth students, greeted by the now famous READY> prompt on their teletype terminals, could write simple programs and send them off to be compiled and run."

But in an oral history interview around a decade after that, Kurtz calls BASIC's May the First birthdate a "pretty good myth." It's even questionable if BASIC was born in the year 1964, since Kemeny had asked William M. "Bill" Zani, an undergrad, to help him code the earliest versions of the BASIC compiler in the summer of 1963 (Zani would transcribe Kemeny's notes onto punched cards). As mathematician Dick Hamming has argued, when it comes to writing history, the names and dates do not matter as much as "the ideas behind the things": "Thus, when Gibbon gives 476 as the date when Rome fell, we realize that this is arbitrary to a high degree. Rome did not fall at one moment, nor does Gibbon so claim." Likewise, BASIC was by no means born overnight, ex nihilo.

What is certain is that by the late spring of 1964 BASIC programs were successfully running on two terminals simultaneously—the key goal set by Kemeny, who was primarily responsible for designing and debugging that first version of BASIC. At the Pioneer Day event, a student in one of Kurtz's classes in the spring 1964 semester revealed that "we started out in that class using BASIC on cards on a GE 225 in the basement of College Hall"—that would have been before the First of May—but later on students in his class were employing multiple terminals, still in the basement of College Hall, to run their BASIC programs. (Before time-sharing, Mike Busch and other students would compete in what they called "one card wonder makers" to see who could squeeze the most instructions onto a single punched card. In the midst of this action, a frequent hazard of programmers in the basement were wastebasket fires, which seemed to sometimes spontaneously combust, Kurtz recalled.)

Despite the ambiguity surrounding the birthdate, in 2019, the New Hampshire Department of Transportation installed a historical marker on the east side of Route 120 memorializing the birth of BASIC. The marker reads as follows:

BASIC: THE FIRST USER-FRIENDLY COMPUTER PROGRAMMING LANGUAGE

In 1964, Dartmouth College math professors John Kemeny and Thomas Kurtz created one of the first user-friendly programming languages, called Beginner's All-purpose Symbolic Instruction Code. BASIC made computer programming accessible to college students and, with the later popularity of personal computers, to users everywhere. It became the standard way that people all over the world learned to program computers, and variants of BASIC are still in use today.

The Historical Marker took ten months to complete; it began with a suggestion by David Brooks, a writer for the *Concord Monitor*. "If you scroll through the list of the 255 official highway historical markers maintained by the state of New Hampshire," Brooks wrote in 2018,

you will find 21 bridges, two memorials to the 45th parallel, several references to Daniel Webster and a few oddities, like the sign labeled "Bungtown."

What you won't find is much geekiness.

Amid all those markers scattered along state roads, there's distressingly little celebration of New Hampshire's technical and scientific accomplishments.

But we're going to fix that, you and I. And we're going to start with something basic— or, rather, BASIC.

Brooks reached out to Tom Kurtz, asking if he thought the marker was a good idea. "He gave me the thumbs-up." Next, Brooks contacted Dartmouth—and the institution gave its approval as well. Retired mathematics professor Scot Drysdale helped Brooks compose the text for the historical marker; they decided that only BASIC, and not the DTSS, should be mentioned, because of the limited space available on the sign. Plus, there would have been too much nuance to explain.

Two years later, the Institute of Electrical and Electronics Engineers (IEEE, pronounced I-triple-E) dedicated their own historical signifier in honor of BASIC: a Milestone marker at the Collis Center for Student Involvement at Dartmouth. IEEE plaques, celebrating achievements in human innovation, dot the landscape, including at Thomas Edison's lab in Menlo Park, New Jersey. The BASIC plaque reads as follows:

IEEE MILESTONE
The BASIC Programming Language, 1964

Beginner's All-purpose Symbolic Instruction Code (BASIC) was created in this building. During the mid-1970s and 1980s, BASIC was the principal programming language used on early microcomputers. Its simplicity and wide acceptance made it useful in fields beyond science and mathematics and enabled more people to harness the power of computation.

The high honor of installing an IEEE marker normally necessitated a public event, which wouldn't be the first time BASIC was celebrated on Dartmouth's campus: for instance, the college set aside an entire day in 2014 for a retrospective of the language on its fiftieth birthday, which included the public premier of the documentary film *Birth of BASIC*, produced by the director of Dartmouth's Neukom Institute for Computational Science, Dan Rockmore. A professor at the college, Rockmore explained that the "marriage of simultaneity and simple language is the birth of BASIC." And National Public Radio (NPR) ran a story in early May 2014, interviewing Tom Kurtz and the station's science correspondent, the latter of whom noted that "[w]ell, the original [BASIC] is totally obsolete, but large sections of the Windows operating system are written in a language called Visual Basic."

Visual Basic has its origins in a program called Ruby, which was "like a set of digital Lego blocks," explained its creator, Alan Cooper. Back in 1976, hot on the heels of Micro-Soft's first professional BASIC product, Altair BASIC, Cooper assisted Gordon Eubanks, Jr., a Naval Postgraduate School student and former IBM employee, with writing CBASIC. An evolution of BASIC-E, created as part of Eubanks's master's thesis, CBASIC was priced at a hundred dollars per copy and sold modestly. Alan Cooper, who wrote the manual for CBASIC, was especially impressed by the "middle layer of code that made programs written in his [Eubanks's] language much more difficult to copy, modify, or steal," explained Steve Lohr in the book *Go To: The Story of the Math Majors, Bridge Players, Engineers, Chess Wizards, Maverick Scientists, and Iconoclasts—the Programmers Who Created the Software Revolution* (2001).

Though he dropped out of high school, Cooper, with a high school equivalency credential in hand, enrolled in a California community college computer programming course. Almost immediately, he was hooked—taking every class he could, "devour[ing] computers and programming," he remembered. In the late 1980s, having attained some success in the computing business, Cooper programmed what he called a "shell construction set": a tool named Ruby that "power" users could employ to manipulate items onto a so-called slate on the desktop. He pitched the product to Microsoft; Bill Gates, suitably impressed, purchased Ruby from Cooper, who chose not to join the company. Ruby was set to be included in Windows 3.0 as a "shell customization tool." However, "that turned out to be a dead end," Cooper recalled. "People did not want to customize the shell that way."

Ruby, though, was not dead. With BASIC losing favor among serious programmers, and C too difficult for novice programmers in corporate environments to easily pick up—especially when it came to writing graphics applications for the Windows environment—Gates saw an opportunity: combine the power of Ruby with the simplicity of BASIC. The potent mixture would bring Ruby's drag-and-drop flexibility on the visual end, while Quick BASIC 4.0 controlled the proceedings.

Why Quick BASIC, rather than GW-BASIC? By that time, recalled Bill Gates in the article "The 25th Birthday of BASIC," development of GW-BASIC had screeched to a halt after the effectively equivalent BASICA was loaded into the IBM PC ROM. "Without IBM's updating the ROM, it was hard to popularize BASIC extensions beyond the interpreter," he added. "When BASIC faltered on the plateau of being an IBM PC-compatible standard, we created Quick BASIC." By 1989, Microsoft was looking to modernize BASIC even further, with object-oriented features as well a "visual component…. With a mouse and a palette of predrawn graphics images, you should be able to combine lines, boxes, and buttons interactively on a screen to design a form for a program," Gates explained. "A visual BASIC program will be a mixture of code, programmer-written objects, and visually specified objects." Gates also envisioned a "universal BASIC," a macro language which could interact with all the applications on a machine.

The appeal of BASIC, waxed Alan Cooper, "was that anybody could bend it and twist it any way they wanted to for commercial purposes and for technical expediency." Two years of bending and twisting finally led to Visual Basic, debuting in May of 1991. With a modicum of training, VB turned designing simple, customizable Windows applications into child's play, and was especially a boon to corporate programmers, whose programs were often in-house, small-scale, tailor-made efforts. The language, with its innovative edit-and-continue feature for debugging, helped secure the dominance of Windows PCs in the corporate world of the 1990s and beyond.

By the time BASIC celebrated its fiftieth birthday in 2014, over 280 variants of the language, including multiple versions of Visual Basic, had spread throughout the world, running on computers (both modern and vintage) as well as on a handful of game consoles. Seven years later, as a consequence of the COVID-19 pandemic, there would be no in-person festivities for the IEEE Milestone marker celebrating BASIC. Nonetheless, the IEEE timed the dedication well: it took place on February 22, 2021, Kurtz's 93rd birthday.

Let's return to the birth of BASIC and the DTSS—or, at least, back to May 1, 1964. Initially, only three user terminals were available. That first month or so, the system was put through its paces by students taking a numerical analysis course. They labored under a mean time to failure rate of about five minutes. It was not for nothing that in the early days, Kurtz referred to BASIC as a "learning machine."

By the middle of June, the system had improved considerably, so the number of available teletypewriters was upped to eleven. Kemeny and Kurtz also began evangelizing the system to fellow professors. Out of about five hundred faculty and staff, almost two hundred sat for three lectures centered on using the DTSS. As homework, attendees were told to practice, which many did, partly because of the teletypewriters' availability—most of the undergraduates were away for the summer, after all.

By the fall, with many incoming freshmen set to be exposed to BASIC, twenty terminals were installed, accessible to both students and faculty; the GE-225 was also upgraded to a GE-235, the machine Kurtz originally requested, with little drama. Access to the DTSS, via networked telephone lines, spread beyond the confines of Dartmouth to nearby universities and high schools, thanks to the NSF grants and some "missionary work," remembered Kurtz. Hanover High School, adjacent to the Dartmouth campus, was the first to receive a networked teletypewriter; by 1965 the public high school had organized a computer club boasting a membership in the hundreds, with HHS's students churning out impressive programming efforts. By 1966, Teletypes had been installed in a number of residential homes in Hanover as well, connecting the small town to an electronic network pulsing through telephone lines—some three decades before the internet established a foothold in the United States. The future had come early—to a handful of New Hampshire residents, at least.

BASIC on the DTSS toggled between two modes: a command mode and a program mode. The operating system differentiated between the two by the presence of line numbers. Statements without line numbers were monitor commands, while those prefixed with line numbers were appended to a program stored in memory. The monitor commands included friendly, "ordinary-sounding English words" (as described by Kurtz) like **HELLO** (instead of LOGON), **GOODBYE** (instead of LOGOFF), **NEW** (to create a new program), **OLD** (to load an already-existing program), **RUN**, and **SAVE**; these were commands designed to navigate the operating system and were not BASIC statements, though some of these commands later (and inappropriately) became part of BASIC when the language escaped the confines of Dartmouth. The first Dartmouth BASIC Manual aided in this confusion by throwing the monitor commands and language statements together in the same document, as one of the undergraduate time-sharing system programmers noted.

Though every FORTRAN program typically had some "line numbers," BASIC required that every statement begin with a line number, "primarily to aid editing," explained Kurtz. (In FORTRAN, line numbers were referred to as *statement numbers*; they were found in columns one to five of FORTRAN punched cards and used as statement labels. What's more, these labels didn't have to be coded in ascending order. In case a FORTRAN card deck was dropped, optional sequence numbers, found in columns seventy-three to eighty, could be used to help reorder the cards.) Indeed, with hardcopy terminals, being able to retype lines made editing a cinch in BASIC, and adding lines within programs—assuming that the lines were numbered in increments of five or ten, thereby leaving space for additional statements—simply involved typing new statements on heretofore unused line numbers. To delete a particular line, the user merely entered the line number as a command into the teletype machine. In addition, Dartmouth BASIC statements, unlike statements in FORTRAN, were automatically sorted in ascending order by line number; a BASIC program's statements didn't need to be (and typically weren't) stored in memory in order but were instead treated as a *linked list*, with one statement pointing to the next.

By contrast, adding instructions within a machine language program was oftentimes tricky, with the tedious task of rewriting jump addresses a consequence of newly inserted code. Furthermore, the user-friendly way of editing lines in Dartmouth BASIC programs stood in stark contrast to the complexity of later line editors, like the UNIX text editors ed and ex.

Kurtz later wrote, "For the first 10 years of BASIC, this design decision"—namely, utilizing line numbers—"remained valid, but eventually video terminals replaced Teletypes and soon supported screen editors." Video terminals like the Digital VT50 permitted full-screen editing, albeit to various degrees of effectiveness. Dartmouth built a video terminal called the Avatar, coupling it with a dedicated editor that greatly increased the functionality of the standard "dumb terminal" by employing a Z80 microprocessor. The early 8-bit microcomputers also offered varying capabilities of on-screen editing, with most lacking robust code editors; typically, commands like **EDIT** offered users a way to avoid retyping lines. In addition, keying in the **LIST** command to display only a portion of the code—e.g., **LIST 50-100**—was yet another workaround to programming without a text editor.

The DTSS offered a one-word command for compiling and executing a program, along with all the steps in between: **RUN**. Unlike more complicated programming languages, Dartmouth BASIC's inherent simplicity permitted single-pass compilation—an important advantage, since multi-pass compilation would have consumed too much computer time. In *Masterminds of Programming*, Kurtz reflected that "in the early days running a program required several steps: Compiling. Linking and loading. Execution. We decided in BASIC that *all* runs would combine these steps so that the user wouldn't even be aware of them."

Single-pass compilation, where the compiler traversed the source code only once, was possible because things were kept so simple. With variable and array names short (and not requiring declaration), along with pre-allocated space for the values of those potential variables, no symbol table lookup (or symbol table at all) was needed in order to parse and generate code. When a BASIC program was run, the compiler didn't make any effort to optimize the object code; after all, the vast majority of the programs being run through the time-sharing system were very small and limited in scope, coded by students and professors. No BASIC programs were being written to obtain nuclear reactor shielding computations, for example; such scientific applications were the province of FORTRAN.

Within two years, BASIC would become interactive thanks to the **INPUT** statement, which paused execution of the program and waited for a user to type a response into a terminal. As John McGeachie rightly noted, "[BASIC] was a combination of immediacy and simplicity that had not previously existed." Prior to the **INPUT** statement, data was assigned to variables using either **LET** or **READ...DATA**, though not interactively during runtime. As an illustration of how programmers worked around the limitations of having no **INPUT** in the earliest versions of Dartmouth BASIC, consider the following program listing, taken from Bill Gates's *Byte* article "The 25th Birthday of BASIC":

```
10 REM 1964 BASIC
20 LET N = 355/113
30 PRINT "MULTIPLICATION TABLE FOR",N
40 FOR I = 1 TO 10
50 PRINT I , N * I
60 NEXT I
70 PRINT "--------------"
80 END
```

As was evident from even the simplest programs, such as Gates's above, BASIC was cut from the same cloth as ALGOL and FORTRAN. "From FORTRAN comes the order of the three loop-controlling variables—initial, final, step—thus permitting the step size to be omitted if it is unity [one]," explained Kurtz. "From ALGOL come the words **FOR** and **STEP**, and the more natural testing for loop completion before executing the body of the loop. These and other similarities are not surprising, since we knew both languages, and we did not hesitate to borrow ideas."

In his classic book *The Soul of a New Machine* (1981), which described the frenetic process of designing a new computer at the Data General Corporation in the 1970s, author Tracy Kidder criticized BASIC as "resembl[ing] a pidgin English." No doubt, Dartmouth BASIC offered a pidgin approach to looping code. Consider the following example, which outputs the numbers 0 to 600 by 2's:

```
10 FOR Y = 0 TO 600 STEP 2
20 PRINT Y
30 NEXT Y
40 END
```

The roughly equivalent program in ALGOL 60 looks like this:

```
for y := 0 step 2 until 600 do
  begin
    print(y);
  end
```

BASIC's **FOR/NEXT** statement was not only simple, it was powerful: non-integer values were permitted, including as a step-size, with calculations performed in the background in binary. There were a few nagging issues, such as with negative decimal step-sizes that wouldn't loop as expected due to two's complement operations on the GE-225. (*Two's complement* is a method of handling signed numbers in binary arithmetic without requiring an additional *sign bit* expressly for that purpose. To calculate the two's complement of a binary number, first find the one's complement of the number by flipping the bits—ones become zeros and zeros become ones. Then, add one to the result. We will return to the problem of negative decimal step-sizes in the third chapter.)

Notice that lines of BASIC were structurally similar to assembly language statements—perhaps even more similar than they were to lines of ALGOL or FORTRAN. If we examine a BASIC line such as

```
20 PRINT Y
```

we can make out the tripartite structure of a typical assembly language statement: instruction number (**20**), operation (**PRINT**), and operand (**Y**). Instructions in BASIC took DARSIMCO code as inspiration as well.

Besides ALGOL and FORTRAN, by the pair's own admission the design of BASIC was also influenced by CORC (CORnell Compiler), written by Richard Conway at Cornell University. Like Dartmouth BASIC, CORC required the **LET** statement for variable assignment but didn't need the user to specify the variable type. Unlike Dartmouth BASIC, though, variable declaration was mandatory in CORC.

The word **LET** was also chosen for BASIC since it sounded like a verbal command in mathematics, "because we were always saying things like: 'Let G be an Abelian Group,'" recalled Kurtz. In addition, the JOSS programming language, developed at around the same time as BASIC, used SET as an assignment statement. Both JOSS and BASIC were termed, in the rapidly evolving nomenclature of the day, "on-line" and "interactive" languages (see writings from the late 1960s to the early 1970s by computer scientists Jean Sammet and Saul Rosen for examples of this usage).

LET helped neophytes understand that an expression involving variable assignment was decidedly not a mathematical equation. For instance, without **LET**, you might be tempted to solve for **X**, as if you were back in algebra class:

$$X=X+20$$

But solving for **X** would result in a false statement, not an equation, since zero does not equal twenty. Inserting **LET** at the start of the BASIC instruction, however, diminishes the temptation to solve for **X**:

$$LET\ X=X+20$$

In many of the non-Dartmouth BASICs to come, **LET** was made optional.

By the early 1970s, six implementations of Dartmouth BASIC had been released. BASIC the First, as its creators later called it, was the BASIC ostensibly born the night of May the First. The implementation offered fourteen programming statements, including **LET, PRINT, END, FOR/NEXT, IF/THEN, READ, DATA, DIM, GOSUB, RETURN, DEF**. A "remark," or comment, was stipulated by the **REM** statement; FORTRAN was among the earliest of the high-level languages to feature comments. And the **GOTO** statement, which offered BASIC programmers an unconditional jump, was modeled after FORTRAN's GO TO; although the pair could have dispensed with **GOTO** in favor of introducing labels pointing to the beginning of blocks of code, for ease of editing they already required prefixing every program statement with a line number—so why not have these line numbers double as labels for **GOTO**? It was a simple, elegant solution to a knotty problem, albeit one that would result in unintended consequences. In addition, recall that the **INPUT** statement, a mainstay of later BASICs, was not a part of this first implementation of Dartmouth BASIC.

Every line of a BASIC program had to start with a line number and then continue with an English word, which happened to be a BASIC statement—there were no exceptions. This HLL structure wasn't unusual for the time; statements in COBOL, for instance, began with imperative English verbs like READ, WRITE, STOP, and DEFINE, which Kurtz believed to be a good approach.

Also recall that monitor commands like **NEW**, **LIST**, **RUN**, and **SAVE** were instructions for the DTSS operating system, and thus not technically a part of the Dartmouth BASIC language. Computer novices using the time-sharing system might not have appreciated the distinction, however, as they typed **HELLO** to begin the session, then entered their six-digit student ID number, next punched in the word **BASIC**, and finally began keying in their program (or loading an **OLD** one)—which they were urged not to save on the system unless it was *absolutely* necessary. (The **SAVE** command didn't store the compiled version of a program, but rather the BASIC source code. True, the program had to be recompiled each time it ran but the compiling times were fast and, from the user's perspective, the DTSS seemed to "speak" BASIC rather than some mysterious machine language.) There was limited disk space memory, after all, and user programs were automatically purged every several weeks, so saving programs in permanent storage amounted to transferring them to punched cards or paper tape. Once a program was executed on the DTSS, the running time would be calculated and output (in seconds) on the Teletype, along with the date (day, month, and four-digit year), the time on the clock (hour and minute), the program name, and the user number.

To keep things as simple as possible for beginners, BASIC the First would automatically adjust to whatever kind of number—integer or floating point (decimal)—was employed in the code, although a double-precision floating-point type was utilized for all numbers internally, with loop terminations requiring special care. Integers were printed without decimal points, and non-integers were output with up to six significant figures before the compiler resorted to scientific notation. "A number is a number is a number," waxed Kurtz, since the GE hardware was optimized for handling floating-point calculations—unlike only a decade earlier, when John Backus and others had to write Speedcoding software to simulate floating point on their IBM machines. A "BASIC the Zeroth" of, say, 1954 could never have treated different types of numbers so casually and processed them automatically using a fixed format, since the few large computers available then weren't equal to the task. Kemeny and Kurtz purposely selected machines with floating-point capabilities built-in to hardware, because they didn't want to write software routines to perform the arithmetic.

Moreover, the abstruse nature of the arithmetic IF statement in FORTRAN, which required arithmetic comparisons—for instance, IF (B − A) 10, 20, 30 transferred control to statement 10 if the difference between B and A was negative, to statement 30 if the difference was positive, or to statement 20 if the difference was zero—was dispensed with in favor of a simpler and more educationally sound **IF/THEN** statement offering direct comparisons with relational operators that students were already familiar with since grade school: =, <, >, <=, >=, and finally <> for not equal to. And unlike in FORTRAN, in which the needlessly complicated FORMAT statement had to be employed to generate any sort of output, BASIC's PRINT statement automatically adjusted the output, always taking into account the type of number being displayed.

FORTRAN offered built-in mathematical functions, as did BASIC—such as SIN, COS, SQR, LOG, INT, and RND. The trigonometric functions used radian measures, rather than degrees; the LOG function used base e, rather than the base 10 (common logarithm) of calculators; and the INT function chopped everything to the right of the decimal point. RND generated a pseudorandom number between 0 and 1, though it required a *dummy argument* to work, like the 1 in RND(1), which Kurtz retrospectively called a "lazy" approach; though the pair shed the dummy argument for successive Dartmouth BASICs, it reemerged like a phoenix from the ashes in BASIC dialects elsewhere—and it wasn't a dummy argument anymore but a real one, affecting the pseudorandom number's generation in one manner or another. Kurtz lamented the proliferation of these later "ugly forms" of RND. It was only one of many ways in which Kemeny and Kurtz lost control over their creation once BASIC escaped Dartmouth's campus.

User-defined functions were also available in BASIC the First by using the DEF statement. For example, DEF FNA, where the naming letters FN were required along with a final letter between A to Z; a statement like DEF FNL(X) = LOG(X)/LOG(10) defined a function that obtained the common logarithm, rather than the natural logarithm, of X). All functions, both built-in and user-defined, had to be three letters in length because of a memory restriction on the word size (20-bit words, but six bits per character) of the GE-225 computer.

Because Dartmouth BASIC performed all arithmetic using floating point, when an integer value was necessary—such as in an array subscript—"[w]e did have to do some complicated stuff internally," Kurtz admitted in *Masterminds of Programming*. If a non-integer was used as a subscript, then the complier automatically rounded the value.

Arrays of one and two dimensions—what were first called vectors and matrices (terms that were mathematical in nature), but which the Dartmouth duo later referred to as lists and tables, respectively—were declared using the DIM statement, although array declaration was optional unlike in other contemporaneous languages like FORTRAN. Following FORTRAN's lead, BASIC arrays were not zero-indexed; subscript bounds began at 1 and extended to 10 if the DIM statement wasn't employed to specify the size of the array. Moreover, in the earliest version of BASIC, the zero subscript wasn't permitted at all. But that resulted in needless complexity with algebra-related programs. To understand why, consider the general form of a polynomial with a single variable x, which could be written as:

$$a_n x^n + a_{n-1}x^{n-1} + \ldots + a_2 x^2 + a_1 x + a_0$$

"In an early revision [of BASIC]," Kurtz recalled, "the zero subscript was added, to allow somebody to represent polynomial coefficients using simple array notation in BASIC, and there's always a zero-numbered coefficient."

Yet we can find numerous examples of one-based, rather than zero-based, indexing in mathematics; consider linear algebra, a field which makes copious use of *matrices* (rectangular arrangements of numbers, symbols, or expressions), such as:

$$\begin{bmatrix} a_{1,1} & a_{1,2} \\ a_{2,1} & a_{2,2} \end{bmatrix}$$

No zero subscripts are used in the matrix above.

Kemeny perhaps found one-indexing more natural, as evidenced not only by the eventual inclusion of matrix math features in Dartmouth BASIC—which were not universally adopted among non-Dartmouth implementations of the language thereafter—but because of his areas of specialization in mathematics, which included matrix-intensive Markov chains. Kemeny coauthored a textbook on the subject, called *Finite Markov Chains*, originally published in 1960 with fellow Dartmouth mathematics professor J. Laurie Snell. In the Preface of the book, they write, "The authors have developed a pair of programs for the IBM 704, one for each type of [Markov] chain, which will find a number of interesting quantities for a given process directly from the transition matrix [representing states of the system]." Unfortunately, they do not include listings of these programs, which, alas, could not have been written in BASIC, which did not yet exist.

Though one-based indexing can still be found in high-level languages like Julia and the matrix-centric (and FORTRAN-derived) MATLAB, zero-indexing hit its stride with languages like C that make use of pointer-based arithmetic, though indexing from zero didn't originate in C; the convention was also found in the language BCPL, from which the B programming language, the predecessor of C, derived.

The topic of zero-versus-one-based indexing has been polarizing for decades, with computer scientists like Edsger Dijkstra voicing opinions on which approach made more logical sense (see, for example, EWD 831: "Why numbering should start at zero") and others arguing that the zero-indexed convention only came about to save precious (and expensive) memory in early computers. Unfortunately, a solution to settle the debate, offered in jest by the British author and computer scientist Stan Kelly-Bootle, is a nonstarter: "Should array indices start at 0 or 1? My compromise of 0.5 was rejected without, I thought, proper consideration."

Loosely structured subroutines, courtesy of the **GOSUB** and **RETURN** statements, were built on *stacks*—abstract data structures that operated exclusively on the most recently added item. But no arguments could be passed to subroutines, nor did subroutines necessarily need to have only one entry or exit point.

For proponents of structured programming, a programming paradigm that gathered steam by the mid-1960s, the **GOTO**s and **GOSUB**s and **RETURN**s of Dartmouth BASIC represented all that was unholy in computer science. Worse yet, BASIC was being presented to students as a prototypical representation of high-level computer programming. No doubt frustrations with this state of affairs led Dijkstra to publicly complain that it was "practically impossible to teach good programming to students that have had a prior exposure to BASIC: as potential programmers they are mentally mutilated beyond hope of regeneration." (In fairness, Dijkstra wasn't a fan of FORTRAN or COBOL, either, and said as much.)

An *xkcd* comic strip called "GOTO" by Randall Munroe literally illustrates the "mutilation" befalling those tempted by **GOTO**'s siren song. A programmer sitting at his desk and absorbed in writing code thinks to himself, "I could restructure the program's flow…or use one little 'GOTO' instead." In the next panel, he's made a decision: "Eh, screw good practice. How bad can it be?"

```
goto main_sub3;
compile...
```

Moments later, the programmer meets his fate as a velociraptor lunges toward him.

The Scott Adams cartoon *Dilbert* also dealt with the unintended consequences of unconditional jumps in code. A 1994 strip features the characters Dilbert and Wally talking to a programmer named Irv. "I've never seen you do any real work around here, Irv. How do you get away with it?" Dilbert asks. "I wrote the code for our accounting system back in the mid-eighties. It's a million lines of undocumented spaghetti logic," Irv replies. His "spaghetti logic" is a reference to *spaghetti code*, where the control structure of a program is so challenging to unpack that if one printed out the listing and attempted to trace the program flow with a pencil, the many resulting crisscrossing lines would resemble a bowl of spaghetti. Dilbert, impressed with Irv's approach, exclaims, "It's the Holy Grail of technology!" after which Irv offers, "You boys may find a little extra in your envelopes this month."

In 1973, six years after Dijkstra's anti-GOTO letter, with everyone having staked out positions on the GOTO debate, R. Lawrence Clark, in an article for *Datamation* titled "A Linguistic Contribution of GOTO-less Programming," satirically proposed the creation of the COME FROM statement—"a new language construct on which…both the pro- and the anti-GOTO factions can agree." Clark hoped that COME FROM, which functioned like an inside-out GOTO, could "at last put to rest the GOTO controversy, [so that] we now may enter the era of the COME FROM conundrum." The COME FROM statement, essentially (but not quite) the inverse of GOTO, was eventually implemented in a dialect of the esoteric and satiric programming language INTERCAL (an acronym for "Compiler Language With No Pronounceable Acronym"), developed by two Princeton students in the early 1970s. The INTERCAL Reference Manual, written by the language's creators, pokes fun at a number of common programming tropes of the era, such as myth-making in the historical record of languages like BASIC. For example, in the section "Origin and Purpose," we learn that "[t]he INTERCAL programming language was designed the morning of May 26, 1972 by Donald R. Woods and James M. Lyon, at Princeton University. Exactly when in the morning will become apparent in the course of this manual."

Although BASIC also parroted FORTRAN in space independence—meaning that the compiler would ignore any spaces in lines of code, except for those in string literals—it diverged in terms of variable naming: either a single alphabetic letter or a letter followed by a single digit were the only options in BASIC. Besides offering the advantages of using less memory and being quicker to code and compile, the pair maintained that these compact variable names would address some of the typographical troubles that had plagued FORTRAN's more flexible variable-naming options. The problem with FORTRAN, Kememy and Kurtz realized, was that the language's latitude with variable names on the one hand coupled with its space independence on the other was a recipe for disaster—like that which struck NASA in the 1960s thanks to a coding error. The organization's Mariner 1 spacecraft, destined for Venus, stopped responding to guidance instructions minutes after launch, so it had to be remotely destroyed. The problem supposedly lay in a single FORTRAN statement, mistakenly coded with a period instead of a comma, causing the compiler to catastrophically misinterpret a string of characters as variable assignment rather than as part of a loop. Kurtz, who recounted the NASA-FORTRAN anecdote—which is likely an urban legend—in his *Masterminds of Programming* interview, underscored that a BASIC line such as

```
10 FOR Y = 0 TO M STEP 5
```

could, with BASIC ignoring blanks, be correctly keyed in by a user like this:

```
10 FOR Y = 0 TO MSTEP5
```

With BASIC's variable-naming rules in place, the compiler would never mistake **MSTEP5** (interpreted as **M STEP 5**) for a variable called **MSTEP5**. Since FORTRAN permitted longer variable names, however, it was primed to make that sort of error.

BASIC the First also offered exponentiation via the ↑ (the up arrow) as only one option when dealing with what were then called "formulas" (we can date the term to at least a decade prior, with it appearing in the early writings of the FORTRAN development team) but which are now called expressions. The ↑ symbol was chosen partly because it sat as an unused button on Teletype machines; plus, form followed function: exponentiation, after all, means to *raise* one quantity to the power of another, such as 4^3 (four to the third power). BASIC suffered from mathematical ambiguity when dealing with negative bases, like -3^4, but these problems were ironed out in BASIC the Third.

The first edition of the Dartmouth BASIC manual, probably written by Kemeny alone (Kurtz wrote the second edition), boasted of the language's facility with mathematics, featuring examples of logarithms, quadratic equations, and matrix products. Indeed, BASIC the Third introduced the **MAT** statement, which could juggle matrices and perform operations with them directly—useful features for mathematicians and students using the language for math classes, but typically not needed for the nonmathematically inclined BASIC user. (In the detailed essay entitled "Very Early Days of Matrix Computations" by English mathematician Beresford Parlett, we learn that matrix calculations have a long pedigree, extending back to the earliest days of computing. Parlett groups these calculations into three categories: solving systems of linear algebraic equations in the form $Ax = b$, searching for eigenvalues, and obtaining least-squares solutions to inconsistent linear systems. "In the United States, anticipating the advent of rapid, non-human computing machines, John von Neumann had already turned his attention to both the eigenvalue problem and the solution of $Ax = b$ by direct methods as part of his larger campaign to harness these computers for fluid dynamics computations." Von Neumann's work in this area, teaming with mathematicians Francis Joseph Murray and Herman Heine Goldstine, "marks the birth of modern numerical analysis," Parlett observes. Matrix computations also entered the purview of James Hardy Wilkinson at the National Physical Laboratory in England. Wilkinson helped to solve a single eighteen by eighteen linear system $Ax = b$ using modest desk calculators over the course of two weeks; such work was frustrating enough to ultimately lead to breakthroughs that Wilkinson wrote up in the paper "Error Analysis of Direct Methods of Matrix Inversion," which corrected errors in thinking by von Neumann and others. Though the center of gravity for matrix work was in the United States and England, notable results emerged from Russia, Germany, and Switzerland as well; besides von Neumann and Wilkinson, Karl Hessenberg, Cornelius Lanczos, Magnus Hestenes, Eduard Stiefel, David Young, and Wallace Givens all contributed to the field.) And BASIC the Fifth introduced subprograms, although that feature was eventually deemed a failure.

Most of the time, the names of the newly released Dartmouth BASICs (the First, the Second, the Third, and so on) corresponded to the manual editions. BASIC the Second rolled around less than six months after BASIC the First, and there were improvements. To facilitate a more seamless integration of mathematics and programming arrays, the zero subscript was added; mathematical terms like A_0 could now correspond to **A(0)** rather than **A(1)**. In the updated manual, the pair urged BASIC programmers to be mindful of aesthetics—"…program in a way that makes it more understandable to both oneself and others in the future"—but did not offer specifics on how to do so. The third edition of the manual, for BASIC the Third, took those aesthetic concerns a step further: by illustrating (optional) indentation for code contained within **FOR/NEXT** loops.

BASIC the Third, released in 1966, most notably offered interactivity courtesy of the **INPUT** statement, as previous mentioned. With the addition of **MAT** statements, users were permitted easy manipulation of and operations with mathematical matrices. The feature was previously tested in a one-off version of the language called CARDBASIC, based on BASIC the Second (but without zero subscripts). CARDBASIC, unsurprisingly, took punched cards as input, and offered users early access to **MAT** statements—which had been planned for inclusion in the first edition of BASIC. By the time BASIC the Third arrived, CARDBASIC was dead but **MAT** statements were very much alive: matrix multiplication, transposition, and inversion were available, as was the generation of identity matrices. The **READ** statement was repurposed to permit matrix redimensioning as well. Although zero subscripts were introduced in BASIC the Second, arrays in BASIC the Third were zero-indexed for the first time, meaning subscript values began at **0** rather than **1**, as was previously the case. Since **MAT** had been developed with BASIC the Second in mind, minor adjustments to how matrix operations were handled behind the scenes had to be made. Needless to say, with **MAT** at the ready, BASIC was now the perfect tool for solving many different types of linear algebra problems.

The time-sharing system had evolved into a marvel of reliability, according to Steven Hobbs, an undergraduate assigned to maintain the system in the mid-1960s. He was amazed by its clock-like dependability, considering its small size and "relatively poor hardware."

Hobbs was a prankster. When learning how to navigate his way around the D-30, he decided to add a command. Along with **OLD**, **NEW**, **RUN**, and **SAVE**, there was now **ZIP**, which *acted* like an illegal command—because when it was keyed in, the response on the terminal would be **WHAT?**, the same as for any other command that didn't work. But **ZIP** secretly opened a door to those in the know, guaranteeing that the person who used it would be the next user swapped in, something that proved "extremely handy for the system programmers," Hobbs recalled. Once, when two system programmers were buried under a mountain of work, they teamed up, **ZIP**ping control of the system between each other to the detriment of the other unaware users, who would be automatically disconnected after ten straight minutes of waiting to swap into the system.

In the fall of 1965, an experimental version of the time-sharing system was being tested at Dartmouth, but only on Sundays. Hobbs noted that "no one could tell the difference that it was experimental." Nonetheless, Hobbs and his fellow undergrads decided to prank users of this one-day-a-week system, so they switched the entries for the numbers 2 and 3 in the character translation tables, which took binary-coded decimal (BCD) and formatted it properly for the Teletype. A BASIC program like this, then:

```
40 FOR X = 10 TO 35
50 PRINT X
60 NEXT X
70 END
```

would produce the following head-scratching output to an unsuspecting user:

```
10
11
13
12
14
15
16
17
18
19
30
31
33
32
34
35
```

Fellow undergrad Ron Martin remembered the challenges associated with writing programs on Sundays: either he avoided the digits 2 and 3 in line numbers or used them in this switched manner. The latter could be a hairy proposition, considering that **END** statements *had* to be at the end of a program or the program would not execute at all, and that **FOR** statements might have to be inserted sequentially after their associated **NEXT** statements, depending on the line-numbering scheme.

"And then there was the case where a slight modification in the program was made so that on March 15 [1966] all output came out in Roman Numerals," Kurtz recalled at the 1974 Pioneer Day event.

Despite its commendable reliability, occasionally the system failed. Ron Martin recalled an incident involving the botched installation of a new monitor program, leading the DATANET-30 to crash every time a user typed **TEST**, a monitor command that reported back the status of a BASIC program. If working correctly, whenever the **TEST** command was entered, the Dartmouth **TEACH** program was invoked; **TEACH** acted like a grading system, methodically checking a BASIC program to determine if it conformed to the requirements of a course programming assignment—and then quickly communicating that information back to the user.

Martin struggled to debug the new monitor program; every time he seemed to resolve the issue, another user would type **TEST** and crash the system yet again. (At this point, the user base of the time-sharing system extended outside of Dartmouth to off-campus locations, so it wasn't just a matter of shutting down the terminals at the college to address the issue.) Kemeny rushed into the College Hall basement and demanded to know why the system wasn't working. "Every time I type **TEST** it seems to fail," Kemeny explained. But Martin had reached his breaking point. "Well," he told the professor, "if people would stop typing **TEST** for a while, I could fix it so it would work." Martin inserted an octal patch from the control terminal into the D-30 to correct the problem.

Sidney Marshall, who helped build DOPE (Dartmouth Oversimplified Programming Experiment) as an undergraduate, was quite the character. A command on the time-sharing system served as a proto-Easter egg: **EXPLAIN**. Akin to a primitive help feature, typing **EXPLAIN JGK** would generate a portrait of the man (John G. Kemeny). But type **EXPLAIN SIDNEY** and the following message would appear: "There is no explanation for Sidney."

Marshall and some of the other students played pranks on the users. A control Teletype, installed in the basement of College Hall, could communicate with any other connected Teletype. But—and here was the kicker—someone receiving these messages on his teletypewriter was not alerted to their point of origin. A user could be minding his own business when, out of the blue, he would be in a text-based conversation with an operator at the control Teletype. "And you'd generally go down there [to the basement] just before a football game or something when everybody was up there typing to impress their dates with the computer," Marshall explained to the Pioneer Day audience. "You'd take control of the computer so they'd be talking to you."

But what if a user on the receiving end didn't realize a human being was pulling the strings? Such was one of the "games" the undergraduates played on unsuspecting users: typing in responses to user questions as quickly as possible, trying to convince them that the computer was in fact answering the questions by dint of its programming, rather than "some stupid person downstairs" offering up responses. Once, when Marshall was stationed at the control Teletype, he fielded this question: "What's the score of the football game going to be?" "14 to 7," he typed back as quickly as possible. Which turned out to be a lucky guess, leading people not only to think Dartmouth had a computer that might pass the Turing Test, but that the college also had possession of an electronic seer.

Marshall also came to discover that if a small radio was placed by the console in the basement, a person could assume control of the time-sharing system. The reason? The computer emitted a sound at a very particular frequency.

Tom Kurtz had to deal firsthand the consequences of that sound. Once, when he and some of the student programmers were down in the basement, a fireman with a radio in his hand came storming in, looking upset.

Some "unauthorized emissions on the official fire department channel" were detected, he told Kurtz. The fireman had raced across town, trying to locate the source of these signals—and the trail had led them to the computer room on campus. "It was a one microsecond machine," Kurtz explained, "so I think it had a strong signal in the meg cycle [sic], wave length, or something of that sort."

Kurtz was at a loss what to do. The machine couldn't be modified to generate a different frequency without a complete redesign, which was well beyond the purview of Kurtz or Kemeny by then. So Kurtz and the fire department struck a compromise: if the fire department needed to use their emergency radio, they would call up the college and the computer would be shut off.

When John Kemeny's son Robert was in grade school, his Hanover elementary school class traveled to Dartmouth to see the operation of BASIC and the recently installed time-sharing system. Kemeny, appropriately, gave the class the full tour. He walked them over to College Hall—the oldest building on campus—and sat them down at the Teletypes, which were upstairs. He typed up and ran several programs on a Model 33 he thought might entertain them. In a fit of mimicry, some of the kids followed suit, typing commands into the Teletypes. Then Kemeny took them downstairs to the basement, where the brains of the operation were located, and showed them the computer.

The next day, Robert's class had a show-and-tell. The kids talked about how much they enjoyed their field trip. "Well, did you have any questions that didn't get answered?" the teacher asked the class.

A young girl raised her hand to speak. "Well, I understood perfectly everything Mr. Kemeny did on the computer," she said. "But then he took us downstairs into the basement and showed us a great big box that looked like a refrigerator. I never did find out what it was."

When Kemeny first heard this story from Robert's teacher, he thought it was funny. But then he reconsidered. What *was* the computer? he asked himself. Was it the hulking machine in the basement that the average user never interacted with, or did it consist of the terminals that the human beings directly interfaced with? (For his part, Steve Hobbs believed that the printed BASIC manuals helped to create some of that confusion between terminal and computer.) Along those same lines, Kemeny thought, what was a telephone? Was it a receiver you held, the entire nationwide network, or some combination of both?

The differences between the second and third editions of Dartmouth BASIC were relatively minor. The pair were awaiting a major upgrade in hardware, since a GE-635 computer, with an operating system written by GE, was due to arrive soon. The GE-235 had served the college community well; *The Dartmouth* school newspaper published an "Ode To A Computer—'G.E. 235 We Sing Thy Praises'" in a December 1966 issue. "Hail to thee, blithe Computer!" the ode begins.

> Man thou'rt not, but far astuter....
> I'd learn to speak to thee in BASIC,
> For who would stir thy electronic bowels
> Must learn to speak in BASIC vowels....
> Time-sharing, answer-bearing,
> Generous but impartial Bard!...
> O Blithe Computer, O G.E. Whiz!
> How insufficient BASIC is
> To sing thy praise!

The new GE-635 united the GE-235 and the DATANET-30. Dartmouth received the hardware in late 1966, and BASIC the Fourth was the first implementation of the language to take advantage of the new machine. To some extent, GE and Dartmouth collaborated on the implementation, in part to ensure that Dartmouth BASIC was compatible with GE's version of the language, called Mark I BASIC, which operated on its Mark I time-sharing system. The college and the company were both able to use the GE-635 on campus under a joint agreement, with GE supplying the Phase I operating system.

By 1967, with computing increasingly difficult to ignore, the President's Science Advisory Committee (PSAC) established the Panel on Computers in Higher Education. Chaired by Bell Telephone Laboratories' John R. Pierce, with Kemeny and Kurtz members of the panel, the group pushed for all institutions of higher learning to offer their students computing services. "In the field of scholarship and education," the panel's final report reads, "there is hardly an area that is not now using digital technology." Unsurprisingly, Dartmouth was offered an exemplar of "educational computing at a level of a relatively advanced school...." But Texas A&M was also described as an institution "in which a majority of *all* undergraduates learn programming and use computing in some part of their course work." Texas A&M alumnus Thomas E. Reddin, who earned undergraduate and graduate credentials in electrical engineering and computer science, respectively, recalled the hardware and programming languages in circulation on campus in the mid-1960s:

> The hardware was all IBM: 709 Computer (later replaced with a 7094), 1401 Computer and 650 Computer, a 407 Accounting Machine, and many keypunch, sorter, and interpreter machines. We learned to program and operate them all. The programming languages we used were: FORTRAN, COBOL, SOAP, FAP, MAP, TAMP, and AUTOCODER.

But no time-sharing or BASIC.

The panel urged faculty members to get acquainted with the new technology. "There is evidence, from experience at schools such as Dartmouth," the panel wrote, "that a nearby console and simple programming languages, if available, make it especially easy for a faculty member to learn and to experiment with the new tool in spare moments and in private." Finally, Appendix K of the panel's report featured statements on the value of computing in higher education; Kemeny submitted a one-page essay that summarized Dartmouth's achievements and concluded, "Even if the student never again touches the computer, he will leave the college with a sensible attitude toward the use of high-speed computers."

The same year that the Panel on Computers in Higher Education issued their report, Dartmouth College began work on a new operating system called Phase II that was more suited to its growing time-sharing needs. Kemeny was chairman of the project, which included among its participants familiar names like Stephen Garland and Robert Hargraves. Phase II required two years to complete, at which point it was officially rechristened DTSS.

As the decade came to an end, that first group of undergraduates who worked with Kemeny and Kurtz on the time-sharing system had graduated, making way for a new generation of young people to rise up and take their place, such as Dave McGill, Dick Lacy, and Greg Dobbs, who all, in various ways, helped to shepherd the time-sharing system from the GE-235 to the GE-600 series mainframes.

Ron Martin, a 1967 graduate who helped Mike Busch develop the very first DATANET-30 executive program and also worked on the first GE-635 time-sharing system, remembered the "immense feeling of power" he had in the College Hall basement. "You knew those people were upstairs pounding away at the terminals and you held their very life in your hands, essentially," he told an audience at the Pioneer Day event.

Martin also recounted a program he developed that became notorious: a random-sentence generator that spit out content that was "obscene." Martin and others were fascinated by the output, which was printed on hundreds of pages of line printer paper in order to test the initial time-sharing-compatible batch BASIC implementation. They drove to nearby eateries like the Four Acres or the Polka Dot and, to the bewilderment of the waitresses serving them, studied the stacks of output.

But it grew tiresome to examine the output that way. So, Martin and his compatriots thought of a new approach: have time-sharing users test the program, albeit unwittingly. They would sit at a control terminal in the basement, modify several internal system pointers, and "pawn our program off on an unsuspecting user," he said. The user would type **RUN**, thinking a program was going to, let's say, solve a differential equation, but would instead be confronted with a series of random, objectionable sentences. Martin and company never knew which user would be targeted next.

In the late 1960s, the time-sharing system emerged from the basement of College Hall and was installed in a brand-new facility: the Kiewit Computation Center. (The DTSS would soon be referred to colloquially as the "Kiewit Network.") At the Kiewit dedication ceremony, held during the two-day "The Future Impact of Computers" conference, Donald L. Kreider, a professor of mathematics at the college, spoke of his experiences with the system—including the time he typed in **RUN** and was surprised by what appeared on the terminal. Martin's sentence-generating program had struck again.

There were numerous changes between BASIC the Third and the Fourth. **RND**'s dummy argument was discarded and the **RANDOMIZE** statement was introduced, which did what it promised: setting an initial random number seed for the pseudorandom number generation. In addition, output options with **PRINT** were added, with **TAB** for setting spacing and the semicolon for conjoined printing. Multiple variable assignment with **LET** was an option, and all numeric variables were initialized to zero. And the **DATA** statement could now handle string literals, with string and numeric data stored in two respective "pools." Variants of a **RESTORE** statement could reset the pointer in the string or numeric data pools, although this was a relatively short-lived feature. There were changes to the **MAT** statements as well.

It was with the transition to BASIC the Fifth that dialects of the language began to proliferate and diverge from Dartmouth BASIC. BASIC the Fourth was the BASIC of the GE Phase I operation system; GE improved upon that implementation, even after Dartmouth moved on to BASIC the Fifth. There was little collaboration between Dartmouth and GE past 1967, and in 1969 the DTSS (along with the associated hardware) was owned by Dartmouth outright. Versions of the language based off GE's BASIC would emerge in the years to come in the most unexpected places.

By the close of the 1960s, Dartmouth BASIC's reach had expanded geographically, with approximately thirty Teletype machines connecting to Dartmouth from other schools, both secondary and postsecondary. The Fifth version of the language, appearing around 1969, was the first to be fully integrated with the DTSS. Users could now read and write different types of files, such as random-access files. In addition, programs could be segmented and run via the **CHAIN** statement, and subprograms could be created and run from within a main program. Kurtz was never able to pin down the origin of these BASIC program-segmentation features—they may have been a Dartmouth original, or they might have been lifted from GE Mark I BASIC. Regardless, the pair ultimately regretted the subprograms feature, despite it resulting in some useful (and large) BASIC programs, including a piece of software that was widely used for analyzing social science survey results. BASIC the Fifth also offered a number of new built-in functions, including ones to process strings more efficiently (e.g., **LEN**, which returned the length of a string). And in-line commenting became available, with the apostrophe indicating a comment to the compiler.

In a detailed report for the American Federation of Information Processing Societies (AFIPS) Spring Joint Computer Conference in May 1969 called "The Many Roles of Computing on the Campus," Kurtz relayed the state of affairs for the time-sharing system and offered a number of compelling statistics. In the late 1960s, there were about three thousand undergrads enrolled at Dartmouth, with a quarter majoring in one of the sciences and the remaining students studying social sciences or the humanities. Roughly 150 graduate students were enrolled in Ph.D. programs, the majority in the sciences. Faculty and administrators numbered six hundred, with about 250 teaching faculty of undergraduates. "Because the computer is so easy to use, practically no one avoids it," Kurtz explained.

In the 1967-68 academic year, around half the faculty "found it convenient or necessary to use computing in some form in their teaching or research," Kurtz reported. The proportions were higher among students, with two-thirds of undergraduates and three-fourth of graduate students using computing—but "computing" didn't simply refer to employing the machines for number-crunching. "Computer services" encompassed a wide variety of modalities: A-computing, or administrative data processing; C-computing, or numerical calculations; V-computing, or computer-assisted instruction; I-computing, or "the types of services needed to support information systems such as are needed for management decision applications or library automation"; and T-computing, or a "being taught" machine involving "simple command and programming languages." Other than for A-computing and some aspects of C-computing (where the number-crunching requirements were extensive), the general-purpose nature of the DTSS was able to satisfy Dartmouth's computing needs.

By 1969, the time-sharing system boasted fast response times and several built-in services, including file creation, file editing, on-line assembly, and DDT (direct debugging technique). Kurtz was bothered by what he called a "myth" of the DTSS, however: "that it is devoted to a single language (BASIC)." Even as far back as 1964, BASIC was not the only programming language on the system; within six months after BASIC's debut, ALGOL became available, too, with LISP and FORTRAN appearing soon after. Before 1970, FORTRAN IV and ALGOL 60, as well as computer simulators (e.g., for the PDP-9), also made their home on the DTSS, as did string processing in the form of either an on-line string editor or "a system patterned on TRAC [Text Reckoning And Compiling]."

Specifically with BASIC, Kurtz explained that it

provides for random access string and numerical files as well as console-compatible "teletype" files. While no string operators as such are included, any string can be mapped into a vector of numerical character values for arbitrary manipulation (the mapping can go in either direction.) BASIC is designed to provide the services it offers in as efficient a way as possible, so that the same offerings in the context of another language might be more costly.

The advent of the DTSS brought about a key realization: that the preponderance of computing jobs tended to be of modest size. The "public library in the Dartmouth computer" offered compact programs for a variety of statistical applications, such as linear regression and analysis of variance (ANOVA), and these programs ran as quick jobs on the system. Faculty would obtain the results of calculations in only several minutes using a terminal, saving hours of time in the process. A Markov chain problem coded in FORTRAN in the 1950s, Kurtz noted, could be (and was) written in BASIC in only fifty lines, a quarter the size of the corresponding FORTRAN program. The BASIC compilers could process between twelve thousand and seventy-five thousand program statements per minute; and BASIC's fixed-output format was a model of efficiency compared to FORTRAN's.

Users connected to the DTSS via Teletypes; besides the standard Model 33 and Model 35, as well as the speedier Model 37, any "terminal device that uses the ASCII code and standard teletype data rates" could be employed. DTSS was scheduled to operate every day of the week from 8:00 AM to midnight, placing particular priority on first-run job requests, though there were frequent power failures and air conditioning system issues. Kurtz detailed how the teletypewriters interfaced with the time-sharing system:

> At the present time, most of the teletypes operate through the regular Centrex switching network using 103-type datasets. Some of the teletypes in the public teletype room are non-switched and use the much cheaper 109-type dataset. Most of the teletypes on the switching network can access the computer through single-digit dialing. Although most of the teletypes are switched, it is common for a department or an outside secondary school or college to dial in at 8 AM and remain on throughout the day.

Attempts were made to save money by using a "multiplexing apparatus" on long-distance charges from teletypewriters dialing in from off-campus. Without using a multiplexer, adding up the rental costs ($45 for the Model 33), the Datasets ($50), and the long-distance line ($225 at $3 per mile for seventy-five miles), the costs of a Teletype during a typical month amounted to $320. But with the purchase of a nine-thousand-dollar multiplexer, Teletype costs over time could be significantly reduced. Mount Holyoke, which dialed in to the DTSS, was among the first institutions to experiment with the approach (women at Mount Holyoke and men at Dartmouth sometimes used the DTSS for courting).

By the late 1960s, there were eighty-eight Teletype terminals stationed on campus: the Kiewit Center Public TTY room had sixteen of them; the Tuck School of Business had eleven; the Thayer School of Engineering had eight; the Medical School had four; the Departments of Arts and Sciences had twenty; the Computer Center "in-house" had nineteen; and ten additional Teletypes were floating around for miscellaneous purposes (in homes, for research projects, and so forth).

Fifty-two Teletypes were installed in secondary schools and colleges dotting the New England landscape. Specifically focused on high schools, the Dartmouth Secondary School Project was facilitated by a National Science Foundation grant expressly geared toward funding telephone lines, Teletype rentals, and support staff for secondary schools; a more informal College Consortium, also funded by an NSF grant, helped increase access to the in-demand time-sharing network among institutions of higher learning. These colleges included Bates (two terminals), Berkshire Community (two terminals), Middlebury (two), Mount Holyoke (five), and the University of Vermont (one). There were twelve boys-only private high schools (sixteen total terminals) and ten public high schools (fifteen total terminals) in five states also connected to DTSS, including Cape Elizabeth High School (Maine, Public), Concord High School (New Hampshire, Public), the Loomis School (Connecticut, Private), Phillips Exeter Academy (New Hampshire, Private), Phillips Andover Academy (Massachusetts, Private), and Vermont Academy (Vermont, Private) that connected to the DTSS. By the early 1970s, non-Dartmouth DTSS users outnumbered those at the college by a ratio of five to one.

The DTSS could theoretically accommodate anywhere between 120 and 150 users at once, although the highest number of simultaneous users ever recorded in the 1960s was 113, which occurred in January 1968 with the time-sharing system still running under the Phase I operating system (albeit the 113 individuals included commercial users who were part of the joint-use agreement with General Electric). (In his 1972 book *Man and the Computer*, Kemeny notes that "[o]n a particularly busy day the system had...a peak of 111 users...[and]...a total of 19,503 jobs for the day.") From October 1967 to June 1968, more than eight thousand people used the DTSS, with only about one out of every four unique users being Dartmouth students or faculty; secondary school students made up about half of the users, with the remaining quarter from other colleges. These users were playing games, writing programs, and even sending messages to each other courtesy of the program **MAILBOX** (high school students, connected to the network at their secondary schools via long-distance phone lines, were prodigious BASIC game and application creators, too). Of course, students were never directly billed; rather, the college was sent a single bill at the end of the year for all student use.

Displacing some laboratory studies of physical systems at Dartmouth, simulation studies were conducted on the time-sharing system, often by students to complete assignments. For example, a marketing game was programmed by Dartmouth graduate student William Jaffee for the Amos Tuck School of Business Administration—one of a number of uses of the DTSS for computer-assisted instruction. (Others included a program that relayed elementary climatology facts for a geography course as well as programs that drilled students in the Spanish language; all the software was written by instructors of the respective courses. More complex projects, such as the IMPRESS interface that offered social science faculty and students access to real data, also employed the DTSS to great effect.) And in elementary statistics classes, students could "investigate the behavior of the t-test under various kinds of non-normality."

A survey conducted in the late 1960s revealed that eighty-two out of six hundred courses—thirteen percent—spanning fourteen departments out of forty made use of computers for coursework. These courses enrolled 5,200 students, out of a yearly student-course enrollment totaling twenty-seven thousand. Unsurprisingly, mathematics courses used the computers the most (sixteen such courses), followed by engineering science (ten courses), sociology (nine courses), physics (seven), economics (six), earth sciences (five), psychology (five), biology (four), chemistry (four), geography (four), classics (four), government (three), and even romance languages (two). But the majority of computer exposure at Dartmouth came in the form of a second course in freshman mathematics taken by eighty-five percent of undergraduates, though Kurtz admits this "formal training" only offered "short exposure."

The "formal training" included two one-hour lectures (initially there were three lectures), delivered in the first week of a ten-week term and serving as an introduction to BASIC, along with four programming assignments; a little less than an hour per week of teletypewriter time was reserved for each student for the remainder of the term (at first only a half-hour per week was set aside, until Kemeny and Kurtz realized how poorly students typed). If a student took freshman calculus, in his second term he could expect to be assigned the following problems to solve by writing (and debugging) programs:

PIE approximate pi by inscribed polygons
TRAP a general trapezoid rule program
SIXE a Taylor series approximation
DIFFEQ a simple differential equation solver

If the student instead elected to take Finite Mathematics, a course Kemeny designed, instead of calculus as their second mathematics course, then the problems assigned to him were

MOD compute A times B mod M
QUINT root of a quintic by bisection
BDAY probability calculation
OZ simulated three-state Markov chain

In both of these second-term courses, the first program—PIE or MOD—served as a warmup, something to "break the ice" (in the words of Kurtz), in anticipation of the remaining three program that were specifically tied to the course content. To reduce the time demands on instructors, a student's program, once submitted, could be automatically checked using simple unit testing, with the student receiving one of two of messages on his terminal: either that the program did not satisfy the requirements of the assignment (and to try again), or that it did.

Note that there were no courses on computer programming, as its own separate discipline, offered at the college back then. There was obviously no computer science department to speak of, either. So, if a student wanted to learn how to program in BASIC or FORTRAN or ALGOL, where could he turn? "[C]onsult the many available manuals and texts," recommended Kurtz. Such an information-scarce environment drove home the power of BASIC's simplicity: "It is a fact that extremely simple constructions in BASIC are sufficient for perhaps 95 percent of the programs needed by students," he added.

⇛

Work on the next edition of BASIC began in 1969. With the release of BASIC the Sixth in 1971, Kemeny, Kurtz, and the student programmers—a number of whom had by then returned to Dartmouth as professors—finally produced a BASIC they were satisfied with for the long haul. With the help of these alumni (and some undergrads), issues with "hastily designed" prior versions were ironed out in this new edition, which was "designed thoughtfully and slowly," reflected Kurtz; even a beta version was tested for several months, with the completed manual appearing ahead of BASIC the Sixth's release.

BASIC the Sixth changed the way in which users dealt with subprograms; in addition, the management of files was improved. String manipulation was strengthened: a new function, called **SEG$**, generated substrings; the ampersand allowed the concatenation of strings; and the **POS** function searched for a substring within a string.

BASIC had been designed for educational use first and foremost, complete with flexibility and ease of use when it came to variable types, the dimensioning of arrays, and error checking. Further, English terms were always given preference over punctuation such as commas and semicolons. "[I]f FORTRAN is the lingua franca," Kurtz observed, "then certainly it must be true that BASIC is the lingua playpen."

In one of her few misperceptions, computing historian and cocreator of COBOL Jean Sammet undervalued the enthusiasm of users toward BASIC. In a 1972 survey of the field called "Programming Languages: History and Future," she claimed that certain languages like ALGOL and APL\360 inspired people and generated enthusiasm, akin to politicians who were blessed with "political charisma" in spades. "It is hard to pinpoint the reason for lack of charisma in a language, and it has very little to do with actual use," Sammet opined. "For example, BASIC and COBOL are very widely used languages, but I doubt whether many people are personally enthusiastic about either of them."

The Dartmouth Time-Sharing System had a far-reaching impact, as computer scientist William Y. Arms, who was Vice Provost for Computing and Planning at Dartmouth, explained:

> DTSS had a direct commercial impact. Since large computers were so expensive, commercial time-sharing businesses sold computer time to remote customers. The market leader was General Electric's GEIS, which was originally developed in a joint project at Dartmouth. Concepts from DTSS were adopted by the early minicomputer systems from companies such as Hewlett-Packard and Digital Equipment. Even the computer HAL in the film *2001: A Space Odyssey* had commands taken from DTSS.

"The most widely replicated of the successful [time-sharing] systems was the [DTSS]," argued Kemeny and Kurtz in their 1968 article for *Science* magazine. "[I]t became the backbone of several commercial time-sharing services as well as making its appearance in numerous industrial and engineering organizations." They claimed that over fifty copies of the DTSS were in operation by then.

Though often copied, the original Dartmouth Time-Sharing System continued to evolve. By the late 1970s, the DTSS could support two hundred users simultaneously, with compilers for BASIC, PL/I, and FORTRAN on tap (though the system was decidedly not designed with the interests of researchers in mind, which is partly why it didn't keep up with the times; another reason: the time-sharing system itself couldn't run commercial software packages, though minicomputers, nominally connected to the system, were temporarily used for this purpose).

DTSS was nimble even running larger programs, despite no virtual memory to speak of, by "automatically swapping procedures within a user's memory allocation," Arms explained. To counteract the unreliability of the disk drives, weekly backups were made on magnetic tape. The computer running the time-sharing system then was a Honeywell 66/40 with two megabytes of memory and containing two processors, each of which could handle one million instructions per second. In addition, two Honeywell 716 minicomputers triaged the operation by directing terminal traffic and transferring batches of keystrokes to the 66/40.

In the early 1970s, the British Open University, which offered distance-learning degrees to students in the UK, operated a functional time-sharing network using Hewlett-Packard HP2000 Time-Shared BASIC. Students accessed the system via time-sharing terminals stationed in study centers; installing a telephone onto an acoustic coupler facilitated the connection—at 110 bits per second. Each HP computer could accommodate up to thirty-two users at a time.

Time-sharing systems proliferated at other universities as well. Digital Equipment Corporation offered three of them: VAX/VMS, TOPS-20 for the DEC-20, and RSTS for the PDP-11 mini. (The PDP-10 mainframe had its own time-sharing operating system called TOPS-10 [Timesharing Operating System-10], complete with BASIC interpreter.) The upshot: "Time-sharing dominated academic computing until the late 1980s, when it was replaced by personal computers," according to William Arms, as the number of users who wanted their own slice of computer time increased exponentially and ultimately overwhelmed the capacity of even the most powerful time-sharing systems.

The personal computer revolution didn't spare Dartmouth, either, with the institution rejecting entreaties by IBM to instead join the Apple University Consortium, thereby procuring new Macintoshes for around one thousand dollars a pop, about half the market price. Dartmouth higher-ups like Arms, then Vice Provost for Computing and Planning, were sold on the Mac's elegant graphical user interface. "These are the subtle signs of a computer revolution that's changing Dartmouth," wrote Fred Pfaff in the June 1985 issue of *Dartmouth Alumni Magazine*. "Knowing that in some ways education would never again be the same, the College worked out a deal with Apple last year…. Parents of incoming freshmen received Macintosh brochures along with letters urging them to buy a personal computer," with nearly eighty percent of the previous fall's freshman class ponying up for the Apple.

The Macintosh featured standalone software applications such as MacWrite and MacPaint. Since Dartmouth hardwired all the dorms (and some fraternities) and converted the network to AppleTalk protocols, the computer also connected with the Kiewit Computation Center via the MacTerminal program (later DarTerminal), giving students access to electronic mail and Dartmouth's mainframe through Apple's Chooser application.

In the span of only one year, the number of personal computers on campus shot up from one hundred to nearly three thousand. Kemeny, who had by then had returned to teaching in the classroom full time after a successful run as college president, gave his blessing to these changes at the university. "This is the right way to do educational computing," he said, as Dartmouth gradually retired its time-sharing system.

By 1991, owning a personal computer, albeit not necessarily an Apple, at Dartmouth was mandatory for all students. By then, there were around ten thousand computers on campus, with nine out of ten of them Macintoshes.

A measure of good luck, perfect timing, and the potent combination of ingredients described in this chapter—including a generalist and visionary leading the mathematics department, in the form of John Kemeny; a man dedicated to the open-stack concept of free computing for all, in the form of Thomas Kurtz; a company (GE) willing to supply the necessary equipment at reduced cost; and a liberal arts college, with a precocious and intellectually vibrant student body along with an administration and a culture open to new ideas (while not institutionally burdened by government-sponsored research on campus)—laid the groundwork for the BASIC language, along with a robust time-sharing system, to take root and flourish at Dartmouth College but not elsewhere. Other institutions were too research-oriented, or lacked the resources, or the staff, or the raw talent (or some combination of these elements) to successfully put all the pieces together, as had Dartmouth.

CHAPTER 2

BASIC SAINTHOOD
The Poetic Truth of
Sister Mary Kenneth Keller

Did computing pioneer Sister Mary Kenneth Keller help
create Dartmouth BASIC?

A war has been raging at a low boil about BASIC's origins for years. Little known, and even less understood, this is a war whose battles and skirmishes are fought on Wikipedia and social media. It is a war with implications far beyond BASIC.

This chapter tells the full story of that war.

Consider the sage words of mathematician Dick Hamming who, in his essay "We Would Know What They Thought When They Did It," wrote, "We now recognize that the mere giving of names is not important; it is the ideas behind the things that matter."

Following Hamming's lead, in the essay "What Makes History?", which appears as an appendix at the end of the book *History of Programming Languages II* (1996) edited by Thomas J. Bergin and Richard G. Gibson, Princeton University's Michael S. Mahoney urges those who write about the history of computing to do more than just list the dates, names, and places of "firsts." Instead, Mahoney argues, "Getting the facts right is important, both the technical facts and the chronological facts. But the reasons for those facts are even more important, and the reasons often go well beyond the facts."

Agreed. But *only* if we can get our facts straight.

Mary Kenneth Keller is easily the most controversial figure when recounting the development of Dartmouth BASIC. Debates have raged on BASIC's Wikipedia page about her for years (scroll through the "Talk" section of the webpage). Before dismissing the importance of Wikipedia out of hand, consider: people who place an internet search for information about BASIC, or the history of BASIC, will likely be directed to Wikipedia first. Plus, those who are responsible for populating other webpages or articles or social media feeds often look to Wikipedia for the first word—perhaps even the last word— about the facts at hand, believing that content littering Wikipedia pages is essentially correct or, even if it is not, then certainly in the ballpark.

When researching any subject, the historian must rely on experts. And not just the historian: we must all lean on the expertise of others when living our everyday lives. "We believe most of what we believe about the world because others have told us so," explains philosopher Sam Harris in his book *The End of Faith* (2004). "Reliance upon the authority of experts, and upon the testimony of ordinary people, is the stuff of which worldviews are made."

To that end, it is seemingly beyond dispute that BASIC was designed by two people: primarily John G. Kemeny and, to a lesser extent, Thomas E. Kurtz. After all, the experts have told us so; Kemeny and Kurtz have themselves told us so; Dartmouth students who were present at the birth of BASIC have told us so. Very few of us were there to see the birth firsthand, so, like much else in life, we must rely on the testimony and authority of others.

Consider the words of John Kemeny. In a long-form print interview with Lynn A. Steen for the book *Mathematical People: Profiles and Interviews* (1985), Kemeny was asked about the origins of the DTSS and BASIC. "Let me give you a bit of history of that," he began.

> It is very important that Tom Kurtz should be mentioned in this connection, because he is a very modest person and I am not. *I seem to have received 90% of the credit, when the effort was strictly 50-50.* Actually the initiative was taken by Tom. We only had a small computer and he came to me when I was chairman of the math department and said, "Don't you think the time has come when all liberal arts students should know how to use the computer?" I said, "Sure, Tom, but there is no way on today's computers that we can teach 800 students." Tom said that he was thinking of a different kind of system, and he vaguely outlined what is now called time-sharing. [emphasis added]

But if you logged on to Wikipedia at various times over the last five years—to take one example, throughout most of 2018—however, you would have encountered a rather startling declaration at the top of its BASIC webpage, prominently displayed:

> In 1964, John G. Kemeny, Thomas E. Kurtz and Mary Kenneth Keller designed the original BASIC language at Dartmouth College in New Hampshire, United States.

In addition, Wikipedia's sidebar panel had the following text:

Designed by	John G. Kemeny
	Thomas E. Kurtz
	Mary Kenneth Keller

Google "BASIC" during that time, and you would have seen a summary panel of these three people—Kemeny, Kurtz, and Keller—pegged, in *equal* measure, as the language's designers.

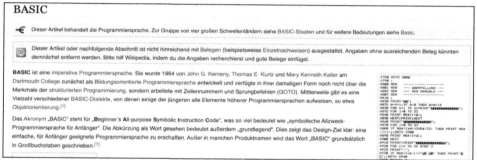

A screenshot of Wikipedia's BASIC page, English website, from June 2018.

Such Wikipedia results are not restricted to the United States. The BASIC entry for the German-language Wikipedia site, as recently as mid-2022, also had her receiving top billing; translated to English, the second sentence of the first paragraph reads, "It was initially developed in 1964 by John G. Kemeny, Thomas E. Kurtz and Mary Kenneth Keller at Dartmouth College as an educational programming language."

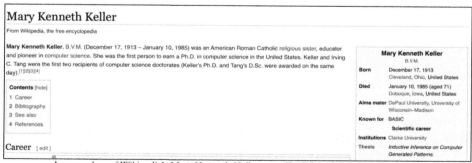

A screenshot of Wikipedia's BASIC page, German website, from June 2022.

And on Keller's U.S. Wikipedia page, we learn that she was "Known for BASIC."

A screenshot of Wikipedia's Mary Kenneth Keller page, English website, from June 2022.

In 2017, an article featuring a biography of Keller was published by *The National Catholic Register*. Called "The First Woman to Earn a Doctorate in Computer Science was a Nun," it included these two lines:

In 1958, she began working at the National Science Foundation workshop at Dartmouth College. And, because they gave this very clever nun a chance, she helped develop the computer language BASIC.

The year 1958 is similarly, but not quite identically, proffered as the *annus mirabilis* in the article "Veiled Figures: Pioneering Women Religious in the Sciences" (2018) written by Jennifer A. Head and published in the scholarly journal *Studies: An Irish Quarterly Review*. The section on Keller, which offers a lengthy biography of the computer scientist, reads in part:

> Sr Kenneth first became interested in the field of computer science while studying for a Master's degree in Mathematics at DePaul University in the early 1950s. In 1958, she applied for a six-month National Science Foundation workshop at Dartmouth University's Computer Center. She was the first woman permitted to work in the computer centre. As part of this workshop, she assisted in the development of BASIC—the first 'easy to learn' computer language.

Notice, though, Head writes that Keller *applied* for the NSF workshop in 1958, not that she attended the workshop that year.

On May 1, 2018—BASIC's fifty-fourth birthday—numerous Twitter tweets and Facebook posts lauded Keller as having either "helped develop BASIC" or "developed BASIC" (implication: solely). The next year, history repeated itself, most notably with several tweets by decorated American game developer Brenda Romero, lauding Keller's accomplishments. In March 2019, Romero tweeted to her more than half a million followers,

> A nun and a pioneering programmer, Sister Mary Kenneth Keller was instrumental in the development of the BASIC programming language, having worked with Kemeny and Kurtz in its development. She was also the first woman to attain a PhD in computer science in the US….

> It's worth noting that during the years Keller was at Dartmouth, it was male-only. Throughout her long career, she worked to establish multiple means of teaching code to women, founding entire programs if need be. #rockon

Another notable mention of Keller comes from the self-described "experimental poet" and MIT digital media professor Nick Montfort, who in December 2019 tweeted out the following:

> Sister Mary Kenneth Keller's involvement with BASIC is quite relevant to #10print but (nostra culpa!) not in the book. Not deeply documented in the scholarly record; this sidebar to Denise W. Gürer's 1995 CACM article mentions it.

The "#10print" hashtag refers to the 2012 MIT Press Commodore 64-centric anthology called *10 PRINT CHR$(205.5+RND(1)); : GOTO 10*, of which Montfort was a coauthor and editor.

The Vatican Observatory, located in Castel Gandolfo, Italy, and established by the Holy See centuries ago, maintains a website promoting its mission of "Faith Inspiring Science." One entry in its online "Religious Scientists of the Catholic Church" series focuses on Keller. "When I was little, my dad bought an Apple II+ computer," recalls Br. Robert Macke, "[and] I learned a very simple computer language called Beginner's All-purpose Symbolic Instruction Code, or BASIC. With it, I made my own games, limited only by my imagination and skill. For the freedom that programming in BASIC gave me, I have to thank a nun: Sr. Mary Kenneth Keller."

There are simply too many other articles, blog entries, and social media posts about the Keller-BASIC connection to list here, and they are ever-growing. The sister's ostensible claim to BASIC fame is also faithfully reported in several recent scholarly books. Take, for example, *The Triumph of Artificial Intelligence* (2021), by Günter Cisek and published by Springer. "In 1964," we learn on page 14, "John G. Kemeny, Thomas E. Kurtz and Mary Kenneth Keller at Dartmouth College developed the education-oriented programming language BASIC (Beginner's All-purpose Symbolic Instruction Code), which was intended to be universally applicable and easy for beginners to learn." Also consider *New Media Futures: The Rise of Women in the Digital Arts* (2018), edited by Donna J. Cox et al. and published by the Board of Trustees of the University of Illinois. An endnote to the Introduction of the book reads, "As a graduate student, Keller additionally studied at Dartmouth, Purdue, and the University of Michigan. At Dartmouth, the university broke its 'men only' rule, enabling her to work in the computer center where she participated in the development of BASIC."

But like a game of telephone, the historical record has become widely distorted. How did this mythology develop around Mary Kenneth Keller?

Born on December 17, 1913, in Cleveland, Cuyahoga County, Ohio, Mary Kenneth Keller entered the Sisters of Charity of the Blessed Virgin Mary (BVM) in 1932, professing her religious vows in 1940. Afterward, she earned two degrees—an undergraduate degree in mathematics and a graduate degree in mathematics and physics—from DePaul University in Chicago. In the 1950s, around the time she obtained the master's, Keller worked as a mathematics teacher at St. Mary's High School for Girls, also located in Chicago, encountering a computer for the first time, as we learn in the 2015 article "Half a Century of Computer Science" printed in *Clarke: The Magazine of Clarke University*. By the 1960s, a document with the heading "List of Members in the Iowa Section of the MAA [Mathematical Association of America] as of March 2, 1964," shows a "Sister Mary Kenneth B.M.V." of Heelan High School in Sioux City, Iowa. An MAA Iowa Section list from two years later devotes two lines to Keller: one line mentioning Heelan High, and the other line Clarke University.

In 1965, after three years of studying at the institution, the plucky Keller earned a doctorate in computer science from the University of Wisconsin-Madison. Her dissertation, titled "Inductive Inference on Computer Generated Patterns" and overseen by mathematics professor and computer scientist Preston Clarence Hammer, detailed the creation of algorithms in CDC FORTRAN 63 that performed analytic (symbolic) differentiation. (In calculus, *differentiation* and *integration* are inverse processes of analyzing mathematical functions; the former deals with rates of change and the latter sums changing quantities. Differentiation is akin to scrambling an egg, while integration is more like unscrambling it.) She considered using list-processing languages better suited for symbolic manipulation, such as LISP and its forerunner, IPL (Information Processing Language; specifically, IPL-V), but ultimately settled on FORTRAN, "based on its availability at the computing center."

Her dissertation leaned on the scholarship of D. H. Potts in the discipline of algorithms as well as that of J. A. Robinson with respect to machine-oriented logic. Keller employed a technique by the Soviet mathematician Andrei Petrovich Ershov, called Ershov's algorithm, to perform what she termed a "pattern generation": syntactically analyzing an expression of input strings of symbols linked by binary operators and transferred to matrix form. Then, analytic differentiation of the expression was carried out using a FORTRAN program, building off the ideas of mathematicians Bruce Wesley Arden and J. W. Hanson.

Of course, she also relied on the direct support of academics to complete the doctorate. "I wish to express my appreciation to Professor Preston C. Hammer for his suggestions which led to the selection of this area of research," Keller wrote in the dissertation, "his invaluable guidance in bringing it to completion, and especially for his patient assistance in my work over a period of years." She thanked "J. W. Hanson, director of the University of North Carolina Computing Center, [who] was kind enough to correspond with me regarding analytic differentiation by computer...." The Acknowledgments section also included Keller expressing her "gratitude" to the "National Science Foundation for its support of my education."

In an oral history interview conducted in 2004 of Seymour Parter, a professor who joined the mathematics department at Wisconsin while Keller was knee-deep in her doctoral work, interviewer Joyce Coleman pointedly asked Parter if he remembered Keller. "Barely. She was a student of Preston's," he told Coleman. "But she was an interesting woman. She learned numerical analysis…. I came in '63, so I guess I must have seen her around. She never took a course with me. I think she was busy writing her thesis by the time [I got to Wisconsin]."

Keller is likely the first woman in the United States to earn a Ph.D. in computer science. Irving C. Tang also obtained a doctorate in computer science (specifically, a D.Sc.) on the same day as Keller—June 7, 1965—but at a different institution: Washington University in St. Louis. Keller secured her doctorate mere months before Richard Wexelblat earned his at the University of Pennsylvania.

Keller then assumed a faculty position at Clarke College in Dubuque, Iowa, founding (and chairing) the institution's computer science department. She advocated for women's involvement in computer science as well as the integration of computers in education, establishing a master's degree in computer applications in education at Clarke (back then, the college was a women's college; now, Clarke is a co-ed university). Keller and "other members of the computer science faculty and staff wrote programmes to assist academic departments on campus," relayed Jennifer Head. "Chemistry students ran simulated experiments while psychology students used a programme to run a hypothetical 'stat rat' through a learning maze, saving time 'both ours and the rat's!'" Furthermore, "She also anticipated the importance computers would have in libraries, recognising that 'its function in information retrieval will make it the hub of tomorrow's libraries.'" In Keller's words, "Since this is the era [in 1965] of automation and since we are fast becoming a computerized society, everyone should at least be acquainted with the appearance and purposes of a computer."

Gail Bukolt Coury, an alumna of Clarke who graduated in 1977, was a student of Keller's. In the 1970s, the institution had a modest IBM mainframe on campus, along with access to more computing power via a dial-up connection to an IBM installation at the University of Iowa. "I remember one of the first assignments in Sister Kenneth's class was to describe how a person stands from a sitting position," wrote Coury for *Clarke: The Magazine of Clarke University.*

> I was a bit frustrated because I couldn't understand what this had to do with computers. In class, we had to read what we described and Sister Kenneth would follow our instructions. In most all cases, we were not detailed enough, which was the point of the assignment—computers will do exactly what you tell them, and only what you tell them. Sister Kenneth acting out the instructions that we all wrote was quite funny.

Another alumna, 1981 graduate Karen Shepard Demello, was intimidated by Keller at first, since "she looked a little gruff and very serious." But Demello's opinion of the sister changed rapidly. "Once in her class I found that she had an amazing sense of humor and was nothing like I imagined. She was very dedicated to her students, telling us that we could ask her for help any time day or night, except for Friday nights when *Dallas* was on TV." (The author of the *Clarke* article also claims that Keller "participated in the development of [the] BASIC computer language.")

Jennifer Head notes that Keller, an author of numerous computer science books, was an acknowledged expert in her field, a "fixture in the early 'IT' world of the Upper Mississippi River Valley," with Keller once boasting that "around Dubuque [in Iowa] nobody buys a computer without calling me!" After she passed away, the computer center at the college was rechristened the Keller Computer Center and Information Service, with a scholarship in her name introduced.

The time period between Keller's graduate school work and the awarding of her doctorate, however, is a source of major questions. In an article published in the January 1995 issue of *Communications of the ACM* (Association for Computing Machinery) (Volume 38, Number 1) titled "Pioneering Women in Computer Science," which offers a comprehensive grand tour of women's achievements in the field, the computer scientist, educator, and author Denise W. Gürer devotes a single, short paragraph to describing this critical time in Keller's life. Here is the relevant paragraph in its entirety:

> As a graduate student, Keller also studied at Dartmouth, Purdue, and the University of Michigan. At Dartmouth, the university broke the "men only" rule and allowed her to work in the computing center, where she participated in the development of BASIC.

In the article, the only "References" endnote directly relating to Keller is of her doctoral dissertation (the ninth endnote). However, Keller does not mention Kemeny,

Kurtz, Dartmouth, DTSS, or the BASIC programming language in the dissertation. Since "Pioneering Women in Computer Science" is cited by many sources (including Wikipedia) that claim Keller was involved in the development of BASIC—indeed, if there are citations in these sources at all—it is unfortunate that the basis of the Keller-BASIC claim is opaque. (According to Google Scholar, "Pioneering Women in Computer Science" has been cited well over one hundred times as of 2022; the article itself has been downloaded thousands of times, as shown in the ACM Digital Library. Of course, Keller's biography is only one small portion of a much larger story about women's accomplishments in computer science. Also, note that there are two published versions of "Pioneering Women in Computer Science"—one from 1995 and the other from 2002 [Volume 34, Number 2 of the *ACM SIGCSE Bulletin*]—but the sections devoted to Keller are effectively identical; we thus treat both versions here as one publication.)

It is not clear if documents were unearthed proving Keller's involvement or if Keller was interviewed for the article. However, note that for the individuals interviewed, a citation is offered to that effect—for instance, endnote "15. Sammet, J.E. Interview with Jean E. Sammet conducted by Denise Gürer, June 1994." No such citation is given for Keller who, regardless, died in Dubuque, Dubuque County, Iowa, on January 10, 1985, a full decade before "Pioneering Women in Computer Science" was first published.

So, then, the question becomes: Based on what we know about the BASIC development timeline, could Keller have had a hand in the creation of the language? And, if so, how did she contribute to the Dartmouth effort?

Let us first examine the history of coeducation at Dartmouth. As relayed in a 1995 article published in the college's newspaper, *The Dartmouth*:

> When serious discussion about coeducation began in the 1960s, the faculty were the strongest supporters of the move. Eventually, the idea grew on the students. But the majority of alumni did not believe women would or could make a positive contribution to the campus.

> The move to coeducation could not have taken place without then College President John Kemeny's commitment to coeducation and his ability to create a plan for its execution that the alumni could swallow. Without Kemeny, the history of women at Dartmouth might be significantly shorter.

Although the admission of women as full-time undergraduate students didn't begin until the early 1970s, it is important to underscore that it was Kemeny, as president, who shepherded the turn to coeducation. As he said in his 1970 Inaugural Address, "It is my personal opinion that if we were refounding Dartmouth College today, we would, of course, not discriminate on the basis of race or religion. But I believe that if we were refounding the institution today, we would also not discriminate on the basis of sex." Kemeny boasted progressive bona fides for the time—speeches he gave in office were focused on increasing diversity in the student body, opposition to American escalations in the Vietnam War, and concerns over the Three Mile Island nuclear accident (see the curated anthology *John Kemeny Speaks* for the full text of these remarks)—lending credence to the possibility that he could have conceivably recruited at least one exceptional woman, such as Keller, to help with the development of BASIC. (Note that of the three dozen programming assistants employed at the Kiewit Computation Center in the four years following Dartmouth's shift to a coeducational institution, likely none was female. In the 1970s, computing at Dartmouth was still dominated by males, as were overall enrollments at the college.)

The *Dartmouth* article also relays several landmark dates involving the college's transition to coeducation: (1) A poll conducted around 1958, in which faculty and students were queried about the possibilities of women on campus; (2) A comment by the president of the college in 1958, John Sloan Dickey, about the possibilities of undergraduate coeducation (he said, "I haven't thought about it seriously. I have great misgivings about its practicality and viability here"); (3) A first-ever summer term, established in the 1961-62 academic year, in which women were permitted to "take classes that would count toward their degrees at their own schools"; (4) A 1965 poll conducted among faculty, students, and alumni about coeducation; (5) A 1969 coeducational "experiment" in which the school bussed women on campus for "Coed Week"; (6) A 1969-1970 college exchange program with a dozen schools; and (7) The recommendation, in 1971, by the Dartmouth Trustee Committee that the college become coeducational. Observe that only items (1), (2), and (3) occurred before BASIC debuted in 1964.

Perhaps, then, Keller was at Dartmouth for that summer term in the 1961-62 academic year, helping Kemeny and Kurtz design BASIC. But there's another problem. Take a look, once again, at the key passage from "Pioneering Women in Computer Science":

> As a graduate student, Keller also studied at Dartmouth, Purdue, and the University of Michigan. At Dartmouth, the university broke the "men only" rule and allowed her to work in the computing center, where she participated in the development of BASIC.

Was there a "computing center" at Dartmouth prior to BASIC's birth? Consider the history related in a brochure called "The Kiewit Computation Center & The Dartmouth Time-Sharing System," written by Kemeny in the mid-1960s:

> The interest of the College in automatic computation was first manifested earlier than that [the 1960s]—in fact as far back as the pre-electronic age.... In 1940 Dartmouth was host to the autumn meeting of the American Mathematical Society. In the world's first publicly demonstrated remote use of a computer, Dr. George Stibitz, then of the Bell Telephone Laboratories, enabled the visiting mathematicians to perform calculations on complex numbers while seated at a Teletype in McNutt Hall....

> But not until 1959 did the College acquire a computer of its own and begin to operate it. In the spring of that year an LGP-30, capable of performing several arithmetic operations per second, arrived on campus. During the summer an enthusiastic group of students worked to wring the utmost from this machine, which by present-day standards was very small and very slow....

So, despite Dartmouth playing host to a computing demonstration in the prehistoric days of 1940, *not until 1959 was there was even a single programmable computer on campus for students to use*. There was certainly no computing center; that would come later, when, in 1962, "Dartmouth mathematicians John Kemeny and Thomas Kurtz proposed building a College computation center," according to the timeline shown on the Dartmouth website's "ITS Tools" page. Kemeny explained the motivation behind building a computation center in the Kiewit brochure:

> The computer system [the DTSS] had become the focus of so much activity on campus that the limits of its temporary quarters in the basement of College Hall were increasingly confining to the team of programmers engaged in the never-ending task of improving the software system and extending its capabilities. An appropriate building, to house the larger new computer that had become necessary, was urgently needed. Thanks to the generosity of Peter D. Kiewit '22 and his wife Evelyn Stott Kiewit, together with further support from the National Science Foundation, this need was magnificently met.

The Kiewit Computation Center was dedicated on December 2, 1966; its first director was Tom Kurtz. From the mid-1950s until June of 1959, when Kurtz, Kemeny, and their wives personally picked up the LGP-30 and then drove the machine back to campus in a station wagon, there were few good computing options for Dartmouth faculty and students. The Massachusetts Institute of Technology made its New England Regional Computing Center available, which featured an IBM 704; Kurtz traveled every several weeks to MIT to use the machine. There was also a computer installation at General Electric of Lynn, Massachusetts, which Kemeny and Kurtz utilized prior to the computing center at MIT opening its doors in 1956. (Kurtz was hired by Kemeny in 1956.)

What year, then, did Keller travel to Dartmouth to help Kememy and Kurtz develop BASIC? Though "Pioneering Women in Computer Science" offers no such date, as we have seen from several other sources, the consensus appears to be 1958. For instance, that is the year relayed in Keller's official biography on the Catholic Archives website, found at catholicarchives.bc.edu. Here is the relevant passage:

> She first became interested in the field of computer science in the 1950s and in 1958, she was the first woman permitted to work in Dartmouth University's Computer Center, where she assisted in the development of BASIC—the first "easy to learn" computer language.

But in 1958, the LGP-30 computer was still a year away from installation at Dartmouth. And there was nothing close to a "Computing Center" on campus yet, either.

A source offering a bit more detail can be found on the Acton Institute website, acton.org. Keller's biography there reads as follows:

> In 1958, Keller started at the National Science Foundation workshop in the computer science center at Dartmouth College, which was an all-male school at the time. While there she teamed up with computer scientists John G. Kemeny and Thomas E. Kurtz to develop the BASIC programming language.

Indeed, National Science Foundation grants funded more advanced computing hardware than the LGP-30—specifically, the GE-225/235 computer and the GE DATANET-30 for time-sharing. But all that happened in the early 1960s, not in 1958, and these grants were not intended to support a "computer science center" at Dartmouth, only computing equipment needed for a time-sharing system.

There was at least one summer session that offered students hands-on access to the LGP-30, though. Perhaps Keller attended that summer session, although it is unlikely that Kemeny taught the class or was involved in any way. Regardless, BASIC was not developed for or on the LGP-30, although predecessors of BASIC, most notably DOPE (Dartmouth Oversimplified Programming Experiment), were programmed for the machine.

In the 1950s, Dartmouth's most significant summer gathering took place not in 1958 but in 1956, when John McCarthy, who would go on to great renown as an MIT professor and creator of the LISP (LISt Processor) programming language—which would solve problems in artificial intelligence—organized the Dartmouth Summer Research Project on Artificial Intelligence, the first such conference of its kind. Marvin Minsky, Claude Shannon, and other computer science luminaries attended. No records indicate that Keller was present at McCarthy's conference.

In March 2019, the University of Wisconsin-Madison, where Keller obtained her doctorate, released an article for their Computer Sciences webpage that boasted of her accomplishments—sans one. The article's key paragraph reads as follows.

> She [Keller] earned her B.S. in Mathematics and M.S. in Mathematics and Physics from DePaul University, and she participated in a summer institute at Dartmouth University in the late 1950s. John Kemeny, Dartmouth's mathematics department chair, explained, "Our vision was that every student on campus should have access to a computer, and any faculty member should be able to use a computer in the classroom whenever appropriate. It was as simple as that." Keller shared this vision in her career as well.

BASIC is not mentioned at all in the article, nor is there any talk of Keller helping to develop the language. Rather, the author seems to imply that Keller, in her time at the Dartmouth summer institute, was influenced by the goal of equal access to computing, just as Kememy professed to be. Yet that Dartmouth vision of computing wouldn't crystalize, either publicly or privately, until around 1962 or 1963, so while Keller may have *later on in her career* been sold on Dartmouth's open-access computing model, she demonstrably could not have been influenced by it in the late 1950s or even in the very early 1960s, since it didn't yet exist. (In fact, Kemeny's words in the block quote above were pulled from a 1991 video interview in which he offered a qualification: that it was Kurtz who had the vision for democratic, open-access computing.)

In Keller's doctoral dissertation, she lists "Colleges and Universities: Years attended and degrees." There was Clarke College, from 1933 to 1935; Mundelein College, in 1935; De Paul University, Chicago, from 1942 to 1952 (A.B., 1942; M.S., 1952); Purdue University, in 1957; University of Wisconsin, from 1962 to 1965 (Ph.D., June 1965); and Dartmouth College, in 1961.

By her own hand, the myth of Keller studying at Dartmouth in 1958 was put to bed.

The case for Keller's involvement in the development of BASIC—certainly in any central capacity—undoubtedly weakens further if we consider the writings of Kemeny and Kurtz. For example, in *Back to BASIC: The History, Corruption, and Future of the Language*, the Dartmouth duo's definitive insider's look at the history of BASIC published in 1985, Keller is not mentioned. But other students, such as John McGeachie and Mike Busch, who helped develop the Dartmouth Time-Sharing System, are repeatedly referenced. In his chapter for 1978's ACM SIGPLAN History of Programming Languages Conference in Los Angeles, California, Kurtz gives credit to John McGeachie and Mike Busch, but Keller is nowhere to be found.

In an extended interview in 2002, Kurtz never refers to anyone named Keller. In a documentary released for the fiftieth anniversary of BASIC, called *Birth of BASIC*, again, Keller goes unmentioned. Even in historian Jean E. Sammet's seminal 1969 book *Programming Languages: History and Fundamentals*, Kurtz and Kemeny are discussed—but Keller is absent.

During Kemeny's *Mathematical People* interview, he claimed that "[i]n the development of the original time-sharing system, it was not just Tom and myself—we were highly part-time. It was twelve undergraduate students, and believe me they worked incredible hours." At no point in the interview does Kemeny speak of graduate students connected with the design or development of BASIC or the time-sharing system, nor does he mention Keller. But, of course, Kemeny not bringing up either graduate students or Keller doesn't rule out the possibility of their presence since he does not explicitly exclude them.

The Dartmouth website lists the following undergraduate "sysprogs" (system programmers), along with their graduation years, who kept the DTSS running smoothly:

Allan (Bicky) Jayne, 1973; Andrew Behrens, 1971; August (Gus) Reinig, 1980; Barry Hayes, 1980; Brig B. (Chip) Elliot Jr. 1976; Charles (Kip) Moore, 1965; Christian Walker, 1973; David Pearson, 1975; David Rice, 1967; David Wright, 1978; Douglas Rice, 1976; Elliot Noma, 1972; G. Blake Meike, 1979; Gregory Dobbs, 1969; James Keim, 1972; Jennifer Kemeny, 1976; John McGeachie, 1965; L. Carl Pedersen, 1973; Louis F. Fernandez, 1973; M. Alexander Colvin, 1977; Phillip DiBello, 1982; Richard Lacey, 1967; Robert Hargraves, 1961; Ronald Harris, 1971; Ronald Martin, 1967; Sidney Marshall, 1965; Stephen Garland, 1963; Steven Hobbs, 1969; Steven Reiss, 1972; T. Gary Broughton, 1966; Thomas Martin, 1963; Warren Montgomery, 1973

But there is no companion list of graduate students who helped Kemeny and Kurtz. Though, in fairness, the names listed above include only those who attended a reunion in June 2007; Keller had passed away two decades earlier. Yet the article describing the reunion makes no mention of Keller, nor of any sysprogs who were not Dartmouth undergrads.

At the first National Computer Conference Pioneer Day Session, held in 1974 and honoring the DTSS (later honorees would include FORTRAN, COBOL, and the EINAC), and which both Kememy and Kurtz attended, Keller was still alive—but she wasn't present at the event (by this point, she had founded the computer science department at Clarke College, establishing her bona fides in both computing and education). A number of the sysprogs, including John McGeachie and Mike Busch, who helped get the DTSS off the ground, were there. Indeed, McGeachie was there *ab initio*—a time when "we used to know our programs by the names of the people who wrote them," he recalled.

A lone graduate student participated on the Pioneer Day panel: Neil Wiedenhofer. As the transcript of the event reads, "I'm Neil Wiedenhofer. I was a graduate student at Dartmouth back in those days. I worked mostly on the BASIC compiler. Now I'm a systems programmer for United Computing Systems, a time-sharing outfit." Which is significant because of Kemeny's last words at the discussion panel, quoted in full below.

> Tom [Kurtz], may I give an acceptance speech on behalf of both of us then? It is customary when accepting an Academy Award to mention your mother, your father, your music teacher, and your coach, and everyone else who really deserves the award. And I'm going to follow that precedent by saying that *for both Tom and me this award would not exist except for the work done by a number of undergraduate students, Dartmouth College, and one graduate student, many of whom are sitting right here.* And some of them are not here. Therefore, I think they deserve about half, each one deserves about half of our award and the other half should be divided equally amongst the other students who did all the work. [emphasis added]

His sentence "And some of them are not here" clearly refers to other undergraduates—or perhaps even to other professors or administrators at Dartmouth—but most definitely *not* to other graduate students, since Kemeny was explicit that there was only "one graduate student" who assisted—presumably Wiedenhofer, who was an attendee on the panel and had earlier introduced himself as "a graduate student at Dartmouth back in those days" who worked on BASIC. Since neither Kemeny and Kurtz, nor anyone else at the Pioneer Day event honoring the DTSS, ever mentioned Keller (who would have been a graduate student then), the probability further diminishes of not only her participation in the development of Dartmouth BASIC but also of her having had any role related to the DTSS.

Moreover, in her recent book *A People's History of Computing in the United States* (2018), which devotes several chapters to how computing in and around the Dartmouth campus of the 1960s and '70s "became increasingly masculine," author Joy Lisi Rankin chronicles the stories of the "women of Kiewit." There was Janet Price, who was hired at Dartmouth as an applications programmer in 1968; she was a FORTRAN expert who also taught the language. There was Ruth Bogart, hired as a social sciences programmer with the mission to support faculty. There was Jann Dalton, the librarian at Kiewit. And there were the two Dianes, Diane Hills and Diane Mather, hired in 1969, who were both assigned applications programming, among other tasks. But Mary Kenneth Keller does not appear anywhere in *A People's History*. Rankin—who conducted an intensive study of archival documents at Dartmouth, including poring over the Records of Dartmouth College computing Services, the Information File for the Computation Center and for Time-Sharing, as well as the Papers of Kemeny, Kurtz, Sidney Marshall, and Stephen Garland—is quite direct on the authorship of the language and the time-sharing system: namely, Kemeny and Kurtz, along with a handful of male student programmers supporting the effort. "Busch and McGeachie triumphed during May 1964," Rankin wrote. "They sat at separate teletype terminals. They each typed a short BASIC program, and they submitted their programs at the same time." Both leading up to and on that fateful early morning of BASIC's birth, Mary Kenneth Keller was nowhere to be found, at least according to Rankin's account.

Yet more damning evidence comes to us from the peer-reviewed academic journal *IEEE Annals of the History of Computing*: specifically, Volume 8, Number 2, published in April 1986. In the issue, we find Keller's obituary, which is reprinted in full below.

> Sister Mary Kenneth Keller, BVM, died in January 1985 at the age of 71 after a long and distinguished career in the use of computers in education. She received her Ph.D. from the University of Wisconsin in 1965. Sister Mary Kenneth established the computer science program at Clarke college in Iowa, one of the first in a small college. She wrote four books on various aspects of computing and was a founder of the Association of Small Computer Users in Education (ASCUE).

If Keller had played a part—*any part*—in the development of Dartmouth BASIC, that fact would have almost certainly been mentioned in the obit.

Perhaps all this could be explained away as something political, as a conspiracy of silence intended to purposely not provide a particular woman her due for the development of a popular programming language—a conspiracy extending to more than half a century. A series of tweets from February 2021 by one Twitter user, named Ana Campón, floats this idea:

> **Seeing is believing.**
> How many of you are able to say three women who have contributed to #science or #engineering without Google? And no, Marie Curie or Ada Lovelace are [*sic*] not an option.
> If you can't do it, don't worry. You're not alone.
> Why does it happen?
> …
>
> **That which cannot be named does not exist.** The lack of references is one of the problems of the low number of women studying a #STEM career.
> …
>
> So on the #womeninscienceday, I propose you a challenge: leave me a comment with a women [*sic*] scientists who has made a difference and share this post. This way all of us will show the female contribution to the advancement of the #STEM field.
> …
>
> I kick-off. She is Mary Kenneth Keller and co-developed the BASIC programming language, basis of the entire digital revolution that we enjoy today. But her name has been forgotten from #history and only those of her colleagues John G. Kemeny and Thomas E. Kurtz are remembered.

But if there has been such a conspiracy of silence, ensuring that the contributions of Keller are memory-holed, then how do we explain the world renown of other women like Grace Hopper, senior member in the pantheon of all-time great programmers? IBM's John Backus already knew of, and reacted to, her seminal work during his team's development of FORTRAN in the 1950s at IBM, publicly saying as much at the time. For that matter, how do we know of Lois Haibt's and Grace "Libby" Mitchell's critical contributions to FORTRAN while working on Backus's team? What about the "First Programmers Club"—that group of a half-dozen women, mathematicians all, who coded the ENIAC during the Second World War—headlined by the legendary programmer Frances Elizabeth "Betty" Holberton? What about Kathleen Booth, among the first to develop an assembly language (at Birkbeck College, University of London) in the 1940s, and Ann Hardy, who overcame sexist discrimination to program the IBM Stretch supercomputer and write a novel time-sharing operating system in 1966? And what of Deborah Davidson, Mary K. Hawes, Sue Knapp, Jean E. Sammet, Nora Taylor, and Gertrude Tierney who helped develop COBOL? Knowledge of contributions by these women, and many others, were very much in circulation in computer science literature well before the turn of the twenty-first century.

So why would Kemeny, Kurtz, and the many Dartmouth students who worked on BASIC and the DTSS remain silent about Keller's contributions—a silence that has now persisted for six decades?

Such questions don't arise in a vacuum; rather, more context is required. The following interlude provides some.

AN INTERLUDE:
GENDER AND RACE AT DARTMOUTH—AND BEYOND

If Mary Kenneth Keller was involved in some way with the creation of Dartmouth BASIC, then her life on campus could not have been easy; she would have been present at the inauguration of Dartmouth's "tech-bro culture" that computing historian Joy Rankin has documented in detail. Rankin, who earned an undergraduate degree at Dartmouth (majoring in mathematics and history) and a doctorate at Yale (in history), was a consultant on *The Birth of BASIC* documentary. "Kemeny and Kurtz," explains Rankin in the article "Tech-Bro Culture Was Written in the Code,"

> believed that computing offered a tremendous opportunity for all students—not just those in the sciences and engineering—and the college's dedication to accessible computing set its network apart from similar computing networks during the 1960s. Its founders referred to participation on the network as computing "citizenship." But that citizenship, and the systems that followed Dartmouth's lead across the country, ultimately mirrored the college's demographics: predominantly male, white, and affluent. And although Kemeny and Kurtz intended computing as an equalizer for their students, the Dartmouth network's computing "citizens" created novel and lasting associations among computing, masculinity, and status.

For instance, in 1966 Dartmouth built the Kiewit Computation Center in front of the Baker Library and adjacent to Webster Avenue, the latter commonly referred to as "Fraternity Row." Since "social life at Dartmouth revolved around its fraternities," Rankin writes, "[t]his placed the new Computation Center in a perfect location for socializing, entertaining dates visiting from the Seven Sisters Colleges, or popping in on the way back from a football game." (Observe Rankin's use of the term *computing citizens* above, referring to those individuals who made use of time-sharing services, differentiated them from mere "users," since computing citizens had a more active role: as both producers and consumers of content, they were dynamic participants in the "social computing" implicit in time-sharing.)

But the Computation Center also offered a new means for young men to show off; these "brogrammers" exhibited their newly-realized "computer prowess" to impress dates in demonstrative displays of machismo. "On the lighter side," Kurtz admitted in the 1969 article "The Many Roles of Computing on the Campus," "the students enjoy using the computer for fun things such as playing a simulated football game or demonstrating to their weekend dates their 'prowess' on the computer." For example, student Francis Marzoni printed out a banner with the text "HEY GIRL I MISS YOU" for his long-distance girlfriend. (BASIC code to create such large-scale lettering can be found in the program *Banner*, part of David Ahl's early 1970s book of type-ins called *101 BASIC Computer Games*.)

After all, as Dartmouth's dean of engineering wrote in a letter at the time, "There would be complete privacy [when using the terminals]. No one would know what the students were doing." Consider Kurtz again: "There is no attempt to control the uses they make of the computer; in fact, there is almost no way of finding out what they are doing except by walking into the teletype room and looking over their shoulders." And when comparing the library open-stack concept with time-sharing terminals, Kemeny wrote, "Similarly, any student may walk into the Kiewit Computation Center, sit down at a console, and use the time-sharing system. No one will ask whether he is solving a serious research problem, doing his homework the easy way, playing a game of football, or writing a letter to his girlfriend."

Rankin adds that as DTSS's net widened, "[it] advantaged a homogeneous group of network users: male students, predominantly white and well-to-do, who could create programs in BASIC." After all, women weren't formally admitted as undergraduates to the college until the 1970s—although some women managed to study there, in various capacities, before then, as well as to work at Kiewit, with applications programmer Janet Price, a FORTRAN expert, being one notable example—and the first set of schools with access to the DTSS were similar demographically to Dartmouth, resulting in a relatively homogenous user base early in the life of the time-sharing system.

John Kemeny made a number of progressive moves as Dartmouth's president in the 1970s, such as shifting the school to a coeducational model as well as redoubling the college's efforts to educate Native Americans. He was also a long-time anti-nuclear war activist, having worked with the World Federalist Movement to inform people about the horrors of nuclear warfare. After leaving the presidency, Kemeny chaired Jimmy Carter's Presidential Commission investigating the Three Mile Island accident.

As a child, Kemeny was hardly the beneficiary of privilege and was certainly no stranger to outright evil. He was born Kemény János György to a Jewish family in Budapest, Hungary, on May 31, 1926, with the rise of Hitler only several years away. Kemeny's father, Tibor, left the country for the United States in 1938, convinced that Hitler's march into Vienna earlier that year was a troubling omen; in two years, his wife and young son would follow. With anti-Jewish laws in effect in Hungary, Tibor persuaded most of the rest of the family to immigrate to America as well; they left in 1940 but lost most of their possessions. Sadly, several family members, including Kemeny's grandfather, an aunt, and an uncle, refused to leave Hungary and perished in the Holocaust. Certainly, John Kemeny's background accounts in part for his progressive views and empathy for others.

Though demonstrably progressive for his time, Kemeny was also a product of his time. Pick up copies of a computing magazine like *Datamation* from the early 1960s, and you'll likely encounter *Mad Men*-style sexist language, where women are often called "girls" and descriptions of their physical characteristics are de rigueur. Consider the article "Tabular Form in Decision Logic," found in the July 1961 issue. Burton Grad, employed at the Thomas J. Watson Research Center at IBM, penned the piece, which begins this way:

> Glancing around the office, I can see three young women busily engaged in the various duties of a typical work day. Let me tell you about them. Blond Marilyn is a chatterbox. Penelope and Theresa enjoy going to the movies. Marilyn is married, but the other two are single. Penelope has an attractive figure, while Marilyn is somewhat on the plump side. Theresa's quiet moods contrast to Penelope's happy ones, but they both seem to enjoy life in native Manhattan. Marilyn has dimples; Theresa may be recognized by her amber eyes and red hair. Unlike the others, Marilyn prefers Shakespeare and country living in Chappaqua.

But why stop at magazines geared toward computers? We can get an even better sense of the zeitgeist by examining an issue of *Cosmopolitan*, which featured an article called "The Computer Girls" in 1967. As author Lois Mandel explains, "A trainee gets $8,000 a year...a girl 'senior systems analyst' gets $20,000—and up! Maybe it's time to investigate..." (the ellipses are hers). And investigate she does, even interviewing Grace Hopper for the piece. "Twenty years ago, a girl could be a secretary, a school teacher...maybe a librarian, a social worker or a nurse," writes Mandel. "If she was really ambitious, she could go into the professions and compete with men...usually working harder and longer to earn less pay for the same job." But new opportunities in pink-collar work had opened up. "Now have come the big, dazzling computers—and a whole new kind of work for women: programming.... And if it doesn't sound like woman's work—well, it just is," she adds. Hopper, then employed at Univac (though Mandel incorrectly gives her credit for helping develop the ENIAC), is happy to explain how they landed in "the age of the Computer Girls." "It's just like planning a dinner," Hopper tells Mandel. "You have to plan ahead and schedule everything so it's ready when you need it. Programming requires patience and the ability to handle detail. Women are 'naturals' at computer programming."

But as author Alana Staiti, who analyzed the *Cosmopolitan* article for the National Museum of American History, pointed out,

> Left unsaid in the 1967 article was the fact that women had already made a lasting impact on computer programming; they were programmers even before the work was called "programming." These (mainly white) women who helped shape the growing field performed calculations and plugged patch cords into the earliest electronic digital machines of the 1940s. However, at the time, few gained recognition for their work, which was distinct from systems design and engineering, jobs overwhelmingly held by white men.

By the 1950s, as companies and other organizations automated many of their processes using large mainframes, skilled programmers were in demand—with "[c]ompanies…keen on recruiting women—a demographic typically considered cheaper and more obedient than men—as programmers, systems analysts, data processors, and [clerical] key-punch operators," according to Staiti. "Whether it was done consciously or subconsciously, citing women's 'natural' talent for this sort of work was one way that (mostly male) managers contributed to keeping women in subservient jobs."

Beginning around World War I, when the term *computers* became widely used, the word referenced people, not machines; these "computers," who performed mathematical computations, were typically women. After World War II, the term shifted gradually to refer to machines. "When computing became the work of business administration and office machines, the people doing computing at that time were most often women," observed Rankin. "And it's why in some ways it's not so surprising that there are so many women doing computing in the United States during the 1950s and 1960s." Even teletypewriters were typically operated by women as far back as the 1910s, when the electromechanical machines were first integrated with the existing telegraph infrastructure.

In his book *The Art of Doing Science and Engineering: Learning to Learn* (1997), mathematician Dick Hamming describes closely collaborating in the 1950s with "a lady programmer from Bell Telephone Laboratories, on one big problem coding in absolute binary for the IBM 701." (Hamming is quoted in the first Dartmouth BASIC manual offering the timeless advice, "Typing is no substitute for thinking.") But then things began to change for women in computing, as Rankin explained in a 2018 talk delivered at Google:

> What we've seen happen is that as it was increasingly clear that computers would be crucial to society and [be] valuable work, sort of multiple processes happened whereby women were pushed out because the work became work seen as more prestigious and therefore, as computing professionalized, [it] became a more masculine field…. So, in some ways, it was a reverse of inclusivity where the women were over time pushed out and the cultures around technology became more masculine in ways that it was harder for [women] to be in that work [and] in that world.

Perhaps the inflection point in the profession came when the term *programmer* replaced *coder*. According to John Backus, the shift in language occurred for the "same reason that janitors are now called 'custodians.' 'Programmer' was considered a higher class enterprise than 'coder,' and things have a tendency to move in that direction."

Martin K. Gay, author of *Recent Advances and Issues in Computers* (2000), in writing of the "First Programmers Club"—that group of a half-dozen women, mathematicians all, who coded the ENIAC (Electronic Numerical Integrator and Computer) during the Second World War—notes that the women coders were not allowed inside the room with the giant machine because they were deemed security risks. Considered "subprofessionals by the government that was relying on them," these women were "forced to work with wiring diagrams and blueprints only. But they did learn how the machine was built, what each relay and tube could accomplish; and finally they were allowed into the room to start testing their procedures." Worse yet, he continues,

> Part of the culture of the time was to keep women out of any limelight, which might be construed as supporting their work away from home. And in a very real sense, the hardware was the news then. ENIAC and the male engineers responsible for its construction were the stars of the day. Until Bill Gates demonstrated the economic value of software, programming was simply a clerical extra.

We hold up Grace Hopper as a paragon of success in a male-dominated field, but she had no easy time of it. Several years before the ENIAC, computing's cutting edge was the Automatic Sequence Controlled Calculator (ASCC), better known as the Harvard Mark I: an electromechanical beast devised by Howard Aiken but brought to life by engineers at IBM. Programming the Mark I was a real chore, involving much physical labor and hand-to-hand combat with the machine. Hopper, who had endured her share of discrimination based on sex as she rose in the ranks of the U.S. Navy—she was permitted entry in the military because the organization was desperate for officers during World War II—was one of only a handful of people who learned how to program the leviathan. Howard Aiken, who directed the operations of the machine at Harvard's Computation Laboratory, could be a severe, stern man, and he was far from sold on Hopper initially, despite her considerable reputation preceding her, largely because Aiken wasn't predisposed to working with a woman officer. Neither were Hopper's fellow programmers, Robert Campbell and Richard Bloch, who were both so concerned that an "old lady teacher" from Vassar was coming to usurp their power that Bloch "paid Bob Campbell to take the desk next to me because he didn't want to have to," recalled Hopper. But she won them all over.

The few other women working with Aiken during this time, such as Ruth Brendel, weren't nearly as simpatico with Aiken as was Hopper, who became an expert at navigating male-dominated spaces (e.g., universities, the military, and professional computing). Brendel thought Aiken an "awful man," and firmly believed he was biased against women.

Despite her racking up successes, Hopper's stresses during the 1940s snowballed, ultimately culminating in divorce from her partner, alcohol abuse, suicidal ideation, and institutionalization. Yet through it all, Hopper was never a feminist, nor did she ever fall under the sway of the women's liberation movement. "They [women] are going to have some choices, they can't have everything," Hopper later said. "And women's lib is trying to encourage them that we can have everything."

Hopper became especially well known because of her association with the COBOL project, since her FLOW-MATIC compiler was one of its key influences (COBOL was ninety-five percent FLOW-MATIC, according to Hopper); FLOW-MATIC had a linguistic flair that was a counterpoint to the cold, analytical symbology of the stereotypical programming language. Consider that Hopper expressly designed FLOW-MATIC (and her earlier, prolix compilers) for the symbol-averse business*man*! One critic decried an early version of COBOL as dead on arrival, "concluding that the fruits of such an unstructured, female-dominated process could not be expected to survive, let alone flourish." But it did, with gusto, and in an increasingly male-dominated computing world to boot.

Yet there were consequences to the language's survival, as noted by the historian of technology Mar Hicks: COBOL became an easy scapegoat when things went wrong, which they sometimes did, catastrophically so. During the pandemic of 2020, several U.S. state governors, like New Jersey's Phil Murphy, complained that legacy systems and COBOL programs caused the collapse of state unemployment benefits websites, which experienced unprecedented traffic thanks to layoffs and furloughs in the early days of COVID-19. Immediately fingering COBOL as the culprit, though, was at best a premature assessment, and at worst terribly misleading, since COBOL code was handling the back-end processes just fine—it was Java, on the front-end, that wasn't keeping up with the web traffic, coupled with the so-called pet servers of these state agencies that strained to handle the greatly increased throughput. Twenty years earlier, COBOL was also famously blamed for the Millennium bug, a misleading assignment of responsibility as well.

Repeatedly turning COBOL into a scapegoat had its roots in "the culture and gender dynamics of early computer programming," according to Hicks. As computer *programming* transformed itself into computer *science* by the 1960s, newly minted, mostly male computer science practitioners resolved "to prove their worth and professionalize what had been seen until the 1960s as rote, unintellectual, feminized work," Hicks explained. "Consciously or not, the last thing many male computer scientists entering the field wanted was to make the field easier to enter or code easier to read, which might undermine their claims to professional and 'scientific' expertise." The newly credentialed men entering the field would ultimately push aside the less-credentialed women, but first "the men needed help" plying the trade, noted Hicks—and ironically turned to the veteran women programmers to learn these skills. Juliet Muro Oeffinger is a case in point: graduating in 1964 with a bachelor's in mathematics, she took up "the next hot thing," she said: COBOL. "I learned COBOL and taught it for Honeywell Computer Systems as a Customer Education Rep."

COBOL was designed in late 1959 by a committee consisting of numerous women programmers. "In a field that has elevated boy geniuses and rock star coders, obscure hacks and complex black-boxed algorithms," Mar Hicks concluded, "it's perhaps no wonder that a committee-designed language meant to be easier to learn and use—and which was created by a team that included multiple women in positions of authority—would be held in low esteem."

How did John Kemeny view women's roles vis-à-vis computing?

In 1966, when Dartmouth opened the Kiewit Computation Center—and took campus computing out of, in his description, "some horrible basement" and into the light—Kemeny, then president of the college, delivered a keynote address at the dedication ceremony of the "Conference on the Future Impact of Computers" which was reported on by the *New York Times* in the article "Computer Hookup to Home Foreseen." Looking forward to the day when computer terminals were installed in every home—as common of an appliance as television sets were in 1966—Kemeny said he envisioned prototypical "housewives" employing the power of these networked terminals to program chores, engage in online shopping, and arrange balanced diets for their families; thus computing would play its part to reinforce gender norms. "That [was] the way he sees women using computing [at that time]," lamented Joy Rankin in a talk delivered at Google, despite the fact that there were women on staff, such as Janet Price, Nancy Broadhead, and others, who were already critical to the technical operations of newly established Kiewit. (William Arms, who taught at Dartmouth from 1978 to 1985, recalled, "My wife was one of the first people to have a [time-sharing] terminal at home [in England], in the kitchen. In those days, it was the ultimate status symbol of the working wife.")

What's more, Kemeny, like many American males, had a deep, abiding love of American football, and he translated that affinity into a computer simulation of the sport. One of the very first football videogames, called **FTBALL***** (abbreviated from *Dartmouth Championship Football*; note that the names of these early Dartmouth BASIC programs were postfixed with three asterisks), was a BASIC program, several hundred lines long, written on the DTSS that virtually pitted Dartmouth's team against arch-rival Princeton's. The human player quarterbacked the Dartmouth team and could call the following plays: a simple run; a tricky run; a short pass; a long pass; a punt; a quick kick; and a place kick. Multiple versions of the game were produced, and other football simulations, like **FOOTBALL** and **GRIDIRON**, followed.

All versions of **FTBALL** were purely text-based simulations of the sport that made extensive use of **RND**, a deterministic mathematical function that generated a pseudorandom floating-point (decimal) number between 0 and 1 to determine which team received the ball first following a coin toss, the yards gained on a play, or if a kick sailed through the uprights. There was even a provision for a dog randomly interrupting play by running onto the field, a common occurrence during real-life competition. Take a look at the following loosely defined subroutine in the code (named "Jean's Special" in honor of Kemeny's wife):

```
1060 REM  JEAN'S SPECIAL
1070 IF RND(1)> 1/3 THEN 940
1080 PRINT "GAME DELAYED.  DOG ON FIELD."
1090 PRINT
1100 GOTO 940
```

By the 1970s, Stephen Garland and John McGeachie programmed an interactive two-person version of the game by creating MOTIF, or Multiple On-Line Terminal Interface, for the DTSS (the time-sharing system was being managed then by a Honeywell/GE-635 computer, three IBM-2314 disc storage units, and two DATANET-30 communication processors). MOTIF was "run as an independent job whenever a multiple terminal conference [was] initiated," McGeachie explained in the article "Multiple Terminals Under User Program Control in a Time-Sharing Environment." "It is linked to the user's BASIC, FORTRAN, or other program," he continued, "by a communication file which appears to the user's program as a conventional terminal communication file. It is also linked to the various terminals participating in the conference through terminal communication files, one for each terminal." MOTIF interpreted control characters, sending the information to the correct terminal, and finally "prefix[ing] data from the various terminals with an identifying string so that the user program may determine its origin." Specifically with respect to prefixing:

> As input is received from a terminal, MOTIF places it at the end of a queue of messages awaiting transmission to the conference program. MOTIF also prefixes each line of input from terminal number k with a string consisting of a two-digit ASCII representation for the number k followed by the ASCII representation for a comma. For example, the characters "05," are prefixed to every line of input from terminal number 5.

A user began a multiplayer session of **FTBALL** by queuing up an existing program using the **OLD** command and running it with the **LINK** command, while another user joined in on the fun by employing the **JOIN** command; the input and output were then multiplexed. Garland and McGeachie later scaled up MOTIF, permitting five people to play poker simultaneously, three to enjoy a game of bridge, or ten to try their luck at a management game—complete with marketing and selling a product—expressly created for students at the Amos Tuck School of Business Administration.

Kemeny himself wrote the original version of **FTBALL**—according to then-Dartmouth undergraduate Steven Hobbs; the Dartmouth emeritus professor of mathematics, Bob Norman, concurred, writing in 2014 that his "recollection is that Kemeny stayed up all night to produce the game"—though Kemeny always refused to take the credit. In late November 1965, undefeated (but underdog) Dartmouth beat Princeton 28-14 to claim the Ivy League championship—one of more than a half-dozen titles won by the college from the early 1960s to the early 1970s—and **FTBALL** was released the next day. In a panel discussion of the DTSS at Pioneer Day held a decade later, Kemeny recalled the circumstances leading to the game's creation. "I don't remember who wrote it but I do remember when that program was written, it was written on a Sunday," he said. "Those were the good days when time-sharing still ran on Sundays. It was written on Sunday after a certain Dartmouth-Princeton game in 1965 when Dartmouth won the Lambert trophy. It's sort of a commemorative program."

In his nontechnical, philosophical book *Man and the Computer*, based on lectures he delivered at the American Museum of Natural History in 1971, Kemeny wrote of the importance of electronic games. "In addition to classroom and research uses there is a great deal of recreational use of DTSS. The computer library contains a wide variety of games, most written by students," at which point Kemeny devoted several paragraphs to a discussion of the logistics of one game in particular: the "old favorite" **FTBALL**. "My father loved football, especially Dartmouth football," recounted his daughter Jenny. "The math department would get blocks of tickets for home games and then take bets on first downs, interceptions, scores...[and] there were plenty of martinis afterwards for the winners." Kemeny was so proud of **FTBALL** in particular, he had an eye toward its future. "By 1990," he said, "I envision two people sitting at terminals quarterbacking opposite football teams in highly realistic matches simulated by computer and displayed with appropriate visual and sound effects." (Of course, his prediction would become a reality much sooner than 1990, with videogames like *Atari Football*, released as an arcade game in 1978, as well as *Temco Bowl*, released for the arcades and the Nintendo Entertainment System in the 1980s.)

When promoting the virtues of the DTSS, however, Kemeny was not only quick to neglect or sell short the art, music, letters, and other types of BASIC programs written on the system, but also gave the football game pride of place on Pioneer Day. Indeed, Kemeny worried so much about the game's functionality that he once placed a phone call solely about **FTBALL** to the time-sharing operator, Nancy Broadhead, in the middle of the night—while she was relaxing at home.

Broadhead was a part-time employee at Dartmouth. About four months into her tenure at the college, she was introduced to time-sharing, becoming an "operator/consultant," as she called it at the Pioneer Day event, adding that she thought of herself "more appropriately [as a] housemother." She worked there during the daytime while the student programmers were the night owls, officially on watch. Luckily, the system was so reliable, Broadhead recalled, that it could mostly run unattended day and night. "So you went down to the basement of College Hall, unlocked the door with a nail file or your I.D. card, whatever you happened to have handy, walked over to the disc, pushed one [small red] button, everything started up, and you went home."

At Pioneer Day, Broadhead brought up **FTBALL**—and was purposely cagey about its author. "A lot of us here know who wrote it," she said, without mentioning Kemeny's name. What was the story of that after-hours phone call? One night, Broadhead's home phone rang off the hook. When she finally picked up the receiver, the voice on the other end of the line sounded at an absolute panic. "**FTBALL** has been clobbered in the library!" It was Kemeny. Though sympathetic, she lived a half-hour away from campus and was certainly not about to race to College Hall and queue up the paper-tape backup that night. "Well, I'll put it back in the morning," she sleepily answered him.

Why the urgency to fix the problem? Apparently, Dartmouth was in the midst of recruiting a new football coach. Football was integral to the campus culture; after all, the Ivy League athletic conference was codified in 1954, with Dartmouth one of the few universities included.

FTBALL wasn't the last sports simulation Kemeny would code, however. According to William Arms, "Kemeny wrote a popular baseball simulation based on the 1955 World Series triumph of the Brooklyn Dodgers. In anticipation of the modern 'open source' movement, these programs were always stored as source code and continually upgraded by colleagues. Whenever we taught a course, it was a matter of pride to extend and improve the programs in the course library," which were "public libraries" of freely accessible and modifiable programs by college course (e.g., statistics and computer graphics courses).

Between the focus on the football team conveyed via numerous BASIC simulation games that were decidedly male-centered (e.g., SALVO42, read as "Salvo for Two," which was a multiterminal battleship-like game; the "42" might also refer to the naval battles of 1942 during the Second World War, Rankin suggests), and cultural appropriation in the form of the school's de facto "Indian" mascot (for example, on the masthead of *The Dartmouth* school newspaper) coupled with public use of the offensive SCALP (Self Contained ALgol Processor) acronym without a second thought, Dartmouth's early computing culture did not match the promise of equal access for all.

One of the key themes in Joy Rankin's scholarship, developed fully in her book *A People's History of Computing in the United States*—the title is meant to call to mind Howard Zinn's *A People's History of the United States* (1980), which offered a counternarrative of the telling of American history—is that the notion of a meritocracy in Silicon Valley, propagated by its denizens and the media at large, is in fact a self-serving myth designed to mask the real truth: that the technology industry perpetuates a heteronormative, cisgender white male-dominated power structure of computing. The tech industry is very much still a "fortress of patriarchy," as Rankin writes, and her book—which was based, in part, on her doctoral thesis—challenges the traditional narrative of "Silicon Valley mythology," where "the personal computer became the hero, the liberator that freed users from the tyranny of the mainframe and the crush of corporate IBM," and with a "history of computing and networking [that] has likewise been dominated by a Great White Men (and now, maybe a handful of women) storyline."

That "fortress of patriarchy" in the digital realm took shape in the 1960s and 1970s on Dartmouth's campus, with the "intersection of Dartmouth's student body and the campus's nascent network yield[ing] a computing culture of masculinity, whiteness, and heteronormativity," we learn in the chapter "Making a Macho Computing Culture" found in *A People's History of Computing*. Although males (students and instructors) operated the Teletypes directly at Dartmouth, a number of women programmed at and provided support for the Kiewit Computation Center, though these women certainly labored under the weight of societal norms (e.g., page through issues of the *Kiewit Comments* newsletter, which reflected the gendered language of the time in its descriptions of the comings and goings of staff; by 1968, the newsletter had a subscriber base of one thousand, as the Kiewit Annual Reports found in the Kurtz Papers reveal).

As the center of gravity of BASIC shifted outside of Dartmouth in the 1970s, BASIC's masculine, heteronormative assumptions could be observed in type-in books like *BASIC Computer Games*, which sold over a million copies. One of the program listings in the text, called *Bunny*, is a non-interactive text rendering of the *Playboy* logo, a rabbit composed of repeated instances of the word "BUNNY." Another program in the first version of the book (*101 BASIC Computer Games*), titled *Ugly*, is described as a "[s]illy profile plot of an ugly woman."

There were consequences to the masculinization of computing that unfolded by the 1980s. Consider an article written by Steve Henn for National Public Radio (NPR) titled "When Women Stopped Coding." The centerpiece of the story is a graph, assembled using National Science Foundation, American Bar Association, and American Association of Medical College statistics. Tracing the percentage of women by field from 1965 to 2014, the trends are stark: while enrollment numbers hover between five and fifteen percent for women in medical school, law school, the physical sciences, and computer science through the 1980s, they rise sharply in the decades thereafter in all but one field: computer science. Around 1984, the CS percentage peaks at a little under forty percent, and then declines, precipitously, until leveling off at around seventeen percent by 2010 and never climbing any higher. In *Broad Band: The Untold Story of the Women Who Made the Internet* (2020), author Claire L. Evans points out the same trend. "In the generation after the pioneering programmer Grace Hopper and her contemporaries, the professionalization of 'software engineering' marked a sea change in the gender demographics of computing," explains Evans. "By 1984, the number of women pursuing computer science degrees in the United States began to dive, and it has kept diving to this day, a decline unrivaled in any other professional field."

But why?

NPR's Henn offers a theory. After observing that some of the earliest computing pioneers were women (Grace Hopper et al.), he then notes that "[t]he share of women in computer science started falling at roughly the same moment when personal computers started showing up in U.S. homes in significant numbers." Though correlation is not causation, these "early personal computers weren't much more than toys," and "were marketed almost entirely to men and boys." In fact, the cultural milieu at the time, Henn adds, was awash in films where young tech geeks—invariably boys—would triumph over adversity: *War Games, Weird Science*, and so on. He cites research from Jane Margolis, who, through the course of interviewing many students attending Carnegie Mellon University, found that families were more likely to purchase home computers for boys rather than girls, even if the girls expressed interest in the machines.

There is a notable omission in Henn's article, however: any discussion of BASIC, which came built-in to most of the popular home computers released from the late 1970s into the 1980s (Apple, Commodore, Tandy, and so on). Moreover, most of these microcomputers in fact booted to BASIC, forcing, at least to some extent, users to interact with the language, even if they employed the most rudimentary commands (for example, to load a game or application on the Commodore 64). Did boys receive a head start over girls, not only in using computers but in (BASIC) programming, thanks to the influx of home computers that were more often than not marketed to males?

The subjugation of females in the history of computing compounds when we factor in race. In 1943, at the National Advisory Committee for Aeronautics (NACA) in Langley, Virginia, the team of all African American "computers" who staffed the West Computing group suffered the indignity, day after day, of walking into the segregated cafeteria only to see the "white cardboard sign on a table in the back of the cafeteria beckon[ing] them, its crisply stenciled black letters spelling out the lunchroom hierarchy: COLORED COMPUTERS," as described by Margot Lee Shetterly in *Hidden Figures: The American Dream and the Untold Story of the Black Women Mathematicians Who Helped Win the Space Race*

(2016). Being a human computer was tedious and thankless work, mostly left to women, usually white but not always; "several of them would work together (a foretaste of parallel processing?) to solve systems of difference equations derived from differential equations," writes the English mathematician Beresford Parlett in the article "Very Early Days of Matrix Computations."

During the Second World War, Shetterly explains,

> For many men, a computer was a piece of living hardware, an appliance that inhaled one set of figures and exhaled another. Once a girl finished a particular job, the calculations were whisked away into the shadowy kingdom of the engineers. "Woe unto thee if they shall make thee a computer," joked a column in *Air Scoop* [a NACA magazine]. "For the Project Engineer will take credit for whatsoever thou doth that is clever and full of glory. But if he slippeth up, and maketh a wrong calculation…, he shall lay the mistake at thy door when he is called to account and he shall say, 'What can you expect from girl computers anyway?'"

The post-war period, coinciding with the advent of large mainframes, spelled a change in the zeitgeist. "The early 1960s were an inflection point in the history of computing, a dividing line between the time when computers were human and when they were inanimate," writes Shetterly, "when a computing job was handed off to a room full of women sitting at desks topped with $500 mechanical calculating machines and when a computing job was processed by a room-sized computer that cost in excess of $1 million." More significantly, though, was that the "function of computing" went from an "all-female service organization with minimal hardware requirements" to a "launchpad and a career path [for] ambitious young men."

Racial norms were also problematic in the early days of computing at Dartmouth, according to Rankin. "[T]he handful of examples of how and when race was invoked [at Dartmouth] demonstrates the social construction of whiteness as the normative college computing culture," she explains. No doubt, there was little racial diversity in the early days of the computing project at the institution, with Black students comprising low, single-digit percentages of the matriculating classes at Dartmouth throughout the mid-1960s but growing to nearly ten percent by the middle of the next decade. (That growth can be partly explained by active efforts taken by administration, including sponsorship of the "A Better Chance" [ABC] scholarship program as well as policies implemented by then-President Kemeny in the 1970s that encouraged student body diversity.)

In 1968, race and BASIC intersected at Dartmouth. To educate its undergraduates, the Dartmouth Department of Anthropology developed BASIC programs along two lines: one for elementary general anthropology and the other for cross-cultural research. For example, there was the program **LIFEWAYS**, which allowed users to explore Charles Morris's "13 Ways of Life." **ETHATLAS** featured an interactive ethnographic atlas. **KINTYPE** offered a tutorial in kinship systems and social organizations. **CENSUS** made tools available for demographic analyses.

The programs **RACEMYTH** and **RACECHEK**, however, explored racial difference. As we learn in the "Final Report: Time-Sharing Computer Applications in Undergraduate Anthropology at Dartmouth College," writing **RACEMYTH** necessitated gathering

[d]ata on the occurrence of 12 physical characteristics…from 35 Old World locations. A display map of the Old World with these locations is printed out. These characteristics are: skin color, hair structure, stature, skeleton index, facial morphology, Mongolian eye, nose index, horizontal cephalic index, height of skull index, and blood factors A, B, O.

When running the program, students were required "to examine the notion of race as 'clusterings' of physical traits by testing for high correlations in the distribution of these traits in selected Old World locations" in a variety of ways.

RACECHEK asked the user to supply personal information—including "blood type, ABO, Rh factor, stature, nasal index, PTC tasting ability, cephalic index, hair texture, hair color and skin color"—and then offered a best guess for the user's race. As explained in the report, "This program is designed to teach the difficulties and vagaries of racial classification…. It is fair to say that this program makes a persuasive attack on stereotypes of self (and other) racial identification." But Rankin argues that, contrary to the ostensible good intentions, **RACEMYTH** and **RACECHEK** further otherized nonwhite students on campus.

END OF INTERLUDE

Did Mary Kenneth Keller have to navigate these problematic cultural waters at Dartmouth? What's more, despite all the countervailing evidence, could Keller have been one of *three key people* (not just one contributor among many Dartmouth students), along with Kemeny and Kurtz, who designed and developed the BASIC programming language?

It seems extraordinarily unlikely. Indeed, as we've seen, it doesn't even appear probable that a toned-down BASIC Wikipedia page, giving Keller a measure of credit for the first BASIC implementation, is true. Here is how that tempered version of the U.S. Wikipedia BASIC page reads (for example, from early 2022): "One of the graduate students on the implementation team was Sr. Mary Kenneth Keller, one of the first people in the U.S. to earn a PhD in computer science and the first woman to do so." A similar claim can be found on the French-language Wikipedia page for Keller; translated to English, it reads, "While women were not previously allowed access to computer centers, she participated—with a dozen other students—in the development of BASIC under the direction of John George Kemeny and Thomas Eugene Kurtz."

Tools used to navigate and communicate on the internet also help to spread exaggerations, misinformation, and untruths; few people take the time to independently verify claims that seem questionable. Wikipedia, even with its numerous checks and balances, is not free from being a medium that spreads untruths or questionable information. Google privileges information filtered from Wikipedia, putting it front and center once a search is initiated. "We no longer search for information," writes the historian Yuval Noah Harari. "Instead, we google. And as we increasingly rely on Google for answers, so our ability to search for information by ourselves diminishes. Already today, 'truth' is defined by the top results of the Google search."

It is beyond dispute that Keller was a pioneer in computing education at a time when few women had positions of institutional power in the profession; for that reason alone, she should be recognized, studied, and celebrated. But elevating Keller to BASIC sainthood is not only very likely factually incorrect, but also—and this is a key point— negatively impacts the rest of her biography: because once the claim that she co-developed or even had a hand in helping to develop BASIC is dismissed as fiction, the rest of her biography becomes open to dispute—the last thing a society needs as it attempts to encourage women and other marginalized groups to garner a greater interest in learning about and ultimately joining the computing profession at all levels. "Coding is currently a male-dominated practice," observes Annette Vee, an associate professor at the University of Pittsburgh who has studied the connection between literacy, programming, and the BASIC language. In "Programming as Literacy," a chapter in *The Routledge Companion to Media Studies and Digital Humanities* (2018) edited by Jentery Sayers, Vee writes, "Because of historical, social, and economic barriers, women and certain minority populations are underrepresented in the population of people who can code…."

Since BASIC's humble beginnings at Dartmouth College, the push to break down historical barriers and teach coding to all has spread far and wide, leading to contemporary initiatives like Code.org, #YesWeCode, Girls Who Code, Black Girls Code, and Vidcode, among many others, that not only advertise the benefits of coding but also feature diversity and inclusivity as part of the package. Which brings to mind the feature of Dartmouth BASIC that has dated the most: it was never enough to teach only a small subset of college undergraduates to code.

By early 2020, I had hit a wall in my research efforts, having searched every nook and cranny. There was nowhere left to look, no further avenues to explore, to learn the full truth of Keller's degree of involvement, if any, in the creation of Dartmouth BASIC.

In the final analysis, there really was only one person who could know for sure, only one person who would be able to definitively settle the issue and set the record straight.

So, on the morning of Monday, March 2, 2020, I sent off a long email to ninety-two-year-old Tom Kurtz, offering background information about my search and pointedly asking him, "Was Mary Kenneth Keller involved in any way at Dartmouth in the implementation of BASIC?"

It wasn't particularly difficult to get ahold of his email address (it can be located online but will not be reprinted here). By all accounts, Kurtz is an intellectually generous, deferential, humble man. But I certainly didn't pin much hope on a response from the nonagenarian.

Yet less than a week after sending off the email, and mere days before the COVID-19 pandemic would wreak mass havoc across the United States, a reply arrived in my inbox.

What follows is Kurtz's email response to me—in full and unedited.

Friday, March 6, 2020 at 9:33 AM

Subject: Re: One BASIC History Question

Fr: Tom Kurtz
To: Mark

Sorry for the delay in answering —

It is unlikely that Sister Mary Kenneth Keller had anything to do with the invention of BASIC. She did attend a summer seminar session using the LGP-30. I don't recall the year.

In the fall of 1963 we (Kemeny and I) selected GE-225 as the best choice for us (over IBM and its 704.) John Kemeny invented BASIC, and wrote the first compiler, using a GE computer somewhere in MA to test his code. I initially preferred to believe that a simplified subset of one of the standard languages (Fortran, Algol,...) made more sense, but quickly agreed with Kemeny. (My reasoning was that BASIC would be completely free of so-called "type-declarations," such as REAL, INTEGER, etc.)

Obviously, Sister Mary Kenneth has absolutely no direct contact with the invention of BASIC by Kemeny, as she had no direct contact with Kemeny. Plus, initially, even I was opposed to it.

And, I cannot imagine any indirect contact. Obviously, I cannot recall any conversations that might have taken place. But I cannot see how she would have had any influence on John Kemeny's work; while I had some influence on his work, it was of a detailed technical nature, as I have described above.

In the course of the history of computing, yes, there were occasions where a simple verbal suggestion turned out to have a major impact. For example, as I reported in one of my papers, at one point John McCarthy, who had been at Dartmouth earlier and was then at MIT, suggested to me: "You guys should do time-sharing". Returning to Dartmouth I said to Kemeny: "McCarthy thinks we should do time sharing," and Kemeny responded: "Okay." That would have been in 1962 or early 1963.

But that sort of conversation with a summer seminar secondary school teacher defies belief. But who can recall all the informal conversations one might have had at that time. But Kemeny's decision to invent BASIC was the culmination of a long stream of internal experience and capability, and the decision to implement the first versions through compilers (rather than interpreters) was also a well-thought-out matter.

In your email you quote the BASIC Wikipedia page "One of the graduate students on the [BASIC] implementation team was Mary Kenneth Keller, ..." That statement is completely FALSE. We didn't even have a "computer science center." A minor point, while Dartmouth at the time admitted only men to its undergraduate BA program, women were present in most of the other activities and in the graduate programs in business, engineering, and medicine.

A complete change of subject...

My present wife, Agnes Bixler Kurtz, was the first female coach in the Dartmouth athletic department. She arrived in 1962, along with the first group of women in the freshman class (and women transfer students in the upper classes.) She started and coached field hockey, women's squash, and women's lacrosse. Those, and all her other activities are readily documented. Oh well .....

Regards.

Kurtz leaves the door open a crack with this statement: "In the course of the history of computing, yes, there were occasions where a simple verbal suggestion turned out to have a major impact."

In the talk "Programming in America in the 1950s—Some Personal Impressions," delivered in 1976 at the International Research Conference on the History of Computing in Los Alamos, New Mexico, John Backus addressed the question of authorship in the frontier days of computing. "Since the programming fraternity was a very small group," he said, "recognition was more likely to be accorded for a colorful personality or for an extraordinary feat of coding or [for] the ability to hold a lot of liquor than it was likely to be accorded for some intellectual achievement."

> Sometimes, looking back, people I'm sure regret how freely [ideas] flowed and how little documentation there was…. There was just [a] huge flow of ideas, and those ideas seemed to just naturally belong to anybody who heard one and could use it. Nobody thought of noting where he got it—since he was probably under the influence at the time anyway.

Consequently, there were typically few references, and even fewer acknowledgments, offered in papers of the era.

Notwithstanding that small chance of indirect influence, Kurtz was as sharp, clear-eyed, and decisive as ever in his email response—which seems, for all intents and purposes, effectively dispositive regarding the controversy at hand.

What a delicious bit of irony it would have been if Kememy and Kurtz had a long-overlooked female BASIC collaborator on a male-only undergraduate campus—and all this time, while we've been lauding Kemeny and Kurtz, we should instead have been giving credit to Kemeny, Kurtz, and Keller in equal measure. But some stories really are too good to be true. As Daniel Patrick Moynihan famously observed, "Everyone is entitled to his own opinion, but not to his own facts." The burden of proof now lies squarely with those arguing in favor of Keller's BASIC canonization.

Admittedly further complicating matters, from an ontological perspective it is nearly impossible to prove a negative—to prove, in this case, that Keller had *nothing* to do with the development of the BASIC programing language. We can't prove that Bigfoot doesn't exist, either, since absence of evidence is not the same as evidence of absence. While we could never completely rule it out, chances are exceedingly high that Keller had nothing to do with Dartmouth BASIC.

Nonetheless, no matter how much evidence has been marshaled in this chapter, those who are dead set against believing anything other than Keller's full or at least partial involvement in the genesis of Dartmouth BASIC may never be moved from their positions. Sure, Jonathan Swift once remarked, "Reasoning will never make a Man correct an ill Opinion, which by Reasoning he never acquired." But if the conclusions reached in this chapter are correct, then it will be as if a woman's contributions to computer science have been "erased"; it will be as if we took a step backward. That is why the topic continues to be so polarizing, and the likely truth of the matter so hard for some to accept.

Yet with the facts arrayed before us, still believing of Keller's involvement in the development of Dartmouth BASIC can be classified as nothing more than a *poetic truth*, a term coined by cultural critic Shelby Steele to mean "a distortion of the actual truth that we use to sue for leverage for power in the world. It is a partisan version of reality, a storyline that we put forward to build our case."

And that's why the facts—the dates, names, and places of those "firsts"—matter so much. Perhaps they matter more than Michael S. Mahoney's "reasons for those facts" and also more than Dick Hamming's "ideas behind the things," since without the facts being correct, all the analysis in the world is nothing more than so much bunk.

POSTSCRIPT

On December 31, 2021, more than a year and a half after I received Tom Kurtz's email reply, a Wikipedian with the username SJGarland edited the U.S. BASIC Wikipedia page, making the following change:

> (→*Origin: Removed inaccurate statement of Mary Keller's contributions to Basic*)

In addition, on that same day, SJGarland modified the Sister Mary Kenneth Keller Wikipedia page to read as follows:

> Many sources claim that Keller began working at the National Science Foundation workshop in 1958 in the computer science center at Dartmouth College, a male-only institution at the time, where she participated in the implementation of the first DTSS BASIC Kernel for the language, working under John G. Kemeny and Thomas E. Kurtz along with about a dozen other students. But this cannot be correct since Dartmouth did not acquire its first computer until 1959. Keller in fact was at Dartmouth sometime in 1961 when Dartmouth ALGOL 30 was being developed and used in undergraduate education.

"The widespread claim that Sister Keller played a role in the development of Basic is an urban myth," Steven Garland explained in the "Talk" sections of the two Wikipedia pages he corrected, continuing, "Some sources place her at the computer center at Dartmouth in 1958. Yet Dartmouth did not acquire its first computer until 1959, three months before I arrived as a freshman." Garland remembers seeing Keller on campus in 1961: "I recall seeing a nun at Dartmouth." "At best, she observed our work on the Dartmouth ALGOL 30 compiler, whose successful use in education was a precursor to the development of Basic," he added. "Keller could well have witnessed how the use of Algol in undergraduate education at Dartmouth served as a prelude to the development of Basic...."

Not content to leave it at that, Garland reached out to computer scientist Dianne P. O'Leary, who looked further into Keller's biographical details. In private communication to Garland, O'Leary wrote the following:

Sister Mary Kenneth Keller (MKK) was at Dartmouth in the summer of 1961, between the time she taught math at St Mary's High School in Chicago and at Heelan High School in Sioux City, Iowa. She continued to teach high school until 1964, and there was no reason for her to need an exception to participate in Dartmouth's summer program.

MKK went to Clarke College in 1965, after receiving her PhD. This was 4 years after the Dartmouth summer program, so since you [Garland] mention the Clarke affiliation, I guess you must have stayed in contact with her. Some of her notes suggest that she did maintain contact with Dartmouth, perhaps through ASCUE [Association of Small Computer Users in Education], or perhaps through her activity in writing a book with Dorn and Greenberg on Mathematical Logic and Probability with BASIC Programming.

What's more, O'Leary told Garland that "although the published references said that Sister Mary Kenneth Keller studied at Dartmouth in 1958, I just found a resume she wrote in 1965 saying that she was at Dartmouth in 1961. This is much more consistent with the likely dates of the summer program for high school teachers, so I believe it is accurate." Recall that it was in Keller's 1965 doctoral dissertation, in which she listed "Colleges and Universities: Years attended and degrees," that the line "Dartmouth College 1961" appeared.

Steven Garland, who had participated in and witnessed history nearly from the beginning, tidied up the loose ends, presumably putting the final nail in the coffin of an urban myth, and now all was right with the world. (Yes, the irony of disproving a Wikipedia claim by using a Wikipedia edit of that claim is not lost on me. In an *xkcd* comic strip titled "Where Citations Come From," Randall Munroe introduces the term *citogenesis* to capture the idea of circular reporting in Wikipedia, where a single source introduces a "fact" in a Wikipedia page that is then later presented as fact by a reputable source—which is then cited in Wikipedia, completing the circle. Regardless, Garland's Wikipedia edits did not serve as the basis for this chapter.)

All was right with the world, that is, until the next Wikipedia edit. Which occurred in May 2022 when the U.S. BASIC Wikipedia page reverted to fiction—only to snap back again to fact later that month. No amount of evidence will ever be enough to stop the spread of misinformation, and so the war over BASIC's origins continues, likely forever.

In the final analysis, let us celebrate Mary Kenneth Keller for the trail she blazed in computer education, and hold her up as an inspiration for others, especially females, to follow—even though she almost certainly had no part in creating Dartmouth BASIC.

CHAPTER 3

FIDDLING WHILE BASIC BURNED
Minicomputers, Microcomputers, and the Quest for BASIC Standardization

Why did the formal standardization of BASIC fail?
What led to additional BASIC language-design decisions?

Even in 1973, only nine years after BASIC made its first public appearance on the Dartmouth campus, many people felt that it was too late to standardize the language. By that point, BASIC had proliferated on numerous time-sharing systems, such as the HP 2000, the DEC PDP/11-RSTS, and the GE Mark I, and it seemed like the genie couldn't be put back in the bottle. As Thomas Kurtz later observed, like FORTRAN prior to its standardization, writing standards for BASIC involved reconciling a "multiplicity of variations…. If anything, the task is more difficult [than it was with FORTRAN] since BASIC grew unchecked for nine years (from 1964 to 1973) before the effort began."

John Kemeny lamented the spread of an "old BASIC." In a mid-1980s interview with Lynn A. Steen for the book *Mathematical People*, he was asked if it bothered him that "computer science departments are trying very hard to get people away from BASIC and to use structured languages like Pascal."

What bothers the people of Dartmouth, Kemeny replied defensively, was that "[w]hen people think of BASIC, too often they think of BASIC as it was in 1966."

> BASIC at Dartmouth is a totally structured language. As a matter of fact the International Standards Committee in BASIC is about to report and they are reporting a highly structured version of BASIC. We all agree that structured languages are far superior. We haven't used the non-structured BASIC in many years at Dartmouth. The problem, however, is that the versions of BASIC that are implemented on microcomputers tend to be the old BASIC. Therefore people tend to think of BASIC as it was ten years ago.

Further, the old BASIC—the BASIC that had first proliferated on minicomputers and then on micros—was the one typically taught to school students. Despite their best efforts to whip the language into shape, Kemeny and Kurtz had lost control of both the narrative and the product. Dartmouth BASIC fell apart; the center did not hold.

What went wrong?

To fully understand how Dartmouth BASIC's fortunes declined, we need to recount the language design decisions made by Kemeny and Kurtz. In a chapter he wrote for the *Encyclopedia of Physical Science and Technology (3rd ed.)*, published in 2001, Kurtz acknowledged that "BASIC is not just a single computer language; it is actually a collection of many languages or dialects, perhaps hundreds that have evolved since the mid-1960s." As these dialects spread outside Dartmouth, certain Dartmouth BASIC rules, such as preceding assignment statements with **LET** or the mandatory inclusion of **END** statements, were relaxed. While Dartmouth BASIC initially allowed only uppercase letters, many of these "Street BASICs"—a derisive term employed by Kemeny and Kurtz to refer to these "illiterate dialect[s] of a lovely language"—permitted the use of upper- and lowercase letters in the same statement.

Back in 1964, mixing the cases of letters wasn't standard practice—after all, it was rare to encounter terminals that offered lowercase—nor was inserting blanks lines between program statements. But indentation to denote the contents of loops appeared a short time after BASIC's debut:

```
10 FOR X=1 TO 10 STEP 2
20    PRINT X
30 NEXT X
```

Kemeny and Kurtz were very intentional with the design decisions they made for the first implementation of Dartmouth BASIC. For instance, though machines of the time usually could perform arithmetic using integer or floating-point numbers, the duo dispensed with integer arithmetic—though it was typically faster—in favor of sticking exclusively to floating point. "While some programs might run more slowly, life was made considerably easier for the beginner," Kurtz noted.

Troubled by the complexity of FORTRAN's FORMAT statement that was used for input and output, Kemeny and Kurtz decided to automate the reading and printing of numbers in BASIC sans special "formats." (In a 1971 *Datamation* article on BASIC that we will examine later in this chapter, author Jerry Ogdin describes the FORMAT statement as "really a cryptic language-within-a-language.") They also found FORTRAN's assignment statements objectionable; for instance,

```
N = N+1
```

could be confusing to a beginner, since it appears as if the variable N is equal to N+1, as in an algebra equation. ALGOL, even with its := representing an arrow pointing leftward, was equally confusing:

```
N := N + 1;
```

They believed that the keyword **LET** cleared up any confusion:

```
LET N = N+1
```

"This made understanding things like X = Y + Z easier for nonscientists," Kurtz explained.

Despite the mandatory presence of **LET**, there was no need to declare variables—or even to dimension arrays. If an array wasn't declared using the **DIM** statement, then the array defaulted to comprising ten elements, subscripted from 1 to 10. However, arrays featured one potential ambiguity: an array name could be the same as a scalar name. For instance, the following program would execute without error, outputting **6**:

```
100 A = 3
110 A(3) = 6
120 LET Z = A(A)
130 PRINT Z
140 END
```

With video screen terminals uncommon at the time, the pair ensured that editing code using a Teletype Model 33, an uppercase-only machine that printed ten characters per second, was as simple as possible via line numbers. Adding to that simplicity was the decision to forgo multiple statements per line—separated by, say, semicolons—in favor of only one per line, meaning a statement and a line were treated as equivalent in BASIC.

In a concession to beginning typists, as well as to those who were not particularly nimble-fingered (such as Kemeny), blanks were ignored by the compiler. (FORTRAN also ignored whitespace outside of string literals.) A line like

```
10 LET N = N + 1
```

could be shortened to

```
10LETN=N+1
```

without introducing error. But there was a consequence to *blank insensitivity*: variable names had to be short, consisting of either a single letter, like **N**, or a letter followed by a digit, like **N1**. Eventually, Kemeny and Kurtz decided that multicharacter variable names took precedence over ignoring blanks. Why can't both be possible simultaneously? As Kurtz points out, if we consider the line

```
10 FOR I = A TO B STEP C
```

there is ambiguity: If BASIC both ignored blanks *and* permitted multicharacter variable names then *perhaps* the loop above begins at an **I** value equal to **A** and ends at the value of **B** incremented with step size **C**, but the loop also might start at the **I** value **A** and terminate at the value **BSTEPC** while being incremented by the default step size of unity (one). So, with multicharacter variables names deemed more important, blank insensitivity was dropped.

The example above also helps us understand why variable names were restricted to either a single letter or a single letter and a digit—that is, $26 + 26 \times 10 = 286$ possibilities: potential ambiguity in the interpretation of statements like this:

```
FOR I = 1 TO J
```

With blank insensitivity in force, the compiler treated the statement as

```
FORI=1TOJ
```

which could potentially be interpreted as

```
FOR I = J TOK
```

or

```
FOR I = JTO TO K
```

but *only if* variable names could be more than two characters, which, initially, they could not be.

The next five years saw a number of changes to Dartmouth BASIC, most notably the addition of the **INPUT** statement. By BASIC the Fifth, strings, matrices, files, and overlays had become part of the language.

With text processing emerging as a necessity, and the GE-235 taking over time-sharing duties, Kemeny and Kurtz added string capabilities, with string variable names denoted with a dollar sign ($) as the last character. "The dollar sign was chosen," Kurtz reflected, "because, of all of the characters available on the keyboard, it most suggested the letter *s* in the word *string*." Like numerical variables, string variables were a primitive data type—the lowest, most basic, atomized level of data—rather than an array of characters, like the derived data type for strings of the C programming language. Manipulations with strings were also possible, with string comparisons made based on which of the string literals came first alphabetically (courtesy of inequality operators comparing the American Standard Code for Information Interchange, or ASCII, codes of the characters, one by one, left to right). In addition, the **CHANGE** statement converted a string to its associated vector of ASCII codes in decimal. Consider the following program:

```
10 REM STRING COMPARISONS AND CHANGE
20 LET A$="ANNA"
30 LET B$="BOB"
40 IF A$<B$ THEN PRINT A$ ELSE PRINT B$
50 CHANGE A$ TO A
60 END
```

When run, the output would be **ANNA**, since **ANNA** precedes **BOB** alphabetically. Then, on line **50**, the following integers were placed into the list **A**: 65, 78, 78, 65. (The ASCII code for A in decimal is 65; for N, it is 78. ASCII was the default *collating sequence* used, with uppercase letters always preceding lowercase letters.)

The **MAT** statement handled matrix operations, which effectively simplified the use of two-dimensional arrays (also referred to as tables). For example, a matrix could be multiplied by a scalar quantity; there was a matrix inversion routine, **INV(M)**, as well. Note that in the earliest versions of Dartmouth BASIC featuring matrix capabilities, matrix names were restricted to only a single letter.

Working with data files in programs offered a natural extension to the **DATA** statement; such capabilities were added to Dartmouth BASIC by 1969. The **FILES** keyword opened a terminal-format file (i.e., a text file), and **#1** denoted the first record in the file—as in the statement **INPUT #1:T\$**, which initially stored the first record into the string variable **T\$**. Each time an **INPUT #1** command was encountered by the compiler, the next record in the file was accessed in a sequential manner (hence this was *sequential access*; *random access*, meaning accessing records anywhere in a file, was possible in some versions of BASIC, too).

Though Dartmouth BASIC offered limited subroutine capabilities in the form of the **GOSUB** and **RETURN** statements, large programs were difficult to write without *overlaying*—i.e., replacing code or data stored in the main memory with other code or data. Therefore, an overlay mechanism was made accessible courtesy of the **SUB** statement, permitting the **GOSUB**ing to subroutines outside of the main program, though the variables of these subroutines were public. By 1970, Dartmouth BASIC offered the capability of private variables in external subroutines—precompiled ones, no less, stored in libraries—along with information sharing between the main program and the subroutines using parameters.

From the mid-1960s into early the next decade, Dartmouth BASIC was clearly improving, transforming itself into a more structured, more robust language. But Dartmouth BASIC didn't have a stranglehold on the BASIC market, despite the compiler serving as the seed from which innumerable BASICs sprouted.

Kemeny and Kurtz intentionally neither copyrighted nor patented Dartmouth BASIC. "People were thus free to modify the language in any way they felt was justified for their purposes and still call it BASIC," Kurtz explained. "In addition, there was no standard, either real or *de facto*." When FORTRAN, developed at IBM for the IBM 704 mainframe, arrived on the scene in 1957, there was also no official standard offered; it took years before such an effort got off the ground. Akin to Dartmouth's approach, IBM neither patented their software nor enforced strict usage controls, and, just as with BASIC, numerous dialects of FORTRAN arose, tailored for the machines they ran on. Kurtz argues that despite there being no official standard, IBM's FORTRAN was *the* de facto standard—"because anyone wishing to provide a FORTRAN compiler would almost certainly base it directly on IBM's FORTRAN. Dartmouth enjoyed no similar preeminence with respect to BASIC."

BASIC first escaped out of Dartmouth College via General Electric, which in 1965 offered a commercial time-sharing product to consumers that included a version of BASIC identical to Dartmouth's for the GE-265. Approximately fifty sites used this BASIC for GE's Mark I time-sharing system. (There were others users of the GE-235, including some educational institutions as well as Call-A-Computer.) By the end of the decade, however, GE BASIC had diverged, with the company including features tailor-made for their customers. Thereafter, as other companies threw their proverbial hats into the ring of the commercial time-sharing business, the BASICs they employed were derivative of GE's, rather than Dartmouth's, version of the language. That included the widely used HP 2000 and DEC PDP/11-RSTS time-sharing systems.

The BASIC genealogy gets more jumbled in the 1970s, first as vendors of minicomputers supplied their machines with hardware-dependent BASICs informally taking GE BASIC as their standard, further distancing these dialects from Kemeny and Kurtz's vision. Then, with the advent of cheap computing brought about by integrated circuits, microcomputers arrived on the scene. These home computers, despite their modest memories, needed a high-level computer language, and BASIC fit the bill, being small, simple, and already widespread on other types of computers. Though these early microcomputer BASICs were similar to Dartmouth BASIC, the implementations diverged as time passed. "By 1979," Kurtz observed, "the incompatibility between the different versions of BASIC had become such a serious problem that one software organization advised its programmers to use only the simplest features of BASIC." Simplified BASIC, but not Dartmouth BASIC, had become the de facto standard for home computers.

In 1978, David A. Lien, a technical author known for computing books such as the *Radio Shack TRS-80 User's/Learning Manual*, published *The BASIC Handbook: An Encyclopedia of the BASIC Computer Language*, which compiled and categorized innumerable versions of BASIC on "Micros, Minis and Maxis," as he put it. "[A]s computers developed in laboratories around the world, over a hundred variations or 'dialects' of BASIC also developed," lamented Lien. "These dialects have much in common, but there are enough differences that non-trivial programs written for one computer will seldom run on another without modification." Each chapter of the comprehensive *Encyclopedia* centered on a BASIC statement, command, or function, and included test programs, sample runs, descriptions of variations in usage from machine to machine, and references to other related BASIC keywords.

The limited memory of early microcomputers, some puttering along with as little as 4K bytes of storage, drove many of the design choices of BASICs for these home computers, of which the prototypical example—but not the only such instance—was the Tiny BASIC family of dialects. With space at a premium, hard choices had to be made. Space-saving measures included compressing each line of code once it was typed in and checked for correctness. Consider a BASIC line like the following:

```
50 IF A = B THEN 100
```

Storing the line in memory, without any changes, requires about twenty bytes since the line is twenty characters in length (one character ≈ one byte). But ignore the six blanks, and only fourteen bytes of storage are necessary. (As a consequence of ignoring the blanks, indentation would be ignored as well, since when a program was LISTed, only a single space would be inserted between items by default.) The relational operator (=) still occupied one byte, but the IF and THEN keywords really only needed one byte each. As long as line numbers were restricted to a maximum of 2^{16}-1, or 65535 (the "-1" is necessary so that 0 can serve as a line number, too), each line number required two bytes (since one byte = eight bits, and two bytes = sixteen bits—hence the 2^{16}). Since variables in these scaled-down BASICs could be up to two characters in length, two bytes were necessary for each variable. Adding it all up, we have scaled down the twenty bytes into only eleven bytes. With 4K bytes of memory, where each kilobyte is 2^{10}, or 1024, bytes, we have 4 × 1024 = 4096 bytes of storage available. Though the maximum line number *could* be 65535, a 4K machine wouldn't come close to storing a single program of 2^{16} lines—numbered 0 to 65535 by 1's—no matter the space-saving tricks employed.

With conserving memory paramount, the decision to dispense with LET in a statement like

```
10 A = A + 1
```

becomes clear: though contrary to the design principles of Dartmouth BASIC, since each statement had to begin with a keyword, a byte of memory is nonetheless preserved by eliminating LET.

Additional memory could be saved if multiple statements were strung together in a single line. The most common separator character for this purpose was the colon (:), although others characters, like the forward slash (/) and the comma (,), were used in BASIC dialects as well. A separator character took up only one byte in memory, while a line number required two. But there were problems with the approach. For one thing, not every version of BASIC offered the feature (of course, Dartmouth BASIC did not). In addition, there could be ambiguity when separator characters were utilized in IF/THEN statements, since an expression included after a THEN would *only* be executed if the condition tested by IF was true. For example, in versions of Microsoft BASIC from this era, the line

```
50 IF A = B THEN PRINT "KEMENY ";:PRINT "& KURTZ"
```

would either print KEMENY & KURTZ if A was equal to B, or print nothing at all if A was not equal to B. But consider the same two statements separated into two lines:

```
50 IF A = B THEN PRINT "KEMENY ";
60 PRINT "& KURTZ"
```
& KURTZ would be output regardless of whether the test condition in line 50 resulted in true or false.

There were stylistic differences between microcomputer dialects that had nothing to do with conserving memory. For instance, though the **REM** statement, indicating a single-line remark, was universal among implementations, the ability to append comments at the end of programming statements was not. For dialects that offered the capability, the most common characters designating an end-of-line comment were the exclamation point (!) and the apostrophe (').

The means of exponentiation, or raising a base to a power, differed between versions of BASIC, too. FORTRAN, as with so much else, set the standard, at least for a while: double asterisks (**) denoted exponentiation, with A**B connoting A^B. Some versions of BASIC employed double asterisks—making exponentiation the only arithmetic operator requiring two characters—but others, including the original Dartmouth BASIC, used the caret (^) for the mathematical operation. Sometimes the up arrow (↑), available on some microcomputer keyboards, was utilized instead. (Note that in 1967, ↑ was replaced by ^ in the ASCII code.)

Interestingly, when dealing with the *unary minus* (the sign denoting a negative quantity), the earliest BASIC compilers didn't perform the order of operations correctly. Though -10^2 = -100, since exponentiation precedes negation in priority, these compilers incorrectly calculated the answer as +100.

"A number is a number is a number," Kurtz repeatedly said, underscoring the simplicity of Dartmouth BASIC's approach to numerical data: all values would be treated as floating point automatically, no matter the deficit in speed. With the advent of minicomputers and microcomputers, however, integer variables were introduced in some versions of BASIC. Oftentimes, if a percentage sign (%) was appended to the end of a variable name, it denoted an integer variable; leave off the **%**, and the variable would be floating point by default. Implementations of BASIC with integer variables took as inspiration FORTRAN's approach: called *implicit typing*, in which the first letter of a variable indicated its type—in early FORTRAN, variables beginning with the letters I to N were of type integer, while all others were of type real—either a **DEFINT** or a **DECLARE INTEGER** statement would set up an implicit typing scheme for a BASIC program.

Even more inconsistencies among BASIC dialects emerged with string manipulations. Take *concatenation*, or appending strings. Some BASICs employed the ampersand (**&**) to perform the operation:

```
50 H$ = "HELLO, " & "WORLD!"
```

Yet others used a comma (**,**), a plus sign (**+**), or even a double pipe (||) instead.

Suppose a string literal is stored into string variable **GH$**:

```
100 GH$ = "IT'S EASIER TO ASK FOR FORGIVENESS THAN PERMISSION"
```

If a user wished to find the first instance of the word **ASK**, she could use the **POS** function in some BASICs:

```
110 T = POS(GH$,"ASK")
```

and the index of the first character in the substring **ASK** would be returned and stored in variable **T**. In this case, since strings were not zero-indexed—the first character of any string was automatically indexed, or subscripted, as 1—the value of 16 would be returned and stored in **T**. If the substring could not be found, then 0 would be returned. Though many microcomputer dialects employed **POS** for searching strings, some utilized **INSTR**, **IDX**, or **INDEX** instead.

There were variations in how BASICs used the functions **SEG\$**, which returned subsets of strings, and **MID\$,** which returned middle characters of strings, as well.

Spurred on in large part by the development of ALGOL as well as computer scientist Edsger Dijkstra's pointed criticisms of the unconditional jump in his famous 1968 letter "Go To Statement Considered Harmful," in the 1960s the structured programming paradigm took hold. Structured programming promised to bring more clarity to program design through the use of block structures and subroutines along with the elimination of GO TOs, among other characteristics. Yet valiant attempts to conform to the new paradigm resulted in implementations of BASIC becoming even more inconsistent with each other.

At Dartmouth, Stephen J. Garland, one of the original student programmers of the Dartmouth Time-Sharing System who returned to the college as a professor, developed a structured version of BASIC the Sixth called SBASIC, or Structured BASIC. New loop structures, the naming of subroutines, and advanced conditionals were only some of the improvements, all in the name of GO TO-less programming (a synonym for structured programming); now, a **GOTO** could be dispensed with in favor of a **DO...LOOP** block (a "general loop," where the number of iterations of the loop was unknown until runtime). And with no need for **GOTO**, line numbers could be eliminated as well. For example:

```
C=5
DO
   PRINT "TYPE THE CORRECT INTEGER, FROM 1 TO 10, TO EXIT:"
   INPUT X
   IF X=C THEN END
LOOP
END
```

Without the **DO...LOOP,** a general loop could be simulated by using a **FOR/NEXT** loop with many iterations, but the form wouldn't be aesthetically pleasing nor would it meet the approval of Dijkstra and his acolytes:

```
10 C=5
20 FOR A=1 TO 100
30    PRINT "TYPE THE CORRECT INTEGER, FROM 1 TO 10, TO EXIT:"
40    INPUT X
50    IF X=C THEN 70
60 NEXT A
70 END
```

Conditional structures beyond merely **IF/THEN** also took pride of place in structured programming in BASIC. Consider the following unstructured snippet.

```
10 C=5
20 PRINT "TYPE THE CORRECT INTEGER, FROM 1 TO 10:"
30 INPUT X
50 IF X=C THEN 80
60    PRINT "INCORRECT!"
70 GOTO 90
80 PRINT "CORRECT!"
90 END
```

With the addition of **ELSE** and **END IF**, the code becomes clearer:

```
C=5
PRINT "TYPE THE CORRECT INTEGER, FROM 1 TO 10:"
INPUT X
IF X=C THEN
   PRINT "CORRECT!"
ELSE
   PRINT "INCORRECT!"
END IF
```

The occasional statement label here or there replaced line numbering an entire program. (A similar feature could be found in a handful of early non-Dartmouth BASICs, permitting users to only assign line numbers to code that would be jumped to, conditionally or unconditionally.)

BASIC the Seventh added even more features to SBASIC. But these structured BASICs didn't travel far outside Dartmouth—unlike GE BASIC, replicated many times over, which was built off of an unstructured BASIC the Fifth. "As the acceptance of structured programming grew, the reputation of BASIC declined," observed Kurtz. "This was a fair assessment for most microcomputer versions of BASIC."

The reputation of BASIC also suffered thanks to "[t]he lack of adequate modularization tools," added Kurtz. The limitations of **GOSUB...RETURN** brought into relief how much BASIC was behind the times. Jerry Ogdin, in his 1971 *Datamation* article critiquing BASIC, writes, "The subroutine facility of BASIC is primitive and most closely resembles COBOL in style."

> The most unfortunate part of the subroutine conventions in BASIC is that no local variables may be declared or implied, and there is no parameter-passing mechanism. All symbols are globally known throughout the program. This is analogous to the simple PERFORM verb of COBOL. This means that any temporary or intermediate results computed are not private, and may destroy important contents saved under the same name elsewhere in the program.

Generic BASIC lacked the power to pass arguments to subroutines, and only global variables could be used; creating local variables was not possible. Moreover, subroutines could only be written in a main program, rather than in external ones. For these reasons in particular, BASIC lost significant ground in the United States by the 1980s to structured programming languages like Pascal in the one realm that mattered most for the future of the language: education.

Pascal, designed by Swiss computer scientist Niklaus Wirth, was the language of choice for the first high school Advanced Placement Computer Science course, introduced by the College Board in 1984. Ironically, it was Stephen Garland himself who, as chairman of the College Board committee tasked with designing the Advanced Placement Program in Computer Science, put the kibosh on endorsing BASIC. The interminable delay in producing a standard, along with innumerable unstructured dialects costing BASIC its reputation among many computer scientists, had turned the creator of SBASIC toward Pascal instead. (For his part, Tom Kurtz wasn't a fan of the presentation of computer programming in high schools in general. As he explained in an interview for the 2009 book *Masterminds of Programming*, "One of the things that bothers me about the education of programming primarily in secondary schools, where they have an advanced placement in computer science, is that it's much too complicated." How would he structure an introductory college-level course in the subject? First, Kurtz would employ BASIC. Second, he would use the language to teach all the CS basics except pointers and allocated storage. When asked, *If you could design a new language for teaching students programming how similar would it be to BASIC?*, Kurtz responded: "Very, because the principles that we followed are still valid." As evidence, he cited University of Maryland's Ben Shneiderman, who penned an article in 1985 titled "When Children Learn Programming: Antecedents, Concepts, and Outcomes," published in *Computing Teacher*, that praised some of the design decisions of BASIC—the structure of loops, conditionals, and so forth—in terms of user friendliness, especially as compared to languages like ALGOL and Pascal.)

At institutions of higher learning around the globe, BASIC's standing had plummeted by the 1970s. For instance, at the Technische Universität Berlin (Technical University of Berlin), BASIC fell out of favor as a teaching language, with Pascal floated as an alternative. Dutch computer scientist Cornelis H. A. Koster, a professor at TU Berlin, helped develop a teaching language called ELAN (Educational Language) that ran on the EUMEL (Extendable Multi User Microprocessor ELAN System) operating system; ELAN was closely related to ALGOL 68. The Arbeitskreis Schulsprache (school working group) approved ELAN for secondary teachers to use throughout West Germany as an alternative to BASIC.

Another example: COMAL, or COMmon Algorithmic Language, a teaching language created in Denmark in the early 1970s by Børge R. Christensen and computer scientist Benedict Løfstedt. A mathematics teacher at the Tønder Seminarium in Tønder, Denmark, Christensen found that his students struggled to decode older BASIC programs, replete with **GOTO**s and undescriptive variable names, running on the school's Data General Nova minicomputer. So, corresponding with Løfstedt, Christensen developed COMAL, an amalgam of the simplicity of BASIC and the structured programming capabilities of Pascal. "In Denmark we have learned that people will turn away from Basic if they are given something better," Christensen told *Your Computer Magazine* in 1981, "simultaneously easier and more powerful." COMAL was eventually implemented on the Regnecentralen (RC) Piccolo series, microcomputers that were mainstays in Danish schools, as well as on a number of other computers.

With the Logo programming language infiltrating elementary schools in the U.S., educators of all stripes were already looking past BASIC by the late 1980s. In his chapter on BASIC for the *Encyclopedia of Physical Science and Technology (3rd ed.)*, Kurtz envisioned a "more modern" and "more convenient" way of programming with subroutines in BASIC, like this:

```
CALL Add (a, b, c)
...
SUB Add (x, y, z)
   LET z = x + y
END SUB
```

More modern and more convenient, but unfortunately too little, too late to save BASIC—in part because there wasn't just *one* BASIC that needed timely modernization in the microcomputer era, but dozens of them. BASIC had gained mindboggling popularity as a result of a Faustian bargain: Though the language had penetrated homes, schools, and even businesses (in the form of Business BASICs) by the 1980s in the United States, Europe, and elsewhere, the lack of standardization of these innumerable dialects rendered any global proposals for change, arising from Dartmouth or elsewhere, effectively impossible to carry out. Structured programming capabilities would become part of many BASICs, but in an ad hoc, inconsistent-between-dialects manner. Features originally intended to circumvent the small memories of underpowered microcomputers persisted in version after version despite newer and powerful computers becoming available, further sullying the reputation of the language. (Modern day probability and statistics has a similar problem: mathematical methods devised prior to the computing revolution to shortcut tedious calculations are still commonly taught in classrooms today: for example, normal distribution approximations to the binomial distribution. Even a mainstay of the field like hypothesis testing—taking a small sample to learn about a larger population of interest—is an anachronism that ignores the advances in *big data* made possible by the computing power of the twenty-first century.)

On the positive side of the ledger, as Kurtz notes, "It is undoubtedly true that, while BASIC fell behind other languages in adapting to structured programming, it led all other languages in embracing graphics." As microcomputers exploded in popularity through the 1980s, inexpensive graphics displays followed suit. Versions of BASIC were expected to offer means to tap into these newly accessible visual capabilities; Dartmouth BASIC circa 1964, running on Teletype machines, offered no template for the future. But by the late 1960s, interactive graphics was being experimented with on the Dartmouth Time-Sharing System—well in advance of the microcomputer revolution.

Unsurprisingly, it was with graphics functionality that features of these many BASIC dialects diverged most radically, with, for example, the Tandy Color Computer's Color BASIC (using simple statements like **SET**, **DRAW**, and **LINE**) differing markedly from the Commodore 64's BASIC v2.0 (using the closer-to-machine-language **PEEK** and **POKE** commands but also having access to sprites). The idiosyncrasies of BASIC graphics on microcomputers extended to the Apple II, the Texas Instruments TI-99/4A, the BBC Micro, the Sinclair ZX Spectrum, the Atari 8-bit family of computers, and more.

Many of the inconsistencies in graphics implementation stemmed from one critical fact: different machines permitted different numbers of pixels (points) on-screen. Compounding the problem was the availability of various graphics modes, each with varying degrees of resolution. A BASIC standardization project had to grapple with more than just the differences in language features, but also had to take into account the underlying hardware that had caused those differences—a quality most apparent in the realm of graphics.

Even by the late 1980s, the evolution of BASIC was already viewed as a cautionary tale. For example, in "Prolog Dialects: A *Deja Vu* of BASICs" (1987), author Raymond Sosnowski begins the article by telling the story of the proliferation of BASIC dialects:

> At the beginning of the so-called microcomputer revolution, there were the dialects of BASIC. It seems as though each different microcomputer had its own dialect of BASIC which doubled as the operating system, and then various BASICs appeared for each different operating system such as CP/M and MS-DOS. As a language that is not covered by a standard, there is no BASIC programming language per se, but rather there is a large collection of dialects that are referred to as BASIC. An effort is being made to create a standard, but with so many hardware and software companies that have a vested interest, the creation of a BASIC standard is certainly many years away.

Many years away—despite BASIC, at that point, being over two decades old.

It shouldn't have taken such a long time to publish standards for BASIC. True, there were de facto standards—"descriptions of a programming language as provided by a dominant manufacturer," Kurtz wrote, with "[o]ther vendors…provid[ing] the 'same' language in the hope that some of the customers might switch from the dominant manufacturer of them." Most obviously, this described the early history of FORTRAN although, if this was the salient example Kurtz had in mind, he understates how poor of a check the informal, de facto standard of IBM FORTRAN turned out to be in the long run—considering the proliferation of dozens of machine-dependent FORTRAN dialects beginning in the late 1950s and continuing into the next decade.

In a talk delivered at the International Research Conference on the History of Computing in Los Alamos, New Mexico, in 1976, John Backus took a question from fellow programmer Betty Holberton. During FORTRAN's development phase, she told the audience, Backus and others on the IBM team delivered numerous presentations across the United States describing proposed features of the programming language. Holberton then said, "To me, that is a real first, because that is an attempt to get consensus. And I consider that to be the beginning of standardization of languages." Such informal efforts, however, didn't bring order to the chaos. (Plus, Backus received little feedback from audiences during those FORTRAN presentations.)

In the early 1960s the American Standards Association (ASA)—which, nearly half a century old at that point, started as a consortium of government agencies and engineering societies called the American Engineering Standards Committee (AESC)—established the ASA Sectional Committee X3 for Computers and Information Processing. Sponsored by the Business Equipment Manufacturers Association (BEMA), a subcommittee was formed to examine high-level languages; the X3.4 Sectional Subcommittee decided on three procedure-oriented languages for immediate standardization: ALGOL, COBOL, and FORTRAN.

FORTRAN was the first high-level language to be standardized. It took several years, but by mid-decade the FORTRAN standards written by the X3.4.3 working group were approved. In fact, there were two sets of standards: a superset called USA Standard FORTRAN (ASA X3.9-1966), and a subset named USA Standard Basic FORTRAN (ASA X3.10-1966). These standards did much to mitigate the "Tower of Babel" that had arisen. (For the best illustration of a tower of programming languages, look at the front cover of Jean Sammet's essential book *Programming Languages: History and Fundamentals*, published in 1969.) Before the decade was out, COBOL received its own first set of official standards as well. Around that time, the ASA was renamed the American National Standards Institute (ANSI).

As early as 1971—half a decade before the release of the Altair 8800 and Micro-Soft's debut product, Altair BASIC—computing experts argued that the train had already left the station, dismissing efforts to standardize BASIC as futile. Look no further than the September issue of *Datamation*, for instance, which contained a scathing indictment of the language by independent consultant Jerry Ogdin called "The Case Against…BASIC."

"The BASIC language was developed at Dartmouth College in the early 1960s," the article begins, "and has suffered mightily since. That the fate of divergent development should befall such an elegantly simple language is a crime." Ogdin then proceeds to identify "good language improvements and bad language extensions," arguing that BASIC wasn't designed for those who now primarily used the language: "It was developed for undergraduates at the college algebra level, and was obviously designed on the premise that something had to be easier to teach than FORTRAN."

> To be sure, there are problems in BASIC. The lack of data files, the single data type (real numeric), the restricted symbol set, and the lack of a subroutine capability with local and formal declarations have all been widely acknowledged. But, the language does meet its objective of being a simple language for beginners.

> Let me reiterate that last phrase: *for beginners*. There's the rub.

Ogdin's dissatisfaction with BASIC's evolution had as its cause the system programmers who transformed BASIC into FORTRAN-lite via extensions. Though some extensions for BASIC surely improved the language, many others "have been absurd." With variations in function definitions and **FOR/NEXT** loops, and extensions for **PRINT** involving the **TAB** function, "About the only statements which have escaped unscathed have been the **READ**, **GOTO**, **GOSUB**, **STOP**, and **END**" statements, he observes.

As minicomputer and microcomputer dialects of BASIC to come compounded standardization difficulties, back in 1971 Ogdin was among the first to identify the cause of the problem: "In each case, because of no central source for control of extensions, each compiler writer has gone a different way from his predecessors." In other words, there was no central authority to turn to for approval, let alone guidance, when writing BASIC extensions. Hence their great variability and sometimes ambiguity, as in this extension for multiple assignment using **LET** illustrates:

```
LET A = B(I) = I = 5
```

Take a moment to consider the statement. If the initial value of **I** is not 5, then compiler X, which interprets the statement from left to right, will use a different index for storing the value of 5 in the **B** array than compiler Y, which interprets the same statement right to left. Thus, BASIC compiler X offering the multiple assignment extension didn't guarantee portability when compiling on BASIC compiler Y, despite Y offering the same extension. Of course, a user could avoid multiple assignment. But then what was the point of the extension?

Ogdin praises the original Dartmouth compiler for stubbornly sticking to one numerical data type: real numbers. "However, there are always special interest groups," he explains. "So at least one compiler has introduced **INTEGER**, **REAL**, and **COMPLEX**-type statements," surely inappropriate in a beginner's language. Also inappropriate: a BASIC implementation that employs SUBSTR, a PL/I convention for manipulating strings that "causes enough grief to PL/I programmers—now it is impressed upon novice programmers that everything has to be tough in useful languages!" Ogdin finds much to dislike about the treatment of data files, too, with so many differing conventions he hardly has the space in his *Datamation* article to list them—let alone all the other extensions, limitations, and changes from one implementation of BASIC to the next. "In the blind objective of making BASIC suit all uses and all users," Ogdin complains, "unnecessary and unreasonable changes have been perpetrated on the flimsy premise that all potential programs should be able to be programmed in BASIC." His conclusions are stark: "I feel that BASIC has effectively been killed as an industry-wide language because no two compilers have even a semblance of compatibility," and "It is already too late for BASIC. The formal standardization channels are either dormant or clogged with rhetoric with no objective."

Two people took great issue with Ogdin's salvo: Tom Kurtz and Stephen Garland. A month after the article's publication, the two Dartmouth professors issued a response. Called "Toward Standardization of BASIC," and appearing in the October issue of *ACM SIGCUE Outlook*, their piece begins by conceding the point: "We at Dartmouth are in substantial agreement with the substance of Mr. Ogdin's article…." But they disagreed that BASIC "suffered irreparable damage" or that "BASIC has effectively been killed as an industry-wide language." After all, Kurtz and Garland argue, consider its popularity in the educational field. Yes, the increasing number of different BASICs is dangerous to the long-term health of the language, but throwing out the baby with the bathwater is not the solution; rather, standardization will be BASIC's savior. And it wasn't too late to standardize, since "you can't standardize until you are sure you have a product worth standardizing," they write. The experience at Dartmouth gained by implementing a half-dozen versions of BASIC allowed Kurtz and Garland to express full confidence that they could propose a standard aligned with the "original philosophy behind BASIC." Plus, the newest version of Dartmouth BASIC largely addressed Ogdin's criticisms.

Kurtz and Garland also raise an interesting point. If standardization had occurred in 1964 concurrent to the birth of the language, then BASIC might not have become widely used outside of Dartmouth, leaving FORTRAN to fill the vacuum in the educational arena. In addition, "premature standardization would have inhibited the natural process—i.e., divergent implementations—by which most widely used languages have been extended to meet the needs of their users."

"Toward Standardization of BASIC" also briefly details the earliest efforts behind the BASIC standardization project. "ANSI/X3/SPARC has expressed its willingness to hear the case for standardizing BASIC," report Kurtz and Garland. "Such a case is now being prepared. If the recommendations of a small ad hoc committee are accepted by SPARC, a working committee to draft a standard will be formed, and the work begun in earnest."

By 1972—only eight years after the language debuted but well in advance of the microcomputer revolution—things were an unstandardized mess. BASIC dialects had proliferated on mainframes and minicomputers. A window into this chaotic state of affairs is provided by "Interdialect Translatability of the BASIC Programming Language," a technical bulletin compiled by Gerald L. Isaacs in 1972 for the American College Testing Program in Iowa City, Iowa, and sponsored by the Office of Education of the U.S. Department of Health, Education, and Welfare. There were at least twenty "different major dialects," we learn from the report, making translations of programs between BASICs difficult in many cases—unless "reasonable [and optional] programming restrictions [were] imposed," an informal strategy that fell short of a set of formal, published language standards akin to FORTRAN's.

For example, ensuring translatability between Xerox BASIC, running on SDS Sigma series computers, and Hewlett-Packard BASIC, running on HP minicomputers, might take a great deal of effort, depending on the machine-specific features and extensions found in the code. But programs written for one computer from a manufacturer's product line would likely work as is running on other machines from the same line.

After putting the twenty BASIC dialects through their paces, Isaacs found much variation in their capabilities, adding further wrinkles to the translatability between them. And, with the exception of the **INPUT** statement, whose implementation was both universal and consistent, translatability wasn't merely a matter of altering a little syntax here or there. For instance, though all the BASICs provided at least six digits of computational accuracy, several boasted upwards of sixteen digits. Likewise with the largest and smallest numbers permitted: at least one BASIC had a numerical range of 10^{-38} to 10^{38}, while others were less expansive. Some dialects offered syntactical variations of **PRINT USING** statements for producing formatted output, while others either didn't offer the option at all (such as HP BASIC and Control Data Corporation 6000

BASIC, with output workarounds possible by creatively using the **PRINT** statement) or utilized a FORTRAN format (namely, MULTICOMP BASICX). Even line-numbering schemes weren't consistent, with some dialects offering a range stretching from **0** to **99999999**, while others, such as PDP-8 BASIC-8, were capped at a maximum of only **2046**.

Then there was the problem of size. For executing larger programs, several options were on the table—at least in theory—including program chaining (chopping up a large program into smaller ones and then running them sequentially), partitioning a program and then swapping these segments in and out of the core as necessary, and external subroutine calls. Nonetheless, a handful of dialects permitted only a "fixed area of core," such as IBM CPS BASIC, National Cash Register Century 100 BASIC 1, and certain BASICs for the DEC PDP-8 (not EduSystem 25 and 50, however), therefore rendering these dialects insufficient for handling more complex programming tasks.

In his report, Isaacs argued that any BASIC worth its weight had to be able to access and create external files (i.e., data files that could be written to and read by a program; memory was saved by having a program offload the results of calculations to external files). Alas, not all BASICs could do so, with the dialects mentioned in the previous paragraph yet again falling short.

A tier above were BASICs that supported *sequential files*, or files containing data stored in a chronological order; these included IBM ITF BASIC, IBM CALL/OS BASIC, Honeywell 200 BASIC, CDC 6000 KRONOS BASIC and 6000 Version 2 BASIC, Burroughs B5500 BASIC, DEC PDP-8 EduSystem 25 and 50, and UNIVAC 1100 BASIC, all of which ran on large machines.

At the top tier were the most functional BASICs—like Time-Shared BASIC for the HP 2000 minicomputers, BASIC for the HP 3000 minicomputer, Mark II BASIC for the GE-600 series mainframes (specifically, Mark I was the name of a time-sharing system, and Mark II was the name of an operating system; by 1973, there would be a Mark III as well), BASICs for the PDP-10 mainframe and PDP-11 mini, BASIC for Data General minis, and Dartmouth BASIC—that could deftly handle both sequential and random-access files. Of course, there were differences in syntax, with some utilizing the statement **FILE**, others **FILES**, and still others **ASSIGN**, all for the same task of opening a file, while **IF END**, **NODATA**, or **ENDFILE** was used to detect the end of a file.

It was in the realms of "file handling, chaining or subroutine calling, and output formatting" that produced the most translatability difficulties, Isaacs noted. "Since there is no exact standard for these areas, a knowledge of the statement formats in these areas can help to minimize the expenditure of time and energy." Though there were dialect differences beyond these three realms, they were less pronounced. For instance, although the symbols for the four arithmetic operations were consistent across BASICs, and the relational operators (<, >, <>, <=, =) were nearly consistent (UNIVAC 1100 BASIC employed three-letter English abbreviations instead of symbols, while Honeywell 200 BASIC used => instead of >=), the operator for exponentiation widely differed: some dialects used ******, others employed ↑, while still others made use of ^. At the time, however, the up arrow was the most common, presumably because BASIC the First had adopted the convention. In addition, the logical operands **AND**, **OR**, and **NOT** received their due on some dialects like Hewlett-Packard's, Digital Equipment

Corporation's, and Univac's, with the latter two also supporting logical equivalence (EQV/EQU) and exclusive OR (EOR/XOR).

Variable naming was restrictive on most dialects, with the vast majority of BASICs following in the footsteps of early Dartmouth BASIC. Numeric variable names could be either a single letter in length or a letter and a digit. Some flexibility was afforded by IBM BASICs, courtesy of special characters like $ and @ as substitutes for letters; IBM CPS BASIC even permitted two-letter variable names. (Only several dialects boasted integer-specific variable types, namely, PDP-11 BASIC and HP 3000 BASIC, the latter of which offered 16-bit integer variables. The fact that so few BASICs had integer-only capabilities led Isaacs to implore readers never to use these variables. He likewise warned against using HP 3000 BASIC's "complex" data type, a 64-bit quantity housing two real numbers: a real portion and an imaginary portion.) User-defined functions required identifiers, too; for those dialects that offered these functions (nearly all did), naming consisted of the letters FN followed by a single letter. And for BASICs that handled strings—even at this late date, not all of them did—-the naming of string variables took one of two forms: a letter and then a $, or a numeric name and then a $.

Strings were handled inconsistently between dialects, with the concatenation (appending strings) operation performed with either an ampersand, a plus sign, a comma, or the function CAT$; some BASICs did not even offer concatenation as a feature. A handful of BASICs, like those for the PDP-8 (excepting EduSystem 25 and 50) and the NCR Century 100 machines, weren't even able to process strings, with no string literals permitted in DATA statements as well (READ and DATA statements were universal among the BASICs, with all dialects resetting the read position using RESTORE, except for Dartmouth's, which employed RESET instead). For BASICs that could handle them, string literals were enclosed in double quotation marks—save for a handful of dialects, like the UNIVAC 1100's, which enclosed string data between single quotes instead. Analogous to numeric data, there was significant variation in the maximum length of strings, with some dialects limiting users to only twenty-two characters (e.g., Burroughs B5500 BASIC and IBM CPS BASIC) while others provided a generous cushion of more than thirty-two *thousand* characters along with substring features. Needless to say, these extreme differences in string-handling capabilities put the kibosh on translatability in certain cases.

As opposed to strings, every dialect examined by Isaacs in 1972 offered some form of arrays (often called subscripted variables) to use, both one- and two-dimensional, with a handful of dialects like Honeywell 200 BASIC and CDC 6600 BASIC 2.0 even offering three-dimensional arrays. Typically, arrays were named with a single letter and not explicitly size-restricted, with the maximum number of elements dependent on the core memory (although CPS BASIC permitted only five hundred elements, an exception that proved the rule). If an array was not explicitly dimensioned (using DIM), then most dialects would default to providing ten elements for each array dimension; BASIC for the PDP-8 and the NCR Century 200 required explicit dimensioning, however. Some BASICs started array indices at zero, while others began them at one. Nonetheless, for all dialects boasting matrix operations (MAT), "the zero elements are ignored anyway," we learn in Isaacs's report. (PDP-8 BASIC-8 and National Cash Register BA-

SICs didn't offer matrix capabilities, although arrays on PDP-11 BASIC could be saved in "virtual storage," which was on disc.)

Starting with Dartmouth BASIC the First, built-in mathematical functions were a mainstay in the language. The dialects examined by Isaacs were remarkably consistent, with all offering **ABS** (absolute value), **ATN** (arctangent), **COS** (cosine), **EXP** (exponentiation), **INT** (integer portion of the number), **LOG** (common logarithm), **RND** (randomization), **SGN** (sign), **SIN** (sine), and **SQR** (square root), while every dialect except one (IBM CPS BASIC) also made **TAN** (tangent) available, too. Except for NCR Century 200 BASIC, the dialects Isaacs reviewed allowed for user-defined functions, with variations in the number of arguments passed (one or two) as well as their composition (single- or multiline).

When it came to control statements, there were several differences between BASICs. For instance, in HP 2000 dialects, a variable or a constant, rather than an expression, had to be used as the initial value for a **FOR/NEXT** loop. In addition, some dialects put a limit on the quantity of nested loops. Though simple **GOTO** and **GOSUB** statements were implemented in all the dialects, only some featured computed versions, where a single **GOTO** or **GOSUB** could branch to any one of a number of lines, depending on the value of a variable; for instance, in the statement

```
ON B GOSUB 1000,2000,3000
```

the value of **B** determined where the program would resume running.

After BASIC spread outside of Dartmouth, Kemeny and Kurtz were especially frustrated by implementations that rendered **LET** optional in assignment statements as well as those that squeezed in multiple statements per line (e.g., BASIC for the PDP-11 and the Honeywell 200). As evidenced by Isaac's technical bulletin, both of these characteristics predated both Tiny BASIC and the microcomputer revolution.

Kurtz and Kemeny never seriously considered writing Dartmouth BASIC as an interpreter; they were wedded to compilers, largely because their single-pass approach churned out compilations quickly as long as the BASIC programs were relatively short. Offering the language in an interpreted form, the pair believed, would tie up the resources of the time-sharing computers too much; they wanted a user to run his entire program as is, and then be confronted with error messages (there could be at most five messages). The duo wanted newbies to *think through* their code *before* running it—and not be given real-time, line-by-line, on-the-fly error messages about syntax. In this way, compiled Dartmouth BASIC resembled FORTRAN more than most later versions of interpreted BASIC.

If Kemeny and Kurtz swore fidelity to compilers, why by the 1970s did BASIC spread most often as an interpreted language? Even General Electric, which released, effectively, a carbon copy of BASIC the Fifth for their machines, stuck by compiled BASIC. But a revolution was afoot: an explosion of minicomputers, machines flexible enough to bring real-time feedback to users. And before all was said and done, BASIC interpreters would be implemented on a great number of them: for the HP 2000, the

Data General Nova, and the DEC PDP-8 and PDP-11, among many others. In fact, in the decade that brought us disco and bell-bottoms, DEC and HP positioned their mini-computers to compete in the burgeoning BASIC educational market, with these minis running various incarnations of BASIC in time-shared environments or otherwise. Indeed, minicomputers are the missing evolutionary link between early BASICs on the one hand, and microcomputer BASICs on the other: minis provided a reservoir for BASIC to spread, flourish, and mutate into forms divergent from Dartmouth BASIC, well in advance of the even more extreme departures that would come to reside in home computers.

Compared with mainframes, minicomputers were small, cheap, and relatively fast. First called "real-time control computers," as their uses expanded outside process control and laboratory work the moniker "minicomputers" was adopted instead. Certainly, there were small computers that predated minicomputers proper. Consider the LGP-30, for instance, which Kemeny and Kurtz brought to the Dartmouth campus. Though compact, relatively cheap, and tailored for a single user, when it came to processing speed the LGP-30 was no match for an average mainframe.

Vacuum tubes powered the LGP-30. But for a small computer to be competitive with its larger brethren, it would have to be engineered with transistors. Enter MIT physicist Wesley A. Clark, who, after joining the MIT Lincoln Laboratory in the 1950s, designed the transistorized TX-0 and TX-2. (The DEC PDP-1, released in 1960 and geared toward laboratory control applications, was inspired by these two machines.) He then helped develop a computer geared expressly toward laboratory work, which became the transistorized Laboratory Instrument Computer, or LINC—arguably the first minicomputer. Engineer C. Gordon Bell has gone further, calling LINC "the world's first personal computer."

Meanwhile, at the Control Data Corporation, engineer Seymour Cray, whose surname would later become synonymous with supercomputing, put pen to paper and designed the 48-bit CDC 1604, a million-dollar transistorized scientific computer that was quite powerful but encumbered by slow I/O processing in the form of paper tape and punched cards. To counteract the bottleneck, Cray built the small, fast, and cheap single-user 12-bit CDC 160, which could be employed for I/O tasks, thereby giving its big brother a hand. The 160, about a tenth the price of the 1604, was later sold as a standalone product, the 160-A, which also might be considered the world's first minicomputer.

Minicomputing blossomed at yet another site in the first half of the 1960s, precipitated by the revolution that supplanted transistors with integrated circuits (i.e., chips). When Digital Equipment Corporation—founded in 1957 by the young American engineers Ken Olsen and Harlan Anderson and sited at an industrial mill in Massachusetts once used to make uniforms and blankets for Union troops during the U.S. Civil War—was tasked with designing a machine to monitor a nuclear reactor in Canada, DEC engineers Gordon Bell and Edson de Castro put their noses to the grindstone, building and programming a general-purpose computer to do the trick. Their computer evolved into the PDP-8 (Programmed Data Processor-8, also known as the "Straight-8"), a 12-bit, general-purpose, high-speed, random-access, magnetic-core memory (4,096 words) computer, with a starting price of less than twenty-thousand dollars, whose various incarnations ended up selling tens of thousands of units. (The PDP-8 utilized the same instruction set as the 12-bit PDP-5, which Gordon and de Castro had also collaborated on.) Early models came packaged with a one-pass FORTRAN compiler, complete with dynamic error checking, as well as a MACRO-8 Symbolic Assembler. These computers were interactive, providing near-real-time feedback to users.

It is with the PDP-8 that the term "minicomputer" first gains traction; a sales report penned by DEC United Kingdom head John Leng included this sentence: "Here is the latest minicomputer activity in the land of miniskirts as I drive around in my Mini Minor." If the minicomputer was being normalized as just another cultural artifact, then the PDP-8 was the prototypical minicomputer: small, fast, ubiquitous, and often imitated.

The first PDP-8 brochure, a technical document as much as a sales pitch, boasted of the variety of applications the machine could tackle: everything from research experiments and measurement; to quality control testing and statistical analysis; to data acquisition, logging, reduction, and analysis (including telemetry, biomedical and oceanographic research, and real-time analog signal monitoring); to process control (e.g., in steel mills and nuclear reactors); to data processing; to communications; and, finally, to education and training. Yet these were rather narrow applications, especially as compared to the machine's creative uses later on. Clearly, the PDP-8 was not initially targeted to the average home consumer, especially since, despite its low price (compared to other similarly powered equipment), at the time it cost as much as a medium-sized house.

As the cost of the machine's components decreased and its sales grew, however, the PDP-8 was put to increasingly novel uses, like controlling the scoreboard at Fenway Park in Boston, the lighting for the musical *A Chorus Line* in Shubert Theater in New York, and the news ticker in Times Square. The PDP-8 also invaded offices and hospitals across the globe, proving its general-purpose bona fides. Numerous BASICs were released for the PDP-8, including BASIC-8 for DEC's TSS/8 time-sharing operating system as well as versions designed to run on the company's OS/8 operating system.

Fresh off the wild success of the PDP-8, Edson de Castro began dreaming up his next project: a family of 16-bit computers. But, stymied by DEC, the engineer left the company and, along with several other DEC employees, founded Data General Corporation in the late 1960s. DG's cheap 16-bit Nova minicomputer, released in 1969, was positioned as a direct competitor to the PDP-8. Next came the successor machines: first the Eclipse and then the 32-bit Eclipse MV/8000 (codenamed *Eagle*), with the development of the latter famously documented by Tracy Kidder in his book *The Soul of a New Machine*.

The rise of personal computing spelled the end of DEC; the company was swallowed up by Compaq in a 1998 merger. Hewlett-Packard, founded by Bill Hewlett and David Packard in a Palo Alto garage in the 1930s, thrived at the dawn of the twenty-first century, acquiring Compaq (and thus DEC) along with a number of other firms. From its humble beginnings manufacturing audio oscillators (the HP 200A), HP's product line grew in ambition, culminating in the 1960s with the HP 2100 family of 16-bit minis.

There were other players in the minicomputer market, like Scientific Data Systems, begun by Max Palevsky and Robert Beck; Computer Automation, founded by David H. Methvin and known for its Naked Mini systems ("naked" because the machines could be purchased stripped-down, sans power supply and other components); General Automation, started by Honeywell salesman Larry Goshorn; Texas Instruments, begun in 1930 as Geophysical Service and later renamed TI, which turned out a slew of 16-bit minis; Wang Laboratories, founded by An Wang and G. Y. Chu and manufacturer of the businessperson-friendly Wang 2200, a minicomputer that could *only* be programmed in a form of microcoded interpreted BASIC; as well as Honeywell and IBM.

As popular as the Digital Equipment Corporation PDP-8 series proved to be, the PDP-11 family put it to shame, beating its predecessor's sales volume by a factor of ten. Arriving on the scene in 1970, a number of programming languages were made available for the machine, including COBOL, FORTRAN IV, APL, and RPG (report generating system). Several BASICs ran on the PDP-11 too, depending on the OS; these dialects were derivatives of Dartmouth BASIC the Fifth, which had spread to DEC via GE BASIC, itself a carbon copy of BASIC the Fifth (GE BASIC had also spread to the HP 2000 series this way).

BASIC-11, an interactive interpreted version of the language similar to BASIC-8 (which ran on the DEC TSS/8, a time-sharing operating system), could "be used for relatively large data processing tasks as well as quick, one-time calculations," boasted a 1977 DEC brochure titled "PDP-11: Variations on a Theme." BASIC-11 ran on the RT-11, RSTS/E, RSX-11M, and IAS operating systems.

BASIC-PLUS offered additional features not found in Dartmouth BASIC, including expanded string operations, extensions for handling fixed-length field records, and program control and storage facilities. BASIC-PLUS was included as part of the RSTS/E operating system.

BASIC-Plus-2 upped the ante, offering compilation capabilities. In addition, BASIC-Plus-2 files "interface[d] directly to the RMS-11 record management system," we learn from the 1977 brochure, "which allows the BASIC-Plus-2 user to create files, do record mapping, and access records sequentially, randomly, or by key." What's more, the **CALL** statement was introduced, permitting access to external subroutines. BASIC-Plus-2 ran under the RSTS/E, RSX-11M, and IAS operating systems.

The 32-bit VAX-11/780 minicomputer, successor to the PDP-11, arrived in 1977. And BASIC soldiered on, with BASIC-Plus-2 being rebranded VAX BASIC and running on the VMS operating system.

Digital Equipment Corporation released a great variety of BASIC dialects over several decades. Mapping out all versions of BASIC for only the PDP-11 is a challenging genealogical task; accounting for all DEC BASICs, no matter the machine, is a daunting one.

Author Russ Walter—best known for the multi-volume *The Secret Guide to Computers*, of which numerous editions were published, and famous for his promise to answer any computer question, day or night, at no charge over the phone—also stepped into the BASIC fray. In the 1977 article "Let's Improve BASIC" for *Personal Computing* magazine, Walter noted that DEC offering BASIC on its PDP-8 computers as an alternative to the high-level language FOCAL (Formulating On-Line Calculations in Algebraic Language) resulted in BASIC becoming the language of choice for the PDP-11. But then, he offered an analogy for what went wrong with BASIC:

> Suppose you try to reach the highest point in the world by always walking uphill. Though you'll wind up higher than you started, you won't reach the top of Mt. Everest: to reach that pinnacle, you must occasionally walk downhill to get to a higher mountain.

> Unfortunately, Kemeny and Kurtz always walk uphill: they adopt a new feature only if it agrees with programs written previously. Following their plan, all the wrong steps we've taken during the past dozen years will never be reversed; all future generations will suffer.

With backwards compatibility paramount, the Beginner's All-purpose Symbolic Instruction Code had turned into a fragmentary language, Walter argued, replete with vestigial elements. BASIC desperately needed, albeit could never receive, a top-to-bottom rewrite.

So, instead, Walter offered a number of recommendations to improve the language, including:

- Use of the colon (:) for defining all ranges, in order to improve consistency. For instance:

  LIST 100:   to **LIST** every line from **100** onward

  FOR I=1:   for **I**=1, 2, 3, and onward

  A$[3:]   a substring of **A$**, beginning at index 3 and continuing to the end

- Indent to define blocks of statements for loops, subroutines, and functions (instead of terminating these blocks with **NEXT**, **RETURN**, and **FNEND**, respectively). So, instead of

```
10 FOR X = 5 TO 1 STEP -1
20 PRINT "TIMER READS:"
30 PRINT X
40 NEXT X
50 PRINT "BLAST OFF!"
```

we should write:

```
10 FOR X = 5 TO 1 STEP -1
20    PRINT "TIMER READS:"
30    PRINT X
40 PRINT "BLAST OFF!"
```

- Avoid thinking negatively. As Walter put it, "Instead of thinking, 'if **N** is less than 3, do the following 10 statements', you must think 'if **N** is greater than or equal to 3, skip the following ten statements', and write it like this:"

```
100 IF N>=3 THEN GOTO 200
```

Arguing that this kind of negative thinking often led to confusion for the beginner, Walter suggested a different approach that again employs indenting:

```
100 IF N<3
110     J=J+1
120     K=K+1
130 IF NOT
140     J=J*2
150     K=K*2
```

- Use of longer variable names like **CIRCUMFERENCE**, yet resulting in no loss in compiler or interpreter speed, since only the first two characters of the identifier would be considered—and, subsequent use of **CIRCUMFERENCE** in the program could be abbreviated as **CI** by the programmer.
- Extending the prior recommendation, statements like **PRINT** could be abbreviated as **PR**, for example.
- Switch the functionality of the comma (**,**) and the semicolon (**;**), directing the latter to generate a single space in output and the former to produce packed output—thus matching the convention in the English language, where a comma indicates a shorter pause than a semicolon. For instance, in Walter's conception, the program

```
10 F$="MA"
20 L$="RK"
30 B=22
40 PRINT F$,L$;"WAS BORN ON AUGUST";B,"ND"
```

would print out the following:

```
MARK WAS BORN ON AUGUST 22ND
```

- Remove "useless junk," like the statements **END, LET, REM, ON...GOTO, SGN, IDN, CON,** and **TRN**. The first five were redundant, and the final three were designed to analyze matrix-intensive Markov chains and thus too specialized for a general audience.

Interestingly, several of Walter's recommendations made their way into Python, which debuted in 1990. (Python is discussed as a potentially "new BASIC" in the fifth chapter.)

Some observers of the BASIC madness, like Russ Walter, offered constructive criticisms to improve the state of affairs. Others, in advance of any formal standards effort, tried to bring the Hydra-like BASIC monster to heel.

Consider J.A.N. Lee, a computer scientist and historian working at the University of Massachusetts in Amherst, who proposed a formal definition for BASIC in 1972. Lee made use of Backus-Naur Form (BNF), named for John Backus and Peter Naur. In the late 1950s, when at work on the International Algebraic Language (IAL)—later renamed ALGOL 58—Backus was disappointed by the lack of precision in the language definition. "They would just describe stuff in English," he lamented decades later. So, in the 1959 paper "The Syntax and Semantics of the Proposed International Algebraic Language of the Zurich ACM-GAMM Conference," Backus struck back, bringing a high degree precision to the syntax of IAL by proposing a *metalanguage* (a language to describe another language) that consisted of a context-free grammar of symbolic notation coupled with mathematical formalism. Originally called Backus Normal Form, Peter Naur improved Backus's metalanguage, leading Donald Knuth to suggest renaming it after both Backus and Naur.

BNF consisted of *production rules*, which were metalinguistic formulas: left-hand-side names (non-terminal symbols) and right-hand-side alternatives (non-terminal symbols and/or terminal symbols), separated by ::= ("is defined as") symbols. There were angle brackets, <>, enclosing classes or metalinguistic variables, and vertical bars, |, denoting ORs that delimited right-hand-side alternatives. For instance, what follows is the BNF definition of a single letter in BASIC:

$$<letter> ::= A\,|\,B\,|\,C\,|\,D\,|\,E\,|\,F\,|\,G\,|\,H\,|\,I\,|\,J\,|\,K\,|\,L\,|\,M\,|\,N\,|\,O\,|\,P\,|\,Q\,|\,R\,|\,S\,|\,T\,|\,U\,|\,V\,|\,W\,|\,X\,|\,Y\,|\,Z$$

The above was an instance of a *concrete syntax definition*, "the definition of the syntactic form of the language used by the programmer," explained J.A.N. Lee; digits, signs, and library functions (like **SIN**, **COS**, and **LOG**), could be defined in a similar, straightforward manner.

Keywords could be expressed using concrete syntax definitions as well. Consider the **GOTO** statement:

$$<goto\ st> ::= \textbf{GOTO}\ \ <line\ no>$$

And the **IF** statement:

$$<if\ st> ::= \textbf{IF}\ \ <boolean\ expression>\ \textbf{THEN}\ <line\ no>$$

Lee modified BNF, denoting repetitive concatenations of objects by using the notation $\{...\}_i^j$, where i represented the minimum number of repetitions required and j stood for the maximum number of repetitions permitted. For instance, consider the definition

$$<for\ st> ::= \textbf{FOR}\ <simple\ variable> = <expression>\ \textbf{TO}\ <expression>\ \{\textbf{STEP}\ <expression>\}_0^1$$

which allowed, at most, one instance of **STEP** in a single **FOR** loop.

Or consider this definition, which rendered the **LET** statement optional:

$$<\!for\ st\!> ::= \{\textsf{LET}\}_0^1 <\!variable\!> = <\!expression\!>$$

Or this, which enumerated exhaustively the valid keyword possibilities for a BASIC line containing a **DEF** statement:

$$<\!def\ statement\!> ::= <\!line\ no\!>\ \{<\!def\ let\ st\!> | <\!def\ read\ st\!> | <\!def\ print\ st\!> | <\!go\ to\ st\!> | <\!def\ on\ st\!> |$$
$$<\!def\ if\ st\!> | <\!def\ for\ st\!> | <\!def\ next\ st\!> | <\!gosub\ st\!> | <\!return\ st\!> | <\!restore\ st\!> | <\!stop\ st\!> | <\!rem\ st\!>\}_0^1$$

As Lee explained it, "The statements defined by the meta component names of the form $<\!def\ n\ st\!>$ have the same structure as the object $<\!n\ st\!>$ except that $<\!simple\ variable\!>$ may be replaced by $<\!function\ variable\!>$ in all components." Thus, we have a definition like

$$<\!def\ next\ st\!> ::= \textsf{NEXT}\ \{<\!simple\ variable\!> | <\!function\ variable\!>\}_1^1$$

where using 1 as both subscript and superscript indicated the mandatory presence of **NEXT**.

Lee not only modified BNF to fit his vision of a rigorous definition for BASIC; he also adapted the Vienna Definition Language (VDL) of Austrian computer scientist Peter Lucas, who had leveraged it to formally define the high-level PL/I. In Lee's conception, besides the concrete syntax of BASIC, there was also the *abstract syntax*, or "the definition of the essential structural form of the language which is to be used as input to the interpreter." In addition, the interpreter of the BASIC machine instructions and functions, which "operates on the abstract text according to instructions and functions defined for the language," had to be considered. The interpreter's state contained the abstract text of the program along with an instruction stack. The instructions handled by the interpreter were of two types: *self-replacing* and *value-returning*. "The former instruction type replaces itself in the stack by one of its defined groups, chosen according to the condition currently existing in the state of the abstract machine," Lee explained. "The execution of a value returning instruction causes changes in the state of the machine and the deletion of the instruction from the stack." Before a program was run, the program stack contained but a single instruction: **execute program**(s-text(ξ)).

The interpreter was the third of three processors constituting the so-called *abstract machine*, which operated over the language definitions; the other two processors were termed the "analyser" and the "translator." The former processor used the concrete syntax to verify the concrete text, in turn generating a parsed text that could be represented as a tree. The latter processor transformed the parsed text into abstract text, which met the standards of the abstract syntax while also being in accordance with the default conditions. More complicated to understand than the concrete syntax, the abstract syntax made use of what were called s-data-components that determined the state of the abstract machine. Each variable, for instance, had attributes stored as s-data-components. A simple variable had the abstract syntax shown below.

$$\text{is-simple-variable} = (<\text{s-name: is-simple-name}>)$$

While an array variable had a more complex syntactical presentation:

$$\text{is-array-variable} = (<\text{s-name: is-array-name}>, <\text{s-subscript-1: is expression}>,$$
$$<\text{s-subscript-2: is expression v is-}\Omega>)$$

The abstract syntax for a **GOTO** statement appeared as

$$\text{is-goto-st} = (<\text{s-line-no: is-line-no}>, <\text{s-st-name: \textbf{GOTO}}>, <\text{s-destination: is-line-no}>)$$

When the abstract machine's interpreter encountered, say, a **GOTO** statement, it would execute it according to these rules:

$$\textbf{execute-statement}(\text{line-no, text, line-no-stack}) =$$
$$\text{is-}\textbf{GOTO}(\text{s-st-name*s-line(line-no)(text)}) \rightarrow$$
$$\textbf{execute-statement}(\text{s-destination*s-line(line-no)(text), text, line-no-stack})$$

The summary of J.A.N. Lee's BASIC proposal above merely scratches the surface. The curious reader is encouraged to obtain the 1972 paper "The Formal Definition of the BASIC Language," published in *The Computer Journal*, for more details.

Using BASIC as a teaching tool in secondary school classrooms, not just in university settings, was well underway by 1972, as documented that spring by Walter Koetke in "The Impact of Computing on the Teaching of Mathematics," written for a joint computer conference of the American Federation of Information Processing Societies (AFIPS).

Koetke worked at Lexington High School in Massachusetts and had a front-row seat to the perils and promise of computing in the mathematics classroom. No matter how schools acquired their computing equipment—through local industries providing computing time, or by schools obtaining their own facilities, or via commercial time-sharing services—each school initially needed an "inside agitator," "a motivated, aggressive member of the mathematics department" to spearhead the effort, he wrote. But especially around 1970 or 1971, as the costs of acquiring these computing services fell (whether through the outright purchase of minicomputers or the rental of time-sharing terminals, or even the lease of batch-processing systems), there was "increased awareness by both teachers and administrators that computing facilities have become a necessary part of the mathematics program." Local school boards saw the writing on the wall. As long as math teachers had the desire and skill to exploit these new technologies, BASIC's widespread availability around this time greatly contributed to the increase of computing in high school mathematics classes. Koetke explained,

BASIC is not here defended as the "best" programming language. It is, however, offered as the most appropriate language for present secondary school requirements. Remember that the primary application of the computing facilities is problem solving, not computer science. The computer is to be used as a problem solving tool, thus the programming language itself should not be a problem for the students. Languages such as FORTRAN and APL are themselves problems for most students. The language used must also be well documented, not just in vendor's operating manuals but in the wider literature of mathematics. Languages like FOCAL, CAL [Conversational Algebraic Language, based on the JOSS programming language] and TELCOMP [also based on JOSS] are certainly easy to learn, but they are not often referenced in the literature. BASIC, however, satisfies both of these requirements—it is very easy to learn and commonly referenced in the literature.

A robust mathematics curriculum involved teaching more than the traditional subjects that the ancient Greeks studied, like geometry and algebra; rather, it made space for calculus and non-Euclidian geometry as well as including, post-World War II, topics in algorithms and computation. Though they were once necessary, brilliant mathematical end-runs around tedious calculations, Koetke maintained, no longer held sway in the computer age. Rather, with these calculations offloaded to machines, higher levels of abstraction could be explored in the secondary school classroom, with mathematical concepts assuming pride of place. (Even a half century after the publication of Koetke's article, mathematics students were still being taught many of these clever computation-avoiding formulas. In the realm of secondary education, old habits die particularly hard.)

In the 1970s, BASIC spread beyond secondary and even higher ed classrooms, as University of Southern California engineering professor Bennet P. Lientz noted in "A Comparative Evaluation of Versions of BASIC" (1976) published in *Communications of the ACM*. "Usage has expanded in universities as well as industrial organization," Lientz contended, offering as evidence three papers documenting BASIC's use in professional laboratory work, transmission line problems, and information and retrieval (i.e., Project FLNP, "an integrated information and modeling system for management," described in a paper coauthored by John McGeachie, who, as an undergrad, programmed the DTSS).

Lientz categorized BASIC's use at the time as "substantial," offering as support research by programmers Jean Sammet and Saul Rosen as well as a DATAPRO survey of over one hundred organizations "reveal[ing] that while Fortran was used by 65 percent of the respondents, BASIC was second with 49 percent." In addition, "Of the 98 timesharing utilities surveyed...over half (58) offer a version of BASIC. BASIC is offered by many utilities in both interactive and batch modes and is available on minicomputers as well as larger computers."

These survey results are explained partly by the popularity of Business BASICs, versions of the language developed in the 1970s that were tailored for business use (typically on minicomputers), bringing many of the data- and file-handling capabilities of COBOL to the Beginner's All-purpose Symbolic Instruction Code. Well known dialects included MAI Basic Four and Data General Business Basic, the latter of which would influence the design of the Atari BASIC interpreter for the Atari 8-bit family of microcomputers. In fact, just as microcomputer BASICs have complex multibranch family trees, Business BASICs have their own rich genealogy, as these dialects migrated from proprietary minicomputers to operating systems like Unix, Linux, MS-DOS, and Windows by the turn of the century.

Taking the bull by the horns, Tom Kurtz became an integral part of the standards effort for BASIC, chairing ANSI committee X3J2 that wrote the draft standard (X3J2/82-17). Stephen Garland rose to the rank of X3J2 vice-chair.

In January 1974—with BASIC used on time-sharing networks more than any other programming language (there were well over one hundred such networks)—X3J2 held its first meeting; "committee X3J2 has been one of the largest and most enthusiastic of the language standards committees," Kurtz wrote around that time.

Four years later, ANSI X3.60-1978, or Minimal BASIC, was released, with cooperation from the European counterpart to X3J2, ECMA/TC21. Kurtz noted that "the standards committee X3J2 was charged to develop a standard for Minimal BASIC first, partly because it might fail if it tried to do more." The European Computer Manufacturers Association's "Standard ECMA-55: Minimal BASIC" report, published in 1978, offers a brief history of the cross-continental partnership. The document reads in part:

> In 1974, the ECMA General Assembly recognized the need for a standardized version of the language, and in September 1974 the first meeting of the ECMA Committee TC 21, BASIC, took place. In January 1974, a corresponding committee, X3J2, had been founded in the USA.

> Through a strict co-operation it was possible to maintain full compatibility between the ANSI and ECMA draft standards. The ANSI one was distributed for public comments in January 1976, and a number of comments were presented by ECMA.

> A final version of the ECMA Standard was prepared at the meeting of June 1977 and adopted by the General Assembly of ECMA on Dec. 14, 1977 as Standard ECMA-55.

The report clearly spelled out the scope of the project: "This Standard ECMA-55 is designed to promote the interchangeability of BASIC programs among a variety of automatic data processing systems." Pivoting to the future, the ECMA observed that "[s]ubsequent Standards for the same purpose will describe extensions and enhancements to this Standard."

Minimal BASIC, similar to the Dartmouth BASICs of the 1960s, included **BASE**, **DATA**, **DEF** (single line), **DIM**, **END**, **FOR/NEXT/STEP**, **GO**, **GOSUB...RETURN**, **IF/THEN**, **INPUT**, **LET**, **ON...GOTO**, **OPTION**, **PRINT**, **RANDOMIZE**, **READ**, **REM**, **RESTORE**, **STOP**, and **SUB**, along with line numbers. Since no keywords were optional, **LET** was required.

Sometimes the results of calculations, depending on the manner in which the machine performed them, did not necessarily materialize as expected. "Standard ECMA-55: Minimal BASIC" contains this warning about the unpredictable (or, more precisely, implementation-defined) behavior of code in a **FOR/NEXT** loop:

Where arithmetic is approximate (as with decimal fractions in a binary machine), the loop will be executed within the limits of machine arithmetic. No presumptions about approximate achievement of the end test are made. It is noted that in most ordinary situations where machine arithmetic is truncated (rather than rounded), such constructions as

```
FOR X = 0 TO 1 STEP 0.1
```

will work as the user expects, even though 0.1 is not representable exactly in a binary machine. If this is indeed the case, then the construction

```
FOR X = 1 TO 0 STEP -0.1
```

will probably not work as expected.

To appreciate the above passage, note that just as not all base 10 decimals terminate— e.g., $1/3 = 0.333333...$—the terminating base 10 decimal 0.1 has an infinite representation in binary, namely, 0.00011001100110011.... (To obtain the binary value, perform binary long division, dividing 1_{bin} by 1010_{bin}.) No matter how much memory is set aside, all the individual binary digits of this repeating binary decimal (also called a repeating *bicimal*) can never be stored because an infinite number of bits would be necessary for the operation. Since floating-point values are represented with a finite number of bits, the bicimal 0.00011001100110011... must be truncated somewhere—and converting that truncated bicimal back to base 10 typically results in a decimal number close but not quite equal to the base 10 decimal 0.1, such as

$$0.1000000000000000055511151231257827021181583404541015625$$

which was found by terminating the bicimal at the fifty-third bit position (the maximum value for double-precision floating-point) and then converting the truncated bicimal back to base 10.

Though not all decimals convert to repeating bicimals, more often than not they do. (Let's put aside the thorny issues involving infinite sets—and the faux precision of the phrase "more often than not they do," which immediately unravels under the scrutiny of anyone with even a passing knowledge of Cantor's theorem—so we can continue our discussion.) If the denominator of the reduced fractional form of a decimal is a power of two, then its associated bicimal terminates (e.g., $0.1 = 1/10$ and 10 is not a power of 2, so the bicimal does not terminate; but $0.0625 = 1/16$ and 16 is 2^4, so 0.0625 converts to a terminating bicimal: i.e., 0.0001). Again, note that if the number of significant digits of the terminating bicimal exceeds fifty-three, then the number cannot be precisely stored as double-precision floating-point, since that numeric type labors under the upper limit of fifty-three bits per number.

Bringing the discussion back to BASIC, while the errors of repeatedly adding or subtracting 0.1 accumulate in a **FOR/NEXT** loop, thereby leading to unexpected loop counter variable values, a construction like the following

```
FOR X = 1 TO 0 STEP -0.0625
PRINT X
NEXT X
```

results in output of the numbers 1, 0.9375, 0.875, 0.8125, 0.75, 0.6875, 0.625, 0.5625, 0.5, 0.4375, 0.375, 0.3125, 0.25, 0.1875, 0.125, 0.0625, and 0—exactly as expected. This decimal **STEP** issue had to be explicitly dealt with as early as the first implementation of Dartmouth BASIC; Kurtz recalled in an interview for the book *Masterminds of Programming* that a "fuzz factor to determine the completion of the loop" was implemented in cases of infinite repeating binary fractions resulting from lines like **FOR I = 1 TO 2 STEP 0.1**.

In Minimal BASIC, keywords, variable names, function names, constants, and line numbers could not contain any spaces, but keywords had to be enclosed in spaces (unless they were at the end of a line, in which case they had to be preceded by at least one space). BASIC statements were restricted to a maximum of seventy-two characters in length. Multiple numeric functions were defined: **ABS, ATN, COS, EXP, INT, LOG, RND, SGN, SIN, SQR**, and **TAN**; the only function that didn't take any arguments was **RND**, which simply returned "[t]he next pseudo-random number in an implementation-supplied sequence of pseudo-random numbers uniformly distributed in the range 0 <= RND < 1," as explained in "Standard ECMA-55: Minimal BASIC." (There is much more on **RND** and pseudorandom sequences in the eighth chapter of this book. But the key point here is that Minimal BASIC left it up to the implementor to establish the mathematical means to generate these highly circumscribed "random" numbers.) From "Standard ECMA-55: Minimal BASIC," we also learn that "[a] number of features defined in this Standard have been left for definition by the implementor," which included the accuracy of evaluation of numeric expressions, the initial values of variables, the input prompt, the print-zone length, and the aforementioned pseudorandom number sequence, among others. Strings lists, files, and graphics commands were not defined by the standard.

Kurtz lamented, "One characteristic of standards work is that major points are usually settled easily, while seemingly minor points may take years to resolve." Indeed, there was one minor Minimal BASIC point of contention that the committee struggled to settle: that of the default starting index for an array, either zero or one. "Every time we took a vote on the subject—and we took many many votes—it came out to be a 14-to-14 tie," recalled Kurtz. "And there we had to resort to a committee compromise, and the two-humped camel that has resulted is what is known as the **OPTION BASE** statement," which specified the default lower bound for an array: zero or one (if the statement didn't appear in a program, the lower bound defaulted to zero). Five years later, the committee shifted course somewhat, permitting users to specify lower bounds for each array. For instance: **DIM YEAR(1979:2022)** declared an array named **YEAR** with forty-four elements, subscripted from **1979** to **2022**.

As Kurtz wrote in "On the Way to Standard BASIC," an article appearing in *Byte* magazine in June 1982, "Minimal BASIC has not caught on because the rapid development of chip technology has made its modest capabilities obsolete." Attempting to write a minimal set of BASIC standards through the 1970s, where by the end of the decade microcomputers hooked up to television sets had invaded homes throughout the world, was like using a rock and sling shot to hit a moving target traveling at supersonic speed. By the early 1980s, as James Harle reported in "The Proposed Standard for BASIC" (1983), "Work is just beginning on defining a subset as a replacement for the Minimal BASIC Standard. The subset is intended to be an appropriate size for microcomputers and smaller minicomputers." In the meantime, software, such as PBASIC (written in PFORT, a subset of FORTRAN), arrived on the scene that checked if BASIC programs adhered to the standard.

With Minimal BASIC a noble but failed effort, that left Full BASIC, which wouldn't be finalized until 1987; an addendum defining modules would be approved in 1991. When Kurtz penned his *Byte* piece in 1982, Full BASIC was "under technical committee mail ballot," and a mandatory public-review period was forthcoming (the public comment period extended from March through July, 1983). The Full BASIC standard, ANSI X3.113-1987, was adopted by the International Standards Organization (ISO) as well. Three committees had cooperated on writing the draft standard: X3J2, the European Computer Manufacturers Association (ECMA) TC21, and the European Workshop on Industrial Computer Systems (EWICS) TC2.

Committee meetings were typically held at locations near committee members' workplaces, with hosting duties cycling between members. From 1974 to 1982, X3J2 gathered for thirty meetings. Some meetings were held in the Eastern U.S., some in the Midwest, some in the South, and still others on the West Coast. X3J2 met yearly with the ECMA TC21, alternating between sites in the United States and Europe.

When choosing places to meet, cost of accommodations was unsurprisingly a key factor. But perhaps the most pressing consideration involved food, according to Kurtz: "Whatever site we choose must have good restaurants." With much of the X3J2 committee employed in San Francisco, and the TC21 members based in London, Paris, and Vienna, Kurtz never feared lacking in "culinary delights."

After years of working together with little turnover, X3J2 participants grew close. At one early meeting, a committee member stood to speak and revealed to the group a custom-made T-shift he was wearing, with "BASIC Standard" printed on the front and "Strings Subco" on the back. The demonstration "brought down the house," Kurtz recalled. At another meeting, a committee member showed the group a brand of toilet paper he found called "Basic," employing it as an apt metaphor for the standard's state of affairs. And at a gathering sometime in the early 1980s, one of the veterans showed up holding a large plastic goose. "When the discussion deteriorated (who can be brilliant for six hours a day all week long?), the goose would appear on the table," Kurtz remembered.

"Developing a standard for BASIC has been difficult because the language serves such a diverse clientele," Kurtz explained in *Byte* magazine. There were educational users, pecking away on their keyboards on minicomputers and microcomputers, expecting an easy-to-learn language "not cluttered with declarations or excessive structure." There were also users who tapped into BASIC on large machines, wanting a "rich, compiler-based language," complete with subroutine libraries and advanced string-processing capabilities suited for interactive programs. And there were business users of BASIC, needing the means to process and output nicely formatted financial calculations, access record-structured files, and successfully run financial applications—especially in Europe, where BASIC was the "primary business data-processing language for small computers."

What's more, not only were the clientele diverse; BASIC dialects floating around in the post-Dartmouth, pre-microcomputer days were diverse as well, and the standards committees had to consider them all. In his aforementioned 1976 report, Bennet Lientz compared vendors' versions of the language; he also put these BASICs up against the proposed ANSI Standard, enumerating their features, limitations, I/O capabilities, and constant and intrinsic functions. Some vendors offered BASIC on different platforms, such as Rapidata, which released the language for IBM (the IBM 370/145), DEC (the PDP 1070 mainframe), and Honeywell (the Honeywell 437) hardware; and Tymshare, which offered BASIC on DEC (the PDP 1070) and Xerox (the XDS 940, first known as the SDS 940 until Scientific Data Systems was acquired by Xerox in the late 1960s) machines. In addition, versions of BASIC implemented by Dartmouth (for the Honeywell 6635), General Electric (for the Honeywell 6080), Hewlett-Packard (for the HP 2000F), International Timesharing Corporation (for the CDC 3300), Service Bureau Corporation (for the IBM 370/158), and United Computing Systems (for the CDC 6500) were also put to the test. Finally, as another point of comparison, Lientz gathered data from two earlier BASICs: IBM ITF BASIC and IBM CALL/OS BASIC.

Even in the smallest of details, these many BASICs could differ considerably from each other. Consider matrix operations—specifically, obtaining the *determinant* of a square matrix (i.e., a matrix with an equal number of rows and columns); determinants have a number of applications in algebra and geometry. For example, the 2×2 matrix

$$\begin{bmatrix} 7 & 4 \\ 5 & 6 \end{bmatrix}$$

has a determinant of $7 \times 6 - 4 \times 5 = 22$. As the dimensions of a square matrix grow, so do the number of steps required to calculate its determinant. Versions of BASIC capable of computing determinants—like offerings from Dartmouth, DEC-Tymshare, GE, IBM, and ITS—provided a function called **DET**. But ITF BASIC and CALL/OS BASIC, as well as BASICs from HP, Rapidata, SBC, and UCS, had no determinant function. And IBM VS BASIC required special software in order to access some of the matrix operations.

While some trigonometric functions like **SIN** (sine), **COS** (cosine), and **TAN** (tangent) were nearly universal, others, like **COT** (cotangent) and **SEC** (secant), were not. Additionally, there was wide variation in intrinsic constants (i.e., built-in constants, such as for π), intrinsic functions for strings and files (for example, **LEN**, which returned the length of a string), I/O capabilities (for instance, reading and writing to the same file, or deleting records), statements (**IF/THEN/ELSE** was absent on most BASICs considered by Lientz), and the maximum number of statements per program (VS BASIC was limited to only one thousand).

Despite the differences between implementations of the language—on mainframes, minicomputers, and, most recently, microcomputers—Kurtz was optimistic in 1982 that the draft standard would be approved within a year, relaying a timetable in *Byte* for "Final approval by ANSI" by 1983, though he did acknowledge that "unforeseen problems" might lead to delays.

At ACM '82, a computing conference held in January, Kurtz participated in a panel session chaired by Ronald Anderson of the Minnesota Center for Social Research. Other panel participants included Jerry Isaacs of Carroll College (now University) in Waukesha, Wisconsin, and J.A.N. Lee. Features of the proposed standard were presented, with the panel taking questions from attendees. Full BASIC, adopting much from Garland's SBASIC, was designed to extend Minimal BASIC; for that reason, X3J2 considered calling Full BASIC "Extended BASIC" or even "Enhanced BASIC," but ultimately decided against it.

The proposed standard was "sufficiently stable to permit examination and discussion," the panel argued, containing "multicharacter variable names, external subroutines, two-dimensional plotting, and several simple file types," along with "[o]ptional extensions includ[ing] additional file types, real-time [applications], and a fixed-decimal module for business applications." The standard had a "core module" along with five optional modules: "enhanced files (direct access and keyed); graphics; real time [for applications]; fixed decimal (for business users); and editing." Details of the standard included:

- *Data types*: String variables, up to 132 characters in length (string variables could be capped at a user-defined maximum size), along with single-precision numeric variables, with fixed decimal as an option (invoked by the **OPTION** statement; for example, **OPTION ARITHMETIC FIXED*5.3** called for fixed-decimal arithmetic with variables allowing five digits before the decimal and three digits afterward).

- *Program comments*: **REM** for full-line comments and **!** for end-of-line remarks.

- *Identifiers*: Multicharacter variable and function names up to thirty-one characters in length, albeit spaces separating keywords were required. Upper- and lowercase letters were ignored except within strings.

- *Numerical operations*: Arithmetic was performed in floating decimal, meaning that 0.1 added to itself nine times would equal exactly 1, and that a ten-digit decimal like 0.9876543210 was ruled strictly less than 0.9876543211. That opened the door to business applications in BASIC, since users could "carry out dollars-and-cents calculations with confidence," contended Kurtz.

- *Built-in numeric functions*: In addition to those of Minimal BASIC, additional trigonometric functions along with other useful mathematical functions were defined—more than forty functions in total. Using **OPTION ANGLE DEGREES** switched the angle measures for the trigonometric functions from radians to degrees.

- *Mandatory keywords*: Like with Minimal BASIC, the **LET** statement was not optional. Also, keywords were reserved, and could therefore not be utilized as identifiers in a program.

- *String operations*: The ampersand (**&**) symbol was employed for string concatenation. Substrings were captured using square brackets along with a range appended to the string variable. For instance, to obtain the second through the fifth characters of the string **A$**, a user could type **A$[2:5]**, a format which bore resemblance to FORTRAN 77 syntax. (Extracting variable-length strings by using parentheses, rather than square brackets, was proposed first.) Consequently, mainstay substring functions like **SEG$**, **MID$**, **LEFT$**, and **RIGHT$** were retired.

- *String functions*: A number of string-related functions, including **CHR$**, **DATE$**, **LEN**, **POS**, **STR$**, **TIME$**, and **VAL**, were included in the standard.

- *Collating sequence*: ASCII defined the order of the characters for comparisons, but other collating sequences, such as EBCDIC (Extended Binary Coded Decimal Interchange Code), could be employed courtesy of the **OPTION COLLATE NATIVE** statement.

- *User-defined functions*: In addition to using **DEF** for simpler functions, function definitions could be multiline, enclosed with the keywords **FUNCTION...END FUNCTION**. Function definitions, like named subroutines, could be internal or external (if prefaced by the **EXTERNAL** keyword) to the main program—thus facilitating the building of libraries of routines. Here is an example of a single-line function to simulate rolling a dodecahedron die straight out of *Dungeons & Dragons*:

```
DEF ROLL = INT(12 * RND + 1)  ! twelve-sided die roll
```

Note that once the **ROLL** function is invoked, the value returned (i.e., an integer from 1 to 12) is stored in the function name. A multiline function required **END DEF** to terminate the function definition, as shown below.

```
DEF FACT(N)   ! factorial calculator
        LET X = N
        LET F = 1
     DO
        LET F = F * X
        LET X = X - 1
     LOOP WHILE X >= 1
        LET FACT = F
END DEF
```

Named subroutines, unlike functions, did not return a value when called (using the keyword **CALL**) but, like functions, parameters could be passed to subroutines. What follows is an example of a simple subroutine.

```
SUB ADDER(X, Y)
   LET Z=X+Y
   PRINT Z
END SUB
```

- *Arrays*: Unlike Minimal BASIC, which permitted array use without prior **DIM**ensioning (these undimensioned arrays defaulted to ten elements in length), in Full BASIC arrays had to be declared with **DIM** statements beforehand. The need for array declaration arose because of potential ambiguity in a statement such as **LET A = X(4)**. Since user-defined functions didn't have to start with the letters **FN**, **X** could be defined as a function with a single argument. In that case, was the **X(4)** a user-defined function named **X** or the first use of an undimensioned array called **X**? True, we could force an interpreter to pre-scan the code or a compiler to make a first pass through the program, checking to ensure that there was no such one-parameter function as **X( )**. Or instead, we could require that all functions be defined at the start of a program.

  In addition, attempting to keep the number of reserved words under control, coupled with the option of very long variable names, further argued for the explicit dimensioning of all arrays. Thus, the committee decided to force the declaration of arrays, "because most arrays have to be dimensioned anyway and it's customary to place the dimension statements early in the program," Kurtz explained. This mandate resulted in the only incompatibility between Minimal BASIC and the new standard.

- *Matrices*: A **MAT** package of operations were available, with linear algebra functions like **INV** (inverse) and **DET** (determinant) at the ready.

- *Logical expressions*: In addition to the relational expressions of Minimal BASIC (e.g., **A < B**), Full BASIC boasted the logical operators **AND**, **OR**, and **NOT**. Comparisons with strings were more robust in Full BASIC than in Minimal BASIC; the latter only allowed for = and <> with strings, but the former added the inequalities < and > as well. So a comparison such as **IF X$ < Y$** would return either true or false depending on the position of the characters (compared one at a time, left to right) in the strings **A$** and **B$** in the collating sequence (the default collating sequence was ASCII).

- *Conditionals*: Unlike with Minimal BASIC, **IF/THEN/ELSE** was available; however the branching construct required that each of the keywords—**IF**, **THEN**, **ELSE**, **END IF**—begin on separate lines.

- *Loops*: In addition to Minimal BASIC's **FOR/NEXT**, Full BASIC included the **DO...LOOP**. Exiting out of such a loop was triggered by an **EXIT DO**, and the **UNTIL** or **WHILE** keyword could be utilized to set the conditions of the loop. The following example, slightly altered from a code snippet found in James Harle's article "The Proposed Standard for Basic," only exits the loop if the user types an integer between one and seven:

```
DO
    INPUT X
IF 0 < X AND X <= 7 AND X = INT(X) THEN EXIT DO
    PRINT "ENTER AN INTEGER BETWEEN 1 AND 7"
LOOP
PRINT "YOU ENTERED ";X
```

- *Multiple paths of execution*: Full BASIC offered the **SELECT...CASE** construct, which branched based on a value. For instance, for the northern hemisphere:

```
SELECT MONTH
CASE 1, 2, 12
    PRINT "WINTER"
CASE 3, 4, 5
    PRINT "SPRING"
CASE 6, 7, 8
    PRINT "SUMMER"
CASE 9, 10, 11
    PRINT "WINTER"
CASE ELSE
    PRINT "NO SUCH MONTH"
END SELECT
```

- *Modularization*: Minimal BASIC offered single-line user-defined functions; Full BASIC permitted multiline functions by employing the keywords **DEF...END DEF**. Minimal BASIC allowed subroutines courtesy of **GOSUB...RETURN**; Full BASIC offered subprograms, too, and these subprograms could be passed parameters of various types. Moreover, the **CHAIN** statement could be utilized to begin running another program—which didn't even have to be written in BASIC—and parameters could be passed to these **CHAIN**ed programs, too, received by a **CHAIN**ed program's **PROGRAM** statement. For example:

```
CHAIN "calcprog"
CHAIN prog$(value, name$)
```

There were five techniques available to segment programs: the aforementioned **CHAIN** to link to call other programs, subprograms that could be called, internal functions, external functions, and graphical pictures. Parameters of internal and external functions were passed by value, and recursive calls were permitted.

- *Input/Output*: In addition to the **DATA, READ, INPUT**, and **PRINT** statements of Minimal BASIC, a **PRINT USING** statement was available for formatting output.

- *Files*: Dozens of pages of the standard were dedicated to files. Full BASIC offered multiple types of file organization, including sequential and random access. Keywords **PRINT, INPUT, READ**, and **WRITE** served double duty by accessing and communicating with files. While a program was running, files could be accessed by linking them with a channel—i.e., a number or an expression prefixed by a hash sign (**#**)—using the **OPEN** statement. For instance,

```
OPEN #5: NAME "dungeons"
```

The file could then be closed by referencing the channel:

```
CLOSE #5
```

To work with files, users employed statements like **READ, WRITE, ERASE**, and **ASK**.

- *Exception handling*: By using the **WHEN EXCEPTION IN...USE...END WHEN** construct, *exceptions*, or events that affected the flow of a program's instructions during execution, oftentimes causing program termination, could be handled. The **WHEN EXCEPTION IN** tested some code—for example, ensuring that user input was of a certain data type (such as a string), or that a particular file could be accessed and opened successfully. If the code ran error free, then control was passed to the statement following **END WHEN**; if not and an exception occurred, then BASIC instead jumped to code in the **USE** block. Consider the following simple example:

```
WHEN EXCEPTION IN
    PRINT "What is your favorite number?"
    INPUT N
USE
    PRINT "You must enter a number, try again..."
    RETRY
END WHEN
```

There were a number of other exception handlers available as well.

- *Debugging facilities*: There were limited debugging options available, essentially consisting of the statements **DEBUG ON** (turning on the debugging feature), **BREAK** (triggering an exception when debugging was on), and **TRACE ON** (outputting a program trace).

- *Graphics*: Rather than being dependent on a particular arrangement of pixels on a screen, graphics in Full BASIC were rooted in what were termed "user coordinates." The optional graphics module, initially developed with ANSI graphics committee X3H3, adhered closely to the Graphics Kernel System (GKS) International Standard, introduced in 1977 and ratified in the mid-1980s. After specifying a **WINDOW** statement, the **PLOT** statement facilitated the drawing of dots and lines, while the **PICTURE** statement coordinated graphics-only subroutines. Keywords for plotting such as **CIRCLE, POLYGON, FILL POLYGON, ROTATE, SCALE**, and **SHIFT**, among many other graphics-related keywords like **GRAPHIC PRINT** for output and **GRAPHIC INPUT** for user input, brought into relief how dissimilar Full BASIC's approach to graphics was as compared to, for instance, variants of microcomputer Microsoft BASIC.

- *Real-time applications:* As Kurtz notes in his *Byte* article, "Most BASIC users would be surprised to learn that BASIC is one of the important languages for real-time applications...." In the twenty-first century, online gaming and videoconferencing might first spring to mind when contemplating RTAs; in the twentieth century, though, Kurtz was specifically referring to industrial-process control and the operation of small machines—activities that necessitated coordination and cooperation between pieces of equipment. The **WAIT** statement facilitated this optional real-time module by pausing a program until some condition, such as a hardware interrupt, was met.

All of these features were a far cry from Dartmouth BASIC the First. Unsurprisingly, though, not everyone was sold on them.

Shortly after Kurtz's *Byte* article appeared, concerns with the proposed ANSI standard surfaced from a number of quarters. Software engineer and author Kurt Guntheroth, whose 1983 piece "The New ANSI BASIC Standard," published in *SIGPLAN Notices*, offered a representative critique.

True, the overall objective of the new standard was sound, Guntheroth argued, the "implementation of which will allow interchangeability among BASIC programs written on diverse hardware." Many stakeholders—in business, industry, and education—helped form the standard, which was doubtless "comprehensive," "well organized and written, and...relatively readable." The optional features were a breath of fresh air as well.

But with its 161 keywords, the standard was much too large and complex—and therefore antithetical to BASIC's core mission of simplicity, of being easy to learn and easy to use. Moreover, a number of language features didn't marry well. "Probably the most serious mistake made by the designers of the ANSI BASIC standard," Guntheroth argued, "is that they have attempted to superimpose a block-structured, compiled language with declared data types onto the older, line-oriented, untyped, interpreted language that people tend to associate with the name BASIC." The structured programming superstructure imposed new restrictions on the form and function of the language, especially with **GOSUB** and **GOTO** line number targets—leading Guntheroth to defend unencumbered versions of these line-oriented control structures, which were long the bane of the **GOTO**-less programming advocates. In fact, the restrictions imposed on control statements, among others, and the resulting network of implicit references, would result in interpreted versions of the standard simply being too complicated and unwieldy to implement. Thus, Full BASIC users would be stuck with compliers, the attendant compiling, linking, and loading a further burden for those accustomed to the real-time feedback of interpreted BASIC.

Worse yet, there was feature duplication. For instance, an array could be dimensioned with **DIM** or **DECLARE**, and arrays could start at index zero, at index one, or at user-specified bounds. The standard offered three ways to set the maximum length of a string, three ways to exit a loop, and five ways to represent a subroutine. It all came down to an overriding problem diagnosed by Guntheroth: a failure to choose. "The ANSI BASIC standard often chooses to avoid the need to make a choice by including all choices in the standard."

When decisions were made, they often led to further questions. The average terminal had eighty columns, so why did the standard mandate a physical line length of 132 characters or more? Why did the line continuation character (&) also serve as the string concatenation operator? Why were there multiple versions for relational operators, such as <= and =< both representing less than or equal to and <> and >< both referring to not equal to? Why, when integers were necessary in many places (e.g., indices of arrays), were they not explicitly supported by the standard, whereas two different kinds of data types allowing for exact dollar-and-cents calculations (i.e., binary-coded decimal floating-point and fixed point) specified? Sure, BASIC had its uses in the financial arena—think of the popular Business BASICs for minicomputers and microcomputers—but BASIC was hardly the first choice of clientele typically served by COBOL.

Guntheroth's most damning critique, however, centered on how much of a departure the proposed standard was from existing BASIC implementations. "A standard should formalize details, but the basic structure should come from an existing language implementation which has proved its popularity and robustness over several years," akin to ANSI FORTRAN. But Full BASIC failed this test, with the "ANSI standard…proposing an entirely new language, with little resemblance to what has been conventionally known as BASIC."

In *The BASIC Handbook: An Encyclopedia of the BASIC Computer Language*, first published in 1978, author David Lien issued a warning. "The efforts…towards standardization of at least a common language core will probably be a major factor in some day having a Standard BASIC," he wrote. "Failing that, the immutable laws of the free market will determine which version[s] of BASIC survive."

Irrespective of criticisms lobbed at Full BASIC, as the personal computer industry exploded in the late 1970s and early 1980s, even more BASIC variants were let loose, set free to compete in the burgeoning computing marketplace. They were everywhere, appearing on machines as varied as the Apple II, the Atari 800, the BBC Micro, the Commodore Amiga, the IBM PC, the Sinclair ZX81, the Texas Instruments TI-99/4A, the TRS-80 Pocket Computer, and the Casio FX-700P calculator—and most made little effort to be in line with emerging ANSI standards. Especially divergent BASIC implementations appeared on videogame consoles.

BASIC Programming, released between 1979 and 1980 for the Atari Video Computer System (VCS, later referred to as the Atari 2600), was programmed by Warren Robinett, who also developed *Adventure* for the console. The non-gaming ROM cartridge, in addition to offering a split-screen IDE (Integrated Development Environment) for coding, graphics, intermediate results, and output, served as a language tutorial. Input came in the form of Atari Keyboard Controllers with overlays specifying the purpose of each button, but the limitations of memory greatly restricted the length, if not the functionality, of the BASIC programs. In fact, throughout the slim *BASIC Programming* manual, readers were encouraged to shorten programs as much as possible to save memory. What follows is a sample program, in its entirety, illustrating several features of the Atari BASIC dialect.

```
1 Hor 2 ← Hor 2 + Key
2 If Ver 1 > 90 Then Ver 1 ← 88
3 If Hit Then Ver 1 ← 9
4 Ver 1 ← Ver 1 + If Ver 1 Mod 2 Then 8 Else 92
5 Hor 1 ← Hor 1 + 7
6 Goto 1
```

The coordinates of an on-screen object were represented by the variables **Hor 1** and **Ver 1**, while the coordinates of another on-screen object were given by **Hor 2** and **Ver 2**. Modular arithmetic and in-line **If** statements powered the program, which, when executed, treated users to a game of *Pong*, albeit without sound.

"The higher-ups at Atari wanted a cartridge that would allow the user to learn simple programming," Robinett told interviewer James Hague for his book *Halcyon Days: Interviews with Classic Computer and Video Game Programmers* (1997), "and I had been vocal in expressing my interest in doing a programming language before management came up with this. I was the only 2600 programmer who had studied computer science. Also they wanted cartridges that used the new keyboard peripheral, instead of the joystick." Robinett labored under some serious hardware limitations, with the VCS sporting a MOS Technology 6502 8-bit microprocessor clocked at one megahertz, along with 128 bytes of RAM and 4K of ROM. Coding a simple game was challenging enough under those constraints, let alone an interpreter for a programming language. Making use of an alphanumeric display routine capable of twelve characters per line (and written by videogame designer David Crane), Robinett directed the VCS to interpret only a single token per frame so that computations could be traced in real time on the screen—an especially effective educational feature of *BASIC Programming*.

Competing with the VCS was the more expensive Bally Professional Arcade, later rebranded as the Astrocade, which appeared on store shelves in 1978. The machine, powered by a Zilog Z80 8-bit microprocessor, offered a front-loading slot for game cartridges as well as a twenty-four-button calculator keypad. Like the Atari, the Astrocade offered its own version of BASIC. Called *Bally BASIC* (also known as *Astrocade BASIC 6004* or *Astro BASIC*), and developed by Jamie Fenton, the cartridge-based implementation took its cues from Li-Chen Wang's Palo Alto Tiny BASIC. Eighteen hundred bytes of usable programmable memory were available—the memory remaining could be obtained at any time by typing **PRINT SZ**—along with color graphics, sound, and I/O commands that tapped directly into the hardware.

Users entered in line-numbered BASIC programs using the standard keypad, in which a plastic overlay—containing color-coded symbols, numbers, letters, and BASIC statements, all toggled between by pressing the appropriate Shift key—was fitted. Like *BASIC Programming*, keying in even the simplest line of code was a cumbersome ordeal, requiring hunting, pecking, and repeated trips to Shift keys. Below is an example program from the manual that draws a never-ending series of connected lines on-screen:

```
10CLEAR
20X=RND(60)+20
20Y=RND(70)-40
30LINE X,Y,1
40GOTO 10
```

Twenty-six integer variables were available (named **A** to **Z**), along with two arrays (named **@** and *****); each array item consumed two bytes of memory, with the maximum number of elements limited by the remaining storage. The **@** array began storing elements where the program ended in memory, starting with **@(0)**. But if the user expanded the program after defining elements of the **@** array, then any overlapping elements would be deleted automatically. Hence the need for the second array, *****, which stored items at the very end of memory, albeit working backward *toward* the end of the stored program in memory. The following example program, slightly modified from the manual, employs an array to output a simple horizontal bar graph:

```
5CLEAR
10PRINT "ENTER NUMBER OF ITEMS"
13INPUT X
15PRINT "ENTER VALUE OF EACH ITEM"
20FOR A=1TO N
30INPUT @(A)
40NEXTA
50FOR A=1TO N
60FOR B=1TO @(A)
70PRINT #1,"$",
80NEXT B
90PRINT
100NEXT A
```

Unlike with Atari's BASIC, *Bally BASIC* programs could be saved, courtesy of an audio cassette interface. *Bally BASIC* proved popular, with a total of four versions released.

In the early 1980s, Sega also dipped its proverbial toe into the BASIC waters with line-numbered *BASIC Level II*, *BASIC Level III*, and *Home BASIC* ROM cartridges, all for the 8-bit Sega Computer 3000. Released in 1983, the SC-3000 was a home computer—complete with a built-in keyboard, which its close sibling, the home videogame console SC-1000, didn't offer—built by the Japanese entertainment company that later became best known for Sonic the Hedgehog. Programs using a full range of generic Microsoft BASIC-like features were possible, such as this one, which output a multiplication table using a two-dimension array:

```
10 CLS
20 DIM A(5,5)
30 FOR J=1 TO 5
40 FOR K=1 TO 5
50 A(J,K)=J*K
60 PRINT A(J,K);
70 NEXT K
80 PRINT
90 NEXT J
```

Graphics statements, such as **COLOR**, **PSET**, and **LINE**, were on tap as well.

In the late 1990s, another version of BASIC for Sega hardware arrived, albeit only in Japan: *Game BASIC*, a line-numbered, interpreted dialect run by interfacing a PC with a

32-bit Sega Saturn (the ill-fated successor console to the wildly popular 16-bit Sega Genesis). *Game BASIC*, which included a serial cable, tapped into the powerful graphical and audio hardware of the Saturn to great effect, resulting in arguably the most impressive multimedia capabilities—including rapid real-time three-dimensional polygonal rendering of worlds—of any first- or second-generation BASIC implementation. Besides its limited availability, the biggest drawback of *Game BASIC* was that it couldn't generate standalone games; any programs (boasting .B file extensions) created with the language could only be run using the interpreter.

Not to be outdone by Atari and Sega, Nintendo released its own BASIC implementation. Commercially available in 1984 for its Family Computer videogame console, or Famicom, *Family BASIC*, priced at ¥14800, was bundled with a keyboard, a textbook, and a ROM cartridge containing the interpreted language offering a direct mode and a program mode. In the original version of *Family BASIC*, users had 2K of RAM available for their line-numbered BASIC creations, while in second version, called *Family BASIC V3*, 4K RAM of storage was accessible. Users had direct access to sprites and hardware-dependent commands, but saving BASIC programs to external storage required a cassette tape recorder. *Family BASIC*, in addition to offering a customizable coding environment, featured several applications, including a word processor and a calculator. Nintendo-themed sprites, such as from *Mario Bros.*, were built in; to call up Mario—stored as sprite animated character number 0—for instance, and display him in the bottom third of the screen, type in and run the following code.

```
5   CLS
10  SPRITE ON
20  DEF SPRITE 0,(0,1,0,1,0)=CHR$(1)+CHR$(0)+CHR$(3)+CHR$(2)
30  SPRITE 0,120,140
```

The keyboard's function keys (F1 through F8) stored preassigned commands, including **LOAD, PRINT, GOTO, CHR$, SPRITE,** and **RUN,** which helped with writing programs quickly.

Family BASIC was a joint effort involving three companies: Sharp, Hudson Soft, and Nintendo. Sharp had collaborated with Nintendo on a combined television-Famicom product; *Playbox BASIC*, effectively the same software as *Family BASIC*, was released for the television. Hudson, for its part, was fresh off developing a BASIC dialect called Hu-BASIC for the new Sharp X1 home computer. Since no BASIC was hard-coded into ROM on the Sharp machine, Hudson's compiler was loaded via cassette tape.

Notably, in 1983, Hiroshi Ishikawa, only sixteen years of age, developed the game *Kagirinaki Tatakai* using Hudson's BASIC on the X1; though obscure, many people are familiar with *Kagirinaki Tatakai* courtesy of the popular shooter *Bangai-O*, initially intended as a remake of the X1 game.

Also writing a influential game using Hudson's BASIC on a Sharp computer—specifically, the MZ-700—was Yutaka Isokawa who, in 1985, programmed the puzzle-platformer *Pitman*, which first appeared in *Oh!MZ* magazine as a type-in before debuting in 1990 on the Nintendo Game Boy as *Catrap*. The *Pitman* BASIC source code is relatively straightforward and of modest length. Some of the mechanics of the main character's movements, for example, are printed below.

```
260 REM _____
270 REM |   MAN MOVE   |
280 REM _____
290 IF SY>1 THEN LOCATEMX,MY:GOSUB 2470
300 X=MX:Y=MY:X1=X:X2=X:SY=1:BEEP0
310 IF CHARACTER$(X+1,Y+3)=" " AND GB=0 THEN MY=MY+3:GOTO 730
320 A$=INKEY$(0):IF A$="" GOTO 320
...
700 REM _____
710 REM |   PRINT MAN  |
720 REM _____
730 BEEP0:LOCATE X,Y: ON GB+1 GOSUB 2410,2420
740 A$=CHARACTER$(MX+1,MY):GB=0
750 IF A$="_" THEN BG=1
760 IF A$="__" THEN G=G-1
770 LOCATE MX,MY
780 ON SY GOSUB 2470,2480,2490
```

Next, we turn to Satoshi Tajiri. The creator of *Pokémon*, Tajiri is on record as having been influenced by Nintendo's Family BASIC. "It became possible to see what was actually going on inside the Famicom, when software for beginners called *Family BASIC* was released," he remembered. "When I completely understood its mechanism, I went to Akihabara [in Japan] to buy a multiuse circuit board, added the terminals from my Famicom, and ran my programs over it."

Tajiri, Ishikawa, and Isokawa were far from the only Japanese developers influenced by BASIC. Home computers, including the Sharp X68000 and the NEC PC-6001, served as proving grounds for future industry luminaries like Yuji Horii. The videogame designer, best known for creating the *Dragon Quest* role-playing games, learned to program using Microsoft N60 BASIC on the PC-6001; among Horii's earliest efforts include the adventure game *Portopia Renzoku Satsujin Jiken* (*The Portopia Serial Murder Case*), written in BASIC, that directed budding detectives to solve a murder mystery.

All told, by the late 1980s, variants of Microsoft BASIC alone were burned into the ROMs of at least fifty different kinds of computers around the world. In fact, as freelance gaming journalist John Szczepaniak relays in his *Game Developer* magazine article "A BASIC History of BASIC," a good proportion of those fifty computers were built in Japan, making Microsoft BASIC the dominant dialect in the land of the rising sun. Besides the Sharp machines, the NEC PC-8800 and PC-9800 series featured a Microsoft BASIC called N88-BASIC; Fujitsu's FM-7 and FM-8 used a Microsoft BASIC dialect (i.e., F-BASIC) as well. The Redmond, Washington-headquartered company even launched a joint venture with the Tokyo-based ASCII Corporation, developing a standardized computing platform called MSX; unsurprisingly, the MSX systems, which proved popular in Japan, arrived with (Microsoft) MSX BASIC stored in ROM.

Microsoft BASIC also made its way to the Netherlands, where a grassroots BASIC standardization effort, independent of ANSI, arose.

Though California transformed into a computer hobbyist hotbed by the 1970s, computer clubs also arose in the UK and the Netherlands. The British Amateur Computer Club (ACC) was up and running by 1973. Dutch tinkerers were electronics and amateur radio enthusiasts, too, leading to "roots of personal computer technology in the Netherlands [that] were established in an atmosphere of experimentation, similar to their American and British counterparts," explained Frank C.A. Veraart in the chapter "Transnational (Dis)Connection in Localizing Personal Computing," found in the book *Hacking Europe: From Computer Cultures to Demoscenes* (2014). Magazines like *Elektuur* and *Electronics TOP International* featured discussions on microprocessors and computer kits; the first Dutch computer club, called the Hobby Computer Club (HCC), was founded in 1977. By early the next decade, many Dutch hobbyists had turned their attention from hardware to programming the machines—specifically, microcomputers imported mainly from the U.S. and UK.

In the late 1970s, with online connectivity the stuff of science fiction for most—not only in the Netherlands but in the United States and the United Kingdom as well—exchanging data between home computers was onerous. There were typically two ways to obtain computer programs: via some form of physical media (e.g., on a cassette tape) or by typing in listings printed in magazines like *Acorn User*, *Compute!*, *Computing Today*, *Creative Computing*, *Personal Computer Magazine*, *Practical Computing*, *The Rainbow*, *RUN*, and dozens more, some multiplatform and others geared to specific hardware.

The Dutch radio program *Hobbyscoop*, transmitted by the public service broadcaster Nederlandse Omroep Stichting (NOS) weekly on the radio station Hilversum 2, offered a third way: airing computer programs that listeners could record on cassette tape and then play back to run on their home computers. Experimenting with radio transmissions was nothing new for *Hobbyscoop*; the radio show was among the first to broadcast in stereo, and even sent telex and videotext pages over the air.

Broadcasts of BASIC code first came about thanks to a television show. Several years before the premier of BBC's popular *The Computer Programme* that featured the BBC Micro, Dutch educational television aired *Microprocessors 2*, a course on computing, with *Hobbyscoop* transmitting Apple II software over the airwaves for the course. Despite *Microprocessors 2* came to an end, *Hobbyscoop* continued broadcasting programs: specifically, in BASIC. Yet transmission difficulties aside—despite a slow transmission rate, the same code had to be repeatedly broadcast thanks to audio quality issues—the programs sent over the airwaves were not machine independent, resulting in precious air time being spent on multiple versions of the same program: one for the TRS-80, another for the Commodore PET, yet another for the Apple II, and finally one for the Exidy Sorcerer, which were the Netherlands' four most popular micros. Accordingly, programs for only one of these BASIC dialects could be broadcast each month. (First released by California-based arcade game manufacturer Exidy in 1978 and powered by a Z80 microprocessor, the Sorcerer offered a version of Microsoft BASIC albeit on a ROM cartridge, known as a ROM-PAC, rather than being stored in the machine's read-only memory. The Sorcerer and the Umtech's VideoBrain Family Computer are among the first 8-bit home computers to offer software in cartridge form.)

If there were a standardized BASIC, however, then only one version of each program would need to be transmitted. Hobbyist teachers, members of the British Association of Microcomputer Users in Secondary Education (MUSE), created a protocol of BASIC: a small subset of the language, coupled with a defined program layout, that permitted a limited level of interoperability. Following the MUSE's lead, the Dutch hobbyist teacher groups utilized the protocol to exchange platform-independent BASIC programs.

In the early 1980s, Philips research engineer Klaas Robers proposed a BASIC translation program, while the Dutch computer hobbyists of *Hobbyscoop* created a BASIC standard called BASICODE—referred to as an "Esperanto for computers"—that used the MUSE protocols as inspiration. When BASICODE was transmitted, an ASCII version of the BASIC program would be modulated over the airwaves in a synchronous FSK (frequency-shift keying) format based on the American Kansas City code, where a zero bit took the form of a single-period 1200Hz tone, while a one bit corresponded to two periods of a 2400Hz tone. (The sound was similar to that produced by a dial-up modem.) Once recorded on audio cassette and played back, the BASIC program was translated, via tailor-made translation software, into native BASIC for that particular machine. The translation software was broadcast over the air—including on television—as well as available for purchase in cassette format through NOS.

However, the first BASICODE format was limited because the proliferation of BASIC dialects resulted in incompatibilities between machines—unless programmers utilized only the most common BASIC statements and instructions, resulting in no graphics commands or other machine-dependent features appearing in programs. ("Producers created and used such variations in BASIC to shield their technology from competitors," Frank Veraart claimed. "Computer models became popular by virtue of the amount of available software rather than their capacities.") To address these issues, 1984 saw the release of BASICODE 2. This enhanced standard specified the statements, commands, and functions of the language, which included `PRINT`, `INPUT`, `GOTO`, `FOR/NEXT/STEP`, `IF/THEN`, `ABS`, `SQR`, `SIN`, `COS`, `TAN`, `CHR$`, `LEFT$`, `RIGHT$`, and `MID$`. But `ELSE` statements were still not permitted, nor were function definitions using `DEF FN`. Variables could be up to two characters in length, but not every two-character permutation was permitted (e.g., `IF` of course was reserved, but `GR` was as well, for reasons explained in the next paragraph); arrays could have at most two dimensions.

The BASICODE 2 translation program appeared on a wide variety of hardware, including the Acorn and Commodore machines, the Amstrad CPC 464, the Apple II, the Colour Genie, the Exidy Sorcerer, the IBM PC, the Mattel Aquarius, the Sinclair ZX81 and ZX Spectrum, the Tandy TRS-80, and the Texas Instruments TI-99/4A. Just as a chain is only as strong as its weakest link, an Esperanto for computers had to account for even the most limited of machines, such as the ZX81. To that end, in addition to its restricted subset of keywords, BASICODE 2 also offered programmers a subroutine library, accounting for operations that these BASIC dialects often performed differently. There were subroutines for clearing the screen, setting and reading the cursor position on-screen, obtaining the keyboard key pressed, beeping, returning a random number between zero and one, obtaining the amount of free memory, and converting a number to a string. Subroutines were called using `GOSUB`. For instance, `GOSUB 100` cleared the screen, then set the cursor position to the top-left corner of the screen;

GOSUB 110 placed the cursor at specific coordinates read from the values stored in variables HO and VE. To convert a number into a string, use GOSUB 300, which retrieved the value in variable GR and then stored its string representation in variable GR$. Besides GR$, the variables HO (horizontal location of the cursor), VE (vertical location of the cursor), and IN$ (keyboard key pressed, the equivalent of the common INKEY$) stored the values returned by certain subroutines. Line numbers below 1000 were reserved for the subroutines and, as such, could not be used in a BASIC program. Line 1000 had the following format, where the value (shown below) relayed the maximum number of characters available for all strings in the program.

```
1000 A=value: GOTO 20: REM program name
```

Line 20 reserved space for string data. Lines 1010 to 32767 contained the main program, with line numbers greater than 32767 not permitted.

Games, applications (like spreadsheets and financial software), and educational programs proliferated in BASICODE 2. Current events were broadcast within BASICODE 2 programs as well, in the form of a *Hobbyscoop* newspaper. An issue of the paper from September 1990, for example, describes a hydrogen leak found in the engine of the Space Shuttle Columbia, which caused yet another launch postponement. Translated to English, a portion of the code reads as follows:

```
25050 DATA "The reason for this was that a "
25070 DATA "hydrogen leak was found in the engine "
25060 DATA "compartment of the shuttle Columbia. Investigation "
25080 DATA "found that this leak was due to "
25090 DATA "a piece of sandpaper left behind in "
25100 DATA "the shuttle supply line! In February "
```

Once a newspaper program was loaded and executed, users had the option to view the text specially formatted for the screen or output the newspaper to a printer.

By the mid-1980s, besides the NOS, the Dutch TROS (Televisie Radio Omroep Stichting) as well as the BBC broadcast BASICODE. On the BBC Radio 4 program *The Chip Shop*, BASICODE was aired four late nights a week, courtesy of their Takeaway service. "Tape record the program off-air," the BBC instructed its listeners. "Record at the right level—too high may distort, too low might not be picked up. 'Load' the translation program for your computer using the Basicode cassette. It will now understand Basicode recorded broadcasts. 'Load' the broadcast software and 'run' in the usual way."

Like the Netherlands and Great Britain, Germany was no stranger to BASIC. In West Germany, the 1985 educational television program *SFB Computer Club*—the SFB stood for Sender Freies Berlin, a public radio and TV service—featured the creation of numerous BASIC programs for several 8-bit home computers, with a focus on the Commodore machines. Hosted by Winfried Göpfert, head of SFB's science department, the series ran for five episodes.

The *WDR ComputerClub*, a West German television show hosted by Wolfgang Back and Wolfgang Rudolph, broadcast BASICODE, at first with an audio signal, and then by visual means: using a technique called VIDEODAT, a flashing area at the top of a television screen transmitted bytes to a Videodatdekoder, containing photodiodes, placed in front of the home viewer's TV.

BASICODE 3 brought several improvements and additions to its predecessor, including monochrome graphics and file storage capabilities. Arriving in 1986, the new standard was not adopted by the NOS but proved especially popular behind the Iron Curtain in East Germany. In the late 1980s, Radio DDR began transmitting BASICODE programs, designed to work on East German state-manufactured Robotron computers; BASICODE translation programs were distributed on vinyl records. Once Germany reunified, Deutschlandsender Kultur briefly took up the mantle, transmitting BASIC programs for several more years.

By the early 1990s, as home computing power skyrocketed and cheap physical media for storing data (like diskettes) flooded the market, the airwaves transmitting BASICODE finally fell silent.

At the same time BASIC was scaling unprecedented heights of popularity and ubiquity throughout the world, appearing on computer and game console alike, the language was also being effectively disowned by its creators—in the form of Kemeny and Kurtz developing a modern form of Dartmouth BASIC that summarily rejected the Frankenstein monster their creation had become. After all, observed Oscar Wilde, each man kills the thing he loves.

In the interregnum between ACM '82 and final approval of Full BASIC, Kemeny and Kurtz released an ANSI-compliant (i.e., a standard-conforming implementation), multiplatform version of structured BASIC. Called True BASIC, the product harked back to many of the original design principles of Dartmouth BASIC, albeit wrapped in modern packaging: no line numbers, robust subroutines, true recursion, matrix operations, access to libraries of code, and more. But by effectively ignoring the evolution of BASICs that had proliferated outside the college—the duo employed the epithet "Street BASICs" to characterize these disreputable dialects—Kemeny and Kurtz did their users a disservice, resulting in True BASIC being a departure from BASIC norms. To take one small example, BASIC programmers had become accustomed to the question mark (**?**) serving as a one-character substitute for **PRINT**, but True BASIC didn't support the convention. As they explain in the chapter "What Went Wrong?" of their book *Back to BASIC: The History, Corruption, and Future of the Language*, which describes the genesis of Dartmouth BASIC as well as serving as an advertisement for True BASIC,

> Some observer has coined the phrase "Street BASIC" for this polyglot. An apt description, we believe. Vernacular street talk varies from location to location and year to year, and is full of vulgarisms not to be used in polite surroundings….

> Although studies of the exact genealogy of the various versions of BASIC (numbering in the hundreds) have not been carried out, it is our opinion that they evolved much like animal species, such as apes and monkeys….

"We are greatly concerned that a generation of students [have grown] up learning Street BASIC," they conclude, "an illiterate dialect of a lovely language." Putting aside the fact that the term and the wording they used to describe it have not dated well, calling a BASIC dialect "Street BASIC" served as a form of gatekeeping not wholly dissimilar to Edsger Dijkstra's, ironically enough. But Dijkstra cast a wider net than Kemeny and Kurtz, seeking to keep everyone away from BASIC in general, rather than just some of the dialects. The Dutch computer programmer hoped to save people from becoming what he rather awkwardly described as "mentally mutilated beyond hope of regeneration."

Regardless, True BASIC differed in some respects from its Dartmouth BASIC ancestors, too. For instance, while BASIC the First employed a single-pass compiler that compiled programs into machine instructions directly, True BASIC used two passes instead. In addition, True BASIC's compiler was written in True BASIC, and its linker was written in a simplified, crude version of True BASIC. To perform the linking, "B code" instructions were executed lighting fast by an interpreter. "In True BASIC we compile into B code," Kurtz explained, "and the B code is very simple, so the execution of B code by a very fast C written loop, as it is now, was originally written for the DOS platforms." The B code was an intermediate language, in the spirit of Pascal's P code. True BASIC's intermediate language used three addresses since BASIC instructions were typically three addresses; for instance, **LET B=5** has three components: an opcode and two addresses. Once compiled, programs in True BASIC were machine-independent.

Over the decades, Kurtz became deeply skeptical of the object-oriented programming paradigm—only encapsulation of data and subroutines mattered, he said, and those ideas predated OOP regardless. In an interview conducted for the book *Masterminds of Programming*, Kurtz cast OOP as a "religion," adding:

> My opinion is that OOP is one of the great frauds perpetrated on the community. All languages were originally designed for a certain class of users—FORTRAN for extended numerical computations, etc. OOP was designed so its clients could claim superior wisdom for being on the "inside." The truth of the matter is that the single most important aspect of OOP is an approach devised decades ago: encapsulation of subroutines and data. All the rest is frosting.

To that end, Kurtz insisted that True BASIC, with its modules (encapsulating data and subroutines) and its structured-programming approach, was every bit as object-orientated as Visual Basic, while simultaneously scoffing at the idea that anyone outside of Microsoft classifying Visual Basic as a true object-oriented language. Most observers would not classify True BASIC as OO either, since it lacked support for, among other features, user-defined types and polymorphism.

It was difficult to write large, complicated programs using generic forms of BASIC. But True BASIC scaled up very well, evidenced by Kurtz's claim that he "personally wrote 10,000- and 20,000-line programs [using True BASIC]…and I could write 30,000- or 40,000-line programs and there wouldn't be any problem, and it wouldn't cause the runtime to become inefficient, either." True BASIC modules, which allowed for the encapsulation of data, set the stage for large-program capability; as described earlier in this chapter, such modules were added to the ANSI BASIC standard by the early 1990s.

It took more than simply modernizing BASIC to attract interest and garner sales. To commercialize the product, Kemeny and Kurtz assembled a team of Dartmouth graduates: there was Chip Elliot ('76), Dave Pearson ('75), and Chris Walker ('73). More accurately, by the early 1980s, the alumni persuaded the Dartmouth duo to go against their instincts and form a commercial software company, capitalizing on the explosion of the microcomputer industry and the success of Microsoft. In 1983, True BASIC Inc., was formed; within two years, the company had released cross-platform versions of a structured BASIC language (based on Dartmouth BASIC the Seventh) for DOS, Macintosh, and Atari. In the coming decades, the software would be written for Amiga, Windows, Unix, and Linux systems as well.

However, all was not roses; in the words of John Lutz, former CEO of the company, "no one seemed to foresee that programming tools would become a VERY small niche product for microcomputers and applications would reign." In early 1990s, with the passing of John Kemeny, the company was at a crossroads. "Without going into all the details, a 'survival' plan was accomplished and, by 2000, all the original shareholders were made whole and I took the company 'private,'" recounted Lutz. By the time Kurtz sat down for an interview printed in the book *Masterminds of Programming* in the late 2000s, the work of porting True BASIC to multiple operating systems had fallen on the shoulders of one programmer (down from a peak of three individuals), helped along by XVT software for building cross-platform applications. True BASIC's underlying code, written mostly in the C programming language, and was riddled with `#ifdefs` directives for conditional compilation of statements.

Right around the fiftieth anniversary of BASIC, Steve Hobbs ('69) procured an old assembly listing of the language dated 1964 from a GE programmer (and untouched by General Electric). He handed over the listing to Kurtz, who "hand copied the source code from the listing, wrote an assembler in True BASIC, and assembled it into octal." After proofreading the octal, he then wrote a GE-235 emulator. "I had to fake the user interface," Kurtz explained, "which was constructed on the companion DATANET-30 hardware, but the result [was] a realistic recreation of what it was like back in 1964."

In 2001, with the days of BASIC's dominance firmly receding into the distance, Kurtz reflected on the Full BASIC standard. Courtesy of the standard's **MODULE** feature, he claimed, BASIC was primed for object-oriented programming, a paradigm shift that eventually swept away structured programming like yesterday's news. But history didn't turn out that way.

> If a computing world in 1987 and 1991, when the standards appeared, had even remotely resembled the computing world of 1974, when work on the standards commenced, the standard for BASIC might have had a major impact, but it has been largely ignored. Why? Because of the microcomputer revolution.

The incredible increase in speed, memory, and power of these small computers precipitated a revolution in software applications as well. And BASIC didn't wait for Kemeny or Kurtz's permission to participate in the revolution. "Features were added [to BASIC] rapidly to allow accessing the specific features of these machines," such as PEEK and POKE commands, Kurtz lamented. Since PEEK and POKE accessed memory at the level of bytes—the former returned the value of a byte at a particular memory address, while the latter set the value of a byte—the commands were "a violation of the Kemeny-Kurtz principle that their higher-level language should liberate the programmer from machine details," writes Steve Lohr in the book *Go To: The Story of the Math Majors, Bridge Players, Engineers, Chess Wizards, Maverick Scientists, and Iconoclasts—the Programmers Who Created the Software Revolution* (2001).

In his *Byte* article "The 25th Birthday of BASIC," Bill Gates took credit for the introduction of PEEK and POKE in BASIC. "We invented new BASIC verbs like PEEK and POKE, and INP and OUT, to let people get at the resources of the machine," Gates asserted. "We devised a way to let programmers call machine language routines from BASIC so they could make critical parts of their programs faster." Indeed, explanations of the capabilities of PEEK and POKE can be found in the 1975 MITS Altair BASIC manual. The POKE command took the form POKE I,J, where the "statement stores the byte specified by its second argument (J) into the location given by its first argument (I)," we learn from the manual, with readers warned that "[c]areless use of the POKE statement will probably cause you to 'poke' BASIC to death."

But consider mathematician Dick Hamming's wise warning: "The history of firsts is also fraught with danger." Steve Lohr notes that PEEK and POKE predate Microsoft, writing, "Programmers at Digital Equipment, for example, had first implemented PEEK and POKE in BASIC on a minicomputer time-sharing system in 1971." PEEK and POKE did not originate in some version of Microsoft BASIC, nor did Microsoft cofounders Gates and Allen invent them; rather, they probably first encountered these commands while using the extended dialect BASIC-PLUS on a DEC PDP computer. PEEK and POKE appeared as monitor calls on early DEC operating systems like DECsystem-10; in fact, in 1974, a year before Altair BASIC first appeared, a DEC RSTS/E time-sharing OS manual offered readers an ominous warning about POKE, calling it a "very dangerous capability."

That said, using POKE in BASIC proved irresistible to a generation of 8-bit computer hackers, with "pokes bec[oming] a popular item in both Western and Soviet bloc magazines as well as Czechoslovak club newsletters," explains Jaroslav Švelch in the book *Gaming the Iron Curtain: How Teenagers and Amateurs in Communist Czechoslovakia Claimed the Medium of Computer Games* (2018). "In one of its most extensive articles on poking, *Mikrobáze* [magazine] justified its inclusion by 'granting the blissful feeling of victory even to those who cannot or do not want to dedicate all their leisure time to entertainment.'"

Adding machine-specific features to BASIC—a trend which began on minicomputers, not microcomputers—was not only antithetical to the spirit of Dartmouth BASIC but also, "[e]xcept in rare instances, ...ignored the standard," Kurtz added.

While most vendors attempted to make their new versions *upward compatible* with their previous versions, there were significant incompatibilities as time went on. The incompatibilities were more marked between versions of BASIC from different vendors.

Thus, the various versions of BASIC grew to provide programmers of applications access to the increased capabilities of computers.

Hence the ultimate failure of either the Minimal or Full standard to rein in the many dialects of BASIC. By the time Full BASIC appeared, the computing world was already moving on from BASIC, leaving only but a small subset of BASICs to become historical curiosities, relics of outdated machines and old-fashioned ways of interfacing with computers, time capsules perfect for those taken to nostalgia.

CHAPTER 4

LONE STAR MYSTERY
The Strange Case of TI BASIC

Did Microsoft develop TI BASIC for the
Texas Instruments 99/4 home computer?

Manufactured by the vertically integrated Texas-based technology company, the TI-99/4 had a tumultuous development and an eventful, albeit short, life.

In 1977, engineers at Texas Instruments were busy at work on three different computers: a cheap videogame console, a personal computer to compete with popular Apple and Radio Shack offerings, and a high-powered business computer. After internal company battles raged, the first two groups merged, while the third group, competing with Texas Instruments' minicomputer products, was shifted to the TI Data Systems Division and then terminated. Ultimately, a home computer was built around the company's 16-bit TMS9900 microprocessor and TMS9918 graphics chip.

When it debuted in 1979, the 99/4 came bundled with a repurposed color television set doubling as monitor, since Texas Instruments' RF modulator failed to meet Federal Communications Commission (FCC) emissions regulations. The computer's chiclet keyboard didn't allow for touch typing and seemed more fit for a calculator, containing only forty-one keys (and no lowercase capability), many of which doubled as function keys if SHIFT were pressed. Not only did Texas Instruments kept the machine's technical specifications close to the vest, the company also didn't publicly release an editor or assembler, effectively shutting out third-party software developers and greatly limiting the number of software applications available. (The 99/4 ran ROM cartridges, which TI called "Solid State Software Command Modules.")

Costing well over one thousand U.S. dollars at launch, partly thanks to the bundled monitor but also as a result of the unique packaging required for the microprocessor's connecting pins, sales of the 99/4 were tepid. Offering rebates and slashing prices greatly increased sales, as did the introduction of novel features like the Speech Synthesizer module, but also reduced the lifespan of the product, with Texas Instruments suffering unprecedented losses. "A joke went around the industry that TI was losing money on every computer it sold, but was making it up in volume," relayed David Ahl in

Creative Computing, a publication that became known for Ahl's Simple Benchmark (short BASIC programs for testing the performance of various computers). At the Consumer Electronics Show (CES) in Las Vegas, Bill Cosby, then a spokesman for TI, joked that getting people to buy computers was easy if you paid them one hundred dollars (in the form of a rebate). The 99/4 was lambasted as an "embarrassing failure" by the *New York Times*, one of a number of postmortems appearing in the press by the mid-1980s.

In 1981, TI rolled out the successor 99/4A, complete with full-stroke keyboard, lowercase capability, and other improvements. (Internally, TI flirted with changing the chip to the popular 8-bit Zilog Z-80, but ultimately stuck with the 9900 for the successor machine.) Although the 99/4A sold nearly three million units, a retaliatory price war with Commodore, coupled with a product recall, took a heavy toll, and in 1983 TI pulled the plug to stop the bleeding, writing off over three hundred million dollars, scrapping plans for follow-up machines (a low-end 99/2 along with a high-end 99/8), and exiting the home computer market entirely.

In early reviews of the 99/4, the press took TI to task. Yet the March 1980 edition of *Creative Computing*, featuring the article "Texas Instruments 99/4 Home Computer" by Steve North, positively gushed about the machine by comparison, heralding the arrival of the first mass-market 16-bit home computer.

"The 99/4 belongs to the very exclusive class of computers which we were able to get up and running without a single adjustment," North wrote. Switch on the computer, and a menu listing is displayed, with "TI BASIC" and "EQUATION CALCULATOR" (more or less equivalent to the functionality of a contemporaneous TI handheld calculator) among the numbered options.

Who developed TI BASIC? Was it Microsoft? After all, the company, then based in Albuquerque, New Mexico, would prove itself more than equal to the task of churning out BASIC interpreters for a range of microcomputers in the 1970s, starting with Altair BASIC for the MITS Altair 8800 and continuing to Applesoft BASIC for the Apple II, Atari Microsoft BASIC for Atari 8-bit computers, Commodore BASIC for the Commodore PET, and TRS-80 Level II/III BASIC for the Tandy TRS-80, to list only a few.

"T.I. BASIC was written by the microcomputer system software house *par excellence*, Microsoft," we learn from *Creative Computing*. But was it? North expresses puzzlement, assuming that "[TI BASIC] was apparently written to T.I.'s specs and is not compatible with the many other Microsoft BASIC implementations…." And several sentences later, after relaying features of the implementation, Microsoft seemingly becomes an afterthought: "However, T.I. has obviously designed this Basic to prevent the user from getting at machine level functions, so the friendly **PEEK**, **POKE** and machine language **CALL** functions are conspicuous by their absence." The author's cognitive dissonance at this point is apparent, manifested by the phrase "T.I. has obviously designed this Basic…" contradicting his earlier assertion that "T.I. BASIC was written by…Microsoft." (In generic Microsoft BASIC, the **CALL** statement was used to transfer program control to an assembly or machine language subroutine. Note that TI would offer a BASIC **CALL** command that directed color graphics, sounds, and various inputs instead. For memory access using BASIC, as well as the option to include assembly subroutines in BASIC code, the Mini Memory and Editor/Assembler cartridges were required.)

David Ahl's March 1984 *Creative Computing* article titled "Texas Instruments" commented on the origins of TI BASIC, too, but more obliquely. Noting that the TI-99/4 arrived on store shelves with a "non-standard Basic," Ahl expounded on what he identified as the company's three mistakes, the second of which was "in trying to keep the software and peripheral market to itself": "But TI seemed to think they could succeed where others had failed. They did not license Microsoft Basic, VisiCalc, WordStar, or any popular games." The clear implication was that TI BASIC had been developed in-house, not by Microsoft.

The *TI-99/4A BASIC Reference Manual*, by Carol Ann Casciato and Donald J. Horsfall, mentions Microsoft nowhere in its three hundred pages. In the Introduction, the authors describe the early history of BASIC:

> BASIC was developed at Dartmouth College for students learning to program on a time-sharing mainframe computer. Because it was designed to be mainly a teaching tool, it was very strong in error detection and diagnosis. Since it had to support many students simultaneously, it was kept simple and was implemented as an *interpreter* rather than as a *compiler*. An interpreter is a good deal easier to write and much easier to use than a compiler.

Though Dartmouth BASIC was in fact only implemented as a compiler, let's continue with Casciato and Horsfall's recounting of history. Though BASIC became the standard language for microcomputers, rather than, say, FORTRAN, because it was "in the right place at the right time," standards for BASIC didn't emerge until after dialects proliferated.

> Only after most of the dust had settled did any officious body—in this case ANSI (American National Standards Institute)—bother adopting a standard for the BASIC language, *ANSI Minimal BASIC*. Texas Instruments, Inc., has adopted this standard in the TI BASIC that you have in your TI-99/4A Home Computer.

> This is a pretty good standard. It has much to recommend it. It's consistent, allows the use of long variable names, it includes powerful program control statements, and it eliminates most of the **PEEK** and **POKE** nonsense that plagues nearly all other home computer implementations of BASIC.

No **PEEK** and **POKE**, but there were **BYE** (to end a BASIC session) and **OLD** (to read a program into memory) commands, harking back to the **GOODBYE** and **OLD** commands of the Dartmouth Time-Sharing System. There were other similarities between TI BASIC and Dartmouth's as well, such as the use of **&** instead of **+** for concatenating strings, **SEG$** in place of **MID$** for obtaining substrings, and only one statement per line permitted. In the 1970s, predating their home computer project, Texas Instruments implemented multi-user BASIC, among other high-level languages like FORTRAN IV and COBOL, for their 16-bit 990 line of minicomputers (some of which were powered by the TMS9900 processor). The features of DX10 BASIC—DX10 was the name of the minis' operating system—not only bore some resemblance to the later 99/4 TI BASIC but also to Dartmouth BASIC. As explained in TI's *990 Computer Family Systems Handbook* (1975), "The language implemented by this system is equivalent to Dartmouth BASIC with certain extensions to enhance its use in the business world."

Of course, TI BASIC offered machine-dependent features, keeping in line with the competition, that went above and beyond either Dartmouth BASIC or the minimal standard, including color graphics, sound, and joystick control. And Extended BASIC, with its extended memory support (i.e., the capability of employing more than the built-in 16K of RAM for programs), even offered up to twenty-eight sprites for the budding graphics programmer as well as memory access commands.

But, despite the advanced features, TI BASIC interpreted programs at suboptimal speeds. To understand why, let us turn to the "TI 99/4 Personal Computer System Software Design Specification," an internal Texas Instruments document dated early 1980 and written by members of the Personal Computer Division. The design features of the BASIC interpreter are described in section 4.3.

> The BASIC interpreter is a GPL application program which is built into the 99/4 console. To provide sufficient speed many of the core execution routines are written in 9900 assembly language. Linkage to these routines is through system defined XML instructions. All of the edit and symbol table generation portions of the BASIC interpreter are written in GPL. Much more of the design of the BASIC interpreter can be found in the TI 99/4 Home Computer BASIC Interpreter Design Specification.

The above initialism, GPL, stands for Graphic Programming Language, an assembly-like low-level, memory-saving, interpreted language that ran slower than assembly language, since GPL instructions had to be converted to equivalent TMS9900 instructions by using an assembler found in the console ROMs. Because instructions from BASIC programs run using TI BASIC—an interpreter—were then being interpreted with GPL—an 8-bit virtual machine in ROM, rather than something that could be run natively—execution speeds on the 16-bit machine were generally slower than comparable BASIC code running on the 8-bit competition. TI BASIC was, in effect, a double-interpreted language.

TI BASIC, itself stored in a Graphics ROM (GROM), stored programs into Video RAM (VRAM). This unconventional architecture further slowed things down, since the CPU didn't have direct access to the VRAM but instead had to work through an intermediary, the video display processor, in order to read from or write to the VRAM—that is, as long as the VRAM wasn't busy handling the video display.

Notice that the text of the "TI 99/4 Personal Computer System Software Design Specification" refers us to the "TI 99/4 Home Computer BASIC Interpreter Design Specification." Written in 1978, this second specification runs to nearly two hundred pages in length. In its "Definition of TI BASIC Subsets" section, three "major identified market segments for TI BASIC" are listed: namely, Industrial, Business, and Educational. TI BASIC syntax, written in a modified style of BNF (Backus-Naur Form) notation, is supplemented with examples and discussions of semantics. ANSI Minimal BASIC is referenced throughout. But there is no mention of Microsoft anywhere in the document.

The 1994 biography *Gates: How Microsoft's Mogul Reinvented an Industry—and Made Himself the Richest Man in America,* by Stephen Manes and Paul Andrews, draws heavily on original interviews with Bill Gates, his associates, and his family to trace the consequential life of the software giant. In Chapter 5, "New Mexican Standoff," we learn of the importance of TI to Microsoft's bottom line: a one-hundred-thousand-dollar deal for "an entirely new version of BASIC for a new machine from Texas Instruments...."

> The new machine, code-named the SP-70, would be a low-cost home unit using the proprietary Texas Instruments TMS 9900 chip. For it, TI was demanding a dialect of BASIC that would be compatible with the developing ANSI standard, which differed in significant respects from Microsoft's version. Much later TI would discover that its adherence to the "official" standard would make its BASIC the odd dialect out in a world that was actually standardizing on Microsoft's edition.

So, in Manes and Andrews's telling, the divergence between typical Microsoft BASICs and TI BASIC was the result of TI's insistence to Microsoft in adhering to ANSI Minimal BASIC, not because Texas Instruments developed TI BASIC on its own.

Continuing the story in *Gates,* we learn how Microsoft planned to handle one of its biggest projects to date: Paul Allen would be designing a program to simulate the new Texas Instruments chip. Monte Davidof would set aside the summer to work on the implementation. And with Microsoft's second employee, Ric Weiland, set to leave, Gates hired a "hotshot programmer he knew from Harvard," Bob Greenberg, to replace him; Greenberg was set "to do much of the TI work." But, explain the authors, "TI wouldn't cough up a dime until Microsoft delivered the code." (The proposal Microsoft handed TI detailing a BASIC implementation called "SP-70 BASIC" was dated May 1977, we read in an endnote of *Gates.*)

Manes and Andrews also describe the day-to-day reality of working at the young software company through the eyes of Bob Wallace, who had just completed a master's degree from the University in Washington only to stumble upon a photocopied "Programmer Wanted" page, dropped off by Paul Allen, in the Retail Computer Store, where Wallace worked. Intrigued, Wallace traveled to Albuquerque, New Mexico, and was hired by Microsoft.

> Microsoft's young cadre had the freedom to experiment, to take an interesting new wrinkle or idea and run with it. "I put in a lot of extra time trying to get the TI BASIC to do funny little things.... In BASIC, you could bring up a line and edit the line. So...suppose you wanted the same line somewhere else. Why can't you just edit the line numbers? And it didn't work that way, so I worked a lot to get it to work that way."

A *Fortune* magazine article from 1995, featuring a sit-down interview with Bill Gates and Paul Allen, finds Gates recounting the company's early bidding strategies. "Our basic business strategy was to charge a price so low that microcomputer makers couldn't do the software internally for that cheap," he recalled. "One of the bigger early contracts was Texas Instruments, where we bid $99,000 to provide programming languages for a home computer they were planning."

In the summer of 1977, Monte Davidoff, a Harvard student who, two years earlier, Microsoft employed to write the floating-point routines and mathematical functions for Altair BASIC, was assigned a new project for the company: program all the routines and functions again, this time for a BASIC implementation set to run on a Texas Instruments processor. "They [Microsoft] had a contract with Texas Instruments to develop a BASIC for them," Davidoff told interviewer Randy Kindig during a Floppy Days podcast recorded in 2022. Kindig, an IT professional with a background in nuclear engineering, then asked Davidoff the sixty-four-thousand-dollar question: "Do you know what processor that was [for]—I mean, it wasn't for their TI-99 home computer, was it?" The former Microsoft employee's answer is revealing:

> Well, it was for the TI, the name of the processor was called the TMS9900, and I believe that's the processor used in their TI-99/4 home computer. And I have no idea, I don't have any direct knowledge about whether the BASIC that I worked on for Microsoft under contract with TI is the one that they put in the TI-99/4. I will say that TI specified how the format of the floating-point number [should look], and I suggested a little tweak to it, a little optimization that made something more efficient to check for, like if it was zero or a negative, or something…. And when the TI-99/4 came out, they had a manual documenting the floating-point format, and it had my tweak in there!

It was the last project Davidoff ever worked on for Microsoft.

In the 2011 *Vanity Fair* article "Microsoft's Odd Couple," written by Microsoft cofounder Paul Allen, TI BASIC's origins are briefly referenced. In recounting what a taskmaster Bill Gates could be, Paul Allen noted that Microsoft employee Bob Greenberg worked over eighty hours in the span of only four days to finish part of TI BASIC, but Gates' reaction was, to put it mildly, not very sympathetic. Here is the key section from Allen's piece:

> Microsoft was a high-stress environment because Bill drove others as hard as he drove himself. He was growing into the taskmaster who would prowl the parking lot on weekends to see who'd made it in. People were already busting their tails, and it got under their skin when Bill hectored them into doing more. Bob Greenberg, a Harvard classmate of Bill's whom we'd hired, once put in 81 hours in four days, Monday through Thursday, to finish part of the Texas Instruments BASIC. When Bill touched base toward the end of Bob's marathon, he asked him, "What are you working on tomorrow?"
>
> Bob said, "I was planning to take the day off."
>
> And Bill said, "Why would you want to do that?" He genuinely couldn't understand it; he never seemed to need to recharge.

What was Bob Greenberg working on over those frenzied, sleep-deprived four days, if it *wasn't* TI BASIC?

Perhaps it was the "TI BASIC Interpreter System Documentation," written by Greenberg in August 1978. Nearly one hundred pages in length, Greenberg's documentation sits on an island by itself, not referenced by other contemporaneous TI internal documents. Whatever BASIC interpreter Greenberg's was, it probably wasn't intended for the 99/4. Following the breadcrumbs, the documentation reads more as if directed toward the 990 minicomputer than the embryonic TI home computer.

Users on the retrocomputing-focused AtariAge website—which hosts forums to discuss classic computers like the Apple II, the Tandy and Commodore machines, as well as the TI-99/4A—helped unearth the Greenberg document, among other historical artifacts.

Contributors to AtariAge have for years taken issue with Microsoft's purported involvement with the development of TI BASIC, no matter the sources cited—especially, in fact, if that source is Bill Gates himself. In 2015, software developer and AtariAge contributor Klaus Lukaschek (user name: kl99) conducted several interviews with former Texas Instruments employees. One of those interviewees, Herman Schuurman, who was hired by TI in 1977 and worked at the company for thirty-six years, tells a very different history of the TI-99/4 Home Computer than described in *Gates*. (In the 1982 Mini Memory cartridge manual, Schuurman is listed as a staff member of the TI Personal Computer Division.) When asked of Microsoft's involvement with TI BASIC, he replied, "Microsoft was not involved with the 99/4 development. They (in the form of Bob Greenberg) were contracted to develop BASIC for the SR-70 (which is also sometimes referred to as the 99/7 [and appears to be called the SP-70 rather than the SR-70 in *Gates*]), but the BASIC for the 99/4 was developed in-house." Schuurman, who had been hired to work on the SR-70, was instead assigned to the SR-62 team after the SR-70 project was transitioned to TI's Data Systems Group. But with the 99/4 falling behind schedule, the SR-62 team was given a new, and urgent, assignment: finish the TI Home Computer. Schuurman picks up the story from there.

> Since my background was in operating system design, I worked on a lot of I/O related stuff such as the audio cassette, thermal printer, etc. I also was responsible for the I/O section of the BASIC interpreter, including formatted I/O, etc... One of the more complex peripherals was the floppy drive. Bill Nale and I split that design, with Bill responsible for the hardware and the low level software, while I took the file system design and implementation. This was the only time I remember having contact with anyone from Microsoft, even though a lot of 99/4 websites seem to think that Microsoft was responsible for a lot of the software on the 99/4. We had Bob Greenberg come out once to validate the file system design (there were no design changes).

Another TI software engineer, Stan Hume, also claims to have been highly involved in writing the source code for TI BASIC.

Most direct, however, are the words of Granville Ott, chief architect for TI-99/4A development. When TI-99 enthusiast Dan Eicher, who interviewed Ott in 2004, asked him about Microsoft's involvement, Ott responded, "We talked to Bill Gates before Microsoft, but didn't buy his because...it would be slow. We wrote it ourselves."

So, in the final analysis, was Microsoft contracted by TI to develop some form of BASIC? Yes. Did Microsoft employees work in various capacities on developing a BASIC implementation for TI? Yes. Was Microsoft involved peripherally in the development of TI BASIC for the TI-99/4? Perhaps somewhat. Did Microsoft develop TI BASIC for the TI-99/4? No.

CHAPTER 5

COMPUTER LITERACY AND ITS DISCONTENTS
The BASIC Language, Logo, and Python

How did the emergence of "computer literacy" spell the end of BASIC?

There were a number of factors that led to BASIC's demise.

In the milieu of education, once a hospitable and welcoming place for BASIC—after all, BASIC was born at a college, designed to be used by students—the language was ultimately rejected in favor of a number of its competitors. In addition, thanks to a botched standardization effort, the proliferation of incompatible non-Dartmouth BASIC dialects, the failure of many implementations to keep up with the latest programming paradigms, and the advent of electronic spreadsheets that automated calculations *en masse* in business, industry, education, and elsewhere, by the turn of the century BASIC had withered on the vine.

The rise of electronic spreadsheets paralleled the fall of BASIC. Spreadsheet software called the "visible calculator," or VisiCalc—developed in the late 1970s by Dan Bricklin and Bob Frankston, who met at MIT while using the Multics operating system—led the wave that drowned BASIC in a sea of redundancy (other spreadsheet programs followed, such as Lotus 1-2-3, Microsoft Multiplan, and Microsoft Excel). BASIC, once vital as a quickly programmable interactive calculator, had been supplanted and was no longer indispensable.

The seed of an idea that led to spreadsheets displacing BASIC—namely, that computer users could and should be further insulated from the workings of the machine—also drove "computer literacy" efforts that started small (within a single college) and grew ever-wider through the decades, targeting more and more people and institutions until, finally, computer literacy came to have little if anything to do with coding.

And it all began at MIT in the early 1960s.

Several years before Kemeny and Kurtz developed their four-part plan to bring BASIC into undergraduate classrooms at Dartmouth, another computer scientist—one who had a way with words, someone whose "epigrams on programming" are still widely quoted—was publicly testifying at the Massachusetts Institute of Technology about the importance of teaching students how to program.

Was it John McCarthy, the MIT professor who told Thomas Kurtz about time-sharing?

No. It was Alan Perlis. He was among the first to suggest what has since become conventional wisdom: all students should be afforded the opportunity to learn to code.

Alan Jay Perlis, whose parents were both Jewish, was born in 1922 in Pittsburgh, Pennsylvania. He attended Colfax Public School, a primary school in the Squirrel Hill neighborhood where he lived. In 1933, Perlis enrolled at Taylor Allderdice High School, a public school with a sterling reputation. Nine years later he was a college graduate, having earned a degree in chemistry (with honors) from the Carnegie Institute of Technology in Pittsburgh.

In 1942, only a week after graduating, Perlis enlisted in the U.S. Army Air Force, Aviation Cadet Meteorology Program. In less than a year, he was a second lieutenant, meteorology services. Assigned to the Army Air Force Intelligence School in Harrisburg, Pennsylvania, Perlis trained in combat intelligence and the interpretation of photographs. His final assignment during World War II lasted a year and a half: while in the United Kingdom, 9th U.S. Army Air Force, Perlis served as an intelligence and weather officer.

With the war at an end, in the fall of 1945 Perlis returned stateside. His first stop: the California Institute of Technology. Although he intended to earn a graduate degree in chemistry, this plan proved to be a nonstarter; Perlis simply lost interest in the field. So, he left Caltech and headed east to Cambridge, enrolling as a graduate mathematics student at MIT and studying under the mathematician Philip Franklin. By 1950, he had a doctorate in mathematics.

Working with Franklin had an unanticipated benefit. Through his advisor, Perlis was exposed to Project Whirlwind that resulted in the construction of Whirlwind I, a vacuum-tube digital computer built for the Navy and intended as a flight simulator. The engineer Jay Forrester, who designed the machine's magnetic-core memory, headed the effort; Franklin was in charge of writing programs for the computer, and Perlis, along with other graduate students with military experience, were asked to assist.

In 1951, Perlis joined the Ballistic Research Laboratory (BRL) at the Aberdeen Proving Ground in Maryland; there, he computed ballistics' firing tables, calculating and reporting the artillery trajectories.

A year later, Perlis returned to MIT and Project Whirlwind, where he worked under engineer C. Robert Wieser building the Cape Cod Air Defense system, a precursor to the Semi-Automatic Ground Environment (SAGE). A complex command-and-control system developed at the MIT Lincoln Laboratory, SAGE was designed to detect enemy bomber activity at the borders of the United States (via early-warning radar) in response to perceived threats by the Soviet Union during the Cold War—and the system used numerous Whirlwind computers.

Perlis left MIT well before SAGE was deployed. In the fall of 1952, he found himself at the Statistical Laboratory at Purdue University, led by mathematician Carl F. Kossac, a man Perlis later called an "unsung hero of our profession." "Within universities as such, however, there was no computing, other than some small punched card calculations being done in various statistical departments around the country," Perlis recalled. "Almost all computing was essentially funded by the federal government and aimed at developing computers that would be directly used within the defense effort [like Project Whirlwind at MIT]."

Concurrent to Perlis making his professional home at Purdue, a new piece of calculating equipment arrived on the campus: the IBM Card Programmed Calculator (CPC), a digital general-purpose computer that could be programmed on standard IBM eighty-column punched cards to perform arithmetic operations. Kossac had pushed for such a machine, specifically to satisfy the educational and research needs of both students and faculty. Thanks to a recommendation from a former colleague at MIT (Alex Orden, who had earned his doctorate at the institution in 1948), Perlis—with his extensive computing experience—was assigned two roles by Kossac: director of the computational division of the Statistical Laboratory and assistant mathematics professor.

At Purdue in the early 1950s, there was no computer science department to speak of, like nearly all other universities of the time. Those who used computers were either numerical analysts or electrical engineers. "The courses on the computer usually were of two kinds: courses in circuitry taught within the engineering department, or courses in numerical analysis taught under the aegis of the mathematics department," added Perlis.

Nonetheless, he was determined to start a campus center dedicated to computing. Like the search and eventual road trip Kurtz, Kemeny, and their wives would take in 1959 to bring the LGP-30 computer to Dartmouth, Perlis conducted his own extensive investigation for a suitable machine. Purdue allotted the young professor five thousand dollars along with a car to explore the East and Midwest of the United States.

"We saw some very strange computers," Perlis, a master of understatement, recalled. For example, he visited a company called Facsimile, with their "headquarters"—that's being generous—located in a third-floor loft on the Lower East Side of New York City, accessible only via a freight elevator. There, Facsimile was developing what they called the Circle Computer. The machine had two rather odd characteristics. First, a socket installed on the top of the computer specially designed for an electric coffee pot. Second, a temperamental personality: it would only work if one its designers was in the room. Perlis wasn't impressed, but National Cash Register (NCR) loved it, purchasing the machine to help them lead a charge in the burgeoning computing industry.

He also visited a small computer company in Minneapolis, Minnesota. Though their hardware was substandard, the company's president had a unique setup in his office: behind him, hanging on the wall, was a clock, with its face and hands reversed; and on the wall facing the president was a mirror, positioned so that he could monitor the clock just by glancing upward—with the image reflected, the clock face was now readable. "A good executive never turns his back on his work," he told Perlis, who later tried to recreate the clever setup for himself.

It took a year of searching, but Perlis finally found the holy grail: a Burroughs Corporation ElectroData Datatron 205, manufactured by Consolidated Electrodynamics. (The computer was later renamed the Burroughs 205.) Its price tag was steep: $150,000, though he managed to talk them down to $125,000. But that was only half the battle. Perlis also had to convince the university to purchase the machine. And it all depended on the selling the administration—and, especially, the president: Frederick Hutde, a former All-American football star.

Perlis walked into Hutde's office and relayed the news: he had found the perfect computer, but the costs were considerable. Perlis assumed the president would be quick to shut down the discussion, asserting that it would be "impossible" to "spend that kind of money on a piece of equipment that no one really understands the benefits of." But what happened next surprised the professor. "Instead, [the president] said, 'Give me two days.' In two days he called me on the phone and said, 'You have $125,000 from the Purdue Research Foundation. Get the machine.'"

Burroughs shipped one of the first Datatrons into the waiting arms of Perlis. Later that year, he and others on campus were already teaching computing to both students and faculty. Since there was little conception of how to teach high-level language programming—FORTRAN was still several years away—those lucky few were taught numerical analysis and electronic circuitry.

Perlis was especially interested in numerical analysis—specifically, Chebyshev approximations, polynomials that approximate more complicated functions. He drew up several algorithms to generate these approximations, but quickly realized that coding them in machine language would be a fool's errand.

So, instead, Perlis got to work developing an algebraic compiler for the Datatron. Eventually called the Internal Translator, or IT (Perlis also called IT the "Interpretative Translator"), the compiler was written between 1955 and 1956 by members of the university's new computing laboratory: Mark Koschman, Sylvia Orgel, Joseph W. Smith, Joanne Chipps, and Perlis. Though first implemented only on the Datatron, the compiler turned out to be quite flexible. In 1956, when Perlis left Purdue for the Carnegie Institute of Technology, his alma mater, he took Smith along with him, and, using copies of flowcharts they brought to Pittsburgh, the team (with some assistance by Harold Van Zoeren) reimplemented the compiler in only three months—this time for a magnetic drum IBM 650 machine. It was at Carnegie that the compiler was first was christened the Internal Translator.

Converting the compiler to work on IBM equipment was greatly simplified by leaning on the SOAP (Symbolic Optimal Assembly Program) assembly language, developed by Stan Poley at IBM Watson Labs in 1955. Each IT program was first translated into a symbolic program called PIT that was written in SOAP; from there, the PIT program was translated into a machine code program aptly called SPIT.

The computer scientist Donald Knuth has called IT the "first really useful compiler." The language was very popular on an already wildly popular machine, the 650. (IBM was practically giving the machines away, offering sixty percent discounts. For those renting the computer, the total cost of the 650 tallied to only fifty thousand dollars per year, including personnel, supplies, and other operating costs.) IT had IF statements, floating-point variables, looping capabilities, and statement numbers (which did not have to be arranged in ascending order). An eight-line Gaussian elimination program, which solved simultaneous equations, was the first program ever successfully compiled using IT. "I will never forget [that] miracle," Perlis recalled, also noting that the eight lines ballooned into one hundred and twenty lines of assembly code.

Knuth recalled using the IT compiler in the summer of 1957 as a college freshman working at the Case Tech Computing Center at Case Western Reserve:

> IT would look at a card that contained an algebraic equation, then the machine would flash its lights for a few seconds and go punch-punch-punch; out would come a deck of cards containing a machine-language program to compute the value of the equation. Mystified by the fact that a mere computer could understand algebra well enough to create its own programs, I got hold of the source code for IT and spent two weeks poring over the listing.

Knuth was one of several people who improved on the functionality of IT, an accomplishment which Perlis praised in a 1981 ACM talk called "Computing in the Fifties": The successor IT was "far superior to the original," he said.

The Internal Translator was positioned, at least implicitly, as a "universal language"; indeed, the compiler was so popular on the IBM 650, a machine lacking a FORTRAN compiler, that it threatened FORTRAN's widespread adoption—until the late 1950s, when Bob Bemer at IBM led the development of FOR TRANSIT, a scaled-down FORTRAN clone for the 650 that ironically needed IT and SOAP in order to run. Perlis once complained that "FORTRAN is not a flower but a weed—it is hardy, occasionally blooms, and grows in every computer." Yet *Perlis helped that happen*, since Bemer received Perlis's blessing to use IT as an intermediary for FOR TRANSIT, thereby eliminating IT as a FORTRAN competitor and clearing a path for FORTRAN's early dominance in the algebraic compiler space.

Regardless, by the late 1950s Perlis's energies were focused on another "universal language" project: the International Algebraic Language (IAL), renamed ALGOL 58, which was a cooperative effort by American and European computer scientists, including John Backus and Peter Naur, in part under the auspices of the Association for Computing Machinery (ACM). By 1960, specifications for ALGOL 60 were released, with ALGOL turning into the de facto standard for imperative programming languages.

Perlis also became deeply invested in computing education. "In 1957 we taught for the first time (although I won't claim at all that there was no previous course offered in the U.S.) a course in programming, independent of numerical analysis and independent of circuitry," he recalled. "The chief issue of this course was: how do you program? In the course we used one of our compiler languages, and we also taught assembly language." Students were given simple exercises to solve, problems that didn't require a deep understanding of mathematics, such as: "if we give you the coordinates of the endpoints of n line segments, how do you tell if these line segments form the consecutive sides of a polygon?" Despite having no previous computing experience, students were still by and large able to develop algorithms *ex nihilo* and find success in these courses.

Several years later, with computer use on campus exploding and causing one bottleneck after another, Perlis made another trek to the university president's office to request a computer. He was given the green light, as long as the machine wasn't too expensive. This time, Perlis picked out a G-20 made by the California-based corporation Bendix. It came packaged with a single piece of software: a binary load routine. There was no compiler for the machine. Carnegie faculty had moved on from IT proper and were using an extension of a compiler called GAT (Generalized Algebraic Translator)—developed at the University of Michigan Statistical and Computing Laboratory— that was a next-generation version of IT. The extension of GAT, created by Perlis and company, was called GATE (GAT Extended). "This excellent language predated BASIC in a way and was much better than BASIC," argued Perlis, "[and was] about the same size, about the same speed."

In 1960, Perlis was awarded a full professorship and made chairman of the mathematics department. By 1962, he was busy at work, as the co-director of the systems and communication science graduate program, developing a graduate course of study specifically for computer science.

Perlis was instrumental in bringing computer science to the academy at large, not just as a professor at Carnegie but also as president of the ACM. "Particularly relevant was the establishment of the ACM Curriculum Committee on Computer Science…. The work of this committee led to the publication of the first recommendation for a Computer Science undergraduate program," reads the ACM A.M. Turing Award Laureate biography of Perlis.

"One of the things we learned about computing in the 1950s was that there are no bounds to the subject," Perlis explained in his ACM talk "Computing in the Fifties." "It cannot be put into a tidy receptacle. Everywhere that computing has been embedded in some other discipline, it has not flowered. Computing is not part of electrical engineering; it is not part of mathematics; it is not part of industrial administration. Computing belongs by itself." Maturing during the Second World War, computing had slipped the surly bonds of the military and academy and began to climb sunward. As Frank Rose noted in *Into the Heart of the Mind* (1984), his book on AI, "The computerization of society…has essentially been a side effect of the computerization of war."

In 1961, Alan Perlis, then director of the Computation Center at the Carnegie Institute of Technology, delivered a consequential MIT talk called "The Computer in the University" that was reprinted in the book *Computers and the World of the Future* (1962) edited by Martin Greenberger. Perlis was joined at the talk by a panel of discussants: Peter Elias, professor of electrical engineering at MIT, and J. C. R. Licklider, vice president of Bolt Beranek & Newman, an engineering consulting firm based in Cambridge, Massachusetts. Donald G. Marquis, a professor of industrial management at MIT, served as moderator.

Perlis proposed an economical purchase for a university—namely, a computer costing several hundred thousand dollars—that could serve as a resource for a "proper freshman course" in programming. At the time, MIT operated an IBM 704 installation; in the years before Dartmouth purchased its first computer, Tom Kurtz shuttled a steel box filled with SAP punched cards on a train to MIT every few weeks. When Perlis delivered his talk, most colleges did not have computers on their campuses.

What would Perlis's first programming course entail?

It is not to teach people how to program a specific computer, nor is it to teach some new languages. The purpose of a course in programming is to teach people how to construct and analyze processes. I know of no course that the student gets in his first year in a university which has this as its sole purpose.

Perlis explained that a chemistry course teaches students facts about chemistry, such as atomic weights, how to balance equations, and the like. A physics class teaches students about physical laws. An English class concerns itself with teaching students about grammar, and expressing oneself in a precise manner. But a computer programming course could offer students exposure to a more general skill: *abstraction*. The course would, in effect, teach students how to think.

[Students would learn about] the abstraction of constructing, analyzing, and describing processes. It is not the particular problem content of numerical analysis or analyzing a statement which is important. Rather, it is possible to skip from problem area to problem area and still stabilize on the concept of process design and analysis. Thus in a programming course, much more than in any of these other courses, it is possible for the student to abstract ideas from the particular examples given....

The point is not to teach the students how to use ALGOL, or how to program the 704. These are of little direct value. The point is to make the students construct complex processes out of simpler ones (and this is always present in programming) in the hope that the basic concepts and abilities will rub off.

It was not enough, Perlis continued, to simply *describe* to freshman what a computer does or could do; rather, the "contact should be analytical...each student during this first course should program and run or have run for him a large number of problems on the computer." Computer programming was a special kind of *literacy*, Perlis argued: "operational literacy." "At least in engineering and science programs, this course should share with mathematics and English the responsibility of developing an operational literacy, while physics and chemistry develop the background toward which this literacy is to be applied."

In the ensuing post-talk discussion, the peerless Perlis presciently noted the "imminence of the time-sharing concept" and how it might contribute to the larger project of operational literacy. He also looked forward to a day when students, who'd been thoroughly educated in computing by the end of freshman year, were set loose in the real world—and then their erstwhile teachers, such as Perlis, could gauge the progress of the educational mission.

As documented in the first chapter of this book, Kememy and Kurtz took up Perlis's educational charge. At Dartmouth, after rolling out a time-sharing system, the pair incorporated required lab classes, featuring application problems that students solved by writing BASIC programs, into second-term calculus and finite mathematics courses. Within several years of implementation, about eighty-five percent of Dartmouth undergraduates had taken at least one of these two courses (hundreds of faculty members gained exposure to BASIC, too). These future leaders of America—who might become key decision makers in government, national defense, business, and industry—were likely to encounter computers in their professional lives, regardless of whether they majored in the sciences or the humanities. As Perlis implied in his 1961 MIT lecture, professors like Kemeny and Kurtz had a duty to expose these students to computing—not merely to ace a class, but to help them become productive citizens in a rapidly changing world. In essence, computing would be taught as a civic virtue.

In a prescient *Daedalus* article published in 1983, Kemeny meditated on the connection between traditional literacy and computing literacy, but argued that only college professors and students should be taught computer programming—that would be sufficient to prepare society for a future of ubiquitous computing. "The Case for Computer Literacy" begins with a warning courtesy of physicist C. P. Snow. "[T]he well educated are splitting up into two cultures, that many in fact lack an understanding of science, is certainly applicable to the United States today," Kemeny wrote. "But while Snow deplored the indifference of the best educated to the Second Law of Thermodynamics, here we complain that most citizens do not understand even the most elementary physical science." Kemeny set a clear objective: "My task is to make the case for widespread computer literacy."

Computer literacy, Kemeny explained, was at least as important as scientific literacy, if not more so. He rejected out of hand the proposition that the coming computer revolution would make Snow's two-cultures schism even more pronounced. Not only was Kemeny optimistic that a significant proportion of people could become computer literate; he also believed that the problem of scientific literacy could be addressed, in part, through increased computer literacy.

In the article, Kemeny foresaw the smart house, envisioning a world in which domestic appliances and gadgets were all interconnected and controlled via a central computer stationed in each home. That computer could also double as a word processor, entertainment system, or information repository—connected to "a national information network that any intelligent home will be able to access." What sort of information would be accessible? News articles from publications like the *New York Times*, to local news, to everything in between. Items for sale at neighborhood stores. Answers to pressing questions, both legal and medical. Access to your congressperson's voting record. A searchable Library of Congress at your fingertips. The ability to read books and magazine articles on your desktop. "Most mail will be received electronically and filed in the memory of the computer," he added. And, to top it off, in this not-too-distant future, printed instruction manuals would be dispensed with in favor of the peripherals being able to understand a common language. "If I am right that intelligent machines will invade the lives of all of us, then the need for [computer] literacy will be even more vital than it is today, and at a level of sophistication higher than that required for using a computer that merely calculates and retrieves information," concluded Kemeny. (Kemeny's idea was not entirely original. Back in 1945, the famed American engineer Vannevar Bush proposed the "memex," "a device in which an individual stores all his books, records, and communications, and which is mechanized so that it may be consulted with exceeding speed and flexibility.")

Computer literacy won't be optional for the jobs of the future—it will be an essential skill, just like traditional literacy:

Today, universal literacy is demanded because the illiterate is [unemployable], and indeed, has difficulty surviving. Someday computer literacy will be a condition for employment, possibly for survival, because the computer illiterate will be cut off from most sources of information. The human brain unaided by computers will appear feebleminded.

"Someday," though, was not 1983, a time when he believed that "most decision-makers in government and industry today are computer-illiterate," in spite of his best efforts to teach the future leaders of America essential computer skills at Dartmouth College.

Here is how Kemeny thought computers would come to aid human beings:

First, although pattern recognition by machines will improve, I believe that, for some time to come, the best results will be obtained by human beings assisted by computers. Second, computers will be invaluable in decision-making, but the final value judgments will be left to humans. And third, creativity will, for the indefinite future, be a uniquely human attribute.

Indeed, the decades since his article's publication have largely borne out these predictions.

Diagnosing the problem of computer illiteracy was one thing; figuring out how to confront the challenge was quite another. Although there were similarities to learning a foreign language, learning to code was more like figuring out how to, in Kemeny's words, "communicate with an alien, the essential difficulty of which is to adjust our thinking to the alien's." Thus, he argued that "[l]earning a computer language is not primarily a linguistic achievement; rather, it requires an adjustment in the way we think."

Adults must consciously put aside their fear of new or strange experiences, while children, who revel in novelty, might master the computer at a rapid clip, Kemeny predicted. Regardless, there was an extraordinary precision in language required when communicating with a computer, much more so than in everyday interactions with fellow human beings. Computers lack common sense, and so are unable to infer meaning or fill in gaps when there is ambiguity in communication; we might believe we have specified a particular procedure to the letter, but the behavior of our computer demonstrates otherwise. Appealing to common sense using phrases like "you know?" will get us nowhere in the face of a cold, calculating machine.

Becoming a competent programmer required a person to communicate with a computer using a compact and simple language like BASIC: "with its small vocabulary and limited number of clearly defined concepts, [BASIC] is extremely simple compared to any human language," according to Kemeny. Indeed, he argued, the wordiness that is a scourge in business and government was a direct result of employees in those professions experiencing difficulty conveying their thoughts with economy.

Beyond even relaying sentence by sentence instructions to a machine, learning programming, perhaps most importantly, required us to think in terms of *algorithms*, recipes of precise logical instructions designed to complete tasks. "The difficulty of writing a given computer program has less to do with the inherent complexity of the problem being solved (complexity as perceived by humans)," Kemeny wrote, "than it has to do with how hard we find it to explain the method of solution to an alien intelligence."

Alan Perlis once observed that "[l]ike punning, programming is a play on words." Program procedures had to be consolidated into small, discrete steps with an underlying logic behind them. Such algorithmic thinking might help people even outside the realm of computer programming, such as medical diagnosticians or executives managing large enterprises, Kemeny believed, since an algorithmic approach involved breaking up large tasks into smaller ones while always maintaining awareness of an inherent hierarchical structure. If bugs should arise, the skill of debugging—of squashing the sources of error—also would translate to environments beyond programming.

Kemeny no doubt remembered that especially in the early days of Dartmouth's time-sharing system, debugging was a chore. Steve Hobbs, a sysprog (system programmer) who graduated in 1969, recalled sitting by the console typewriter, anxiously staring at the lights, waiting for a pattern that resembled his program. When he spotted the correct pattern, Hobbs quickly pressed the carriage return, dumping all the memory onto the printers and then poring through the results. "If that wasn't good enough," he continued, "I went to the D-30 [DATANET-30] and flipped the switch that prevented that jump the boot instruction from being loaded into memory." Once the program was loaded into memory, Hobbs would manually "single step" through, invariably tying up the whole time-sharing system.

Concomitant to humans stretching their language skills to improve precision in task specification, computer scientists might stand to make some improvements to the computer languages themselves, Kemeny suggested. Refining the structure of languages, for one thing, had been a boon to the discipline. Kemeny said, "a good structured language helps an inexperienced person avoid many of the usual kinds of mistakes and helps the expert to write a large, complex program that is readable and reasonably easy to debug." But machine-dependent programming commands, such as for employing graphics, were an impediment to teaching coding cogently. Kemeny rather unsurprisingly recommended the use of Dartmouth BASIC, "a highly structured language of great power, with simple commands for drawing pictures built into it," as a remedy.

He was most excited for the day when computers invaded college classrooms around the U.S. Many scientific and mathematical skills, such as calculating definite integrals or interpolating values in a trigonometric table, could be automated by using a computer, freeing students from "arithmetic bondage" to instead learn—and even enjoy—the principles of Newton's laws or trigonometry. "[S]pending an hour in front of a computer screen trying to put a satellite into orbit around the earth, or landing a space ship on the moon, will do vastly more for a student's physical intuition than trying to solve complicated equations," he maintained.

Therefore, Kemeny concluded that "computer literacy cannot help but bring about a much wider understanding of the principles of physical science." Biology and social science, likewise, would benefit greatly by computer literacy, since data retrieval and calculations could be offloaded to machines in favor of spending more time exploring basic principles. And in mathematics class, with the use of computer graphics, concepts came to life—as evidenced by Kemeny himself, who regularly employed graphics in his classes and also directed students to write programs to solve problems. "Even after more than three decades of teaching, I acquire a deeper understanding of well-known techniques by writing a computer program for them."

Kemeny wondered if only a single introductory course in computing was enough. "Although freshman English is very important, it cannot carry the total responsibility for the teaching of writing"; a variety of other courses, up and down the curriculum (and not just in an English department), had to feature instruction in writing, too, and hold students to high standards to ensure that they wrote well. Analogously, widespread computer literacy would not be achieved with a single computing course; it could only take effect if computing was a necessary skill for success in many courses. But, Kemeny explained, a large obstacle to computers invading classrooms wasn't cost, but rather the rampant computer illiteracy of the instructors themselves. Which is a shame, since the teaching of mathematics and science using algorithms—in the form of computer programs—rather than with traditional methods would "improve human thinking…[and] human thought of a clarity and precision rare today."

In fact, computer programming, which easily "cross[ed] national boundaries," might be better thought of as fulfilling an age-old dream of humankind: that of a universal language. "Thus the first universal language may turn out to be neither English nor Esperanto, but a language like BASIC," concluded Kemeny in his 1983 *Daedalus* article on computer literacy.

Interestingly, as we learn from the book *10 PRINT CHR$(205.5+RND(1)); : GOTO 10*, John Kemeny only merited a single mention in computer scientist Edsger W. Dijkstra's innumerable papers. In EWD 858, "Trip report E.W.Dijkstra, USA, 10 June – 3 July 1983," Dijkstra writes of an airplane flight he took from Eindhoven in the Netherlands to New York. The flight wasn't smooth, having a "very strong headwind."

> As a result I did not write; I read the latest issue of "Daedalus" instead, which was devoted to the topic of "Scientific Literacy". (John G. Kemeny, co-inventor of BASIC and for 11 years president of Dartmouth College, gave a striking example of superficiality: he argues that computer literacy is more easily attained than scientific literacy because programming languages are simpler than natural languages.)

And that's it: not an argument against Kemeny's position, but a casually tossed off opinion, unsupported by evidence. Which, of course, was Dijkstra's prerogative—his manuscripts could take whatever form or shape he wanted them to. They did not have to be term papers, tightly argued one way or another. Nonetheless, his barely contained disdain for BASIC, and by extension Kemeny via guilt by association (or creation), seeps through EWD 858.

Regardless of Dijkstra's feelings, however, BASIC spread like wildfire. "BASIC was once looked down on by elitists as a simple-minded computer language of the unwashed mases, and, [though] phenomenally powerful, not worthy of respectability,"

David A. Lien wrote in 1978 in *The BASIC Handbook: An Encyclopedia of the BASIC Computer Language*, adding parenthetically, "*So was the Volkswagen.*" BASIC beat its critics, at least for a time, by multiplying like a virus, but there were consequences: namely, mutations. "Because of BASIC's simplicity, computer programming (and thereby control) has escaped the grasp of just a select few."

Indeed, BASIC proliferated to such a great degree largely because Kemeny and Kurtz didn't erect barriers for other institutions, such as New York University, that wished to adopt Dartmouth's set up: the creators ceded control of their creation without a fight. As Annette Vee notes in her book *Coding Literacy: How Computer Programming is Changing Writing* (2017), Kemeny and Kurtz offered "generous licensing terms" for both DTSS and BASIC. "Efforts to teach programming broadly were focused on undergraduates in the 1960s, in part because computers could be found only in government offices, large corporate centers, and some campuses," Vee writes. "But as the technology and culture of computing spread, the movement branched out from college campuses in the 1970s." Whereas the East Coast was the "epicenter of programming innovation" in the 1960s, the West Coast took up the mantle in the next decade.

Out of the U.S. hacker and hobbyist culture of the 1970s organically emerged two noteworthy organizations: the People's Computer Company (PCC) and the Homebrew Computer Club, both of which originated in Menlo Park in the San Francisco Bay Area of California. The PCC was founded by former Control Data Corporation programmer Dennis Allison, Stanford lecturer Bob Albrecht, and George Firedrake; its first newsletter argued that computers were weaponized against people, and often used to control them—so, in response, it was "[t]ime to change all that" and to "free" people from the chains of computing. In 1970, Allison started a nonprofit foundation called PCC, and also established a walk-in time-sharing computer center in Menlo Park, with computer terminals connected to a PDP-8 minicomputer (later on, Hewlett-Packard offered computer time over telephone lines, which permitted the installation of more terminals). The programs running at the computer center—games, small-business applications, and puzzles—were in BASIC.

The information technology pioneer Ted Nelson, who coined the term *hypertext*, was a frequent visitor to the PCC. Annette Vee notes that Nelson held even more radical views against establishment computing than did the PCC. In his 1974 two-part countercultural book *Computer Lib/Dream Machines*, Nelson wrote, "COMPUTER POWER TO THE PEOPLE. DOWN WITH CYBERCRUD!"—the "cybercrud" referring to impenetrable technology jargon. He foresaw the integral role computers would play in democracy and the exercise of power: "If you are interested in democracy and its future, you'd better understand computers. And if you are concerned about power and the way it is being used, and aren't we all right now, the same thing goes." In the first part of his book, titled *Computer Lib: You Can and Must Understand Computers Now*, Nelson encouraged people to learn BASIC.

Back in 1962, well before the decade's cultural upheaval reached its climax, future PCC cofounder Bob Albrecht, then a senior applications analyst at the Control Data Corporation, accepted an invitation to speak about computers to a group of students at

George Washington High School in Denver. Though he had never taught high school students before, Albrecht had run one-day courses on remedial FORTRAN for those "who had been to IBM school and hadn't learned anything." After delivering his talk to the high school students and inquiring if any them were interested in learning programming, all thirty-two hands in the classroom shot up eagerly.

So, he invited the students to Control Data for evening classes. Kids practically tripped over themselves for an opportunity to engage with the 12-bit CDC 160-A minicomputer. The classes resulted in part-time jobs for students, with four of the best hired at a salary of one dollar per hour to program the machine. These student hires were also designated apostles, tasked with spreading the programming gospel to other students; they would lead a "medicine show" at George Washington that involved twenty mathematics classes. "After showing the students some math tricks, [Bob] Kahn [one of the four student hires] was asked if the computer could do the exercises in the back of a math text—and he proceeded to do that day's homework assignment," we read in *Hackers: Heroes of the Computer Revolution* (2010) by Steven Levy. The medicine show was an unqualified success, leading four dozen students to sign up for computer classes. Not content to restrict the show to just one high school, Albrecht visited several, eventually exhibiting the spectacle at a National Computer Conference.

Control Data was headquartered in Bloomington, Minnesota. The state was not only a central hub of computer companies in the second half of the twentieth century, but also featured Total Information for Educational Systems (TIES), which networked a cluster of Minnesota school districts, as well as the more expansive Minnesota Educational Computing Consortium (MECC). TIES and MECC connected users via timesharing systems. The Minnesota time-sharing experiment began with a single school, University High School in Minneapolis, connecting to the DTSS in 1965; UHigh was on the hook for the cost of the long-distance telephone bill.

In the years ahead, MECC would become famous for its educational games, among them *Number Munchers, Word Munchers, DinoPark Tycoon, The Secret Island of Dr. Quandary*, and, most notably, *The Oregon Trail*. In 1971, three student teachers—Don Rawitsch, Bill Heinemann, and Paul Dillenberger—enrolled at Carleton College in Northfield, Minnesota, teamed up to write a computer game for Rawitsch's eighth grade American history class. "I was excited and maybe a little naïve," Rawitsch said. "I really wanted to do some things in the classroom that the students were not necessarily used to." Initially, Rawitsch conceived of a board game illustrating the westward expansion of nonnative American settlers in the mid-1800s. But Dillenberger and Heinemann, both studying to be math teachers, convinced their colleague to translate the idea to code instead.

The fruits of their labor: *Oregon*, later renamed *The Oregon Trail*, written in two weeks in a form of time-shared BASIC running on a UNIVAC mainframe. The text-based adventure game, played on the school's Teletype, modeled an arduous two-thousand-mile wagon train trek from Missouri to Oregon; players encountered treacherous obstacles during the journey, including severe food shortages and diseases like dysentery (the latter potentially resulting in a message that became iconic: "You Have Died of Dysentery"). "We spent a week on Oregon Trail, and so [the students] had four or five days to try it out," Rawitsch recalled. "And they were...compared to the usual nonexcitement of reading about history…extremely excited to do this and fascinated by the computer." Groups of five students at a time gathered around the Teletype to play the game, with each student taking turns. December 1971 marked the end of the semester, so the three student teachers printed out the source code and then unceremoniously deleted the game from the mainframe.

Three years later, Rawitsch was hired by MECC. Sick with a cold during the 1974 Thanksgiving holiday, he decided to submit a program to the share library. First, Rawitsch brought home a portable teletypewriter. Next, he connected to the MECC computer from his kitchen phone and keyed in the lines of the *Oregon Trail* printout. Once they played it, MECC staff were "enthusiastic," Rawitsch remembered. "So, then [the game] became available to Minnesota schools that were using that mainframe computer, and over the next couple of years it became extremely popular." In 1978, *Creative Computing* published an article written by Rawitsch about *The Oregon Trail* that included the BASIC code listing (much evolved from earlier efforts). The game, which migrated to microcomputers like the Apple II—MECC and Apple operated in lockstep in the 1980s, ensuring that the Cupertino company's computers were shipped to as many American schools as possible—eventually sold over sixty-five million copies. But Rawitsch, Heinemann, and Dillenberger reaped no financial rewards from their creation.

Bob Albrecht moved to Minnesota, eager to take his medicine show on the road. While teaching programming at the University of Minnesota Laboratory High School, which was connected to the DTSS, Albrecht was introduced to BASIC. Immediately understanding the great potential of the language, he publicly turned against FORTRAN—cofounding the Society to Help Abolish FORTRAN Teaching, or SHAFT—and promoted BASIC to organizations such as the National Council of Teachers of Mathematics (NCTM); in turn, the NCTM published *Computer Facilities for Mathematics Instruction*, a book encouraging BASIC adoption in schools.

Albrecht's next stop was San Francisco, where he teamed up with Woodside High School teacher LeRoy Finkel, another evangelist for teaching computing to young people. Together they founded Dymax, a publishing company funded by stock holdings from Albrecht's time at Digital Equipment Corporation. Before long, Dymax landed a contract with DEC to write BASIC instructional books. Gearing up for the effort meant relocating their new company to Menlo Park; there, a PDP-8, along with several terminals, were gifted by DEC to Dymax so the upstarts could write the book *My Computer Likes Me When I Speak in BASIC* (1972)—which ended up selling over a quarter million copies while simultaneously advertising DEC's minicomputers (the company sold around forty thousand PDP-8s by the late 1960s, with the Straight-8 becoming the best-selling computer in the world by the middle of the next decade).

The tone of *My Computer Likes Me*, with its mishmash of fonts and simple illustrations, was established on the second page: "This book is about people, computers and a programming language called BASIC," Albrecht explained. "We will communicate with a computer, in the BASIC language, about population problems." The page features the heading "TTY," abbreviating teletypewriter, which was introduced as follows: "Tele-typewriters are the Volkswagens of computer terminals…rugged, dependable, inexpensive, ugly and noisy!" Then, BASIC programs were presented to illustrate population growth. For instance, the chapter "Division of Labor" displayed the exponential increase per year of the human population, while other examples made use of population figures and growth rates in various regions around the world to underscore, in apocalyptic language, the dangers of overpopulation—an overriding concern of the time as illustrated in books such as *The Population Bomb* (1968) by Paul and Anne Ehrlich. Program listings in *My Computer Likes Me* were kept short, with the focus on BASIC concepts, like subscripted variables (arrays) and subroutines, assuming pride of place.

Albrecht never shook the teaching bug, packing a PDP-8 into a Volkswagen Bus (a Straight-8 in a flat-four) and traveling to schools across the Golden State to offer demonstrations. He also helped start the "computer education division" of the nonprofit Portola Institute, which published Stewart Brand's countercultural *Whole Earth Catalog*.

In 1972, the first issue of the *People's Computer Company* newsletter, boasting a similar style as the *Whole Earth Catalog*, was circulated. The success of the newsletter resulted in Dymax spinning off the nonprofit People's Computer Company. The PCC operated the computing center, sited at the Menalto Avenue shopping center, that featured terminals connected to a PDP-8 and, via telephone lines, a Hewlett-Packard minicomputer. As Steven Levy described it in *Hackers*, "Sometimes housewives would bring their kids in, try the computers themselves, and get hooked, programming so much that husbands worried that the loyal matriarchs were abandoning children and kitchen for the joys of BASIC."

But BASIC was far from universally loved in the hacker community. Albrecht in particular came under heavy criticism by hackers because he was a BASIC partisan; "hackers considered [BASIC] a 'fascist' language because its limited structure did not encourage maximum access to the machine and [therefore] decreased a programmer's power," Levy explained.

Views of BASIC among these intelligentsia had hardened by the time *The Computer Contradictionary, Second Edition* (1995), a cynical lexicography by British author and computer scientist Stan Kelly-Bootle, was published. An update of the author's *The Devil's DP [Data Processing] Dictionary* released more than a decade earlier, the satirical dictionary, written in the style of Ambrose Bierce's *The Devil's Dictionary*, was especially biting in all matters BASIC. Look up the definition of BASIC, for example, and readers learn that it was "[o]riginally…a simple mid-level language used to test the student's ability to increment line numbers, but now available only in complex, extended versions. *See* EXTENDED BASIC, VISUAL BASIC." Flip to the definition of *Extended BASIC* to see the language drawn and quartered:

> **Extended BASIC** *n.* [From *extended* "fully stretched, prolonged" + BASIC.]
> 1 "Sh-t with icing" (P. B. Fellget). 2 Any BASIC compiler or interpreter enhanced with features stolen from COBOL and C and meeting any two of the following conditions: (1) the cost exceeds $39.95, (2) line numbers can be incremented automatically or omitted, (3) labels can be alpha-numeric, (4) tape cassettes are not supported, (5) **A$** is an object.

The implication, of course, is that BASIC is "sh-t" and adding functionality to it in the form of Extended BASIC is the "icing." (This sh-t take calls to mind Kurtz's opinion of object-oriented programming: "The truth of the matter is that the single most important aspect of OOP is an approach devised decades ago: encapsulation of subroutines and data. All the rest is frosting." Also, P. B. Fellget was Peter Fellget, a physicist with a number of academic papers to his name. No word on whether he actually harbored a distaste for BASIC, though.)

But the slights against BASIC don't stop there. Look at the definition for *disability*, for example:

> **disability** *n.* (pc) A hidden or euphemised deficiency.
> ~Thus 8080 SEGMENTED memory is "address-challenged." Similarly, an employer can no longer ask job-seekers if they are addicted to alcohol, absenteeism, or BASIC.

Page to the definition of *identifier* to find the following sarcastic take:

> Likewise, a programmer declaring `Net_Income` as `double` immediately saddles a chunk of memory with extraneous semantic baggage well beyond its machine-specific floating-point representation. Subsequent code, for all we know, might dictate that
>
> ```
> Net_Income = Gross_Income + Deductions;
> ```
>
> leading some to view "identifiable identifiers" as a mixed blessing. Parnassian fields, named (by me) for D. L. Parnas ("On the Criteria to Be Used in Decomposing Systems into Modules," *Communications of the ACM 5*, no. 12 [December 1972]) are deliberately non-mnemonic. Parnas would prefer the arbitrary `A1`, `X3`, etc., as forced on us by early BASICs. Maintainabilty, he claims, which depends on understanding what the code actually does, should never rely on the "natural language" interpretation of `Net_Income` as someone's net income.

And in the definition of the term *top-down*, Kelly-Bootle warns that "[t]he dispute [top-down versus bottom-up approaches] affects only largish software projects, although one hears of classroom exercises where two weeks are spent discussing the correct programming strategy for a five-line BASIC assignment to list factorial N until the paper runs out." Clearly, BASIC was being treated here more like a scourge or contagion at worst, and the butt of a joke at best, than as a utility with which to solve programming problems efficiently.

The Jargon File, "a comprehensive compendium of hacker slang illuminating many aspects of hackish tradition, folklore, and humor," wasn't kind to BASIC, either:

> **BASIC:** /bay'-sic/, *n.*
> A programming language, originally designed for Dartmouth's experimental timesharing system in the early 1960s, which for many years was the leading cause of brain damage in proto-hackers. Edsger W. Dijkstra observed in *Selected Writings on Computing: A Personal Perspective* that "It is practically impossible to teach good programming style to students that have had prior exposure to BASIC: as potential programmers they are mentally mutilated beyond hope of regeneration." This is another case (like Pascal) of

the cascading *lossage* [definition: "The result of a bug or malfunction"] that happens when a language deliberately designed as an educational toy gets taken too seriously. A novice can write short BASIC programs (on the order of 10-20 lines) very easily; writing anything longer (a) is very painful, and (b) encourages bad habits that will make it harder to use more powerful languages well. This wouldn't be so bad if historical accidents hadn't made BASIC so common on low-end micros in the 1980s. As it is, it probably ruined tens of thousands of potential wizards.

Despite the hacker community's growing displeasure with the language, in 1975, Albrecht and the PCC released *What to Do After You Hit Return*, a "cookbook" of type-in games and programs—many of which had already been published in PCC newsletters—written for Hewlett-Packard's HP 2000 line of minicomputers in HP Time-Shared BASIC (specifically, HP 2000F BASIC). As we learn in *10 PRINT*, "Not once did the acronym BASIC appear on the front or back cover, perhaps indicating that the language was so prevalent for recreational programming that it need not be named."

"If your computer speaks a different dialect of BASIC," advises *What to Do After You Hit Return*, "Many of the programs should 'almost' work as is. Strings and disk references (if any) may require modifications." REMs and text explaining the rules of games could be excised from code to save memory, the book's authors suggest.

With its BASIC listings, narrative exposition, entertaining cartoon illustrations, sample runs, and educational program-flow diagrams, *What to Do After You Hit Return* offered a wide variety of games and applications for readers to type in and run. There were number guessing games like *Abase* (the user guesses a computer-generated value output in any base) and *Button* (a multiplayer game of "find the button"); word games such as *Abagel* (the user must guess a three-letter word) and *Hangmn* (a variant of hangman); Nim-like games including *23Mtch* (a game of Nim that start with twenty-three matches in the pile); hide-and-seek games such as *Hurkle* (with as few moves as possible, the user must locate the "Hurkle" hidden in a grid world); pattern games like *Life* (an implementation of mathematician John Conway's cellular automaton game); board games including *Qubic5* (three-dimensional tic-tac-toe); cave exploration games like *Wumpus* (the player hunts a "Wumpus" in a "world of caves, superbats, and bottomless pits"); science fiction games such as *Sttr1* (the player assumes command of the starship *Enterprise*, taking her into interstellar battle; readers discover that "AS CAPTAIN OF THE *ENTERPRISE*, YOUR MISSION IS TO FIND AND DESTROY ALL UNITS OF THE KLINGON INVASION FORCE WITHIN 30 STARDATES. IF YOU FAIL, THE FEDERATION WILL BE CONQUERED"); business and social science simulations including *Hamrbi* (the user plays as Hammurabi, governing the ancient kingdom of Sumeria), *Stock* (a stock market simulation), and *Polut* (a "real-life simulation that permits you to create a water pollution situation and try to clean it up"); and miscellany like *Lunar* (the user lands a spaceship on the moon). Page vi of *What to Do After You Hit Return* lists the many people who wrote the book's programs, with John Kemeny among them.

Espousing the ethos of the counterculture and positioning themselves as a bulwark against the corporatization of computers—then largely in the form of IBM—the People's Computer Company ultimately adopted not Dartmouth BASIC but Tiny BASIC, a bare-bones version of the language whose design specifications were laid out by Dennis Allison in a 1975 PCC newsletter titled "BUILD YOUR OWN BASIC." Tiny BASIC was to be interpreted, rather than compiled; it might have "fewer statements, fewer features," than its big brother, but it would be free to all—unlike Bill Gates's Micro-Soft (the hyphenated company name combined the first part of the words micro-computer and software) BASIC for the Micro Instrumentation and Telemetry Systems (MITS) Altair 8800, the first popular hobbyist computer, famously featured on the cover of the January 1975 issue of *Popular Electronics*. The PCC newsletter plastered the Altair on its January 1975 cover as well. (The Altair 8800 was not the first time an electronics magazine had a "build it yourself" computer on its cover. For example, the July 1974 issue of *Radio-Electronics* featured the Mark-8, "Your Personal Minicomputer," on the cover. When fully assembled, the Mark-8 was powered by an Intel 8008 CPU.)

By the mid-1970s, hobbyists' groups like the Homebrew Computer Club, of which the PCC's Albrecht was a member, had angered Gates: they were pirating his company's software, costing him royalties. So Gates penned an open letter, dated February 3, 1976, accusing the hobbyists of theft, which ultimately resulted in "prevent[ing] good software from being written." Dartmouth BASIC, first making its home in the commons, had, in the span of a decade, been reimagined as a commercial product—one in which Gates demanded that those who stole it "pay up." (Along with Albrecht, the Homebrew Computer Club's membership also included future luminaries like Steve Jobs and Steve Wozniak; Nelson's *Computer Lib/Dream Machines* was one of the "bibles" circulating at club meetings, Wozniak remembered.)

Bill Gates would presumably find a measure of closure after an amendment to the Copyright Act of 1976 was passed that recognized computer programs as a type of literary work as well as a form of written expression—thus putting the full power of the U.S. government behind ensuring that such intellectual property, in this case the source code (and even the object code, the machine-readable form of a program), was protected.

Less than a year later, though, another crisis arose, one that threatened ownership over Micro-Soft's Altair BASIC interpreter. In 1977, Ed Roberts, cofounder of MITS, sold his company to Pertec Computer Corporation, a deal that included rights to Micro-Soft BASIC. But Gates argued that Pertec had no claim over the software, and Gates and Paul Allen attempted to terminate their contact with MITS. In response, MITS and Pertec took them to court; the legal battle culminated seven months later with a ruling in favor of Micro-Soft: not only was the small company now free and clear of its contract with MITS, but Pertec was on the hook for royalty fees if they ever used Micro-Soft BASIC. As Allen later explained it, "Bill and I recovered all rights to our BASIC interpreter"—during the arbitration, Micro-Soft was not permitted to take on any new BASIC contacts—"and could now sell it to whomever we pleased—and better yet, keep all the revenue. Our one big roadblock was gone." In short order, Micro-Soft employees were busy at work implementing BASIC for the TRS-80 and Commodore PET.

If the hobbyists wouldn't "pay up" for Altair BASIC, then they would write and distribute Tiny BASIC instead.

One of a number of implementations which Kurtz said "[t]he microcomputer folks adopted…for their teeny machines," Tiny BASIC served as the perfect response to Gates's open letter: a free alternative to commercial BASIC software. A newsletter—called *Dr. Dobb's Journal of Tiny BASIC Calisthenics & Orthodontia, Running Light Without Overbyte*, and later shortened to *Dr. Dobb's Journal*—was at first devoted to the dissemination of all things Tiny BASIC (the small size of the language would run light and hence avoid "overbyte").

Unsurprisingly, it didn't take long for new forms of Tiny BASIC to emerge: there were over a half-dozen published in *Dr. Dobb's* alone, with perhaps the most notable dialect being Li-Chen Wang's Palo Alto Tiny BASIC. This version of the language offered a copy*left* license, which gave users the right to freely distribute and modify the software (presaging open-source licenses), as it expressed with the following message: "@COPYLEFT ALL WRONGS RESERVED." Wang, a computer engineer, was a member of the Homebrew Computer Club.

Dr. Dobb's was inspiring programmers to write their own BASICs on the East Coast, too. In 1975, an IBM 5100 Portable Computer, complete with BASIC, landed in Robert Uiterwyk's office. Bringing the machine home from work, far from an everyday occurrence, nonetheless led his twelve-year-old son Ted to develop an all-consuming interest in both the computer and BASIC. By the end of the year, exhausted from transporting the nearly sixty-pound machine back and forth between work and home, Uiterwyk ordered an SWTPC (Southwest Technical Products Corporation) 6800 computer kit, powered by a Motorola 6800 microprocessor chip, that he spotted in *Popular Electronics*. Though intending to hand the computer to his son as a Christmas gift, Uiterwyk could not get the device to run properly—until several acquaintances helped him get it working.

Just in time for the winter holidays, Uiterwyk wrote a machine language program that output, in a loop, "Merry Christmas Ted" on a Teletype. But his son was not moved by the demonstration, since he had seen BASIC on his father's IBM perform far greater feats. Losing patience waiting for a BASIC interpreter from SWTPC that ultimately never arrived, and encouraged by what he read in *Dr. Dobb's*, Uiterwyk had an idea: to write his own BASIC. Which he did, by hand, on a yellow legal tablet; the result of his efforts, MICRO BASIC version 1.3, took about a month to finish. In June 1976, the SWTPC newsletter printed Uiterwyk's BASIC, which was limited: no string variables, a maximum of twenty-six single-letter variable names, integer arithmetic only, multistatement lines not allowed. A symbol table—with hexadecimal (base 16) entries such as `0C13` and `0A44` corresponding to keywords **IF** and **LET**, respectively—rounded out the machine code listing. But, as limited as MICRO BASIC was, it was still functional, even featuring seventeen error codes to assist debugging.

A 4K floating-point version of MICRO BASIC followed, with arithmetic operations performed in BCD (Binary Coded Decimal) to nine digits of precision. By August of that year, at the Personal Computing Convention held in Atlantic City, SWTPC was proudly selling the newly released 4K BASIC for five dollars a pop. And a later 8K version upped the ante by including trigonometric functions, string variables and functions, and **PEEK** and **POKE** commands. SWTPC advertised the two versions of Uiterwyk's BASIC in the December 1976 issue of *Byte* magazine. The attention-grabbing headline of the ad offered a tongue in cheek warning: "It has been determined that reading this ad may be hazardous to your health, if you own another type computer system. We will not be responsible for ulcers, heartburn, or other complications if you persist in reading this material." An order form, found on the bottom-right corner of the page, was prefaced with yet another warning: "You guys are out of your minds, but who am I to complain"—the implication being that the prices for the 4K and 8K BASIC cassettes were too low ($4.95 and $9.95, respectively) for SWTPC to make a profit.

In 1978, the source code for Uiterwyk's BASIC was purchased by Motorola, marking the end of Uiterwyk's short-lived but very successful involvement in the write-your-own-BASIC craze.

Furthering the democratizing spirit of BASIC in the early 1970s was the book *101 BASIC Computer Games* (1973) by David Hollerith Ahl, who founded *Creating Computing* magazine. (Yes, his middle name is Hollerith—an open-and-shut case of nominative determinism.) "When the mainframe priesthood was at the pinnacle of its power, Ahl was one of the original promoters of computer literacy for the masses," wrote John J. Anderson in a 1984 profile of the magazine's founder. "And from the start, he promulgated the idea that computers should be fun."

Growing up in Malverne, New York, on the south shore of Long Island, Ahl's passion for computing began during a 1951 Malverne Junior-Senior High School photography club field trip. Ahl had no interest in photography, joining the club simply because he had a crush on the club's advisor: science teacher Ms. Natalia Dugas. The fateful field trip took students deep into the heart of New York City, where they snapped pictures while walking uptown. On Cortlandt Street he encountered "Radio Row." Though it would disappear in the mid-1960s to make way for the World Trade Center, early the previous decade Radio Row was the home of World War II surplus parts— electronics such as aircraft radios, oscillators, relays, transformers, solenoids, diodes, and vacuum tubes.

Ahl visited Radio Row repeatedly, filling up cardboard boxes with all the parts he could lug home. Spending countless hours experimenting with the equipment and building projects that had been featured in *Popular Electronics*, Ahl monetized his newfound talent by starting a modest radio-repair business. He also won essay contest sponsored by RCA despite never having used any of their products; an RCA vacuum tube voltmeter was the prize, which Ahl and a friend jury-rigged to create a specialized teletypewriter, with some success.

By the mid-1950s, Ahl was enrolled at the School of Electrical Engineering at Cornell thanks to a full scholarship from the Grumman Aircraft Engineering Corporation. But during his junior year at the university, he struggled, failing an AC Machinery class. A timely conference with the dean served as a course correction, permitting Ahl to complete an experimental five-year engineering program that mixed science with a hefty dose of liberal arts and humanities classes.

In 1957, Cornell procured its first computer, a Burroughs, and offered students two computer courses. Ahl enrolled in both—the classes "barely scratched the surface," he recalled—and, in his fifth year, he wrote a computer program that simulated the acoustics in a room. He also worked, for two summers (1960-61), at Grumman's computer group, developing programs to "calculate the distortion coefficient of radar signals" and to "simulate practically everything about the [as yet unbuilt] Orbiting Astronomical Observatory," Ahl recalled.

Carnegie Mellon was Ahl's next stop. Pursuing a graduate degree at GMU exposed the young programmer to many kinds of computer applications, like linear programming, game theory, and queueing theory, in a range of courses. Ahl was especially drawn toward using computers to perform real-world simulation studies; to that end, he wrote parts of a management game that modeled a detergent company competition on a Bendix G-15—a machine comparable to the LGP-30, Dartmouth's first computer for student use—and then translated the low-level code to FORTRAN.

After completing a two-year stint in the ROTC (Reserve Officers' Training Corps), he found work with a former professor, who had started a market research company. There, Ahl wrote a number of programs designed to forecast new product sales. In the late 1960s, he was on the move again, this time to the Educational Systems Research Institute, having been tapped to create computer models that could predict vocational students' success. Meanwhile, Ahl pursued a Ph.D. in educational psychology at the University of Pittsburgh, taking night courses. But short several credits and a dissertation, he left Pennsylvania and traveled north, taking a job with Digital Equipment Corporation in Maynard, Massachusetts.

Shunted into DEC's PDP-8 product group, Ahl was tasked with researching educational markets for the company's machines. He assembled EduSystem, a "total system" kit of hardware, systems software, and applications software delivered to every school that ordered a DEC machine, and *Edu*, a newsletter intended for the company's educational customers that circulated to tens of thousands of educators—some of which weren't even DEC users. "It dawned on me then what a wonderful idea it would be to do an educational computing magazine that wasn't wedded to one particular computer manufacturer," Ahl explained. The pages of the newsletter frequently included listings of BASIC games, some of which were sent in by readers.

In 1973, Ahl agreed to join the research and development group at the company. While there, he penned a lengthy brochure for the RSTS time-sharing operating system. He also compiled programs for a book titled *101 BASIC Computer Games*, which, in two printings, sold around ten thousand copies—more than the total number of computers on the planet at the time.

Within a year, Ahl—frustrated that company brass wouldn't move forward with a nascent personal-computer proposal—tendered his resignation and left for Morristown, New Jersey, taking a job with AT&T. Within months, he also laid the groundwork to publish his own magazine, *Creative Computing*. Despite an initial subscriber count of only six hundred, Ahl printed eight thousand copies of the first issue—of which he had written articles, edited others' work, took photographs, and drew illustrations—more than enough to bombard schools and libraries throughout the United States with excess copies of the magazine. The strategy paid off, with his subscriber count ballooning to over sixty thousand by the late 1970s. Ahl quit AT&T in 1978, putting all his energies into publishing. In addition, he obtained the rights to republish *101 BASIC Computer Games*, which would pay off dramatically in the years to come.

David Ahl sat down several years ago for an interview with the Atari historian and web publisher Kevin "Kay" Savetz, who is no stranger to BASIC. Savetz is the author of *Terrible Nerd* (2012), an autobiography that resonates with a generation of self-styled tech nerds—mostly members of Gen X—whose formative years were spent pecking away on the keyboard of a "1977 Trinity" microcomputer (Apple II, Commodore PET, or Tandy TRS-80) or, in Savetz's case, an 8-bit Atari 800 purchased by Savetz's father. "I created many games and utilities in Atari BASIC," writes the author of *Terrible Nerd*, after waxing nostalgic about the hours spent typing in and debugging program listings printed in computer magazines; the budding programmer pored through the type-ins in Ahl's *BASIC Computer Games* and *More BASIC Computer Games* books as well. (Many years later, after forming a friendship with Ahl, Savetz—who is a prolific collector and cataloger of retrocomputing artifacts—procured a number of foreign-language editions of *BASIC Computer Games* from him.) We learn how Savetz approached solving vexing coding problems in one of a number of relatable passages in the book:

> Early on, programming taught me the unexpected lesson that it's possible to solve a problem by not thinking about it. I'd be stuck on a particular dilemma, unsure how to make a program do what I wanted it to do, or with a bug that I didn't know how to fix…. The answer would only come to me at breakfast the next day, or while watching a movie with Dad—the solution would appear when I wasn't actively thinking about the problem.

Thinking about something without explicitly thinking about it sounds counterintuitive only to those who have never programmed a computer.

As a child, Savetz quickly ran up against the limitations of Atari BASIC, which could "make the computer walk, or chew the gum, but not both at once." BASIC was no match for assembly language, the young Savetz realized; for those interested to learn it, assembly could direct the Atari to walk and chew gum at the same time. *Terrible Nerd* traces a direct line from these early computing experiences to Savetz's later career exploits in technology journalism and website publishing.

In the interview with Savetz, David Ahl commended Kemeny and Kurtz for making Dartmouth BASIC available sans license fee. Although Ahl sold record numbers of BASIC books, he speculated to Savetz of a very different path educational programming could have taken, courtesy of Digital Equipment Corporation's FOCAL (Formulating On-Line Calculations in Algebraic Language) interpreted language.

First built for the PDP-8 family of minicomputers in 1968, FOCAL was "designed to help scientists, engineers, and students solve numerical problems," reads an early manual. It continues: "The language consists of short imperative English statements which are relatively easy to learn. Mathematical expressions are typed, for the most part, in standard notation. The best way to learn the FOCAL language is to sit at the Teletype and try the commands…." There was the TYPE command to output the result of an expression, and the SET command to set variables equal to numerical values. The

IF conditional was available, as were various features with which to manipulate string data. Unconditional jumps were made possible with GOTO, and the DO command—which transferred control to a subroutine and then returned back to the statement following the DO—gave FOCAL the same sort of flexibility as BASIC's **GOSUB...RETURN**.

Ahl was impressed with FOCAL, noting that "FOCAL in many regards was more efficient than BASIC, because they were running it on many computer[s] and there was less memory to work with." He then compared the BASIC-FOCAL debate to the VHS-Betamax format competition of the 1980s: "Sony [was] saying, 'Betamax is ours and it is a better format that VHS,' which it was. But then, JVC [was] saying, 'We have VHS and Toshiba. Hey do you want to use it? Fine, we'll license it to you for next to nothing.'"

I think it [FOCAL] could have been very big. I think…there could have been very serious competition between the two languages, but by Digital limiting it only to their own computers and specifically to their minicomputers, not even the big mainframes, it really limited the spread of FOCAL. In fact, it forced me, at DEC, to go out to the developers, and people in educational institutions [because] they wanted BASIC.

There were few schools and colleges in Boston area, near DEC, that were OK with FOCAL. But stuff was getting published by Minnesota Educational Computer Consortium [MECC] and others in BASIC…. So they wanted BASIC.

The January/February 1977 issue of *Personal Computing* offered a simple explanation for BASIC's rise—one that happened to hinge on FOCAL's demise. "But the big clincher came when Digital Equipment Corp. decided to put BASIC on its PDP-8 computers as an alternative to FOCAL," explained *The Secret Guide to Computers* author Russ Walter in his article "Let's Improve BASIC." "PDP-8 users preferred BASIC to FOCAL so much that Digital chose BASIC to be the main language for its PDP-11." In the 1984 *Creative Computing* profile of the magazine's founder, Ahl noted that he had to hire outsiders to design BASIC interpreters for various DEC machines, because the DEC software development group "wasn't the least interested in [BASIC]." Which also explains why there were so many DEC BASIC dialects. "My goal was to get the product out as fast as possible," Ahl explained, adding that "if I had been a stickler for consistency, it would have taken another two years."

Ahl first encountered BASIC around the time the sixth edition of Dartmouth BASIC was released in 1971. Two years earlier, he joined DEC's PDP-8 product group; before long, Ahl found himself marketing minicomputers to schools, including colleges. Back then, FOCAL was the only high-level language available for these small DEC computers, much to the disappointment of high schools and colleges; these institutions wanted computers that "spoke BASIC," Ahl told John Szczepaniak for *Game Developer* magazine.

With BASIC unregulated but public, and FOCAL proprietary—DEC would not license the language out to competing manufacturers—the writing for FOCAL was on the wall. Sticking only with BASIC led to absurd situations, such as *six* different dialects of the language being developed for the PDP-8 family alone, as new BASIC implementations shifted from being written for mainframes and time-sharing systems and toward minicomputers instead. While the company played FOCAL close to the vest, DEC simultaneously enthusiastically sought out vendors to write BASICs for models of the PDP-8: a 4K standalone machine called the EduSystem 10; a multiuser 8K EduSystem 20; a batch-processing EduSystem 30, complete with card reader; and a time-sharing EduSystem 50. The 4K version of BASIC was especially limited, with the interpreter consuming a whopping 3.5K of memory—thus leaving a paltry five hundred 12-bit bytes available for programs.

Ahl points to games as the key to BASIC's spread. He began "converting FOCAL demo programs to this low-end BASIC," Ahl recalled, in addition to developing his own unique, playable creations. Also, users who wrote games were encouraged to submit them to DEC. By 1972, he had enough BASIC games to assemble them into a book of type-in listings—*101 BASIC Computer Games*—geared toward DEC BASIC and published shortly thereafter. By 1983, well over a million copies of the book, repackaged as *BASIC Computer Games*, had flown off shelves, making it the first computer book to surpass one million sales, a landmark achieved in 1979. Though the majority of programs in *101 BASIC Computer Games* were, as the title promised, games—users could play type-ins of auto racing, baseball, basketball, blackjack, boxing, bull fighting, checkers, craps, darts, dog racing, European roulette, football, golf, hangman, horse racing, ice hockey, Monopoly, Nim, pizza delivery, poker, Russian roulette, slot machines, tic-tac-toe, Tower of Hanoi, war (the card game), and Yahtzee, among many others—there were also simulations like *John Conway's Game of Life*, modeled after the eponymous mathematician's well-known creation; *Poet*, in which the computer generated random poetry; *Rocket*, in which the player took the reins of a spaceship landing on the moon; *Stock*, a stock market simulator; and *Zoop*, which imitated a BASIC compiler but rendered it noncooperative (it was a "BASIC programmer's nightmare," Ahl warned), as well as several examples of non-interactive ASCII art—images composed of ASCII characters—including *Snoopy*, in whose description Ahl writes,

> There must be 7,000 various computer pictures of Snoopy around dating from the ENIAC I. Just why Snoopy was universally adopted as the programmers' mascot is hard to say, but it's clear today that he was—overwhelmingly. Here are a couple of pictures of that ubiquitous dog.

(Though Ahl is presumably joking here, nevertheless note that ASCII art dates to the mid-1960s, two decades after the ENIAC debuted; ASCII was created in the early 1960s. However, images comprised of characters that were output using line printers predate ASCII.) Underneath the description, readers were treated to designs of Snoopy kicking a football and waving his paw at the Red Baron. The program *Diamonds* drew diamonds on-screen, composed of various characters in user-defined sizes, while the program *Love* recreated American artist Robert Indiana's famous pop art work, albeit using a user-input message of up to sixty characters in length.

Ahl wrote a number of sequels to *101 BASIC Computer Games*, including *BASIC Computer Adventures*, published in the mid-1980s. Programs in that book had no spaghetti code, he noted; in addition, Ahl claimed that "some of the efficient routing routines (think travelling salesman problem) from *Subway Scavenger* are being used today by Google Maps and some GPS mapping software."

Let's examine *Subway Scavenger*, whose premise is as follows.

> You have a job with a messenger/courier service located in mid-town Manhattan. To-day, you have five packages to deliver and five packages to pick up for delivery to other locations in the city. So, in total, you must visit 15 different locations.
>
> You can use 264 stations of the New York City Subway System which are serviced by the following 11 trains: A, B, CG, D, E, F, N, 1, 2, 4, and 7.
>
> You must complete all your deliveries and pickups by 5:00 PM. Your boss has given you $20 for tokens....

In addition, you must avoid trip hazards when traversing the city, including fire on the tracks, sticky train doors, and muggings.

The program, around six hundred lines long (half of those lines were **DATA** statements), used a series of arrays to keep track of subway stations and subway lines. As described in the book:

> First are the data about the nodes of the system, in this case the subway stations. To each node (or station) we must assign a number (**STA**), and we probably want to give it a name as well (**STATION$(STA)**). We must also know how many lines of transportation (subway lines) intersect the node (**STANU(STA)**) and which ones they are (**STATR(STA, n)**).
>
> Second, to each line of transportation, we must assign a number (**TR**) and possibly a name (**TRAIN$(TR)**). In addition, we must know how many nodes it intersects (**TRSTOP(TR)**) and which ones they are (**TRSTA(TR, n)**). For convenience, we may also want to know the starting and ending point, so we can differentiate point-to-point routes from circular or continuous ones. In fact, the New York Subway System has on-ly point-to-point routes, unlike the London Underground which has a mixture of circu-lar and point-to-point routes.

Arrays also kept track of the packages, which were shuffled up by the program.

One particular BASIC game that Ahl had a hand in developing proved especially popu-lar. *101 BASIC Computer Games* included a *Star Trek* game, with variants of the text-based adventure spreading everywhere: on minicomputers like the Data General Nova in the 1970s to microcomputers like the Tandy TRS-80 and BBC Micro by the next decade.

Ahl's game was based on the canonical version, the brainchild of one Mike Mayfield, who programmed it in BASIC using a Scientific Data Systems (SDS) Sigma 7 main-frame in 1971. Then only in high school, Mayfield managed to obtain user credentials that gained him access to the machine, found in the computer lab at the University of California in Irvine, despite not being enrolled as a student.

Inspired by the videogame *Spacewar!*, running on a PDP-10 also present in the UCI lab, Mayfield designed his game to work around the limitations of the Sigma 7, which lacked the vector graphics display so artfully employed by *Spacewar!* Instead, he used the ASR-33 teleprinter to maximum effect, allowing players to captain the starship *USS Enterprise*, searching for Klingon warships while navigating the (usually) sixty-four quadrants/sectors of the galaxy that were displayed as maps composed of ASCII characters. The count of sixty-four quadrants on "standard CG" (Cartesian Galactic) maps, as opposed to only four (since the root *quad* means four), were later explained by Ahl as the result of an understanding called the "2^6 Agreement" at the "Third Magellanic Conference," attended by many cultures across the Milky Way. "In that historic document, the participant cultures agreed, in all two-dimensional representations of the galaxy, to specify 64 major subdivisions, ordered as an 8×8 matrix."

Clashes between the *Enterprise* and Klingon battle cruisers were turn-based, with phasers and photon torpedoes the weapons of choice. There were other *Trek* elements present, such as warp engines, shields, short- and long-range sensor scans, starbases, stardates, and the Federation (United Federation of Planets), that would have been familiar to those who watched episodes of the three-season original series, then flourishing in broadcast syndication.

Mayfield's program is relatively easy to understand. For instance, code prompting players for a command was as follows:

```
1270   PRINT "COMMAND:";
1280   INPUT A
1290   GOTO A+1 OF 1410,1260,2330,2530,2800,3460,3560,4630
1300   PRINT
1310   PRINT "    0 = SET COURSE"
1320   PRINT "    1 = SHORT RANGE SENSOR SCAN"
1330   PRINT "    2 = LONG RANGE SENSOR SCAN"
1340   PRINT "    3 = FIRE PHASERS"
1350   PRINT "    4 = FIRE PHOTON TORPEDOES"
1360   PRINT "    5 = SHIELD CONTROL"
1370   PRINT "    6 = DAMAGE CONTROL REPORT"
1380   PRINT "    7 = CALL ON LIBRARY COMPUTER"
1390   PRINT
1400   GOTO 1270
```

And while players certainly wanted to avoid this block of code executing:

```
3920   PRINT "THE ENTERPRISE IS DEAD IN SPACE.  IF YOU SURVIVE ALL
       IMPENDING"
3930   PRINT "ATTACK YOU WILL BE DEMOTED TO THE RANK OF PRIVATE"
3940   IF K3 <= 0 THEN 4020
3950   GOSUB 3790
```

They were surely overjoyed when this block ran:

```
4040   PRINT
4050   PRINT "THE LAST KLINGON BATTLE CRUISER IN THE GALAXY HAS BEEN
       DESTROYED"
4060   PRINT "THE FEDERATION HAS BEEN SAVED !!!"
4070   PRINT
```

```
4080  PRINT "YOUR EFFICIENCY RATING ="((K7/(T-T0))*1000)
4090  T1=TIM(0)+TIM(1)*60
4100  PRINT "YOUR ACTUAL TIME OF MISSION ="INT((((T1-T7)*.4)-T7)*100)"
      MINUTES"
4110  GOTO 230
```

Mayfield didn't stop his *Trek* work with the Sigma 7; if he had, the game may have met a premature end. Contacting a local Hewlett-Packard sales office to purchase an HP-35 calculator, he regaled the HP staff with stories about his game—so much so that they handed him the keys to an HP 2000C parked in the office, requesting that he translate *Star Trek* to their minicomputer. Which the eighteen-year-old did, after completely rewriting it in HP BASIC in the fall of 1972. Renamed *STTR1: Star Trek* and loaded into the HP public domain software library in early 1973,

```
1    REM ****   HP BASIC PROGRAM LIBRARY   ****************************
2    REM
3    REM        STTR1: STAR TREK
4    REM
5    REM        36243  REV B  --  10/73
6    REM
7    REM ****   CONTRIBUTED PROGRAM   ********************************
100    REM ****************************************************************
110    REM ***                                                      ***
120    REM ***     STAR TREK: BY MIKE MAYFIELD, CENTERLINE ENGINEERING   ***
130    REM ***                                                      ***
140    REM ***        TOTAL INTERACTION GAME - ORIG. 20 OCT 1972
150    REM ***                                                      ***
160    REM ****************************************************************
```

Ahl stumbled upon the program and, along with Mary Cole (who worked with Ahl at DEC), rewrote it in BASIC-PLUS for the DEC RSTS-11 compiler, "add[ing] a few bits and pieces while I was at it." The code listing was then printed in the *DEC User Society* newsletter, spreading word of the game to a wider audience. It was also published in *101 BASIC Computer Games*, but under the title *SPACWR* ("Space War—in retrospect, an incorrect name," Ahl admitted); recall that Bob Albrecht's *What to Do After You Hit Return* included a version as well, called *Sttr1*. As Ahl noted in *BASIC Computer Games* (1978), there were *Trek*-type games circulating around college campuses as early as the late 1960s—before the television show was canceled. "I recall playing one at Carnegie-Mellon Univ. in 1967 or 68, and a very different one at Berkeley." But these programs couldn't compare to the mature, polished version written by Mayfield, which became the standard *Trek*.

Westinghouse Electric employee Bob Leedom, captivated by *101 BASIC Computer Games*, spent time after hours implementing *SPACWR* on the company's Data General Nova 800 mini. Based on suggestions from colleagues, Leedom altered the gameplay as well as some of the game's dynamics; for instance, numeric commands (e.g., *4* = fire photon torpedo) turned into three-character commands (e.g., *TOR* = fire photon torpedo). Then, Leedom wrote an article for the *People's Computer Company* newsletter detailing his modified *Trek*. Spotting the piece, Ahl obtained the code listing and published it in *Creative Computing* under the title *Super Star Trek*. Four years later, a Microsoft BASIC version of *Super Star Trek* was featured in a chapter of *BASIC Computer Games*—with Paramount Pictures' blessing.

"Like a virus," author Tony Smith recounts in the article "*Star Trek*: The Original Computer Game," "the game spread from system to system."

> Ahl's Basic version would ultimately lead to *Apple Trek,* the version Apple itself released commercially for its Apple II microcomputer in 1979. It was written by W Sander, and the name was changed to avoid copyright issues, of course, and that was true of all the other commercial releases. AcornSoft's release was called *Galaxy*, for instance; Tandy's *Space Trek. Apple Trek* wasn't the only version published for a late 1970s microcomputer—*Star Trek* appeared on the Commodore Pet, the Tandy TRS-80 Model I and…the [Research Machines 8-bit] RML 380Z—but the popularity of the Apple micro and the decision to release the software commercially, undoubtedly means its influence was far reaching.

Versions were written for Altair BASIC as well as Tiny BASIC. The game was implemented in other languages, too, such as FORTRAN (*UT Super Star Trek*, the UT standing for University of Texas) and C (*BSD Trek*). As the years passed and the technology improved, *Trek* exploited new hardware, with more advanced graphics and playability features regularly appearing.

Like Bob Leedom, Steve Wozniak was greatly influenced by *101 BASIC Computer Games*. In 1975, with the release of Altair BASIC—an implementation that Ahl claimed was "largely based" on DEC BASIC for the RSTS-11 time-sharing operating system—Wozniak "sniffed the wind," despite not programming in BASIC himself.

"There was a book out, *101 BASIC Computer Games*," Wozniak recalled, "So I said: You've got to have these games, it's going to be the heart of a computer that's worth anything to people." Wozniak had never developed a computer language before, so he procured a BASIC manual from his workplace, Hewlett-Packard, and took note of all the language's commands, writing out a comprehensive syntax chart. "I included floating point arithmetic, decimal points, numbers and everything," he recalled. DEC BASIC—the dialect of the programs in Ahl's book—differed from HP BASIC, especially in its treatment of strings.

At this point, Woz realized he could save a month's worth of work if floating-point arithmetic wasn't included in his implementation; at bottom, "all you need for games is integers," which he proved with efforts like *Breakout*, written in BASIC practically overnight and functional enough to impress the likes of a young Steve Jobs. Writing games with software instead of directly into hardware turned out to be a faster, cheaper, and more flexible alternative. Woz figured, "I'll save a month and I'll become famous like Bill Gates if I write it the fastest I could." Unable to afford a time-share assembler, he wrote Integer BASIC (so called because it lacked floating-point capability; Woz also referred to the effort as "GAME BASIC") entirely by hand in machine language. But not including floating point in Integer BASIC became Wozniak's only Apple II regret.

Despite its success and influence, David Ahl believes *101 BASIC Computer Games* was only one among a multitude of factors—such as libraries of BASIC games and other programs that emerged at Dartmouth (from the user-compiled program library called DARTCAT, among other sources), the Huntington Computer Project (headed by electrical engineering professor Ludwig Braun, the NSF-funded project featured educational BASIC programs of various computer simulations serving as laboratory exercises for primary and secondary school classes; the curricular materials were disseminated by DEC), and the Minnesota Educational Computer Consortium, coupled with little competition in the interactive-educational programming language sphere—that launched BASIC to stratospheric heights by the early 1980s while it crushed worthy competitors like FOCAL.

Though FOCAL wasn't adopted as a teaching language, a programming language developed at MIT was set to take schools by storm.

If Alan Perlis envisioned computer programming classes for some undergraduates, and John Kemeny and Thomas Kurtz believed in exposing all college students to programming, then Seymour Papert's mission was to educate children of all ages in computing.

Called the "father of educational computing," Seymour A. Papert was born in 1928 in Pretoria, South Africa, during the time of apartheid. He engaged in a number of anti-apartheid activities in his youth, including establishing classes for Black servants, which led to consequences with the law: found to be a dissident, Papert was barred from leaving the country. So he attended University of the Witwatersrand in Johannesburg, earning an undergraduate degree in philosophy in 1949 and then a doctorate in mathematics in 1952 from the institution.

Yet despite the order to remain in South Africa, in 1954, lacking a passport, he still managed to travel to the University of Cambridge in the United Kingdom. By 1959, Papert secured a second doctorate, this time in mathematical topology. Some of the most important work of his career occurred during the next four years, where he collaborated with famed psychologist Jean Piaget at the University of Geneva; together, they studied how children make sense of mathematics. Papert complemented Piaget's theory of constructivism with a theory of "constructionism"—of gaining knowledge through an active process of building things. He was greatly influenced by the notion that "[c]hildren learn by doing, and by thinking about what they do." Maybe Papert was inspired by one of Perlis's pearls of wisdom: "Perhaps if we wrote programs from childhood on, as adults we'd be able to read them."

Papert's next stop was in Cambridge, Massachusetts. Marvin Minsky invited Papert to MIT, where he would co-found (with Minsky) and co-direct the MIT Artificial Intelligence Laboratory. Here, Papert would help develop Logo, the first programming language expressly designed for children to use; he worked with several employees of Bolt, Beranek and Newman (BBN), including Cynthia Solomon and team leader Wallace "Wally" Feurzeig, to craft the language.

Logo was a dialect of LISP (LISt Processor), a language created by John McCarthy in the late 1950s that was particularly suited for solving problems in artificial intelligence.

As Steve Lohr explained in his book *Go To: The Story of the Math Majors, Bridge Players, Engineers, Chess Wizards, Maverick Scientists, and Iconoclasts—the Programmers Who Created the Software Revolution*:

> For artificial intelligence, McCarthy needed a programming language that could accommodate symbolic problems as well as numeric problems [FORTRAN could only do the latter]. The language also had to be uncommonly flexible, so that the symbols could be manipulated freely to explore different interfaces, assumptions, and new facts—just as a human might.

To accomplish this feat, "McCarthy chose to structure his language as a series of lists of information that are then processed…. All kinds of 'information about the world' can be represented as lists, which then can be manipulated to make deductions and logical inferences." LISP thrived on *recursive code*—that is, code that called itself—because LISP programs and LISP data were effectively interchangeable. The language was also among the first to automate "housekeeping" tasks like clearing out a computer's memory while a program ran, which is commonly called *garbage collection*.

But LISP was not the first list-processing language; that distinction likely goes to IPL (Information Processing Language), presented by John Clifford Shaw, Allen Newell, and Herbert Simon at the 1956 Dartmouth Summer Research Project on Artificial Intelligence. Early IPL was a machine-dependent language, however, and that machine was the JOHNNIAC (John von Neumann Numerical Integrator and Automatic Computer) built by the RAND Corporation. IPL was used to write a "Logic Theorist" program, designed to mimic the kind of thinking human beings engaged in to prove mathematical theorems—and the program successfully proved some theorems from Russell and Whitehead's three-volume *Principia Mathematica*.

As Lohr observes, though there were other symbolic programming languages that debuted in the 1960s—SNOBOL, COMIT, and FORMAC, for example—none of them, including LISP, would catch on, largely because list processing didn't corner a large market of users like FORTRAN (in science, mathematics, and engineering) or COBOL (in business data processing) did. LISP also looked intimidating, with line after line of code buried in parentheses; worse yet, LISP programs ran in plodding way.

Logo became known as the "turtle language" since its users programmed mathematical instructions to move a "turtle"—either a small robot or a virtual object on a CRT (in effect a cursor, typically in the form of a triangle)—that drew lines in its wake. Mathematics came to life as images were generated via turtle geometry; "[p]rogramming commands or instructions were created for didactic purposes and related to 'the movement,'" as one author of a retrospective on Logo put it. Let's take a look at some example code.

A procedure for drawing a box using an early implementation of the language might take the following form:

```
TO BOX
1 FORWARD 100
```

```
2 RIGHT 90
3 BOX
END
?BOX
```

The question mark (?) followed by BOX executes the procedure, which has the turtle moving forward one hundred units while tracing its path with a pen, then turning ninety degrees and moving forward again, until finally returning to its starting point. (When using a computer-controlled mechanical turtle, the PENDOWN command lowered the device's pen, while PENUP retracted the pen. These same commands also worked to lower and raise the turtle's "metaphorical pen" on the screen.) The coordinate system in which the turtle navigated was relative rather than absolute, meaning that a turtle's movements were based on its current position, not on some variant of the Cartesian coordinate system in which lines were drawn between fixed points.

Consider the following procedure that directed the turtle to draw a hexagon by employing repeated sixty-degree turns:

```
TO HEX
1 FORWARD 100
2 RIGHT 60
3 HEX
END
?HEX
```

Additional flexibility of movement was possible by utilizing the associated BACK and LEFT commands.

Logo could also accept string input from a user and echo it, as the following procedure called AGREE illustrates:

```
TO AGREE
10 PRINT [TYPE SOMETHING YOU LIKE]
20 PRINT (SENTENCE [I LIKE] REQUEST [TOO])
END
?AGREE
TYPE SOMETHING YOU LIKE
>STAR TREK
I LIKE STAR TREK TOO
```

The prompt character (>) above waits for a REQUEST to be keyed in by the user. SENTENCE combines the inputs together into a single list.

The square brackets "indicate that something is to be taken literally as a list," reads an early Logo manual, while "[p]arentheses indicate grouping of inputs." Both of these syntactic conventions betray Logo's LISP roots, since LISP programming is arguably best known for employing parentheses to excess. Note that double quotation marks could be used in place of square brackets, as shown in the following:

```
?PRINT "HELLO
HELLO
```

```
?PRINT [HELLO]
HELLO
```

Arithmetic operations were employed courtesy of infix operators like $+$, $-$, $*$, $/$, and $\backslash$. (The backslash obtained the remainder of integer division.) Consider this statement:

```
?PRINT 4*(5-4)*5
```

After following the traditional order of operations, Logo output 20.

Another type of infix form available to the Logo programmer: conditional expressions comparing two quantities. For example,

```
?PRINT 53 = 53
TRUE
?PRINT 22 > 53
FALSE
```

Conditional expressions using `IF/THEN`, pseudorandom numbers, arrays, and operations to manipulate list structures were also available.

Papert and others at the MIT Artificial Intelligence Laboratory penned a great many "LOGO Memos" in the 1970s and early 1980s that mixed raw Logo code with speculative ideas on child psychology and pedagogy. For instance, one memo detailed how to play and code a robust game of Nim, while another, called "Grammar as a Programming Language," described *generative grammars*—thus directly connecting Logo to linguistics.

Conceptually, Logo was revolutionary, but the language needed to be put through its paces outside of MIT. It needed a proving ground.

In the 1968-69 school year, a small subset of seventh graders attending Muzzey Junior High in Lexington, Massachusetts, were the first to experiment with Logo over an extended period of time. A set of Teletypes (models 33 and 35) were installed in one of the school's classrooms; the Teletypes were connected to a Digital Equipment Corporation PDP-1 Logo-dedicated time-sharing system at BBN. "Much of what went on that year is foundational to Seymour's book, *Mindstorms*," Cynthia Solomon later explained. "The first graphics turtle and a floor turtle were built and running by 1970." Over the next few years, students in elementary schools across Massachusetts, such as a group of fifth graders at the Bridge School in Lexington, would get the full Papert Logo treatment. By 1972, Logo had come into its own, running at MIT on a "PDP-11 with special turtle graphics stations which we showed at a math education conference in Exeter, England," added Solomon.

Papert had finally found the perfect vehicle with which to spread his theory of "constructionism": a computer. With small computers flooding the home market by the late 1970s, the MIT Logo Group (an offshoot of the MIT AI Lab) eventually adapted the language for the Apple II and Texas Instruments TI-99/4, though there were differences in the implementations. "[T]he computer being used to program the child" was the wrong approach, Papert explained. Instead,

> the child programs the computer and, in doing so, both acquires a sense of mastery over a piece of the most modern and powerful technology and establishes an intimate contact with some of the deepest ideas from science, from mathematics, and from the art of intellectual model building.

In 1968, a young Alan Kay visited Papert at the Massachusetts Institute of Technology. Kay had first heard of Papert—and Piaget, for that matter—while attending an education conference in Park City, Utah, delivered by Marvin Minsky, who spoke "about how we think about complex situations and why schools are really bad places to learn these skills," though in the talk Minsky didn't explicitly suggest pairing students with computers in the classroom.

Kay was left breathless by what he saw at MIT: children, on their own, exploring mathematics in an interactive, visually entertaining way. "Here were children doing real programming with a specially designed language and environment," Kay remembered. "As with Simulas leading to OOP [object-oriented programming], this encounter finally hit me with what the destiny of personal computing really was going to be." It was clear as day to Kay: personal computing would not serve as "a personal dynamic vehicle," à la Douglas Engelbart; it would instead be "a personal dynamic medium" that extended from childhood to adulthood. He was taken by Marshall McLuhan's dialectical notion of us shaping our tools and then, in turn, our tools shaping us. (Edsger Dijkstra once said something similar: "The tools we use have a profound and devious influence on our thinking habits, and therefore on our thinking abilities.")

On the flight back home from his visit to MIT, Kay made the first sketches of what became the Dynabook: "a personal computer for children of all ages," as the 1972 proposal read. Referring to Papert, Piaget, and John Dewey repeatedly in the proposal, Kay—then employed at the Xerox Palo Alto Research Center (PARC)—envisioned a future teeming with portable and inexpensive personal computers, each with keyboard and flat screen, that were geared toward children's education and play. The Dynabook, in Kay's drawings, resembled a tablet-sized BlackBerry phone circa 2010; he presented the ideas at an ACM conference in 1972. Kemeny and Kurtz later reflected on the impact of that presentation, writing in *Back to BASIC: The History, Corruption, and Future of the Language* that

> [a]s we entered the decade of the seventies, there was scant warning about the computing revolutions brewing. We settled back to enjoy our new version of BASIC the Sixth. Little did we realize the impact that fancy graphics and structured programming would have by the end of the decade....

> ...We said above that we had no hint of the personal computer revolution about to hit us. Actually, we did have a hint. Some of us had heard Alan Kay's presentation..., in which he described the technical feasibility of a personal computer the size of a notebook, having the power of a large computer, and costing $100....

Kay would go on to pioneer GUIs (graphical user interfaces) at Xerox PARC, which inspired Steve Jobs—who was much less interested in the OOP operating under the hood of the Xerox Alto computer than what the machine was displaying on-screen—to direct his team at Apple to reverse engineer and implement in the Lisa (released in 1983) and the Macintosh (released in 1984).

The genesis of a number of these interfacing-with-computers ideas is often attributed to Douglas Engelbart, who demonstrated them using the NLS, or oN-Line System, in a 1968 talk that would later become known as "The Mother of All Demos." Indeed, Kay attended Engelbart's groundbreaking demonstration. But Kay was also influenced by the Programmed Logic for Automatic Teaching Operations, or PLATO, a networked interactive computerized education system originating at the University of Illinois in the early 1960s. Later versions of PLATO offered plasma touchscreens on terminals and other novel user-interfacing technologies. (For much more on the underreported PLATO story, see chapters 6 and 7 of *A People's History of Computing* as well as 2017's *The Friendly Orange Glow: The Untold Story of the PLATO System and the Dawn of Cyberculture*, which author Brian Dear assembled by stitching together archival research with interviews of still-living participants of PLATO's history.)

"We've got to push computers into schools," Grace Hopper argued in a 1980 interview. "They should be in every school, so kids can grow up with them."

Logo ballooned in popularity throughout the 1980s, finding its way into countless schools. Hundreds of dialects of the language were implemented on many platforms: 8-bit Atari machines, IBM PCs, BBC Micros, TRS-80s.

Kids in the 1980s couldn't avoid Logo, even if they didn't have a home computer, since educational children's television programs highlighted the language. For instance, a number of episodes of *Mr. Wizard's World*, a science-themed show staring Don Herbert, included vignettes with kids explaining their Logo programs to the titular character. In one episode of the series, a "New Frontiers" segment features a child named Jason showing off his knowledge of Logo by writing three programs: one that draws a triangle of a set size, another that creates a triangle with a user-defined side length, and a third that generates a colorful spiral on the screen. Below is the aforementioned second program, which includes a looping structure; notice the abbreviated FORWARD and RIGHT commands as well as the absence of statement numbers:

```
TO TRI :SIDE
REPEAT 3 [FD :SIDE RT 120]
END
```

Passé when watching the television episode now, it was certainly a novel, if not revolutionary, viewing experience when it first aired. (BASIC programs also made appearances on *Mr. Wizard's World*, such as in a "How It Works" segment in which Herbert tested a child's reflexes using a loop-intensive BASIC "stopwatch" program.)

Logo was even being used to program machines built of LEGO; called LEGO/Logo, the product was developed at the MIT Media Lab in the late 1980s. The next decade saw more LEGO-Logo collaborations, such as the Programmable Brick and LEGO Mindstorms. Logo Blocks, made for the Programmable Brick, were a reimagining of Logo, replacing lines of code with on-screen blocks that snapped together. By the early twenty-first century, this block-programming paradigm would find a new home in another MIT Media Lab creation called Scratch, which exposed children to the principles of computation sans the text of the code itself.

Scratch was not the first Visual Programming Language (VPL), though, like all such languages, the Media Lab's product added yet another abstraction layer atop programming a computer, further insulating users from the machine language and hardware running the show underneath—but also reducing the barrier to entry for new programmers even more. VPLs can be traced back to the 1960s, such as with the electronic painting program Sketchpad, running on a transistorized MIT Lincoln Laboratory TX-2 computer and designed by MIT graduate student Ivan Sutherland in 1963. Using the painting program, simple shapes could be drawn and scaled on a screen using a light pen in an early form of CAD (computer-aided design). With Sketchpad, we not only see the earliest incarnations of a graphical user interface—presaging "The Mother of All Demos"—but of object-oriented programming, with discrete lines grouped together as geometric objects for manipulation.

Flowchart-based programming languages like GRAIL (GRAphical Input Language), developed by the RAND Corporation in 1968, allowed users to do more than just draw pictures: now, writing software in a visual manner became possible. By wielding a stylus to sketch on the revolutionary RAND Tablet, a computer program composed of flowcharts could be created, edited, and run, all on a CRT display. What's more, sophisticated handwriting recognition technology not only recognized letters and numbers but symbols and shapes as well.

The flowchart-based language Pygmalion, named for the sculptor in Greek mythology who carved an ivory statue of a woman so beautiful he fell in love with it, further refined these ideas. With Pygmalion, implemented in 1975 using the object-oriented Smalltalk, "Communication between human and computer is by means of visual entities called 'icons,' subsuming the notions of variable, data structure, function and picture. Icons are sketched on the display screen." So said computer scientist David Canfield Smith, who coined the term *icons* while writing his doctoral thesis at Stanford. At PARC, Smith would play a key role in developing the Xerox Star interface, with its icons and dialog boxes and desktop metaphor—all of which were replicated later in Apple's GUIs and Microsoft Windows. (Smith would later partner with Alan Kay to write educational software for children.) "*Pygmalion*," Smith explained, "was an early attempt to change the process of programming from one in which algorithms are described abstractly in a programming language to one in which they are demonstrated concretely to the machine." He continued:

> Its design was based on the observation that for some people blackboards (or whiteboards these days) provide significant aid to communication. If you put two scientists together in a room, there had better be a blackboard in it or they will have trouble communicating. If there is one, they will immediately go to it and begin sketching ideas. Their sketches often contribute as much to the conversation as their words and gestures. Why can't people communicate with computers in the same way?

The icons, shapes, and drag-and-drop nature of the Pygmalion interface are also obvious precursors to the block interface of Scratch, with software like Henry Lieberman's Tinker—a LISP-centric VPL developed at MIT in the early 1990s—bridging the gap between the two.

Lieberman worked with Papert's group at the MIT AI Lab. "Despite Logo's initial success in teaching children techniques of learning and problem solving," Lieberman recalled, "we found that teachers experienced some difficulty introducing Logo to younger children." The difficulty didn't involve using the turtle, which kids learned to move with ease. Rather, the "trouble came when the teachers tried to introduce the notion of procedures." Consider the following code:

```
To Triangle
Repeat 3 (Forward 100 Right 120)
End
```

Lieberman detailed why students were confused by this procedure:

> But when the student types Forward 100 this time, the turtle doesn't move! Why not?! Was something wrong with the computer, the student wondered? The teacher then had to patiently explain that the computer was just remembering that it was supposed to do the Forward 100 as part of the Triangle procedure, and you couldn't actually get it to do anything until you finished the procedure (with End) and called it by typing Triangle. But this explanation seemed very abstract to a beginner, who was just trying to learn the concept of a procedure.

> Furthermore, it seemed to require that you type everything twice! Once you performed the turtle commands that drew a triangle on the screen, why did you have to type those commands all over again just to have the computer remember them to make a Triangle procedure?

To help bridge the conceptual divide, in 1971 Cynthia Solomon wrote Instant Turtle, an interface that packaged a procedure into a set of turtle commands which could be accessed instantly in code via the command Teach. In essence, the Instant Turtle was among the first "macro recorders," Lieberman claimed, and served as inspiration for Tinker.

Once desktop computers offered enough processing power, VPLs proliferated, with languages like 1995's CUBE—which offered a three-dimensional syntax—being merely the tip of the iceberg.

Though nascent VPLs were around when Papert was conceiving of Logo, they weren't yet a viable alternative to text-based coding on the underpowered microcomputers of the day, machines which by and large offered BASIC. So why didn't Papert adopt BASIC as his educational language for children? In his 1980 book *Mindstorms: Children, Computers, and Powerful Ideas*, he offers a number of trenchant criticisms of the Beginner's All-purpose Symbolic Instruction Code. For one thing, BASIC did not encourage the sort of deep thinking that Logo engendered. "[E]ven when children are taught by a parent, a peer, or a professional teacher to write simple programs in a language like BASIC," explains Papert, "this activity is not accompanied at all by the kind of epistemological reflection that we see in the LOGO environments." BASIC was the default language employed by educators not because it was the best language with which to learn programming per se, but because of historical reasons—akin to the QWERTY keyboard that, in retrospect, offered a suboptimal arrangement of letters which nonetheless quickly attained ironclad dominance. "[P]ast choices can often haunt us. There is a tendency for the first usable, but still primitive, product of a new technology to dig itself in. I have called this phenomenon the QWERTY phenomenon."

What's more, as personal computers became cheaper and more accessible, BASIC, which may indeed have been one of the few viable options with the "primitive technology" of the past, nonetheless continued to be taught in high schools—despite the more robust hardware available, "despite the existence of other computer languages that are demonstrably easier to learn and are richer in the intellectual benefits that come from learning them." Papert argues that justification of the status quo was a strain of "conservatism" that paradoxically plagued a computer revolution still in its infancy.

Though BASIC boasted few keywords, that didn't necessarily imply it was an easy language to learn, let alone master. Which brings us to Papert's definition of computer literacy, which expanded upon both Perlis's and Kemeny's. Even if we ask ourselves to "think like a computer," we do not leave our other modes of thinking—our other ways of understanding the world—at the door. "This phrase"—*computer literacy*—"is often taken as meaning knowing how to program, or knowing about the varied uses made of computers. But true computer literacy is not just knowing how to make use of computers and computational ideas. It is knowing when it is appropriate to do so."

Papert wasn't a fan of BASIC, and told his readers as much. But what did Kemeny and Kurtz think of Logo?

In *Back to BASIC*, published in 1985, Kemeny and Kurtz devoted a chapter to comparing their then-new structured implementation of Dartmouth BASIC called True BASIC to a number of other languages—including FORTRAN, COBOL, Pascal, and Ada—invariably finding them wanting. For instance, FORTRAN was a terrible language for the beginning programmer, they claimed, largely because of its "ugly" features and syntax. Take the DO loop, for example. Consider this FORTRAN code snippet:

```
    DO 10 I = 1,3
       N = N + 1
 10 CONTINUE
```

The equivalent True BASIC code is as follows:

```
    FOR i = 1 to 3
       LET n = n + 1
    NEXT i
```

"It is sobering to realize that typing a single wrong character can cause that FORTRAN loop to be changed completely, while still remaining legal," sometimes with catastrophic consequences, they claimed. "In fact, just a single typing error caused the destruction of an unmanned satellite several years ago—the programmer accidently typed a period instead of a comma in the first line." Though Kemeny and Kurtz are surely referring to the NASA Mariner 1 spacecraft, which did indeed explode (it was purposely destroyed 293 seconds into its flight because the rocket wasn't properly responding to guidance instructions), the supposed cause of the malfunction—that of a misplaced comma in a FORTRAN DO loop—is almost certainly untrue, though this apocryphal story circulated widely and found its way into numerous textbooks, tarring FORTRAN's reputation.

They level a more valid criticism of FORTRAN with respect to its memory management, however. Because it was "invented in the prehistoric 1950s," when computers were costly and slow, the FORTRAN compiler that John Backus and his team at IBM developed had to be as efficient as possible, generating object code that could execute relatively quickly. To save time, the compiler didn't check to ensure that array subscripts stayed within bounds. Which could wreak havoc unbeknownst to the programmer with code like this:

```
    DIMENSION X(10)
    DO 10 I = 1,50
       X(I) = 22.53
 10 CONTINUE
```

The number 22.53 was stored in fifty different memory locations, but only ten of them had been set aside for the X array. Where were the other forty numbers stored? That was a mystery. Code the equivalent snippet in True BASIC,

```
    DIM X(10)
    FOR i = 1 to 50
        LET X(i) = 22.53
    NEXT i
```

and the compiler's error-checking routine would generate a "subscript out of bounds" message.

A portion of the same *Back to BASIC* chapter also critically examined Logo, then "one of the most highly touted languages for schools." But most of Kemeny and Kurtz's criticisms of Logo fell flat; they had used up their venom on easier targets like FORTRAN and COBOL. While praising the language's graphics capabilities and ease of use, especially for the lower elementary set, they argued that True BASIC's absolute graphics—i.e., a Cartesian-like coordinate system overlaid onto the screen—rendered it more naturally suited for mathematical graphing applications like plotting curves of functions.

Furthermore, despite its facilities with "list structures," Logo was limited when it came to dealing with strings and fractional numbers (some versions of the language couldn't handle either). Unlike BASIC, there was no ELSE statement in many dialects of Logo, which led to added complexity when coding certain algorithms requiring conditionals. Ultimately, though, Kemeny and Kurtz gave Logo its due: "What LOGO does, it does very well; namely, it gives beginning students an extremely simple language for learning the concepts of programming, including recursion, through plotting."

A singular event upended both the political and technological landscape in the United States in the twentieth century: the successful launch of *Sputnik*, the first artificial satellite, by the Soviet Union in 1957. Young people rushed to major in mathematics and science in the wake of the 1958 National Defense Education Act, which dramatically ramped up federal funding for education. The U.S. government shifted funding priorities for scientific research as well, including deploying the complex SAGE (Semi-Automatic Ground Environment) air-defense system, powered by Whirlwind computers, during the early years of the Cold War.

By the 1980s, moral panic had set in that American children were lagging behind their international counterparts; this fear was stoked especially by the 1983 U.S. Department of Education report *A Nation at Risk: The Imperative for Educational Reform*. "Our Nation is at risk," the report warns readers. "Our once unchallenged preeminence in commerce, industry, science, and technological innovation is being overtaken by competitors throughout the world." The report recommended one-half a year instruction in computer science in all high schools, for these reasons: "The teaching of computer science in high school should equip graduates to: (a) understand the computer as an information, computation, and communication device; (b) use the computer in the study of the other Basics and for personal and work-related purposes; and (c) understand the world of computers, electronics, and related technologies."

To make high school computer science a reality, American schools needed thousands of computers. A year before *A Nation at Risk* was released, albeit with its ideas percolating in the ether, Steve Jobs reached out to his state representative, Pete Stark, to help push an initiative called "Kids Can't Wait" that ensured every school had a computer (Apple Computer was pushing the Apple II at the time). Stark in turn drafted HR 5573, the Computer Equipment Contribution Act, but the bill died in Congress despite Jobs's personal lobbying efforts.

Nonetheless, Apple donated its computers to nine thousand elementary and secondary schools in California. Although the computer giveaway seemed a natural avenue toward teaching Logo to young people, it instead proved emblematic to the problems inherent in scaling Papert's creation. Training sessions for teachers on using the new machines were spotty and inconsistent. An issue of *InfoWorld* from 1983 enumerated the problems: a "[fear] that teachers who have inadequate computer training will just 'give out so many recipes' on how to use [Apple] Logo to students…. [T]he Logo instruction at many ill-prepared schools will be 'superficial.'" Though the push for teaching Logo in U.S. schools was a means of "preparing the next generation to fight in the Cold War," researcher Annette Vee notes, thanks to inconsistencies in teacher training (among other issues), Logo initiatives did not catch fire and soon disappeared from elementary schools.

"[A]lmost as soon as computers arrived on college campuses in the United States, computer programming was proposed as a burgeoning literacy akin to reading and writing," asserts Vee. This "coding for everyone" movement bore resemblance to the mass literacy project which, though sometimes subservient to "larger projects of cultural homogenization, like 'Americanization' in the early twentieth century," still resulted in wildly successful outcomes—especially in industrialized countries like the U.S., with literacy rates near one hundred percent and literacy, in and of itself, treated as a "moral good."

But this new form computer literacy didn't necessarily entail teaching coding, such as in BASIC or Logo. Rather, a shift to the code-free visual abstractions of VPLs was part and parcel of a change that had swept through computing and redefined what computing literacy entailed. Essentially, being able to program a computer using a traditional high-level language was no longer a prerequisite of computer literacy. "[T]here's a reason why [BASIC] isn't taught in schools anymore," argues Tim Danton in his expansive history *The Computers That Made Britain* (2021). "[I]f you want to teach young children the principles of good programming, the visual, block-based language of Scratch is a far better starting point. Once children become more adept, or simply older, Python is now a common choice due to its easy-to-understand syntax."

By the late 1980s or early 1990s, personal computers, boasting GUIs and mouse controls, coupled with "the commercial software era [and] severed computer programming from computer usage," Vee observes.

> Because people no longer needed to know how to program in order to use computers, the idea of computer literacy came to mean knowledge of file structures, saving work to disks, and menu operations.... This utilitarian and skills-based idea of computer literacy stripped it of the optimism associated with earlier initiatives.

Think of the computer scientist Alan Kay, who helped pioneer GUIs at Xerox PARC. In 1972, a "typical PARC hallway bullsession" (Kay's words) found Kay, Ted Kaehler, and Dan Ingalls debating programming languages. During the conversation, the idea of power came up, leading them all to wonder: What was the minimum size of a language that would nonetheless have great power? Kay thought of John McCarthy's "self-describing LISP interpreter"—its definition took up only about a page, he recalled—and resolved that he could accomplish the same feat, but this time with an object-oriented language. Kay confidently told them that the "most powerful language in the world" could be defined in only "a page of code." Kaehler and Ingalls retorted, "Put up or shut up."

So, Kay went to work. For the next two weeks, he arrived at PARC before dawn, at four o'clock, and plugged away at the problem until eight, when the morning rush of work intervened. Leveraging ideas he had formulated when writing his master's thesis at the University of Utah on the FLEX system—a "flexible extended language" that "merged 'hardware' and 'software' that is optimized toward handing algorithmic operations in an interactive, man-machine dialog"—Kay nonetheless ran into some trouble early in the process, as he documented in the article "The Early History of Smalltalk" (1993):

> It turned out to be more difficult than I had first thought for three reasons. First, I wanted the program to be more like McCarthy's second non-recursive interpreter—the one implemented as a loop that tried to resemble the original [IBM] 709 implementation of Steve Russell as much as possible. It was more "real". Second, the intertwining of the "parsing" with message receipt—the evaluation of parameters which was handled separately in LISP—required that my object-oriented interpreter re-enter itself "sooner" (in fact, much sooner) than LISP required. And, finally, I was still not clear how send and receive should work with each other.

The first couple versions of his language, called Smalltalk, that Kay presented to the group were roundly shot down. By the eighth morning, though, Kay appeared to have solved the problem: "symbols were byte-coded and the receiving of return of return-values from a send was symmetric," he recalled.

But Kay hadn't actually *implemented* Smalltalk; rather, he had just defined it on paper. "I had gone to considerable pains to avoid doing any 'real work' for the bet," he explained, "but I felt I had proved my point. This had been an interesting holiday from our official 'iconic programming' pursuits, and I thought that would be the end of it." Kay was blindsided only several days later, however, when Dan Ingalls showed him a working version of Smalltalk. Ingalls had done more than just coded from Kay's blueprint—he added a list maker, a token scanner, and some other additional features. "Dan loved to bootstrap on a system that 'always ran,' and over the next ten years he made at least 80 major releases of various flavors of Smalltalk," recalled Kay. But how did he implement that first version so quickly?

Ingalls implemented Smalltalk using Data General's Extended BASIC (derived from Dartmouth BASIC) running under DG's Advanced Operating System (AOS) on an in-house Data General Nova 16-bit minicomputer. Which is why in the book *Coders at Work: Reflections on the Craft of Programming* (2009), author Peter Seibel writes, "If Alan Kay is Smalltalk's father, Dan Ingalls is its mother—Smalltalk may have started as a gleam in Alan Kay's eye, but Ingalls is the one who did the hard work of bringing it into the world." In the book, Seibel asks Ingalls to recount the early history: "You've famously been involved in five or seven or however many generations of Smalltalk implementations. Let's start with the first Smalltalk that you did in BASIC. You have a couple pages of notes from Alan Kay that you had to make real. What did you do?" Ingalls responded:

> I just started typing in code. I think the first thing was to validate the execution model. There were just a couple of basic structures that were needed, the equivalent of a stack frame. So I just made, it must have been an array, in BASIC, to do that and put together enough that would execute a piece of code.

> …I remember the first thing we got to run was six factorial [6! = 6 × 5 × 4 × 3 × 2 × 1 = 720]. It's a really simple example but it involves the process of dynamic lookup and creating new stack frames. And then once you've got that working, you come to understand how things are going to go and you find out what's difficult.

Ingalls called this technique "breadboarding"—"just do[ing] what you need to do to put a structure in place that's the structure you think you're doing to want to interpret and then try to make it work."

Once Ingalls had the BASIC "primordial Smalltalk" (Seibel's term) up and running, he next turned his attention to coding a version for the Nova using assembly language. Around that time, the Xerox Alto was being built, which would feature an operating system based around a graphical user interface.

When Steve Jobs visited Xerox PARC in late 1979, he was shown Smalltalk on the Alto as well as the GUI (with its desktop metaphor) and mouse control that interfaced with it. Jobs, greatly inspired by some of what he saw, ordered his engineers to recreate the GUI experience at Apple, and Bill Gates, at Microsoft, fashioned Windows in the image of the Apple GUIs. By the 1990s, people were interfacing with computers running point-and-click GUIs, further insulating average users from the underlying operations of the machine—and changing what it meant to be "literate" with a computer.

Upon reflection, an irony is apparent: If GUIs rendered BASIC superfluous by re-branding computer literacy, then, at least in a small way, BASIC sowed the seeds of its own demise—since primordial Smalltalk was first implemented using BASIC. Al-though, it must be added, Ingalls didn't *have* to use BASIC on the Nova to bring Kay's first definition of Smalltalk to life; he didn't even have to use a Nova to do it. Both the minicomputer and BASIC were readily available at Xerox PARC, so Ingalls used them—it was all rather incidental to the task at hand.

By the 2000s, the teaching of BASIC programming in U.S. schools was all but dead. But that didn't sit well with everybody.

In 2006, science fiction writer David Brin published an essay for the online magazine *Salon* called "Why Johnny Can't Code"—the title alludes to Rudolf Flesch's 1955 book *Why Johnny Can't Read*, thus implicitly connecting coding to literacy—lamenting the de-clining popularity of BASIC. An imperfect language to be sure, BASIC nonetheless "liberated several million bright minds to poke and explore and aspire as never before," Brin wrote.

> BASIC was close enough to the algorithm that you could actually follow the reasoning of the machine as it made choices and followed logical pathways. Repeating this point for emphasis: You could even do it all yourself, following along on paper, for a few it-erations, verifying that the dot on the screen was moving by the sheer power of math-ematics, alone. Wow!

In those grand old days of truly personal computing, youth curious about BASIC didn't have to look far to encounter lines of code in the language. BASIC educational books, such as Donald Alcock's *Illustrating BASIC* (1978)—with its bold cartoon style and informal manner ("…I would only remark that a careful reader might diagnose a severe astigmatism in my eye and a persistent shake in my hand," we read in the Pref-ace)—proliferated in North America, in Europe, and even across the Iron Curtain. The Elektronika MK-90, an LCD pocket computer with BASIC built in, was a product of the USSR. And a BASIC book published in Russian, its title loosely translated to English as *Make Friends With Me, Computer!*, was geared toward children.

In the 1980s through the early '90s, high school students couldn't avoid encountering lines of BASIC even if they tried, since mathematics and science textbooks of the time often included type-in "TRY IT IN BASIC" programs that enriched math lessons with a helping of programming. For example, flip through the pages of the multi-edition 1990s textbook *Algebra 2 and Trigonometry*, published by McDougal Littell/Houghton Mifflin, and you were treated to BASIC programs simulating the handshake problem; calculating best-fit lines (using the least-squares method); evaluating a polynomial $P(x)$ at a given value of x; and outputting ordered pairs for polynomial functions. Variants of these same programs could have, and probably were, written for Dartmouth classes nearly three decades earlier. If we set aside certain contextual elements of application problems in *Algebra 2 and Trigonometry*, such as predictions for population growth "by the year 2000" and references to technology (e.g., audiotapes and compact disks), the presentation of the mathematical content is effectively indistinguishable from similar math books three decades later—save for the absence of BASIC listings.

Textbook type-ins were writ-small examples of widely circulated BASIC type-in "cookbooks," of which Ahl's *101 BASIC Computer Games*, *BASIC Computer Games*, and *More Basic Computer Games* were progenitors. Restricting our attention only to the Tandy Radio Shack TRS-80, for example, we find dozens of books containing BASIC type-ins that were published either specifically for the TRS-80 or could, perhaps with a few modifications to the code, work on the machine. Ira Goldklang, who runs TRS-80.com, the most comprehensive site on the internet devoted to all things TRS-80, lists these BASIC books, some intended for business use, others for pleasure—like *222 BASIC Computer Programs for Home School & Office* (1984), *30 Computer Programs for the Homeowner in BASIC* (1982), *55 Advanced Computer Programs in BASIC* (1981), *BASIC Programs for Scientists* (1981), *57 Practical Programs and Games in BASIC* (1978), *Announcing Computer Games for Business School and Home* (1980), *BASIC Fun with Adventure Games* (1984), *Writing BASIC Adventure Programs for the TRS-80* (1982), *24 Tested Ready-To-Run Game Programs in BASIC* (1978), *70 Programmes BASIC TRS-80 I and III* (1981), and *Basic BASIC* (1978).

There were even *actual* cookbooks featuring BASIC, of which 1984's *Computer Programs for the Kitchen* by Terence F. Dicker and published by Tab Books is the best example. Sporting the discordant cover photograph of a multi-course table spread topped off by a prototypical Apple microcomputer (complete with monitor and disk drive) being lightly caressed by Chef Dicker, the first half of the book—promising "[e]xciting ways to ease kitchen and cooking chores with a personal computer!" and explaining that "[t]he role of food in the information age will be no less decisive than it has been in past ages"—serves as an introduction to computers, including a short history, and a tutorial of programming in BASIC, albeit with cooking-themed examples such as how to build a culinary database. The second half of the text reads more like a traditional cookbook, with enough recipes and bite-sized edible delights to open a restaurant. Note that back in 1978, Tab Books published *The BASIC Cookbook*, a dictionary of

BASIC commands that leaned into the cooking/recipe theme but was not a literal cookbook.

A subset of BASIC type-in books were departures from mere thematic collections of programs; rather, they were more properly described as storybooks or novelizations containing code listings. By typing in and running BASIC programs presented at various points in the story, more of the plot would unfold for the reader. Prototypical examples include the *Computer Storybooks* series by Stuart and Donna Paltrowitz and the *Micro Adventure* series published by Scholastic. Such type-in storybooks certainly linked literacy with coding, BASIC style.

For instance, open up *The Science Fiction Computer Storybook* (1983) to feast on twenty short stories, one per chapter, that each contain several BASIC type-ins designed to reveal critical information and excite the imagination. The stories are written in first person, with the reader doubling as the protagonist. One chapter, titled "The Beating Heart," has the protagonist steal a "piece of gleaming jewelry outside a basement window ledge" that is "heart shaped and studded with real gems." But the jewel is clearly haunted, as the reader quickly discovers: no matter where it is hidden, the protagonist's heart beats louder and louder, in a deafening cacophony, until, finally, the jewel is returned and its secret revealed.

> Immediately the pounding in your chest stops and you breathe a sigh of relief. Now that you are calmer, you notice that there are letters engraved in the window ledge. They look as if they have been there for a long time. You examine them closely and run your fingers over each letter. Type in the program to find out what the words say. Then go back to the story.

By keying in the included BASIC program—which uses inverse (also called reverse) lettering, producing a black background surrounding each character, like this: **THE CURSE**—"the curse" of the jewel is revealed on-screen: "Blessed you will be if you admire my stones, but if you steal my heart I will pound your bones." Now it makes sense why the heart jewel wasn't stolen, despite it being left out in the open.

The tale concludes with an old woman appearing at the window. "You may take it home if you want to," she says, but the protagonist backs away. "I always offer it," she continues, "but for some strange reason, even in our modern world, people believe the ancient curse." The protagonist hurries home, anxious for a peaceful night's sleep.

Like the industry of type-in books that effectively disappeared overnight, the "TRY IT IN BASIC" programs found in school textbooks might as well be ancient history. As Brin observes, "a bright kid doesn't need to actually do it"—"it" being exploring the abstraction layers of coding, from machine to assembly to HLL programming—"in order to be computer-literate." Computers had become black boxes, even if they were beige on the outside.

Thirteen years later, Brin wrote a follow-up essay on the topic called "Johnny…Janie and Jamal Still Can't Code…Though Ivan Can." Unlike "Why Johnny Can't Code," this new piece reads more like it was written during the height of the Cold War. "Are we in the West—and especially the U.S.—losing our ability to innovate or command the central technology of our era?" he begins. "The news seems filled with stories about fiendishly clever Russian hackers and tricks embedded in Chinese hardware, while Silicon Valley firms desperately seek immigration waivers to import foreign coders, because young Americans appear generally clueless about skills that we invented."

A key theme of Brin's *Salon* essay—that the disappearance of type-ins in textbooks took away a key source of programming exposure for students (and especially for his son, Ben, then in the fifth grade, whose curiosity about programming wasn't easily sated)—is the central focus of the newer essay, posted on his *Contrary Brin* blog.

Brin expresses a nagging frustration: that despite the trivial memory requirements involved with including programming languages on desktop computers or personal devices (such as smartphones), it is not a standard practice of manufacturers. Nor is it standard practice for textbook publishers to include short programs, those "turn-key, simple, introductory exercises that teachers [could] assign, luring millions of youths into trying their hands at programming." He proposes that the big computer manufacturers like Apple, Dell, IBM, and Microsoft agree on including a set of *"five very simple, introductory programming languages* [his italics, in the quotations both here and in the paragraph below]" in their operating systems, and then coordinate with textbook publishers and teachers—in essence, recreating the state of affairs in the 1980s, which was a kind of "Goldilocks Zone" for BASIC (and Logo), albeit with more programming language options. That way, coding assignments could escape the confines of computer science courses and appear in mathematics, biology, statistics, and chemistry classes as well. He suggests Python, BASIC, or even Squeak—an open-source dialect of Smalltalk—as candidates for programming novices to sharpen their skills.

Brin notes that unlike decades ago, when there was "shared *lingua franca* introductory language" (i.e., BASIC or Logo), no such standard exists today; few of our devices arrive with introductory programming languages preinstalled, ready to use right out of the box. Compounding the problem, the "bewildering array of languages, variations, implementations and instructions has left only *truly dedicated young people* able and willing to plow ahead." While this lack of standardization permits entities in the technology field to remain nimble and creative, it is that same lack of standardization, along with the ever-changing currents and eddies in tech, that led publishers to realize that textbook type-ins might become outdated quickly. Thus, an avenue exposing students to BASIC or another introductory language simply no longer exists—and doesn't look to be resurrected any time soon.

AN INTERLUDE:
BASIC CONTESTS, BASIC POETRY, AND A "NEW BASIC"

That sense of experimentation and play with the BASIC programming language David Brin wistfully described in his two essays perhaps reached its fullest flowering in the BASIC contests of the 1980s, which often took the form of single-line programs called *one-liners* that users submitted to magazines like the Commodore-centric *RUN*. When the following line of code was executed on the Commodore 64,

```
10 PRINT CHR$(205.5+RND(1)); : GOTO 10
```

a maze-like pattern of characters was generated on-screen. Partly thanks to the MIT Press anthology of the same name—indeed, the book leans in to the concept, devoting a whole chapter to one-liners—the **10 PRINT** line has arguably become the quintessential example of a BASIC one-liner program.

Kenneth Iverson's compact high-level language APL (A Programming Language), implemented at IBM in 1960, offered the earliest examples of one-line programs, although not in the same form they would later take in BASIC. "In APL there is no limit on the length of a line," reads *10 PRINT*, "[so] anything that a programmer can express as a single statement counts."

Microcomputer magazines of the 1980s offered efficient examples of single lines of BASIC code. Consider the article "Tl BASIC One-Liners" by Michael A. Covington, found in the May 1983 issue of *Compute!* Mathematically-oriented ways of employing the **DEF** statement to great effect on the Texas Instruments TI-99/4 home computer were explored. For example, the function

```
DEF DEG(X) = X*57.29577951
```

converted radians to degrees ($180 \div \pi \approx 57.29577951$), while the function

```
DEF ROU(X) = INT(((10^N)*X) + 0.5)/ 10^N)
```

rounded a number to *n* decimal places.

BASIC code printed in *Compute!* and *Compute!'s Gazette* often included a checksum value appended to the end of each line, like this:

```
40 READ CS:IF CS<>SUM THEN 90     :rem 120
```

Magazine readers were instructed not to type in the **rem** statement with its associated checksum value. As each line of a BASIC program was entered, BASIC software called the Automatic Proofreader displayed a checksum at the top of the screen. These checksums helped safeguard against transcription errors as programs made the leap from glossy magazine page to glowing CRT screen.

The Automatic Proofreader listing was printed in the magazine. Readers had to save the Proofreader to tape or disk after *very carefully* keying it in—the utility couldn't check itself, after all—and then run it prior to typing a BASIC listing, at which point the Proofreader would be **POKE**d into memory and activated.

The earliest versions of the Automatic Proofreader couldn't catch every transcription error. To understand why, let us explore how the program worked. The checksum on a line equaled the sum of the ASCII codes (in decimal) of the individual characters on that line, including the line number but not accounting for any whitespace; the maximum value of the resultant ASCII sum was 255, since the addition took place using eight bits. (The decimal number 255 = 11111111 in binary, with no larger number possible using eight bits; sums exceeding 255 simply reset back to 0 decimal = 00000000 binary. Think of 8-bit arithmetic as the equivalent of performing operations using the hour labels on an analog clock, but with the hours marked from 0 to 255 instead of 1 to 12. Suppose the hour hand is pointing to 150 on our modified clock. Three hundred hours from now, the hour hand will point to 194, since $150 + 300 = 450$, which is the equivalent of 194 "o'clock.") For example, for the following line of code,

```
60 NEXT
```

the checksum is 165, since

6 = ASCII code 54
0 = ASCII code 48
N = ASCII code 78
E = ASCII code 69
X = ASCII code 88
T = ASCII code 84

and $54 + 48 + 78 + 69 + 88 + 84 = 421$. Sums exceeding 255 are not possible in eight-bit arithmetic, so, to find the checksum value, we take 421 modulo 256, which finds the remainder when 421 is divided by 256. The answer is 165—the checksum value.

Typing in the entire line of code *including* the checksum value, as shown below,

```
60 NEXT     :rem 165
```

would result in the Automatic Proofreader displaying a checksum differing from 165, thereby defeating the purpose of the utility.

In addition, the Proofreader would not catch the transposition of characters; typing in

```
60 NXET
```

would still result in a checksum value of 165.

And since the Proofreader did not check for tokens, only for characters, using an abbreviation like **?** in place of a statement like **PRINT** would throw off the checksum calculation.

The checksum utility was first made available for the Commodore VIC-20 and Commodore 64; eventually, versions for Atari, Apple, and IBM PC computers became available. Instead of numbers, the Atari Proofreader used two checksum letters corresponding to the left and right half-bytes added to 33. The following is a sample line of Atari code from the magazine that shows the checksum.

```
CG 1450 IF K=24 THEN PRINT ANIM=4:RETURN
```

For its part, the IBM PC Proofer could catch transposition and spacing errors, too.

In 1986, *Compute!'s Gazette* introduced the New Automatic Proofreader for the 8-bit Commodore family, one that finally caught errors of transcription and also took into account the spacing between quotation marks for string literals.

As Nate Anderson noted in a recent article about type-ins for *Ars Technica, Compute!* urged people to subscribe to the magazine by using full-page advertisements that boasted, "Get up to 30 new programs and games for less than 15 cents each—every month in *COMPUTE!*" The tradeoff involved "[s]aving money by spending time," explained Anderson, who, as a child, pecked away on an Atari 600XL. But as software grew ever more complex, the cost of physical storage media like floppy disks decreased, and people found themselves more willing to shell out cash for code, the writing was on the wall: In May 1988, the magazine stopped including type-in programs, and a *Compute!*-ing era came to an end.

The "Magic" section of *RUN* encouraged reader participation. Likewise, open up an issue of the TRS-80 Color Computer-specific *The Rainbow* magazine, and winning entries for the monthly one-liner contests—expanded to a two-line option by 1986—filled its pages. The specifications for these CoCo programs were as follows:

> The program must work in Extended BASIC, have only one or two line numbers and be entirely self-contained—no loading other programs, no calling ROM routines, no poked-in machine language code. The program has to run when typed in directly (since that's how our readers will use it). Make sure your line, or lines, aren't packed so tightly that the program won't list completely. Finally, any instructions needed should be *very* short.

> Send your entry (preferably on cassette) to:

> THE RAINBOW One-Liner Contest
> P.O. Box 385
> Prospect, KY 40059

No machine code was permitted, but **POKE**s and other hardware-dependent Color BASIC commands were allowed, even encouraged. To that end, take a look at this single-line entry, courtesy of Lonnie McClusky from Toney, Alabama, and printed in the August 1986 issue (the formatting below is identical to that shown in the magazine):

```
0 POKE65495,0:CLS0:A=1248:B=9:C=
128:FORT=0TOA*A:POKE1472+RND(30)
,96:D=2-RND(3):FORS=0TO4:B=B+D:B
=B-(B=0)+(B=19):POKER,C:R=JOYSTK
(0)/2+A:PRINTSTRING$(B," ")STRIN
G$(13,CHR$(C)):IFPEEK(R)=C THENP
OKER,86:NEXTS,T ELSECLS4:PRINT"T
IME="T;PLAY"O1L3G2":RUN
```

When run, the player used a joystick to navigate an obstacle course. "For this winning one-liner contest entry," we read in the magazine, "the author has been sent copies of both *The Rainbow Book of Simulations* and its companion *The Rainbow Simulations Tape*."

Mike Cooney of Mansfield, Ohio, submitted a winning two-liner program, printed in the September 1986 issue, that used CoCo high-resolution graphics commands to simulate a horse race.

```
0 POKE65495,0:DIMH(20,20):PMODE3
,1:PCLS:DRAW"BM100,99U8R10U6R8D4
L2D10L4U3L8D3L4":GET(90,83)-(121
,101),H,G:PCLS:SCREEN1,0:FORX=1T
O191STEP27:PUT(0,X)-(31,X+18),H,
PSET:U=U+1:P(U)=X:NEXTX:DRAW"C3"
:LINE(240,0)-(255,191),PSET,BF:E
XEC44539:PLAY"O3L18CL4F"
1 FORX=1TO7:M(X)=M(X)+RND(10):PU
T(M(X)),P(X))-(M(X)+31,P(X)+18),H
,PSET:IFPPOINT(M(X)+33,P(X)+9)<>
1THENPLAY"O3L115CDDEFFGAAB":FORT
=1TO10:PUT(M(X)),P(X))-(M(X)+31,P
(X)+18),H,PRESET:PUT(M(X),P(X))-
(M(X)+31,P(X)+18),H,PSET:NEXTT:E
XEC44539:RUNELSENEXTX:GOTO1
```

Both of these winning programs, top to bottom, were deeply antithetical to Kemeny and Kurtz's vision of programming well in BASIC, since they contained multiple statements on one line; machine-dependent commands; arguments for **RND** functions—the list goes on. In a roundabout way, the authors of *10 PRINT* agreed with the critiques of these compact programs that (presumably) would have been levied by Kemeny and Kurtz. "Computers, such as those in the Atari and Apple series," the *10 PRINT* authors wrote, "had BASIC multimedia commands (**COLOR**, **GR**, **PLOT**, **HLIN**, **PSET**, to name a few) to access their platform hardware, and could be said to have led to more impressive one-liners that were not possible on the Commodore computers—something that only increased the value of the most impressive Commodore one-liners, including **10 PRINT**."

A much more intelligible—and presumably less offensive to Kemeny and Kurtz's sensibilities—one-liner contest winner appeared in the September 1986 issue of *The Rainbow*:

```
0 CLS:INPUT"ENTER # OF GRADES TO
BE ENTERED";N:FORX=1TON:INPUT"EN
TER GRADES";G:S=S+G:NEXTX:A=S/N
:PRINT"NUMBER OF GRADES"N:PRINT
"TOTAL POINTS"S:PRINT"AVERAGE"A
```

Submitted by Tom Baylie of Chicago, Illinois, this utilitarian program averaged any number of grades the user cared to key in and was, for the most part, platform-independent.

Fast forward to the 2010s. With the explosion in retrocomputing spurred by mailing lists, BBSs, online forums, eBay, and the internet in general, BASIC contests rose again—most notably, with the BASIC 10 Liner Contest.

Run by the Eider-Treene-School in Friedrichstadt, Germany, programs for the 10 Liner Contest were restricted to 8-bit computers and line-oriented BASIC dialects (albeit "[o]nly BASIC variants that were originally installed in the computer system," we learn in the rules). Since the judges didn't necessarily have access to all possible platforms on which to judge the contest entries, it also had to be possible to emulate the computer hardware.

There were four categories to which users could submit:

- PUR-80: "Program a game in 10 lines (max. 80 characters per logical line, abbreviations are allowed)"
- PUR-120: "Program a game in 10 lines (max. 120 characters per logical line, abbreviations are allowed)"
- EXTREM-256: "Program a game in 10 lines (max. 256 characters per logical line, abbreviations are allowed)"
- SHOW: "Program a program in 10 lines (max. 256 characters per logical line, abbreviations are allowed); the program can be a demo, a tool or an application program"

There were several additional requirements: data or program parts could not be reloaded; no machine code was permitted; code had to be completely visible in the program listing, with no self-modifying code or hidden initializations; and compiling the program was acceptable, as was **POKE**-ing to storage locations.

Calling for entries once per year, the popular contest began in 2010. Back then, it was a humble effort: a mere half-dozen people organizing a small, live BASIC programming competition at the NOMAM (Not Only Marvelous Atari Machinery) event held in Schleswig-Holstein, Germany, where the town of Friedrichstadt is located. Known at first only to the ABBUC—the Atari Bit Byter User Club—the competition expanded to Atari users worldwide and then, finally, to programmers of all 8-bit systems in every corner of the globe.

Rather than stuffing as much as functionality possible into only a few lines of BASIC, and thereby exploiting the worst unstructured tendencies of the language, another online BASIC contest requires programs be written in as structured a manner as possible: without **GOTO**s littering the listings, and instead employing **GOSUB**s and **RETURN**s (with **RETURN**s only allowed as the final line of subroutines). Called the Pascalated BASIC Contest—the title obviously tips its hat to the language that helped sweep BASIC out of the classroom, with "Pascalated BASIC" being a structured style of BASIC taking its cues from Pascal—and inspired by the release of the structured NextBASIC for the modern ZX Spectrum Next 8-bit home computer, the contest offers two categories for submissions: games and "everything else," with entries permitted in either English or Portuguese.

Writing BASIC code for contests was more art than science. But writing poetry using BASIC? Now that was pure art.

In 1984, Canadian poet Barrie Phillip Nichol, better known as bpNichol, penned a dozen poems using Applesoft BASIC running on an Apple IIe. Taking nearly a year and a half to program, and packaged together as *First Screening: Computer Poems*, the twelve poems were distributed by the imprint Underwhich on 5¼-inch floppy disks with a limited run of one hundred signed and numbered copies. Unlike traditional poems, however, bpNichol's were dynamic, kinetic works, each featuring only a handful of words being shifted, manipulated, permuted, or repeated on-screen. For example, the poem "Letter" began by displaying the following white words centered on a black background:

SAT DOWN TO WRITE YOU THIS POEM

After a few seconds, the word "SAT" shifts off the left side of the screen, only to reappear on the righthand side:

DOWN TO WRITE YOU THIS POEM SAT

"DOWN" then follows suit:

TO WRITE YOU THIS POEM SAT DOWN

As do the next several words, until the final two permutations are displayed in sequence, effectively turning the original phrase on its head:

THIS POEM SAT DOWN TO WRITE YOU

POEM SAT DOWN TO WRITE YOU THIS

By the end of the presentation, we're left wondering: Who wrote what?

In the electronic poem "Reverie," we are treated to about a minute's worth of animation in the form of the word "SUN" rising over the word "(field)," with a "HOE" snaking slowly from right to left as it tills the soil, crossing the field's plane and then leaving the letters "rizon" in its wake—thereby enabling a concatenated "HOErizon" to materialize.

Other poems contain lines that comment on themselves. "Self-Reflexive No. 2" features the sentence "THE BOTTOM LINE IS WHERE CHANGE IS" filling the screen infinite loop-style, with the conceit that the bottom line of text flickers as it is redrawn repeatedly—unlike the lines above it, which remain static (hence, the bottom line is literally where change is). Similarly, the poem "After the Storm" successively displays the words "THIS," "IS," "THE," "SENTENCE," "THAT," "THE," "WIND," "BLEW," "HERE," as if each of the letters were swept in by the wind.

Arguably the most impressive effort is "Off-Screen Romance," which replicates a Fred Astaire and Ginger Rogers dance routine by playfully coupling, interlocking, and decoupling the words "FRED" and "GINGER" around the screen with elegant simplicity. Cleverly, "Off-Screen Romance" was a hidden poem, buried in the BASIC code:

```
108 GOSUB 1900: REM AFTER THE STORM
110 REM FOR THE CURIOUS VIEWER/READER THERE'S AN 'OFF-SCREEN ROMANCE' AT
    1748. YOU JUST HAVE TO TUNE IN THE PROGRAMME.
```

To watch the Astaire-Rogers routine, the user had to execute the program from line **1748** by typing

```
RUN 1748
```

In the printed matter included with each floppy, bpNichol explained how poetic forms and content he had experimented with in the mid-1960s, such as "filmic effects that [he] hadn't had the patience or skill to animate at that time," could finally be realized via programming a computer. He also lamented the Tower of Babel that had developed around both BASIC and programming languages in general. "As ever, new technology opens up new formal problems, and the problems of babel raise themselves all over again in the field of computer languages and operating systems," he wrote.

> Thus the fact that this disk is only available in an Applesoft Basic version (the only language i [lowercase in original document] know at the moment) precisely because translation is involved in moving it out further. But that inherent problem doesn't take away from the fact that computers & computer languages also open up new ways of expressing old contents, of revivifying them. One is in a position to make it new.

Though bpNichol was far from the first person to realize the possibilities of poetry in code—as early as 1959, the German computer scientist Theo Lutz used a Zuse Z22 computer to generate digital poetry—or even the first to use BASIC to compose poetry—Marco Fraticelli, who also wrote poems using an Apple and inspired bpNichol, as well as Silvestre Pestana, who used a Sinclair ZX Spectrum, are two notable examples—his *First Screening* is one of the great and enduring works of microcomputer-created art that, thanks to the painstaking efforts of a conservation group, can still be enjoyed today.

One member of the conservation effort was Geof Huth, a visual poet. Like bpNichol, he began creating digital poetry using an Apple IIe. *Endemic Battle Collage*, a collection of digital poems from the mid-1980s, was the first of four such poetry series Huth produced. All of *Endemic*'s poems were squeezed onto a 5¼-inch floppy, including "INCHWORMS," in which the titular word slowly snaked across the screen, and "HAVOC," which Huth termed a "masterpiece": "a poem designed to fill the entire computer screen space by space, word by word. Faster than a reader could follow, words would appear on the screen, sometimes accompanied by a surprising beep," as he later described it.

Greatly influenced by *First Screening*, he "learned how to write my own digital poems by following Nichol's example and by reading a book on programming in Apple Basic," Huth recalled. The poet held on to a floppy of *First Screening* for over two decades, leveraging his skills as an archivist to help recover bpNichol's work for modern audiences.

More recently, Nick Montfort—MIT digital media professor, editor of *10 PRINT CHR$(205.5+RND(1)); : GOTO 10*, and self-described "computational artist" (where the artistic medium is computation itself, with the "working program as the core artwork," he explains)—has used high-level languages like Python and BASIC to generate digital poetry. *The Truelist* (2017), for example, is a book-length poem, featuring dozens of quatrains, that was unfurled by running a short Python program printed in the book. "You can flip to the end of the book and type the program in, if you like," Montfort tells the reader. "So, in fact, it's a software artwork that manifests in print form, as was the case with programs that appeared in computer magazines of the 1980s and in books such as *101 BASIC Computer Games*." (*The Truelist* was one of a number of *Using Electricity* computer generated books; the series title is a reference to a line in the poem "A House of Dust," itself computer generated by a FORTRAN program written in the mid-1960s by Alison Knowles and James Tenney.)

Montfort's BASIC poetry project, begun in the early 2010s and titled *101 BASIC Poems*, "is an initiative to develop just more than a hundred computational artworks, each one not simply a digital text but also a computer program that can and should be run," he explains. When composing the poems, Montfort adheres to a self-imposed constraint: "I must be able to write them as one-liners." Realizing that such one-line programs can be difficult to read, he expands them into a "canonical" form that is then published.

"On the computational end of things, a major inspiration [for *101 BASIC Poems*] is *101 BASIC Computer Games*," he admits,

> a collection of BASIC programs that fired the imaginations and scaffolded the programming ability of many people in the late 1970s and early 1980s. My BASIC poems are shorter than the programs in this book, in part because attention spans are shorter these days. They are also inspired by specific work by particular poets, artists, and other creative people.

For instance, "File Not Found" takes as inspiration a poem by American poet Ron Padgett consisting of fourteen lines that each contain the phrase "Nothing in that drawer." Montfort's BASIC code is as follows:

```
10 PRINT "Nothing in that drawer."
20 FOR I = 0 TO 999
30 NEXT I
40 GOTO 10
```

Of course, the program slips into an endless loop, searching through an infinite number of drawers and invariably coming up empty handed, never finding the electronic file sought. Montfort wonders, "Does that make my endlessly looping extended remix of the poem infinitely sad?"

Other works in *101 BASIC Poems* include "Polytropon," which randomly spits out a subset of lines from Caroline Bergvall's "Via" (which itself is composed of forty-eight English translations of the opening lines of *The Inferno*), as well as "Complaint" and "Sketches," both of which are platform dependent (unlike "File Not Found" and "Polytropon"), only executing correctly on Applesoft BASIC for the Apple II. The poem "Flag," generating a Jasper Johns-style American flag comprised of ASCII characters when run, is also platform dependent (because it contains multiple **POKE**s), albeit for the Commodore 64.

"Complaint" is especially clever, taking as its point of departure writer and attorney Vanessa Place's appropriation of terms from the judicial system in order to output random Applesoft BASIC error messages, such as "ILLEGAL QUANTITY" and "RETURN WITHOUT GOSUB," stored in the Apple II's ROM. The program—employing the PEEK command with arguments ranging from 53856 to 53856+239, thus covering nearly the entire gamut of possible error messages—generates an endless string of "complaints" perhaps akin to those directed at Place, Montfort suggests, who is "a controversial figure in poetry."

No doubt there is an element of nostalgia in still using BASIC to write poetry. That sense of the longed-for past is explored in online literary magazine *Taper*'s eighth issue, appropriately titled "8-Bit Nostalgia." Click on Jan de Weille's piece "ZX," for instance, and watch as a BASIC program for the ZX Spectrum is keyed in on-screen, line by line, and then run:

```
10 REM 8 BIT NOSTALGIA
20 LET ZX=8
30 BORDER ZX-1
40 INK ZX-3
50 PRINT AT 7,20; "A MESSAGE"

RUN

THE MEDIUM IS THE MESSAGE
```

Atari historian Kay Savetz, whom we met earlier in this chapter, teamed with design engineer Angela Chang to contribute the computational piece "Sunday Afternoon" to the issue. In it we travel back to 1981 or thereabouts, taking the perspective of a child who's been dragged to the mall by Mom. Making the best of things, the child rushes to a store's electronics department to play with an Atari 400 on display. Knowing it's only a matter of time before Mom breaks the reverie, the child tries to put the microcomputer through its paces as quickly as possible. Tapping into the power of the BASIC cartridge was a must. "A one-person speed programming challenge. What little program can I create in a few moments?" Meanwhile, as the story plays out in text form, "the Fuji" (the Atari logo) is drawn on-screen, element by element. "Tick, tick, tick, tick"—and before long, Mom comes calling and the fun's over.

Taper is published by Bad Quarto, a "very small press publishing experimental and poetic work in non-traditional formats" based in New York, we learn from their website. And who is Bad Quarto's proprietor? None other than Nick Montfort.

Line-numbered BASIC has also been employed to critically comment on contemporary digital culture; rather than BASIC poetry, this approach could be more properly termed BASIC prose.

Edmond Y. Chang, an assistant professor of English at Ohio University, attempts to fashion a modern analog of C. P. Snow's "The Two Cultures"—the lecture that influenced Kemeny and Kurtz—in the chapter "Why Are the Digital Humanities So

Straight?" found in *Alternative Historiographies of the Digital Humanities* (2021). The piece takes the form of a text-based interactive BASIC program, a conceit explained in the **REM** of an early line number: "An essay in the form of a program, a program in the form of an essay."

Once a user executes the program and sails past the title screen, Chang makes no secret of his intentions, which are pedagogical in nature (the curly single and double quotation marks, populating the code in Chang's essay, are left intact below).

```
149 REM PARAGRAPH 1
150 PRINT "*Code names.* *Secret code.* *Code of law.*"
151 PRINT "*Code of conduct.* *Moral code.* *Computer "
152 PRINT "Code.* Code, in whatever form, is never "
153 PRINT "empty, homogenous, neutral. The material, "
154 PRINT "embodied, virtual, and performative worlds "
155 PRINT "imagined, enacted, and augmented by code, "
156 PRINT "particularly the languages and practices of"
157 PRINT "digital computers, are inflected and infec-"
158 PRINT "ted by race, gender, class, desire, nation,"
159 PRINT "and other intended and unintended meanings "
160 PRINT "mapped by and onto algorithms and alphanu- "
161 PRINT "meric lines. Tara McPherson says this best"
162 PRINT "arguing, 'We must remember that computers "
163 PRINT "are themselves encoders of culture...compu-"
164 PRINT "tation responds to culture as much as it "
165 PRINT "controls it. Code and race [and other sub-"
166 PRINT "jectivities] are deeply intertwined, even "
167 PRINT "as the structures of code labor to disavow "
168 PRINT "these very connections' (155). What fol- "
169 PRINT "lows then is a challenge to the regulatory "
170 PRINT "fantasy that perpetuates the story that the"
171 PRINT "creators of code, our machines full of "
172 PRINT "code, and the consumers of code are ration-"
173 PRINT "al, objective, and free. "
```

From this didactic code, we learn that "Why Are the Digital Humanities So Straight?" takes as its point of departure a chapter in *Debates in the Digital Humanities* (2012) called "Why Are the Digital Humanities So White? or Thinking the Histories of Race and Computation" by University of Southern California professor Tara McPherson. In her essay, McPherson recounts a conference of the American Studies Association (ASA) she attended in 2008, in which the prevailing attitude among the membership was, at best, equivocal toward computation. "It is largely accurate, if also a generalization, to say that many in the membership of the ASA treat computation within the humanities with some level of suspicion," McPherson explains, "perceiving it to be complicit with the corporatization of higher education or as primarily technological rather than scholarly." A hallway chat with a fellow scholar at the ASA conference unmasks the underlying reason for the suspicion, in the form of a question posed to McPherson: "Why are the digital humanities, well, so white?"

[T]he difficulties we encounter in knitting together our discussions of race (or other modes of difference) with our technological productions within the digital humanities (or in our studies of code) are actually an *effect* of the very designs of our technological systems, designs that emerged in post–World War II computational culture.

McPherson goes on to explore how the histories of Multics and UNIX on the one hand, and the concurrent cultural and political upheavals in the United States during the mid- to late-1960s on the other, are in fact interconnected—despite "attracting the interest and attention of very different audiences located in the deeply siloed departments that categorize our universities," she writes. McPherson, employing the lenticular lens (a ridged coating typically used on three-dimensional postcards to trick the eyes into perceiving depth or motion on a two-dimensional surface) as a metaphor, concludes that "the very structures of digital computation develop[ed] at least in part to cordon off race and to contain it…." UNIX, with its emphasis on *modularity*—an "insist[ence] that code be constructed of discrete and interchangeable parts that can be plugged together via clean interfaces"—might be advantageous for coding, "but…also underscore[d] a worldview in which a troublesome part might be discarded without disrupting the whole."

Hence, McPherson indicts an approach to software design, conflating it with a real-life worldview—since that worldview, she argues, informed the manner in which the software was coded, with the "modularity" and the "covert" of digital computation paralleling existing social organization in the U.S. involving race: namely, segregation, urban uprising, and containment (*encapsulation*, in programmer-speak). "As programmers constituted themselves as a particular class of workers in the 1970s, they were necessarily lodged in their moment, deploying common sense and notions about simplicity to justify their innovations in code," McPherson explains, adding that "this moment is overdetermined by the ways in which the United States is widely coming to process race and other forms of difference in more covert registers…even if the programmers themselves do not explicitly understand their work to be tied to such racial paradigms." If McPherson had examined the design decisions of BASIC rather than (or in addition to) those of UNIX, perhaps she would have reached a similar conclusion, albeit with respect to gender rather than race: that sexism was *encoded* in the language, regardless of whether or not its creators thought in explicitly sexist terms when developing BASIC.

Let's return to Chang's didactic BASIC program.

After learning of McPherson's work—and questioning, on-screen, whether "this same culture seek[s] to segregate gender and sexuality, queerness and desire from digital media"—the user is then treated to pop culture references from tech-centered movies like *War Games* and *Hackers* while navigating a text-based adventure game in the persona of Alan Turing, Ada Lovelace, or Purna Jackson (a character from the 2010s videogame *Dead Island*). Cultural commentary is sprinkled throughout; consider these code fragments depicting choices for avatars of Turing and Lovelace:

```
5100 REM Alan's Only Choices
5102 REM The correct commands are predetermined but give
     the illusion of choice.
5103 REM Unable to see the code, the player's commands
     are arbitrary and contained.
5105 IF Action$="look" THEN GOTO 360
5110 IF Action$="sit down" THEN GOTO 5160
5111 IF Action$="sit chair" THEN GOTO 5160
...
5600 REM Ada's Only Choices
5602 REM The player's commands are constrained by narrative, expectation,
     and code.
5603 REM Narratives, expectations, and code often produce gendered choices
     and commands.
5605 IF Action$="look" THEN GOTO 552
5610 IF Action$="sit down" THEN GOTO 5660
5611 IF Action$="sit bench" THEN GOTO 5660
...
```

The presence of computing-history standbys like Turing and Lovelace in Chang's BASIC program is unsurprising. But what is Purna Jackson doing here? In a word: *intersectionality*, the notion that there is an interconnected and overlapping nature to discrimination or disadvantage based on gender, class, and race.

```
829 REM PARAGRAPH 11
830 PRINT "Purna Jackson understood this all too well."
831 PRINT "Although Jackson is a fictional character "
832 PRINT "from Techland's *Dead Island* (2011), an "
833 PRINT "action role-playing survival horror video "
834 PRINT "game, she represents the intersection of "
835 PRINT "code, culture, race, gender, and sexuality."
```

It all ultimately leads to Chang's central point, expressed as output on-screen:

```
Given that coder and gamer culture is often characterized and experienced
as a 'boys club,' it is no surprise that '[y]ou don't have to look hard
for to find hundreds of results for controversial terms of every stripe.
Simply inputting racial slurs, misogynistic words turns up code in several
languages--Java, HTML, Python, Ruby, and so on'... Technonormativity is a
preexisting condition, a feature, whereas race, gender, sexuality, and
other difference are bugs, errors, easter eggs, and inside jokes....

...Computers are encoders of culture, culture is the encoder of computers.
The digital is infected with technonormativity, technonormativity is em-
bedded in the digital.
```

Technology isn't race-blind, gender-blind, queer-blind, or otherwise neutral, Chang argues in BASIC code, "...it was the normative man-woman pairings that were also highlighted, never the possibility of the range of queer pairings beyond those that would yield a nuclear family." There is a "hardcoded normativity of computers," seen with, for instance, the deterministic nature of pseudorandom number generators, Chang writes, that is inescapable. In modern computing, politics imbues all, as surely as the tech-bro culture, emerging with the birth of BASIC and the DTSS at Dartmouth as described in *A People's History of Computing*, shaped the early digital universe.

There is no shortage of introductory programming languages today, available at the click of a button; nor is there any lack of tutorial videos and various other multimedia designed to ease anyone in to the basics of high-level coding. No doubt these are all, on balance, positive developments; notwithstanding David Brin's pessimism for the future, the barrier to entry in computer science has never been lower—thanks to the internet coupled with changes in tech culture, including the drive for diversity and inclusion. BASIC once resembled network television: in a world dominated by only a few channels, most viewers were watching the same program at the same time. At its peak, *I Love Lucy* was so popular that, as the *New York Times* put it, "The nation's reservoirs dipped whenever [the show] broke for a commercial. A whole country, flushing as one." TV milestones transformed into cultural touchstones as tens of million tuned in to see the Beetles on *Ed Sullivan*, to learn who shot J.R. on *Dallas*, and to bid goodbye to *M*A*S*H*.

BASIC, in its heyday, enjoyed an effective monopoly over the introductory programming space. Like with network TV, BASIC's dominance came about thanks to a perfect storm of factors that can only in retrospect be appreciated as a unique moment in the history of computing—and one unlikely to be replicated. As surely as cable television and then streaming services chopped up the TV viewing audience into tiny slices, the plethora of choice in the programming language arena ensures that in the years and decades to come there will be options on top of options for those interested in learning how to code.

Which renders debates like "Is Python the new BASIC?" or "Is JavaScript the new BASIC?" beside the point. There is not, nor will there ever be, a "new BASIC" or "modern BASIC" since the elements that made BASIC's rise to fame—and consequent ubiquity—possible are mostly no longer in play. And that ubiquity cannot be overstated: as one user on a Hacker News discussion board titled "Python is the new BASIC" recalled, "I didn't start learning to program because I wanted to program, I learned to program because I saw a file called **GORILLA.BAS** in one of the folders on my MS-DOS machine. Once I figured out I could open it in QBASIC and just press F5…that was it…I would be a programmer for my next 20+ years and counting."

Nonetheless, even if the BASIC experience itself was *sui generis* and can't be recreated, perhaps the spirit of BASIC—namely, its accessibility for beginners—continues in languages like Python and on microcontrollers, as some people argue. Let's take some time to consider these claims.

For the absolute beginning programmer, learning the basics of the scripting language Python, developed in the late 1980s by the Dutch software engineer Guido van Rossum, is remarkably straightforward; the language bears at least some resemblance to a generic version of BASIC. To print out a string like "Hello, World!" requires nothing more than a single line in Python:

```
print("Hello, World!")
```

That one line captures the entirety of the program. Writing the same program in Java necessitates several more lines, since Java wears its object-oriented nature on its sleeve, while Python manages to keep its OO structure in the background. Take a look at Java's verbosity:

```
public class Hello {
    public static void main(String[] args)  {

        System.out.println("Hello, World!");

    }
}
```

Notice that we had to place our code to print the string "Hello, World!" inside a method (the `main()` method) that is itself contained within a class (the class `Hello`); conforming to this configuration takes attention away from the programming concepts in favor of the syntax, debatably counterproductive for a beginner.

Java is *strongly typed*, meaning that every variable, when declared, must be assigned a data type—integer, double-precision floating point, Boolean, character, or string, to take the most common examples—and there are strict rules when mixing values of different data types. Consider the following Java program:

```
public class Type {
    public static void main(String[] args)  {

        double x = 7.2;
        int y = 3;
        double z = x + y;
        String s = "The sum is ";
        System.out.println(s + z);

    }
}
```

When declaring variables in Python, however, the type is assigned automatically, based on the kind of data stored in the variable. Here is the (roughly but not exactly) equivalent Java program translated into Python:

```
x = 7.2
y = 3
z = x + y
s = "The sum is"
print(s, z)
```

Unsurprisingly, conditional statements are available in both languages. First, Java:

```java
public class Main {
    public static void main(String[] args)   {

        int x = 7;

        if (x == 7)
           System.out.println("The variable x is equal to 7");
        else
           System.out.println("The variable x is not equal to 7");

    }
}
```

Then, Python:

```python
x = 7

if x == 7:
  print("The variable x is 7")

else:
  print("The variable x is not equal to 7")
```

Unlike in Java, note that the indentations, which define blocks of statements while enforcing readability, are required in Python.

We could keep on going, comparing elements of Python and Java—or, for that matter, Python and other contemporary languages—and likely arrive at a consensus: that Python is on average more user friendly, especially for the novice programmer, than its peers. To underscore this point, as a nod to Logo, Python even includes a pre-installed Turtle graphics module. The following program draws a rectangle in a Turtle window:

```python
import turtle
t = turtle.Turtle()
for i in range(2):
    t.forward(100)
    t.right(90)
    t.forward(50)
    t.right(90)
turtle.done()
```

The language includes a number of other useful libraries as well.

Not only is Python easy to pick up, but Python interpreters are freely available on the web for download (and some are web-based). Sometimes, however, setting up and using standalone software might be tricky, getting used to an IDE (Integrated Development Environment) can take some practice, and deploying applications could be difficult. Not to mention the complexities attendant with the GUI toolkits necessary to write programs that use even the most basic graphical elements. "[P]ython's problem is that while it goes the distance to make the simplest possible program as simple as possible, simplicity bleeds off very quickly as you add functionality," asserted a Hacker News discussion board user.

The software engineer Ilya Tulvio perceptively noted that "the actual arguments for and against [BASIC] are still alive and well today, they are just applied to different programming languages." Indeed, there are other languages that might arguably fit the bill as an introductory language as well as, if not better than, Python, including JavaScript (with ubiquity its strength), Swift (with expressive syntax its strength), Ruby (with flexibility its strength), or Processing (with simplicity yet similarity to Java its strength). (As described in the Command Line Heroes podcast called "Learning the BASICs," Yukihiro Matsumoto, creator of Ruby, developed an interest in programming thanks in part to BASIC.) If we stretch our definition of an HLL, perhaps even the Java-based Minecraft environment might serve as a suitable introduction to coding à la BASICs of yesteryear.

Less convincing is the argument for Visual BASIC as the "new BASIC." Claiming that VB took up the mantle, bringing BASIC into a new century while becoming more popular than ever—and citing data from, for instance, the TIOBE Index as proof—is disingenuous, since VB, despite some obvious similarities to Dartmouth BASIC, is decidedly not a beginner's language in the same vein as its first- and second-generation namesakes, nor were average computer users ever forced to interact with it.

For a period of around three decades, unstructured BASIC was effectively peerless. Viewed with the benefit of hindsight, the conditions were ripe for BASIC to thrive: from the mid-1960s, when it was the exclusive province of a small college; through the 1970s, as dialects of it appeared on minicomputers, hobbyist machines, and home computers; and finally to the 1980s, when personal computing still offered some version of the language. Especially with those early home computers, which booted to BASIC—meaning, when the user turned the machine on, the computer immediately loaded BASIC, which was packaged in ROM; this was true on the TRS-80, the Commodore 64, the BBC Micro, and many others, with BASIC serving as the de facto operating system—the average user was forced to interact, in at least a small way, with BASIC in order to coax the computer to do much of *anything*, since BASIC was integrated with the hardware. For instance, the Commodore 64 required some variation of BASIC's **LOAD** command, such as

```
LOAD "*",8
```

or

```
LOAD "$",8
```

or

```
LOAD "file",8,1
```

in order to load files, including games. Booting to BASIC also "certainly contributed to the popularity of homebrew, amateur programming efforts," Jaroslav Švelch notes in the book *Gaming the Iron Curtain: How Teenagers and Amateurs in Communist Czechoslovakia Claimed the Medium of Computer Games*:

> On the other hand, the ubiquitous BASIC interpreters could not hide the simultaneous existence of multiple incompatible hardware platforms. A program for the Sinclair ZX Spectrum would not run on a Commodore 64 and vice versa. Platform differences have tremendous emic significance for our story, and structured local gaming culture, including user practices and community network building. People did not join Atari clubs or Sinclair clubs because of their aesthetic preferences or exposure to persuasive discourses, but for pragmatic reasons: they benefited from information and software for their particular platform.

On the ZX Spectrum, Commodore 64, and other 8-bit micros, users were not as insulated from the idiosyncratic inner workings of the machine as they would later become. Put simply, in the past, when it came to programming, you couldn't completely opt out; these days, you have to actively opt in. Once computers booted to something other than BASIC, the language became detritus, relegated to the sidelines; it was no longer indispensable, it was no longer everywhere, and it wasn't swapped for a new programming language: it was replaced with GUIs like Windows, rendering text-based interactions with computers passé. Likewise with other electronic equipment, such as phones, radios, televisions, even cars: users are now more insulated than ever from the inner workings of these increasingly-complex machines, making the exploration and learning that attends to tinkering more difficult to engage in than ever before.

Which raises another pertinent issue. Like phones, radios, televisions, and cars, computer software has evolved tremendously over the last sixty years, offering users more functionality than ever. When Dartmouth BASIC debuted, interactions with computers were primarily text-based, linear affairs. BASIC offered newbie programmers a highly accessible gateway for the creation of programs that could be more or less commensurate, in terms of potential features and UI, to the quality of the software available at the time. But as the decades passed, the gap between the program-development capabilities of even the best unstructured (or loosely structured) BASIC variants and professional-grade software grew to chasm-level proportions as consumers came to expect polished, feature-rich, multimedia experiences. Any language claiming to be the "new BASIC" would have to offer neophytes accessibility coupled with power on a par with the capabilities of contemporary hardware—a tall order indeed.

Forget Python. Perhaps there are versions of BASIC out there satisfying at least some of these "new BASIC" conditions.

Consider QB64, an effective cross-platform modern take on QBASIC and Quick-BASIC developed by Rob Galleon, as one notable example. Liberty BASIC and Run BASIC are two others; Carl Gundel, who developed them both, successfully implemented the BASIC language to work smoothly with the newest UIs. Like David Brin, Gundel—who moderates an active BASIC Facebook group boasting thousands of members—has written of the "Real Computer Literacy" that attends to those who learn how to program computers, arguing that "[i]t can be really hard to create software with the programming languages endorsed by the mainstream. We have gotten away from simpler languages like BASIC, perhaps under the assumption that more complexity is better, but good computing avoids needless complexity," adding, "People like to say that BASIC is a bad language for teaching programming. The early versions of BASIC do have their weak points, but newer versions of BASIC are very strong for students and end users. An entire industry of computer software came out of young people using computers that started up in BASIC programming mode."

Let us assume, however, that young people, unaware of the magic of the language, won't seek out modern versions of BASIC such as QB64 and Liberty BASIC. In that case, where are the most likely places that they could still nonetheless encounter BASIC? Certainly on the Texas Instruments series of graphing calculators, such as the TI-83/84 and TI-89, which come packaged with versions of TI-BASIC; these calculators have been ubiquitous in schools for decades. Intrepid students might find their way, via a few well-placed button presses, to the TI-BASIC menu-driven editor—and then proceed to explore the terrain.

Also consider microcontrollers, or small, programmable computers embedded on a single integrated circuit (IC) that can control other electronics—everything from LEDs to robots—as a means of leading young people back to BASIC. The BASIC Stamp, distributed by the California-based company Parallax, Inc., is a microcontroller with an interpreted BASIC called PBASIC built into ROM. PBASIC offers three dozen commands, some of which are specially designed to interface with the hardware. BASIC programs, once written on a PC using the Stamp Editor application, could be downloaded to the BASIC Stamp II microcontroller.

Let's look at a PBASIC example. First connect an LED to pin #5 (signal name P0) in the breadboard housing the BASIC Stamp module, and then key in the following:

```
output 0
blink:
    out0 = 0
    pause 500
    out0 = 1
    pause 500
goto blink
```

When run, the LED connected to the device will blink on and off.

The cofounder of Parallax, Chip Gracey, was a long-time BASIC programmer, having first encountered the language as a high schooler in 1979 on an Apple II. He wrote BASIC code to display graphics on-screen and then took apart the computer to try to understand its inner workings. Gracey didn't stop there: dismantling videogame systems and other household electronics followed. By the time he reached his senior year, Gracey had turned his hobby into a business in the form of software duplication hardware for the Commodore 64. Four years later, along with his friend Lance Walley, Gracey founded Parallax; a sound digitizer for the Apple II was among their first offerings. The release of the BASIC Stamp in the early 1990s, though, heralded a new chapter in the company's history, since well over one hundred thousand Stamps were sold during the decade.

The Maximite Microcomputer, powered by the PIC32 microcontroller, also illustrates the vast creative possibilities of microcontrollers. Designed by Geoff Graham to purposely recall 1980s microcomputers like the TRS-80 and the C64, and available in several versions, such as the Colour Maximite and Colour Maximite 2 (which upgrades the PIC32 with an ARM Cortex-M7 CPU), the machine features a BASIC implementation called MMBasic. The interpreter-based MMBasic is not only nearly backward compatible with Microsoft MBASIC (designed for the CP/M operating system, a precursor of MS-DOS) but also mostly conforms to the ANSI Full BASIC standard and thus permits structured programming. Written in ANSI C, MMBasic requires a 32-bit microcontroller to run. The language has been ported to other devices, such as the Raspberry Pi.

Originating in the United Kingdom, and inspired by the BBC Micro, the Raspberry Pi is a compact, low-cost, fully functional, single-board computer (SBC), first built to help teach computer science, although its use expanded well beyond the confines of education. Tiny BASIC has been ported to the machine, though Scratch and Python are the featured languages on the Raspberry Pi. (There are numerous Tiny BASICs available for the microcontrollers found on Arduino boards as well.)

Smaller than a Raspberry Pi, the BBC micro:bit is a single-board computer powered by a 32-bit ARM Cortex M0. Though packaged with two programmable buttons, an accelerometer, a compass, and various sensors, and boasting Bluetooth connectivity along with a USB port, the micro:bit offers no means of connecting to an external display. There is a five-by-five grid of LEDs affixed to the board, however, that can display messages or patterns. And the micro:bit really shined when connected to other electronic devices or sensors by using the included five built-in Input and Output (I/O) rings.

There were multiple ways to program the device—including with the Scratch-like MakeCode (which was converted to JavaScript; users could switch between the block environment and the equivalent JavaScript and Python code), Python (MicroPython), or C/C++ (using the Mbed IDE, a platform for Arm microcontrollers)—via a computer, tablet, or phone. A Magic 8 Ball program, for example, might work by having the user asking a yes-or-no question aloud and shaking the board, thereby triggering the device's accelerometer, with various answers (e.g., "YES," "NO," or "MAYBE") then displayed on the LED grid in response. In MakeCode, this simple micro:bit program appeared as follows:

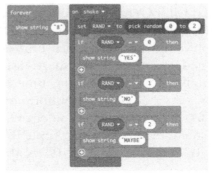

In JavaScript, the code looked like this:

```
let RAND = 0
input.onGesture(Gesture.Shake, function () {
    RAND = randint(0, 2)
    if (RAND == 0) {
        basic.showString("YES")
    }
    if (RAND == 1) {
        basic.showString("NO")
    }
    if (RAND == 2) {
        basic.showString("MAYBE")
    }
})
basic.forever(function () {
    basic.showString("8")
})
```

And in Python, the code took the following form:

```
RAND = 0

def on_gesture_shake():
    global RAND
    RAND = randint(0, 2)
    if RAND == 0:
        basic.show_string("YES")
    if RAND == 1:
        basic.show_string("NO")
    if RAND == 2:
        basic.show_string("MAYBE")
input.on_gesture(Gesture.SHAKE, on_gesture_shake)

def on_forever():
    basic.show_string("8")
basic.forever(on_forever)
```

Once a program for the device was written, the code was stored in the micro:bit's flash memory.

BASIC was also available for the micro:bit (e.g., thanks to Coridium); the device could even interface with a Microsoft Small Basic program. The creative possibilities were endless.

Like its older namesake, the BBC Micro, the BBC micro:bit was geared toward educating the youth of Great Britain. While around four out of every five British schools had an Acorn Computers-built BBC Micro on campus by the end of the 1980s owing to the BBC's Computer Literacy Project—leading BBC BASIC to become the lingua franca on the island (much more on this in the next chapter)—around a million micro:bits were distributed, free of charge, to Year 7 pupils in the United Kingdom in the latter half of the 2010s. Just like the BBC Micro and BBC BASIC greatly influenced a generation of children, the micro:bit was poised to do the same, albeit in a digitally interconnected world.

Ubiquity, flexibility, and simplicity: these are the three preconditions for a programming language, or digital technology at large, to gain widespread adoption. Though the micro:bit ecosystem is obviously not a "new BASIC," the device's ubiquity, flexibility, simplicity, low cost (or no cost), and BBC pedigree allow it to come the closest, perhaps, to satisfying the spirit of Kemeny and Kurtz's vision—but reimagined for a new century of learners.

END OF INTERLUDE

As the years went by and BASIC's fortunes rose and fell, the definition of computer literacy underwent a concomitant transformation: from that of a deep and intimate understanding of high-level programming found in the writings and creations of Perlis, Kemeny, Kurtz, Papert, Solomon, Kay, and other visionaries, to what Annette Vee terms "a surface notion of computer literacy": operational tasks of computer use, like navigating the internet, opening and saving files, creating word-processing and spreadsheet documents, and even using HTML markup language to create webpages—though the code powering webpages, and all other software, for that matter, was hidden by default and thus had to be purposely sought out.

Computer scientist Donald Knuth has spoken of the connection between writing and programming. His discussion of literacy, though, is very different contextually than Perlis's, since Knuth focuses on writing's relationship to computer program clarity rather than considering programming as an analogue to a *fundamental* skill like literacy. In the article "Literate Programming," published in *The Computer Journal* in 1984, Knuth stresses the need for improved program documentation.

> I believe that the time is ripe for significantly better documentation of programs, and that we can best achieve this by considering programs to be *works of literature*. Hence, my title: "Literate Programming."

> Let us change our traditional attitude to the construction of programs: Instead of imagining that our main task is to instruct a computer what to do, let us concentrate rather on explaining to human beings what we want a computer to do.

He compares a literate programmer's practice to that of an essayist's, "whose main concern is with exposition and excellence of style"—someone who is careful to select logical variable names and expand upon their meaning cogently while maintaining comprehensibility at all times in the construction of a program.

But the connection to literacy is tenuous at best, despite Knuth's use of the term "literate programming." In fact, the coinage in his article is something of a joke; Knuth, a polymath, is a master wordsmith and more literate than many essayists (and a more accomplished programmer than nearly any other). In retaliation for being guilted into writing "structured" programs in the 1970s—lest his "unstructured" programs be founding wanting—Knuth imposed a "moral commitment on everybody who hears the term [literate programming]; surely nobody wants to admit [to] writing an *illiterate* program." In the piece, Knuth describes his experiences with the WEB system, a collection of programs used at Stanford. "I chose the name WEB," wordsmith Knuth writes, "partly because it was one of the few three-letter words of English that hadn't already been applied to computers." By the 1990s, of course, "WEB" would be employed widely as a synonym for the internet.

Though she doesn't explicitly make the connection to Knuth's notion of literate programming, Vee explores the salient idea of shaming others through the style of one's code. In an article titled "Coding Values," Vee takes issue with the "Platonic Ideal of Good Code," describing a "rhetorical dimension to code" that is frequently ignored by those in software engineering who have come to expect a certain type and style of coding, down to the documentation (comments) in the programs themselves. "As if digital humanists, biologists, web hackers, and sociologists couldn't possibly bring their own values to code," Vee adds. But context very much matters, she argues, since "like grammar, code is also rhetorical. What is good code and what is bad code should be based on the context in which the code operates."

So, while an Edsger Dijkstra might not approve of using the **GOTO** statement in a BASIC program or of the prolix Logo code that Vee shares with her readers (which she ironically calls "codewell"), "the values of hacking for fun or for other fields are devalued in favor of the best practices of software engineering—that is, proper planning, careful modularity, and unit testing," Vee laments. Such a narrow view of coding—a perspective that rigidly enforces a Platonic ideal even outside the field of software engineering—is exclusionary, dogmatic, and should be, in a turn of phrase familiar to Dijkstra fans, "considered harmful."

Hence we encounter yet another reason why the bloom came off the BASIC rose: people didn't want to be shamed for writing "unstructured" code.

When Don Knuth was a college freshman, poring through the listing of Perlis's IT compiler and extending its capabilities with the help of newfound friends, research in linguistics was in full swing, with linguists like Noam Chomsky formulating rules of grammar in ways that struck Knuth as decidedly mathematical. In fact, on his honeymoon in 1961, Knuth packed a copy of Chomsky's *Syntactic Structures* to read. "Here was a marvelous thing," the computer scientist recalled, "a mathematical theory of language in which I could use a computer programmer's intuition!" Whereas before, "the mathematical, linguistic, and algorithmic parts of my life had previously been totally separate," once the connections between languages and computing came to the fore, "those three aspects became steadily more intertwined."

Taking a cue from Knuth, in the final analysis, perhaps we shouldn't be thinking of computer literacy in isolation. In fact, we probably shouldn't be considering it in binary terms, either. According to Mark Sample, an associate professor at Davidson College and contributing author to *10 PRINT CHR$(205.5+RND(1)); : GOTO 10*, the term *literacy* is "loaded with historical and social baggage. It's often misused as a gatekeeping concept, an either/or state; one is either literate or illiterate." Instead of literacy, we might instead think of *competency*, "[b]ecause the thing with competency is, it's highly contextualized, situated, and fluid," explains Sample. "Competency means knowing the things you need to do in order to do the other things you need to do."

"It goes against the grain of modern education to teach students to program," Alan Perlis once observed. "What fun is there to making plans, acquiring discipline, organizing thoughts, devoting attention to detail, and learning to be self-critical." For young folks who found coding to be enjoyable, those associated benefits—making plans, acquiring discipline, developing other good habits—naturally followed suit as a result of the exposure to programming.

Two years after BASIC first appeared, Dartmouth hosted the influential "Anglo-American Seminar in the Teaching of English," of which Annette Vee devoted several years of her academic life to researching. Later referred to as either the "Dartmouth Seminar" or the "Dartmouth Conference" and funded by the Carnegie Corporation to the tune of $150,000, the seminar brought together forty-nine American and British educators of English—from elementary English teachers (mostly the British) to professors of English (mostly the Americans)—to the campus over a four-week period late in the summer of 1966. In addition, about two dozen consultants organized workshops. Up for discussion and debate: the English curriculum's past, present, and future.

Planning for the seminar had begun two years earlier when contacts were made with the Carnegie Corporation by Boris Ford of the University of Sussex, James Squire from the National Council of Teachers of English (NCTE), and Albert Kitzhaber of the University of Oregon (and formerly Dartmouth); later, John Fisher of NCTE rival organization the Modern Language Association (MLA) became involved in the planning as well. Dartmouth College was chosen because of its library, resources, and cost—cheaper than an equivalent UK venue—as well as being relatively free of distractions (one participant noted that Dartmouth was "protected, isolated, pastoral—was, in short, dull"). There were numerous plenary sessions, held mostly in Sanborn Hall, the English department building, as well as various working groups; faculty navigated discussion topics like "What is English?" and "English: One Road or Many?" Working papers and study group papers were generated, all in an environment of personality clashes, ideological battles (the literature-centric F.R. Leavis faction was particularly dominant), and other attendant drama. Luckily, alcohol flowed liberally, lubricating the proceedings.

In the 1950s, Americans were especially unhappy with the writing skills of incoming college freshman; though this was hardly a novel concern (the previous century, Harvard faculty complained about the same problem), in a post-*Sputnik* world preparedness in English was viewed as a matter of national defense. Project English, funded by the U.S. Congress, was one response to these concerns; Kitzhaber was involved in Project English efforts. Another response entailed the passage of the National Defense Education Act (NDEA) of 1958, which funded Project English.

Plus, conferences to address curricular issues had precedent, most notably with the Woods Hole Conference, held in 1959 in Massachusetts. Poring through the science curriculum in the wake of the *Sputnik* launch, Woods Hole bore fruit: not only was education in mathematics and science transformed—with New Math and New Science, respectively—there were also changes implemented in pedagogical practice (the spiral curriculum) and educational planning in general. In fact, the time period featured a number of what Vee calls "big, field-defining conference[s]" besides Woods Hole, such as a structural linguistics conference (at Johns Hopkins) involving intellectual heavy-weights Jacques Derrida and Paul de Man, John McCarthy's AI conference (at Dartmouth), and "other computational research on programming languages and operating systems by John Kemeny and Thomas Kurtz" (also at Dartmouth).

Though titled as an "Anglo-American Seminar"—"ostensibly because it brought British and American educators together," Vee explains—"John Trimbur notes that the name was indicative of a larger postwar neocolonial project of consolidating and exporting English as a commodity." Unsurprisingly, the seminar attendees did not come from all races or walks of life, with most participants white men of a certain intellectual class. In light of the Watts riots in and around Los Angeles in 1965, as well as the increasing attention to racial inequality in the United States especially, the lack of attention to learners of diverse backgrounds proved particularly tone deaf.

Yet "[t]he influence of the Dartmouth Seminar remains significant in university and K-12 English education in the US and the UK and the rest of the Anglophone world, although this influence is largely indirect," Vee notes, with "[s]everal books…written based on the findings and discussions of the conference, and they generally proposed that English courses should emphasize student growth and literacy processes, rather than specific content to be mastered." She concludes, "A whole generation of teachers were trained in the wake of Dartmouth, and then others—my generation of scholars—were trained by them. In true Bakhtinian fashion, the Dartmouth Seminar's influence is refracted and now rarely cited."

Which leaves us with an important question. What does the Dartmouth Seminar have to do with BASIC?

By the time she learned about the seminar, Vee had already begun her research into BASIC. At first, she believed that "see[ing] my disciplinary history and my research in programming overlap was an exciting serendipity." She continues:

> I wondered: did the Anglo-American Seminar choose to locate itself at Dartmouth because of the exciting work Kemeny and Kurtz were doing to make computing more accessible? Were the participants of the Seminar and those working on BASIC aware of each other? Did they run into each other at the local bars and restaurants on campus? What if these educators found common ground in supporting creative work in composition, in supporting students, in progressive literacy work?

But the seminar's archival record contained no mention of Kemeny, Kurtz, BASIC, or computing in general, so the next step was reaching out to any still-living participants of the Dartmouth Seminar—of which there were only four. Vee attended the seminar's fiftieth anniversary conference, but came up empty on any connections to BASIC.

Which left one avenue remaining: Thomas Kurtz. She emailed him in 2016, and interviewed him the next year.

> We had a lovely conversation in which I learned a lot about the context of BASIC, Kurtz's progressive vision of general education, and Kemeny's ingenuity. I also learned,

without a doubt, that the BASIC team had no knowledge of the English Seminar. Yet both the BASIC and English Seminar initiatives emerged from a general progressive trend in general education as well as the flush funding of the early 1960s.

"So there was a connection, albeit an indirect one," Vee concluded.

"The human mind flows…sometimes in swirling rapids. Thoughts and ideas come and go. BASIC allows the same freedom," argued author David Lien. "Need a variable? Pick one out of thin air and toss it in…. [L]ike a favorite chair, or shoes, BASIC may not be the state of someone's art, but it sure is comfortable."

For a whole generation of kids, BASIC was a comfortable, well-worn sandbox. Without that sandbox to code in—one that freed young spirits from having to worry about conforming to the rules of whatever programming paradigm happened to be dominant, or concerning themselves with Platonic ideals, while still gaining a degree of coding competency—the democratizing spirit of electronic play that imbued those lucky children who grew up programming in BASIC—and in Logo, too—would have been lost to the sands of time.

CHAPTER 6

THE UK CONNECTION, PART I
Where the Sun Never Set on BASIC

Why did BASIC explode in popularity in the United Kingdom in the 1980s?

BASIC began in the United States. And in the United States, BASIC was everywhere by the early 1980s. The Netflix television series *Stranger Things*, set in 1983 rural Indiana, brilliantly comments on that ubiquity—as channeled through the interests of a main character on the show.

In episode eight of the second season, titled "Chapter Eight: The Mind Flayer," Bob Newby (played by Sean Astin), manager of the local Radio Shack, hacks into a mainframe system of a government facility by using an IBM 3180 Display Station terminal. "If you want to unlock the doors," Newby explains to the chief of police, Jim Hopper (played by David Harbour), "you need to completely reboot the computer system and then override the security codes with a manual input."

"Fine. How do I do that?" Hopper asks.

"You can't! Unless you know BASIC."

We are then treated to an over-the-shoulder shot of Newby quickly keying in green code on the black background of the terminal screen:

```
10 DIM FourDigitPassword INTEGER
20 FOR i = 0 TO 9
30    FOR j = 0 TO 9
40      FOR k = 0 TO 9
50        FOR l = 0 TO 9
60             FourDigitPassword = getFourDigits (i,j,k,l)
70             IF checkPasswordMatch(FourDigitPassword) = TRUE THEN
80                  GOTO 140
90             END
100       NEXT l
110     NEXT k
120   NEXT j
130 NEXT i
140 PRINT FourDigitPassword
```

```
150 END
```

The program is stereotypical microcomputer-style, line-numbered BASIC, albeit reimagined through a modern lens: complete with (optional) indentation, (optional) variable declaration courtesy of the **DIM** statement, a questionable mixture of upper- and lowercase characters along with appearances of lower CamelCase words, and calls to several functions (namely, **getFourDigits** and **checkPasswordMatch**). In short, the program boasts much of the syntax of a generic version of unstructured BASIC, not corresponding precisely to any particular dialect of the language, yet is coded more like Pascal—i.e., by using a structured programming aesthetic.

In terms of the program's functionality, "It somehow obtains the access code to regain control over automatic door locks after a power outage," notes Martin Müller, who analyzed the code. "To achieve this, the code performs a so-called brute force attack on the four-digit password prompt which basically means that all possible combinations are tried until the right one is found." Four nested **FOR/NEXT** loops cycle through digits **0** to **9** in four place values (ones, tens, hundreds, thousands), which are then (perhaps) concatenated into a single string that is converted into an integer by the function **getFourDigits** or is instead (perhaps) calculated by summing products of the digits and powers of ten by calling the function **getFourDigits** within the innermost loop. We can't be sure because the workings of **getFourDigits** are never revealed in the story, though we do know that the function takes four arguments: one for each of the four values of the loop counter variables.

Next, **getFourDigits** returns an integer, storing this value into the previously-declared integer variable **FourDigitPassword**. Finally, the **checkPasswordMatch** Boolean function, invoked with a single argument (the value of **FourDigitPassword**), checks to see if there is a match, returning either true or false. If true, control is passed to line **140**, where the matching password is output. If false, the program increments the innermost loop by one digit until that loop counter has exceeded **9**, at which point the loop counter resets to **0** and the preceding outer loop increments by one digit, and so on, until all one thousand unique four-digit integers have been tested as the potential password.

However, as YouTuber The Retro Coder observes, there is one glaring bug in the code: the **END** statement on line **90**. The first time BASIC encounters that line, the program will terminate; thus, unless the correct password is **0000**—the very first permutation checked with the **checkPasswordMatch** function (though not affecting its functionality, note that since **FourDigitPassword** is of type integer, **0000** would likely be stored as just **0**)—the program will stop prematurely. Presumably, Newby meant to type **END IF**, rather than **END**, to create the **IF/THEN** block.

In addition, there is perhaps an error in syntax on line **10**. Instead of **DIM FourDigitPassword INTEGER**, Newby should have typed **DIM FourDigitPassword AS INTEGER**. More problematically, the program itself is much too long; an equivalent algorithm could be compactly rewritten in this generic form of BASIC. For example, as suggested by one poster on a Reddit thread:

```
FOR X = 10000 TO 19999: FourDigitPassword = RIGHT$(STR$(X),4)
```

Stranger Things reminds those of a certain age that BASIC was once the lingua franca for communicating with computers. Another American television series, the animated *Futurama* (1999-), has featured a number of nerdy in-jokes, several of which involve BASIC. For example, in the episode "I, Roommate" (season 1, episode 3), the characters Fry and Bender hang a sign in their new apartment that reads

```
10 HOME
20 SWEET
30 GOTO 10
```

And in the episode "Hell is Other Robots" (season 1, episode 9), a banner is prominently displayed above the altar of the Church of Robotology during a baptism ceremony:

```
10 SIN
20 GOTO HELL
```

Which is as frightening as anything in Dante's *Inferno*.

But BASIC references weren't the exclusive province of American television. Though BASIC was born in the United States, it was adopted by the world; the language seeped into art, literature, and pop culture around the planet.

In Germany, the comic book *Abenteuer in BASIC* (*Adventures in BASIC*) by publishing company Klett charted the adventures of two intrepid children as they learned BASIC. Author Rüdeger Baumann was an old hand at writing books on BASIC and computing, having published at least five during the 1980s.

Next, consider Umberto Eco's esoteric novel *Foucault's Pendulum*, originally published in Italian as *Il pendolo di Foucault* in 1988. In the book, readers were treated to an exploration of the Kabbalah, a strain of Jewish mysticism, in the form of a BASIC program designed to output all permutations (arrangements) of four English letters of God's name. As Jacopo Belbo, a central character in the novel, explains to a colleague called Diotallevi, "The problem is to find all the permutations of the name of God, isn't it? Well, this manual has a neat little program in Basic for listing all possible sequences of four letters. It seems tailor-made for YHVH [or Yahweh, God's Hebrew name]. Should I give it a whirl?" Belbo then shows the program to Diotallevi. (Note that the program will not work on any BASIC dialect requiring array declaration.)

```
10 REM anagrammi
20 INPUT L$(1), L$(2), L$(3), L$(4)
30 PRINT
40 FOR I1=1 TO 4
50 FOR I2=1 TO 4
60 IF I2=I1 THEN 130
70 FOR I3=1 TO 4
```

```
80 IF I3=I1 THEN 120
90 IF I3=I2 THEN 120
100 LET I4=10-(I1+I2+I3)
110 LPRINT L$(I1); L$(I2); L$(I3); L$(I4)
120 NEXT I3
130 NEXT I2
140 NEXT I1
150 END
```

"Try it yourself," he tells him. "When it asks for input, type in Y, H, V, H, and press the ENTER key. But you may be disappointed. There are only twenty-four possible permutations."

Although the anagram program does output twenty-four arrangements for the four letters, not all of them are unique. For example, when YVHH is output, it is followed by YVHH. The reason for such repetitions is subtle. Because the letter H appears twice in the four-letter set, YVHH cannot be distinguished from YVHH—the latter permutation switching the placement of the H's. Put another way, if the H's *were* distinguishable—let's call these distinguishable H's H_1 and H_2—then we *would* have two unique arrangements of letters, YVH_1H_2 and YVH_2H_1. But, since the H letters are indistinguishable, YVHH and YVHH only count as one permutation, not two. Meaning there are in fact fewer than twenty-four unique permutations, despite the program's output—which would be printed on paper rather than on-screen thanks to the **LPRINT** statement. Specifically, since the H's can swap positions with no discernable effect, the number of unique permutations of YHVH is $4 \times 3 \times 2 \times 1 \div 2 = 12$, rather than $4 \times 3 \times 2 \times 1 = 24$. However, in Belbo's Kabalistic conception, the H's of the Tetragram in fact correspond to *different* letters, hence there are twenty-four unique permutations after all, despite the repetitions in output.

Several pages later, a man called Casaubon attempts to crack Belbo's six-character password, *Stranger Things*-style, by modifying the anagram program. Narrowing down the possibilities through some clever detective work—"But he might have played with the Italian transcription [of God's name], which contained two vowels. With six letters—IAHVEH—he [Belbo] had seven hundred and twenty permutations at his disposal," we learn—Casaubon recognizes the indistinguishable permutations issue, only to dismiss it. "The repetitions didn't count," he explains, "because Diotallevi had said that the two [H's] must be taken as two different letters. Belbo could have chosen, say, the thirty-sixth or the hundred and twentieth." The output generated by the modified program, all "seven hundred and twenty names of God" (that's $7 \times 6 \times 5 \times \ldots \times 1$) is printed in the novel, although the modified program listing is not.

The British Invasion brought the Beetles, among other musical acts, from England to the United States in the 1960s, leading to seismic cultural shifts. But by the late 1970s, England was contending with an equally consequential invasion from the U.S, albeit in the form of a programming language. Arguably more than any other country in Europe, BASIC—the high-level language built-in to popular microcomputers, including several home-grown models—would reshape Britannia's tech culture by bringing accessible programming to a generation of young people.

To underscore how much BASIC infiltrated England and the UK at large, look no further than the popular though understated and sly BBC British television comedy show *Look Around You* (2002), which, in its first series (season), satirized the dry, self-serious educational films of the 1970s produced by the BBC and ITV. The first episode, called "Calcium," which explored the element's properties scientifically (and became progressively more and more outrageous, culminating in experimentation with a sentient form of calcium called "intelligent calcium"), begins with a close-up shot of a BBC Micro. We see a man keying in a BASIC program that pops up on a CRT screen:

```
>10 PRINT "LOOK AROUND YOU ";
>20 GOTO 10
```

When he types **RUN** and presses RETURN, the phrase "LOOK AROUND YOU" is repeated in an endless loop on-screen. This short segment served as the title sequence for every episode of the first series.

The second series of *Look Around You* boasted a different format, spoofing the pop-science shows of the 1980s, especially *The Computer Programme* (which featured the BBC Micro). For example, in "Computers," the fifth episode, we find out that by 1990, there could be upwards of—gasp!—ten thousand computers in Great Britain. We also learn about two special computers: the most powerful one ever built in the country, called the Bournemouth (its chief programmer: Computer Jones), as well as the first one designed exclusively for women, called the Petticoat 5 (its creator: Patricia, with a silent surname). By the end of the episode, the Bournemouth and the Petticoat 5 have run off together to, predictably, Bournemouth.

Make sure to write that down in your copy book *now*.

In 1978, a program broadcast on the BBC called *Now the Chips are Down* warned viewers of the disruptive changes in society to come because of microprocessors, which, the narrator claimed, will "totally revolutionize our way of life"—particularly in the automation of jobs—and then accused the British government of ignoring the new technology:

> Perhaps the survival of a nation depends upon its people finding meaningful lives. The questions shout. What is shocking is that the government has been totally unaware of the effects that this technology is going to create. The silence is terrifying. It's time we talked about the future.

The program tapped into the deep fears of Britons, who had suffered through a hard-scrabble decade of widespread unemployment, ballooning inflation, long lines, and high prices. But had the nation truly been left behind from the rest of the industrialized world? Would it now be forced to watch the coming technological revolution from the sidelines?

Now the Chips are Down was likely screened for the British Cabinet. Officials from Prime Minister James Callaghan's government reached out to the BBC to see "if there was anything it could do to raise awareness," explained author Tim Danton in *The Computers That Made Britain*. Sheila Innes, the BBC's Head of Continuing Education Television, directed two subordinates, David Allen and Robert Albury, to travel around the world and "go and see if there is anything in this microelectronics business."

Consequently, the BBC, with backing from the Manpower Services Commission, the Department of Industry, and the Department of Education and Science, developed a three-part series called *The Silicon Factor* (1980) that introduced viewers to silicon chips and their many applications, along with releasing a printed report, called *Microelectronics*, that landed in the hands of British policymakers. The report prompted the BBC Continuing Education Department, which had just completed an adult literacy series starring actor Bob Hoskins called *On the Move*, to begin a *computer* literacy project. *On the Move* was not a standalone television program; instead, it offered associated training and activities to millions of viewers, helping them become active participants in their education rather than just passive spectators. Likewise, a series on computer literacy would need to be more than just a television program; books, manuals, and even software had to be a part of the package, too.

The BBC planned a ten-part TV series focusing on the practical implications of these new technologies. But, with the great number of programming language dialects floating around, Executive Producer John Radcliffe, head of the BBC Computer Literacy Project, realized that the BBC needed to settle on one language, and one dialect, to teach to viewers before the new series could proceed. BBC advisors, among them a teacher at the Arundel School and chairman of Micro Users in Secondary Education (MUSE) called John Alexander Coll, pushed for a standardized version of BASIC, one that viewers could use to try running code shown on TV. MUSE had already developed Adopted BASIC for Computers, or ABC, a structured version of the language that, alas, had not yet been implemented. At a contentious meeting in London, the BBC tried to persuade British computer manufacturers to implement this new common language. But without financial support from the Department of Trade and Industry (DTI), which was not forthcoming, all the manufacturers refused.

Plan B involved roping in the government instead of the manufacturers. The DTI had recently acquired Newbury Laboratories, a consequence of a falling out with Clive Sinclair. The computer pioneer headed Sinclair Research, which produced the Jim Westwood-engineered ZX80 and ZX81 micros; the former was priced at only £100 at launch, less than half the cost of imported VIC-20s, but cost-cutting measures resulted in both ZXs being saddled with touch-sensitive membrane keyboards that were frustrating to use. Sinclair BASIC, developed in the late 1970s by John Grant, fit snugly into only 4K of ROM; when coding lines of BASIC, users employed keyword shortcuts and were alerted to their mistakes via messages. But the display screen flickered whenever a key was pressed because the machine had no dedicated video chip, and the output was strictly in black and white. The ZX81 somewhat improved matters, permitting non-integer data in BASIC and eliminating the flicker by increasing the percentage of time the Zilog Z80 processor dedicated to displaying output.

Newbury Laboratories had built a special Z80 computer with the codename New-Brain, and the BBC looked to modify this machine for the literacy project. Six months of work yielded little progress, however, so the NewBrain idea was abandoned.

Next, John Coll and David Allen, the latter a producer of the literacy project, hastily drew up plans for a microcomputer during Christmas 1980. Color, graphics, and sound were must-haves, as was a robust, fully positive (solid keys) keyboard and the ability to connect to either a monitor or a television set. The micro also had to be expandable and backward compatible. And it had to be cheap.

Seven companies—Acorn, Nascom, Newbury, Research Machines, Sinclair, Tangerine, and Transam—were commissioned by the BBC to submit bids. Research Machines declined to participate, believing the goals were unrealistic, but all the other companies put in bids. From there, the BBC selected only several companies to produce a prototype for consideration; the development teams were given less than one week to demonstrate a finished product.

Acorn was especially determined to win the competition. The company manufactured the Atom, an 8-bit home computer featuring a fast but unusual form of BASIC chock-full of oddities like semicolons, rather than colons, separating statements on lines. The two cofounders of Acorn, Christopher Curry and Hermann Hauser, along with Steve Furber, Chris Turner, and Sophie Wilson, worked tirelessly over the course of three days and two nights to build a working prototype for the impending BBC visit. (In the early 1970s, Curry had designed the best-selling Sinclair Executive Calculator before decamping to start Acorn with Hauser.) The team was helped by the fact that Furber had already been working on a similar design: the Acorn Proton, then still in the planning stages. They were also assisted by Ram Banerjee, "the fastest gun in the West," who was recruited to wire wrap the prototype board.

At around 2 AM, mere hours before the BBC's visit later that Friday morning, the machine still refused to turn on. Hauser, in a fit of frustration, suggested "cut[ting] the umbilical cord from the prototype to the development system [to] let it run on its own"—which worked. Wilson then ported the Acorn System BASIC and part of the Acorn's OS to the board and set up the monitor's controller, with only minutes to spare. "By the time they got upstairs," remembered Wilson, "there was BASIC running on the machine prototype and the Mode 0 display was displayed." Visitors from the BBC saw a simple graphics demo program, and, impressed with the prototype and the can-do attitude of the employees, went for drinks in Cambridge with Acorn's team.

Conversely, the BBC contingent was decidedly unimpressed by Sinclair's ZX80 and ZX81, believing the machines were not up to par; that, coupled with the fact that Clive Sinclair would not peel back the curtain on the Spectrum, then still in the development phase, made the decision easy: the contract to build the BBC Micro—nicknamed the "Beeb"—would go to Acorn.

Under tremendous pressure, Acorn's team had to overcome many technical challenges. Commissioning the UK electronics firm Ferranti—known for their Uncommitted Logic Arrays (ULAs), or gate arrays—to design the machine's graphics chip ultimately led to mass production delays, with the computer not ready to ship in time for the January 11, 1982, premier of the weekly BBC computer literacy ten-episode series, *The Computer Programme*. Nonetheless, "[t]he television programmes brought the Computer Literacy Project directly into the living room," explained Tilly Blyth of the Science Museum in London, "and constructed a vision of a new engaged electronic consumer."

In the opening episode of *The Computer Programme*, titled "It's Happening Now" and first broadcast on BBC Two, the format of the series is established: a blend of historical discussion, on-location reporting, and educational vignettes in a studio, all no more than twenty-five minutes in length. *The Computer Programme* would be geared toward an older audience rather than precocious youngsters. As John Radcliffe put it:

> Generally the material would have to be chosen so as to appeal deliberately to those sections of the audience which had been identified by the research as being less well motivated. Examples of impressively competent youngsters, which would be likely to increase the anxieties of older viewers, would be carefully avoided.

To give viewers of "It's Happening Now" a sense of how fast computers had evolved, studio cohost Ian McNaught-Davis (nicknamed Mac), who had significant experience in the mainframe computing sector, tells fellow cohost and computer newbie Chris Serle that

> it turns out that the Volkswagen Beetle went into production at about the same time as the first large computer was made. And if that had improved in price-performance as much as computers had, then you would have had a Beetle today doing six hundred miles an hour, thirty thousand miles to the gallon. It would have lasted ten thousand years without a service, and it would have cost you fifty p (pence).

By the end of the second episode, "Just One Thing After Another," Mac, after explaining how the Jacquard loom led to punched cards and subroutines, helps Serle write a simple BASIC program.

```
10 PRINT "WHERE IS THE VATICAN ?"
20 INPUT CITY$
30 IF CITY$ <> "ROME" THEN PRINT "WRONG"
40 IF CITY$ = "ROME" THEN PRINT "RIGHT"
```

The BASIC dialect running on the Beeb, called BBC BASIC, was a modified version of Acorn BASIC. Although Sophie Wilson, who was most responsible for Acorn BASIC, was inching toward removing line numbers and replacing them with statement labels, the BBC vetoed that idea. BBC BASIC had to be a structured language, insisted the BBC engineering department's Richard Russell, but compatibility with generic Microsoft BASIC was paramount—hence the line numbers.

Acorn cofounder Hermann Hauser moderated the "standards committee" meetings between Wilson and Russell. "And these were not always easy meetings because [they] didn't always agree on what BBC BASIC should be like," Hauser recalled, "but Sophie normally prevailed because she knew this, of course, backwards and she knew what she could implement efficiently. BBC BASIC then became one of the most celebrated BA-SICs ever, I think, because it was a particularly nice language to write in."

Despite the mandatory line numbers, BBC BASIC offered more advanced features than typical BASICs of the time, such as local variables, recursion, long variable names, and multiline procedures. The interpreter also boasted a fully integrated inline assembler. Far more than merely a Microsoft BASIC clone, BBC BASIC had qualities of structured programming languages like Pascal. In fact, Wilson "guided it [BBC BASIC] towards Pascal," she told UK-based *Your Computer Magazine* in November 1981. "My level of interpreter skill was such that I could write a single-pass Pascal compiler."

In episode three, "Talking to a Machine," Mac complains to Serle that although BASIC is the most popular language for microcomputers, "it has certain problems with it. First of all, it's very easy to make mistakes in BASIC. And secondly, there isn't really a standard BASIC that you can use on every microcomputer—they're all, in some way, a little bit different." By the end of the episode, a BASIC program controlling a small robot arm is queued up and run on the in-studio BBC Micro.

Data storage and retrieval is the focus of the fourth episode, "It's on the Computer," demonstrated with a BASIC program on the Beeb that pulls up the birthdates of keyed-in names. In the fifth, "The New Media," word processing is discussed—in the future, there will be significantly less demand for paper, the hosts assure us—and the following program is presented:

```
10 CLS
20 PRINT "WHAT IS YOUR WORD ?"
30 INPUT WORD$
40 PRINT "THE LENGTH OF YOUR WORD IS " LEN WORD$
```

Loading BASIC subroutines from cassette tape, rather than typing them in, is a recurring motif of the series; episode 6, "Moving Pictures," centerpieces a graphics subroutine pulled from cassette. (The Beeb came bundled with a "Welcome Pack" containing a cassette with sixteen sample programs that demonstrated color, sound, graphics, teletext lettering, and databases, among other features.) After keying in and running the following code,

```
10 GOSUB 500
20 FOR MONTH = 1 TO 12
30     PRINT "SALES";
40     INPUT SALES
50     DRAW MONTH * 100, SALES
60 NEXT MONTH
70 END
```

viewers are treated to a line graph of monthly sales, drawn one input number at a time, on-screen.

In the next episode, "Let's Pretend," games and simulations are discussed, all demonstrated with a BASIC program that models water loss using a visual display similar to the sales graph shown in the previous episode. The animation of water draining out of a pond is an especially effective touch.

The eighth episode, called "The Thinking Machine," focuses on artificial intelligence. Although the BBC Micro appears—it's busy learning how to play noughts and crosses (tic-tac-toe) courtesy of a simplistic form of machine learning—no BASIC code is featured on the show.

In episode nine, "In Control," viewers learn how computers can be programmed to control equipment. Mac hooks up a Beeb to a temperature sensor, directing Serle to run a program that turns on a desk fan if the temperature is too hot (higher than twenty-five degrees centigrade), turns on a heater if the temperature is too cold (lower than fifteen degrees centigrade), or turns both the fan and heater off if the temperature is neither too hot nor too cold:

```
100 TEMP = ADVAL(1)
110 IF TEMP > 25 THEN PROC_SWITCH (1)
120 IF TEMP < 15 THEN PROC_SWITCH (2)
130 IF TEMP > 15 AND TEMP < 25 THEN PROC_SWITCH (0)
140 GOTO 10
```

Speaking of too hot, the prototype BBC Micro used for filming the series tended to overheat; the machine's video processor had to be cooled by spraying it with a can of Freez-It. "And this wasn't the only smoke-and-mirrors trick," writes Danton in *The Computers That Made Britain*, "with the BBC Micro box on the table being for display purposes only: the actual computer was hiding underneath," placed atop a large heatsink and connected to an Acorn System range machine doubling as a disk drive.

The final episode of the series, called "Things to Come," deals with the future of computing. And BASIC code is nowhere to be found on the show—one of *The Computer Programme*'s better, albeit in this case unintentional, predictions.

Producer John Radcliffe acknowledged later on that "although we recognized the value of 'hands-on' experience on personal micros, we began to place less emphasis on programming and more on wider understanding," along with "explanation[s] of computing principles...." The series, rather than being singularly devoted to teaching BASIC, was instead "aimed to help Britons get situated," as we learn from the website *Two-Bit History*. "Where had computing been, and where was it going? What can computers do now, and what might they do in the future? Learning some BASIC was part of answering those questions, but knowing BASIC alone was not seen as enough to make someone computer literate."

About one-sixth of Britons watched at least one episode of *The Computer Programme*, during either original weeknight airings or reruns on Sunday and Monday afternoons. The show's popularity spawned two additional series, both with Ian McNaught-Davis hosting: *Making the Most of the Micro* and *Micro Live*. As Radcliffe wrote in the BBC News article "BBC Micro Ignites Memories of Revolution" (2008), "We were surprised by the reaction. We had audiences between 500,000 and 1.2 million late night on BBC One. We managed to reach 16% of the adult population with one programme or another; so our reach was very wide." All told, nearly 150 Computer Literacy Project programs were produced, with 166 programming exercises supplementing them.

⇍

The BBC initially set a production run of only twelve thousand of the two-megahertz, 8-bit BBC Micro, which offered eight colors on-screen, was powered by a MOS Technology 6502 processor, but lacked a hard drive. Eventually, more than one and a half million BBC Micros were sold in a half-dozen varieties with differences in memory and screen resolution modes (at launch: the 16K Model A for £235 and the 32K Model B for £335; later on: the Model B+64 and the Master 128, among others); over one hundred thousand units were sold in the first year alone. A companion BASIC manual entitled *The Computer Book* sold eighty thousand copies in only six months, and over one hundred thousand people signed up to take a special course, delivered at colleges in England, that taught students BASIC in thirty hours.

These BBC Micros could be decked out with custom ROMs, such as the word processing program EDWORD that was tailored for educational use. In the mid-1980s, Ken Webster, a teacher in the village of Dodleston, borrowed several Beebs from his school for personal use; on them he supposedly discovered a series of cryptic messages saved as files in EDWORD that were written in a style of English dating to the sixteenth century. Thereafter, Webster, his girlfriend, and a friend attempted to communicate with the poltergeist by typing messages on the Beeb, all while paranormal events became commonplace around Webster's home. In the book *The Vertical Plane* (1989), Webster documents his experiences with this ghost in the "box of lights."

Microcomputer fever was thick in the early 1980s UK air, and not just among ghost hunters. Computing magazines—*Micro User, Dragon User, Electron User, Sinclair User, Acorn World, Commodore Horizons, Practical Computing, Your Computer Magazine*—sprouted like weeds. A Micros in Schools initiative was launched, partially funding a computer for every secondary school in Great Britain; the program was soon extended to include primary schools as well. Each school could choose among several microcomputers, such as the BBC Micro and the Research Machines 380Z; the cost of the selected machine would then be partially subsidized by the Department of Industry. Denton notes that "in the mid-1980s, it would have been hard to find a British school that didn't contain a Micro," which resulted in "a generation of computer-literate children, arguably the most computer-literate children in the world at that time. Is it any coincidence that Britain remains a powerhouse of games creation and innovative tech thinking?"

An older 8-bit offering from Research Machines in Oxford, the 380Z ran Digital Research's CP/M operating system; BASIC was packaged into ROM. Recall that Research Machines declined to participate in the BBC Micro bidding war. In fact, by that point, 380Z units could be found in a number of schools throughout the UK. By the mid-1980s, micros manufactured by Research Machines were mainstays in British schools.

The 380Z and the Beeb weren't the only game in town, of course. The ZX Spectrum—or, as Clive Sinclair jokingly called it during the computer's announcement event at the Churchill Hotel, "Not the BBC Micro"; he was still smarting after BBC rejected Sinclair in favor of Acorn—debuted in 1982 and featured color graphics at a low price point (£125). It was cheaper than the Beeb and arguably offered the better value.

The Spectrum's version of Sinclair BASIC, a superset of the ZX81's BASIC, ran slower than BBC BASIC. John Mathieson, in charge of producing the Spectrum, later observed, "The programming was right there: everybody played a little bit with the BASIC, even if they were mostly playing games on it. And so I think there's a generation of game writers in the UK that grew up with the Spectrum." Case in point: as a teenager, British computer game designer Julian Gollop used the ZX81, BBC Micro, and ZX Spectrum to develop his earliest games—including *Rebelstar Raiders*, written with Spectrum Sinclair BASIC.

The Micros in Schools initiative added the ZX Spectrum, nicknamed the "Speccy," to their list of government-sponsored computers for primary schools. Though it never made significant inroads in UK schools, the 8-bit Spectrum models sold over five million units worldwide, making the Speccy Britain's best-selling computer of the 1980s.

The Spectrum even crossed the Iron Curtain, making its way to Czechoslovakia where enthusiasts like electronic scoreboard engineer Jiří Pobříslo excitedly programmed in BASIC on the machine. "Sometime in early 1983…I was reading up in *Amateur Radio* about how Englishmen invented the [Sinclair ZX] Spectrum and what it's capable of," Pobříslo remembered. "At the same time, I got hold of a BASIC course…and I eventually learned the language." Thanks to the difficulty of procuring micros, it was not unusual for young Czechoslovak programmers like Pobříslo and Vlastimil Veselý to learn BASIC prior to ever owning a computer—running machine-less BASIC programs using only pencil, paper, and brainpower.

Indeed, the scarcity of electronic computers in Czechoslovakia led many to employ paper computers similar to the American CARDboard Illustrative Aid to Computation (also known as the CARDIAC Cardboard Computer) and the German WDR Paper Computer (also called the Know-how Computer): educational aids to teach programming via a functional albeit human-powered, paper-made representation of a computer (calculations were manually completed). In 1981, the seventh issue of the magazine *ABC of Young Technicians and Scientists* (*ABC mladých techniků a přírodovědců*) featured such a paper computer: the Computer Game System, a paper model with ten memory registers, a modest instruction set, two included games, and oodles of self-modifying code (a typical characteristic of the programs for these educational aids).

As the availability of microcomputers in the country increased, the Czechoslovak homebrew community tinkered and "adapt[ed] programs from BASIC listings and images in domestic and imported magazines," according to Jaroslav Švelch in *Gaming the Iron Curtain*. For example, *Amateur Radio* published BASIC listings of several text-based games, including the *Lunar Landing Game* popularized by David Ahl. The "Golden Triangle"—a group of three Czechoslovak teenagers who met at the Station of Young Technicians in Prague, which in the mid-1980s was a hotbed of microcomputer activity—programmed the ZX Spectrum, at first in BASIC. But later, they mostly stopped using the language because it ran too slowly. Nonetheless, Golden Triangle member František Fuka developed an influential (and unlicensed) text-based adventure game in Spectrum BASIC loosely based on the Indiana Jones movies. And Miroslav Fídler, another Golden Triangle member, wrote the anti-socialist "protest" game *RECONSTRUCTION* in BASIC anonymously.

Sinclair teamed up with the U.S.-based Timex Corporation to manufacture the ZX81 at its plant in Dundee, Scotland. The Timex Computer Corporation was formed to sell Sinclair computers in the United States, thereby expanding Sinclair's reach beyond the island. The U.S. version of the ZX81 was called the Timex/Sinclair T/S 1000, while the Spectrum was rebranded the T/S 2068 for the States.

In 1984, Sinclair released the upmarket Sinclair QL (Quantum Leap), with Super-BASIC—originally intended as the BASIC interpreter for the canceled SuperSpectrum—included in ROM along with the operating system, QDOS. Developed by software engineer Jan Jones—an actual "Computer Jones"—SuperBASIC brought a procedure-based structure to the language. Within a few years, the Sinclair QL was history, and Jones left the company and became an award-winning novelist.

Despite the success of the BBC Micro, Acorn couldn't rest on its laurels—in part because of intense competition from Sinclair. As Acorn engineer Steve Furber remembered it, "Once the BBC Micro was launched, there was a feeling that the machine was great but that it was a bit expensive, and that there was a big market out there comprising people who would buy machines if only they were a bit cheaper." With the low-priced Spectrum eating into the Beeb's market share, and the BBC Model A—cheaper but less functional than the Model B—not selling well, cofounders Curry and Hauser looked to compete with Sinclair by fashioning a microcomputer less expensive than the Model A. Hauser envisioned "a miniaturised BBC Microcomputer with higher resolution graphics than those offered by the Spectrum," he told *Popular Computing Weekly*, promising compatibility with existing BBC Micro software.

Called the Electron, its release date was set for the second half of 1982. Costs were lowered by drastically reducing the number of chips on the board while selling its expansion potential to the public. Plus, the machine would come packaged with BBC BASIC II, adding more functionality to BBC BASIC—including the ability to enter a BASIC command with a single keypress. But history repeated itself: costly delays involving Ferranti's ULA plagued the Electron, so the machine didn't make its debut until the summer of 1983. When it arrived on store shelves, advertised at £200, the Electron lacked Mode 7 (Teletext mode), a graphics mode that ate up only one kilobyte of the 32K available memory. Nonetheless, Acorn took more orders than it could fill, leading to a backlog that required more than half a year to eliminate. By the time the company ramped up production, however, demand for the machine sunk as the British home computer market wilted.

Delays also hobbled Intelligent Software's 8-bit Z80A-based micro. Though announced in 1983, the machine—which went through a number of name changes, from Samurai to Elan to Flan to, finally, Enterprise—shipped in 1985. BASIC wasn't burned in ROM but was instead available as a ROM cartridge. IS approached Microsoft to write the interpreter, but the software giant balked at the modifications requested. Instead, IS developed a BASIC that checked line syntax prior to execution, held multiple programs in memory simultaneously (parameters could be passed between programs), and adhered to the ANSI standard.

Another home-grown micro, the Dragon 32, was born in Wales. Very similar in design to the Tandy TRS-80 Color Computer, the "CoCo" never gained much traction in Britain. Powered by an 8-bit Motorola 6809 processor, the £200 Dragon was set to ship with 16K of memory—until the Spectrum arrived on the scene, leading Dragon Data, in a fit of competitive fire, to shoehorn in a daughterboard at the last minute that bumped up the Dragon's memory to 32K. The Dragon 32 also came packaged with a

Microsoft Extended BASIC interpreter nearly identical to the CoCo's. Despite the many common elements between the two micros, Tandy UK declined to sue. (The TRS-80 was also effectively cloned by the Hong Kong manufacturer EACA, with its Video Genie family of computers. The Genie, like the Spectrum, made its way across the Iron Curtain to Czechoslovakia where videogame designer Vít Libovický appreciated how the EACA machine instantly loaded to a BASIC interpreter—unlike mainframes of the day, which could take fifteen minutes to boot up.)

Even with the arrival of a 64K version, and despite partnering with the Tano Corporation to sell the Dragon 64 in the U.S. market, the Dragon's days were numbered. Besides offering only limited software support, Dragon Data was rocked by a series of financial crises, which led Spain-based Eurohard S.A. to purchase the company in 1984, effectively spelling the end of the machine.

Tangerine Computer Systems, based in the UK, also contributed to Britain's microcomputer boom, developing the 8-bit 6502-based Oric-1 in 1982. The company followed up with two additional 8-bit machines: the Oric Atmos and the Oric Telestrat. Sound commands in Oric-1 BASIC were unusual: three separate tones, along with a noise channel, could be accessed with the keywords **ZAP** (producing a laser gun sound), **SHOOT** (a gunshot sound), **EXPLODE** (an explosion sound), and **PING** (a bell-type tone).

Self-made British billionaire and entrepreneur Alan Sugar, who founded the electronics company Amstrad (Alan Michael Sugar TRADing) when he was only twenty-one, wasn't interested in the tech industry until the success of Commodore and Sinclair changed his mind. Sugar was certain he could improve upon the ZX81, so in 1983 Amstrad began development of what eventually became the 8-bit Amstrad CPC (Colour Personal Computer). The company contracted out the development of a BASIC interpreter to Locomotive Software; at the time, the software house was busy writing Mallard BASIC, a speedy Business BASIC interpreter named after the London and North Eastern Railway 4468 *Mallard*, the fastest steam-powered locomotive in the world. Locomotive BASIC, the result of their efforts for Amstrad, was burned into the CPC's ROM.

Though we could list many more British home computers—the Camputers Lynx, the Grundy NewBrain, and the Apricot machines come to mind—let's wrap up with the Jupiter Ace. A Z80-powered microcomputer, it employed a Forth programming language environment—a kind of mix between high-level and low-level coding—that offered a number of advantages over BASIC. Jupiter Cantab, the computer's manufacturer, was founded by Richard Altwasser and Steven Vickers, both of whom had helped design the ZX Spectrum at Sinclair Research. Although innovative, the Ace earned only limited acceptance in the BASIC-dominated marketplace.

Imports flooded the island, too, with Apple, Atari, and Commodore computers being the most notable. The Commodore 64, a machine purchased by tens of millions worldwide, arrived in Great Britain in 1983 to wide acclaim. And the Atari ST ended up selling even more units in Europe than stateside.

By the early 1980s, Britons clearly had developed a love affair with home computers, and the computing press in the United States took notice. A *Byte* article from January 1983, headlined "Microcomputing, British style," reported from the Fifth Personal

Computer World Show held at the Barbican Center in London in which nearly fifty thousand people attended—significantly more than the concurrent and similarly staged West Coast Computer Faire that "was—until now—the world's largest microcomputer show." Concluded *Byte* senior editor Gregg Williams, "There's ample evidence that, compared to the U.S., proportionally more of Britain's population is interested in microcomputers."

Usborne Publishing, based in London, was ready to take advantage of that, as we'll see in the next chapter.

CHAPTER 7

THE UK CONNECTION, PART II
A Guide to the World of Home Computing

What can we learn from the 1980s Usborne BASIC books?

The 1980s, with its vibrant microcomputer scene, saw an explosion of books about BASIC programming—or at least featuring BASIC code. Among the best and the most recognizable of these were volumes of the Usborne series, compact computer books geared toward a younger audience and released by Usborne Publishing Ltd, headquartered at 20 Garrick Street in London.

Usborne Books got its start in 1973 thanks to publisher Peter Usborne, who, a decade earlier, cofounded the British satiric magazine *Private Eye*. With its characteristic cartoon drawings, vibrant palette of colors, prodigiously illustrated diagrams, clear layouts, annotated code listings, and trademark red hot air balloon logo, Usborne computer books were mainstays in the homes of children on both sides of the pond and are considered cult classics today. These texts were especially appealing because, though appearing simple superficially, they were not watered down, did not spare readers the technical details, and thus could serve as an introduction first and a reference later. Numerous books were available, most around fifty pages in length and aimed at a range of skill sets; all were priced between 99p and £5.00 at the time of publication.

A prototypical offering was *Practise Your BASIC: Puzzles, Tests and Problems to Improve Your Skills* (1983) by Gaby Waters and Nick Cutler. In the text, we were treated to a basic introduction to the language, carried out via exercises whose answers were found at the back of the book. For instance, page 12 presented **IF/THEN** exercises, extending to examples featuring a simple guessing game and a text-based horse race. Page 14 introduced random numbers, culminating by writing a game of chance in order to escape from the alien planet Zorgos. A spot-the-bugs challenge was shown on page 15. Breezy sections followed, focused on teaching readers about **READ** and **DATA**, arrays, subroutines, and ASCII (the American Standard Code for Information Interchange, an international standardized 7-bit character code for electronic communications). On page 27, underneath the heading "Fruit machine program to write," the reader was challenged to build a slot machine simulation. A screenshot illustrating a sample run, along with hints and other explanatory passages, guided the budding BASIC programmer to the finish line. Programs requiring more complex logic, like a treasure hunt, were detailed over the course of several pages (28 to 33)—complete with flowcharts of subroutines, diagrams of game logic, and snippets of code.

In the final section of *Practise Your BASIC*, which contained the answers to exercises as well as listings of programs, readers were given a warning: "The programs are written in a standard BASIC, so you may have to convert some of the non-standard commands, such as **RND** and **CLS** to suit your computer." Indeed, despite the push toward standardization spearheaded by ANSI and Thomas Kurtz himself—resulting in the publication of a Minimal BASIC standard in the late 1970s and the development of Full BASIC—microcomputer dialects of BASIC varied widely, with even the relatively simple and highly circumscribed programs of *Practise Your BASIC* not guaranteed to always work on every machine.

A BASIC conversion chart between popular dialects, found on page 47 of the book, contained two tables. The first displayed three columns: one for **CLS** (clears the screen), one for **INT(RND(1)*N+1)** (selects a random whole number between **1** and **N**), and one for **INKEY\$** (returns a character read from the keyboard). Rows of the first table were populated by names of the micros—BBC, VIC 20/PET, Dragon, Oric-1, TRS-80, Apple, ZX81, and ZX Spectrum—along with the converted code. For instance, the Commodore VIC-20/PET did not support **CLS**; rather, **PRINT CHR\$(147)** cleared the screen. In addition, there was no **INKEY\$** command; to obtain a keypress from the user, **GET X\$**, where **X\$** was a string variable, had to be utilized. On the Apple, **HOME** cleared the screen, while these lines were used to detect a keypress:

```
X$=""
IF PEEK(-16384)>127 THEN GET X$
```

The second table on page 47 showed additional conversions for Sinclair (and corresponding Timex) micros. **LEFT\$**, **RIGHT\$**, and **MID\$** functions wouldn't work on these machines; substrings were obtained in the following manner instead. The code

```
LET X$="LORENZO"
PRINT X$(1 TO 4)
PRINT X$(5 TO )
PRINT X$(2 TO 4)
```

would output:

```
LORE
NZO
ORE
```

Dimensioning a string array was also idiosyncratic on Sinclair micros. The array took two arguments: the number of strings in the array and the length of the longest string. So, **DIM A\$(6,10)** set up a string array of six elements with the longest of these strings containing ten characters.

Odder still was the presence of **DATA** and **READ** on the Spectrum despite these statements not being part of BASIC on the ZX81. For the latter micro, the nearest equivalent looked something like this:

```
10 FOR A=1 TO 6
20 INPUT T$(A)
30 NEXT A
```

Even ASCII was handled differently on these machines. Instead of **ASC**, the keyword **CODE** was required. And while the Spectrum used ASCII as its collating sequence, the ZX81 employed its own unique set of one-byte characters (the set was dissimilar to IBM's EBCDIC, the Extended Binary Coded Decimal Interchange Code, as well). The ZX81 character set contained sixty-four glyphs (graphical representation of characters), from 0 to 63, that included block graphics (0 to 10), punctuation (11 to 27, including the conveniently located code for the British pound: 12), the ten digits (28 to 37), and the capitalized letters of the alphabet (38 to 63). The remaining character set codes, from 64 to 255, were assigned to inverse video versions of the first sixty-four characters, to BASIC keywords, and to control characters (there were some unused codes). The following program output the entire character set:

```
10 LET C=0
20 PRINT CHR$ C
30 LET C=C+1
40 IF C<256 THEN GOTO 20
```

The ZX81 membrane keyboard served as a masterclass in packing as much utility in as small a space as possible, with some keys offering up to five possible options when pressed. Besides letters and numbers, character set symbols such as $ and £ could be typed directly from the keyboard when the **L** cursor appeared on-screen. The **G** cursor indicated graphics mode, whereby the user could press keys printed with graphics symbols. Inverse video characters also could be input.

Usborne Guide to Better BASIC: A Beginner's Guide to Writing Programs (1983), by Brian Reffin Smith and Lisa Watts, was in the same vein as *Practise Your BASIC*. Included were short programs introducing keywords and concepts, along with detailed (and colorfully illustrated) explanations of longer programs. But *Better BASIC* had more real-world, applied examples, rather than simulations or games, lining its pages than *Practise*, including a section titled "Making a soccer database" that explained how to build a database with the reasoning behind each step detailed. In addition, sorting algorithms were demonstrated (bubble sort and Shellsort), bar chart and line graph programs were proffered, and a simple chatbot (though it was not called that) was presented, rounding out a discussion of string capabilities. Like *Practise*, pages near the end of *Better BASIC* were devoted to answers to exercises (there weren't many) and program conversions between machines (there were a fair number of them, especially considering the differences in syntax for strings and graphics commands. For instance, the Tangerine Computer Systems Oric-1 and the Spectrum both drew lines in a relative way, from the previously plotted point to a set of new coordinates, rather than in an absolute manner as measured from the origin at the top left corner of the screen).

Lisa Watts also wrote a companion book to *Better BASIC* called *Usborne Guide to Programming Tricks & Skills: Professional Tips and Hints for Better Program Writing* (1984). Despite its generic title, all the tricks and skills and tips and hints were presented exclusively in BASIC, with the exception of a snippet of Pascal code. The book was tailor-made for readers interested in pushing BASIC to its limits.

One section, devoted to increasing the execution speed of programs, offered several suggestions: explicitly typing integer variables, if available (by postfixing a percentage sign, as in **A%** instead of **A**); utilizing integer variables, if possible, as counter variables for **FOR/NEXT** loops ("[t]hey run twice as fast as those with ordinary variables," wrote Watts); rearranging the order of subroutines by frequency of their use; shortening a program by deleting comments (remarks); including more than one statement per line (if permitted); and eliminating as many spaces as possible on each line. *Programming Tricks & Skills* also contained sections on naming variables, defining functions, cross-referencing arrays (i.e., having a one-dimensional array serve as an "index" for a two-dimensional array), writing menus, checking real-time input (**LET I$=INKEY$** was explained, albeit the technique was far from standard on all computers, with the C64 and VIC-20 using **GET I$** instead), and packing data with ASCII codes.

Though the commands were not available on all micros, *Programming Tricks & Skills* detailed how to use **PEEK** and **POKE** to pack data. **PEEK**, in which the computer "peeked" at the contents of a memory location (i.e., the byte stored at that location), and **POKE**, in which the computer stored a value at a specified memory location, were not only powerful but also sufficiently dangerous to merit a warning in the book: "You have to be very careful using this method as if you poke data in the wrong memory locations you may confuse the computer by wiping out essential information," requiring that the machine be turned off and back on again. Thus, when packing data with these commands, you had to be deliberate and cautious—and the steps were far from intuitive for a neophyte BASIC programmer.

Here's how the process worked. If you knew the first memory address in which BASIC programs on your computer were stored, then replace **A** with this address in line **20** below; next, insert your numerical data starting at line **100**. When the following program was run,

```
10 REM(**********etc.—the number of stars = the number of numbers you wish
to store)
20 FOR I=A TO A+100
30 LET C=PEEK(I)
40 PRINT "ADDRESS ";I;" = ";
50 IF C<31 OR C>117 THEN LET C=46
60 PRINT CHR$(C)
70 NEXT I
80 STOP
100 DATA list your numbers here
120 DATA etc.
150 FOR I=X TO X+(number of data items)-1
```

```
160 READ N
170 POKE I,N
180 NEXT I
```

BASIC would **PEEK** into each memory location and store those contents into variable **C**, one iteration of the loop at a time. If **C** was classified as an unprintable character, then the value stored in **C** was replaced by the ASCII code for a full stop/period (**.**)—which is 46 in decimal—and output as such on-screen. Also, at some point during runtime, stars appear on the screen; copy down the address of that first star, making sure there are as many stars as numbers in the lines of **DATA**.

With all that done, we can now pack the numeric data. Type in the following as direct commands (i.e., with no line numbers):

```
LET X=address of the first star
GOTO 100
```

This restarts the program, albeit from line **100**. As the **FOR/NEXT** loop (lines **150** to **180**) iterates, numbers are read into **N** and then **POKE**d into **I**. Once completed, all the numbers were packed into memory.

To access a number, we had to use the address of the first star with a **PRINT PEEK**, as shown below.

```
PRINT PEEK(address+data position-1)
```

However, were weren't out of the woods quite yet; there were several more steps to go. As Watts explained it,

> To check [that] the numbers are in the memory you can run the program again. Now you can delete lines **20** onwards and add line **10** to the program which needs the data. You must not list line **10** as the computer may crash when it tries to display data on the screen. You can list the rest of the program, though, by typing **LIST** with a line number.

As usual, the programmer had to be mindful of different BASIC dialects, and not only because of variations in system memory addresses. For example, some BASICs employed hexadecimal (base 16) addresses of memory locations, rather than decimal (base 10) ones, when **PEEK**ing and **POKE**ing. In addition, if you had a BBC Micro or an Electron, instead of the keywords **PEEK** and **POKE**, a question mark (**?**), called the *query operator*, was used; thus, **PRINT PEEK(address)** became **PRINT ?address**, while **POKE 4057,64**—which **POKE**d the number 64 into memory location 4057—was replaced with **?4057=64**. (In an 8-bit microcomputer, each memory address took up two bytes—that's sixteen bits—with the highest decimal memory location addressed as 65536, which is 11111111 11111111 in binary. Each **POKE** statement **POKE**d a single byte into memory, since each memory location contained one byte; bytes ranged from 00000000 to 11111111 in binary, equivalent to 0 to 255 in decimal.)

What's more, note that obtaining the correct first address **A** for the program above required research on the part of the programmer; such information was available on a *memory map*, typically found in the computer's manual (there was even one printed in the *Family BASIC* manual, detailing the innards of Nintendo's Famicom). A memory map revealed the layout of the computer's memory, including the beginning addresses corresponding to each area of memory. An example memory map is shown below; the addresses (in both hexadecimal and decimal form) mark the beginning of each area.

Input/output   *(&6000 / 24576)*
Screen memory (or "display file")   *(where information for the screen display is stored)*   *(&5C00 / 23552)*
Variable storage   *(data for variables and arrays)*   ---the border between variables and RAM varies, depending on the amount of storage needed for the variables---
User/free RAM   *(BASIC programs are automatically stored here; the highest address in RAM is called the "RAMTOP" or "HIMEM")*   *(&2E00 / 11776)*
Reserved for OS (or "monitor") use   *(keeps track of the operations of the machine)*   *(&2400 / 9216)*
BASIC   *(ROM program interpreting BASIC)*   *(&0400 / 1024)*
operating system or "monitor"   *(directs the machine)*   *(&0000 / 0)*

These were the days when most home computers had between 32K and 48K of RAM (random access memory), although BASIC programs couldn't make use of all that space. Around 3K was set aside for what Watts called "housekeeping tasks"—"for storing information it [the computer] needs while it carries out the program." In addition, high resolution graphics modes ate up even more of the memory pie, leaving perhaps as little as 10K for programs. **PEEK**ing into any of the locations shown in the memory map was technically possible, but one could only **POKE** into RAM (strictly off limits was the ROM, or read-only memory, since such storage was by definition not modifiable).

Programming Tricks & Skills, perhaps as useful for a precocious young programmer as a veteran adult, culminated with the *Flip-file program*, which crammed most of the book's tips and techniques into a single functional package. Watts also suggested obtaining a so-called programmer's toolkit, which assisted with debugging as well as automating tedious tasks such as deleting **REM**s, moving and renumbering lines, merging programs, listing variables, and replacing variables names.

Recall that Lisa Watts partnered with Brian Reffin Smith to write *Usborne Guide to Better BASIC: A Beginner's Guide to Writing Programs*; that book served as a sequel to an easier albeit more comprehensive text, *Introduction to Computer Programming: BASIC for Beginners* (1982), also by Smith. *BASIC for Beginners* presents a mostly generic version of the language; hence, no section for conversions between microcomputer dialects is included, though there are a handful of nonstandard statements used (e.g., **CLS**, **LEFT$**, and, surprisingly, **PLOT/UNPLOT** for controlling pixels; in addition, **LET** is employed anytime a variable is initialized to a value). The scope of the text is wide, covering a great many introductory programming concepts like control statements, I/O, and subroutines. Although *BASIC for Beginners* was available in the United States and Canada, it wasn't published by Usborne for those countries; rather, Hayes Books/Publishing, based in Tulsa, Oklahoma, and Ontario, Canada, took the reins.

For a more pared down approach than presented in *BASIC for Beginners*, look no further than two books by Gaby Waters: *First Computer Library: Computer Fun* (1984) and *First Computer Library: Simple BASIC* (1984). *Computer Fun* features text-only programs, mostly basic BASIC games (e.g., an obstacle course and a find-the-key game) but also several clever applications. For instance, one program called "Birthday fact-finder" calculates a user's age in years, months, and days based on the birthdate entered. "If you add these lines to the program," Waters suggests, "the computer will work out how old you will be in the year 2000," back when kids (and even some adults) couldn't conceive of the end of the century:

```
170 PRINT " IN THE YEAR 2000 YOU WILL BE"
180 PRINT " ";2000-Y2;" YEARS OLD"
```

There were also applications to generate "computer postcards" and thank-you letters. Unlike in *Introduction to Computer Programming*, in *Computer Fun* there are a handful of pages at the end of the book detailing code conversions for computers like the BBC Micro, the Commodore 64, the VIC 20, the Spectrum, and the Electron.

First Computer Library: Simple BASIC is similar to *Computer Fun*, but scales back the complexity even further; short programs, each illustrating a single concept such as input, random numbers, and loops, are included.

⇸

Usborne also published books of type-ins. In the twenty-page *Computer Spy Games* (1984) by Jenny Tyler and Chris Oxlade, readers were treated to BASIC games written in a text-based form of the language requiring a handful of changes between systems; symbols appearing to the left of BASIC lines indicated the need for alterations, with each symbol corresponding to different hardware: ▲ for the VIC and Commodore 64, ★ for the BBC Micro and Acorn Electron, ■ for the TRS-80, ● for the Apple, and ˢ (or, sometimes, a six-pointed star) for the ZX Spectrum. For example, a line of code to store a random letter from A to Z might be shown as

```
ˢ★■▲●100 LET M$=CHR$(INT(RND*26+38))
```

The line required changes for all of the above microcomputers, since there were differences in how these machines handled the output of character codes (**CHR$** to display ASCII characters), or the generation of pseudorandom numbers (**RND**), or both. The BBC Micro and Electron produced a random letter from A to Z this way:

```
CHR$(RND(26)+64)
```

while the Apple and Commodore machines performed the same task using the expression

```
CHR$(INT(RND(1)*26+65))
```

In addition, sometimes adjustments to BASIC programs were the result of the variation in screen sizes between the microcomputers, with the VIC-20 offering a maximum of twenty-two characters across the screen and twenty-three lines downward; the TRS-80 boasting sixty-four across by sixteen characters down; the BBC/Electron operating at twenty/forty/eighty across by twenty-five/thirty-two down; the ZX81 and ZX Spectrum displaying thirty-two across by twenty-two down; and the Apple and C64 both offering forty across by twenty-five down.

A warning was issued to readers early on in *Computer Spy Games*: "Some games depend on the speed of both your reactions and your computer. You may find you need to adjust the speed." For example, the "Beeb" (the BBC's nickname) and the "Speccy" (the ZX Spectrum's nickname) typically ran the programs too quickly, with late-model Beebs executing them at a clip that made the games mostly unplayable. Correcting the problem usually meant increasing the multiplicative constants lodged at the end of **FOR** statements:

```
100 FOR I=1 TO G*3
```

Computer Spy Games included listings for programs like *Searchlight*, in which you crossed dangerous enemy territory while trying to avoid a searchlight; *SpyQTest*, an educational exercise with numbers; and *Morse Coder*, a utility for sending and receiving Morse code messages. The book offered annotated line-by-line explanations of the code, encouraging novices and experts alike to appreciate the workings under the hood.

Weird Computer Games (1984), written by the same two authors as *Computer Spy Games*, followed an identical format. Again, readers were warned of possibly having to alter the speed of the programs. Notable games in the slim volume included *Skulls of the Pyramid*, in which the player was reduced to nothing more than a mind without a body; *Jaws*, in which you played as Jaws, attempting to eat as many people as possible while avoiding the "Hunter"; and *Micropuzzle*, a bizarre adventure game with only one objective: escaping the clutches (and claws) of a very large cat.

Although *Creepy Computer Games* (1983) was assembled with the help of a number of authors (it was edited by Jenny Tyler), the structure followed in lockstep with *Computer Spy Games* and *Weird Computer Games*. In the game *Ghost Guzzler*, the eponymous weapon was brandished to defeat attacking ghosts. Mastering *Number Wizard* required the player to perform some quick mental arithmetic. And completing *Seance* necessitated successfully interpreting messages from the great beyond.

Two longer volumes of type-ins, titled *Computer Battlegames* (1982) and *Computer Space-games* (1982), both by Daniel Isaaman and Jenny Tyler, were brighter and more colorful than the aforementioned three, which had a decidedly noir-like aesthetic predominated by shades of gray. Despite the visual differences, the format of these two earlier books was similar: symbols next to lines of code requiring changes (to work properly on various micros), along with copious annotations of program lines unpacking form and function. The games were relatively simple efforts, with the authors promising that "many were short enough to fit into the ZX81's 1K of memory." What's more, concluding pages of both books presented suggestions for improving the games as well as concise BASIC tutorials offering guidelines for writing original, fully-featured programs. Sprinkled throughout the many type-ins were puzzles, with answers found in the back of the texts, that challenged budding programmers to make minor modifications to the code.

Computer Battlegames offered a *Shootout* game to test one's reflexes: once the words "HE DRAWS" pop up on the screen, the player must press a key—but not before. In *Secret Weapon*, all that stands between you and a crippling robot attack is a device capable of slicing through solid rock: aim the weapon blindly by repeatedly entering in guesses for x and y coordinates, hoping for a successful strike. *Missile!* was especially unique, since it employed graphics commands. To account for the significant differences in graphics syntax between machines, multiple versions of the game were listed to ensure compatibility. The book *Computer Spacegames* also featured a graphics-oriented game called *Touchdown*, requiring the player to gently land a lightweight craft on the surface of the moon; once again, numerous versions of the game, accounting for the wide variations in microcomputer graphics features, were listed. Plus, text-based games like *Evil Alien*, in which the player positioned bombs on a three-dimensional grid to stave off the evil Elron; *Monsters of Galacticon*, involving fighting off "the nastiest monsters in the known Universe" with a choice of weapons; and *Death Valley*, a fast-paced race down a bottomless ravine—querying the user for the width of the valley, which was inversely correlated with the difficulty level—rounded out the volume.

Four additional type-in books, classified as an adventure game series, were a departure from previous Usborne efforts. What was an "adventure game," in the publisher's view? "When you play an adventure game," explained the authors of one of these books,

> you become the hero or heroine of the adventure. You have a dangerous quest and you need all your ingenuity and cunning to succeed. You may meet monsters or enemies whom you have to outwit. You may come up against obstacles such as a raging torrent or a landslide blocking your way. You will come across objects as you play the game (a lamp or a rope, for example) which, if you use them properly, will help you overcome hazards.

The Beeb and TRS-80 needed 32K of memory to run these Usborne adventure games, whereas 48K of memory was required if using the Spectrum. With the 16K expansion, the VIC-20 ran the programs, too.

In *The Mystery of Silver Mountain* (1984) by Chris Oxlade and Judy Tatchell, seventeen of the first thirty-four pages were devoted to world building, as the sights and magic of the imaginary land of Sylvani unfolded before the readers eyes courtesy of prodigiously illustrated images and descriptive text. Then, the lengthy "Mystery of Silver Mountain" BASIC text-based adventure program listing appeared, consuming the remainder of the book—complete with the tedious nips and tucks in code necessary for successful execution of the adventure game on a variety of platforms.

The Island of Secrets (1984), written by Jenny Tyler and Les Howarth, offered readers more of the same: over a dozen pages of world building—clearly influenced by *Lord of the Rings*—followed by gaming instructions, a short section on debugging BASIC programs, and a lengthy program listing of the eponymous text adventure, filled to the brim with puzzles to solve. As usual, a number of changes to the code, cosmetic and otherwise, were necessary for compatibility on all machines. The book does contain one notable passage, however: in a short panel titled "About adventure programs," the authors write, "You have probably heard about adventure games even if you've never played one. They were invented in the U.S.A. in 1976 and first played on mainframes with huge memories." Although the date of creation seems rather late—considering the work of programmers like David H. Ahl in the early 1970s, not to mention the efforts of creative Dartmouth undergrads pecking away on their Teletypes almost a decade earlier—the Usborne authors have a very specific style of game in mind (another of the Usborne books, detailed below, will add a little more context to the historical description).

The complexity ramps up in Les Howarth and Cheryl Evans's *Write Your Own Fantasy Games for Your Microcomputer* (1984) and Jenny Tyler and Les Howarth's *Write Your Own Adventure Programs for Your Microcomputer* (1983). These books mostly flip the script of the previous two, leaving some elements of program creation and world building in the hands of readers.

Write Your Own Fantasy Games evoked *Dungeons & Dragons*, and unabashedly so. The book opens by describing the prototypical fantasy game—"an adventure game with a difference," the authors explain. "An adventure game usually involves a dangerous expedition, or Quest, with obstacles to overcome, enemies to face and treasure to find. In fantasy games the added challenge is that players do not play as themselves but take on a character, or role." Hence the RPG, or role-playing game. Stressing the importance of creating consistent rules to keep the attendant complexity under control, *D&D* is cited as an exemplar. "The first people to publish the rules they had developed for their fantasy game [*D&D*] were two Americans, Gary Gygax and Dave Arneson. They called their game *Dungeons and Dragons* and it appeared in 1974." Around this time, fantasy games debuted on mainframes, migrating their way to micros as well—though early on the playability and scope of these games had to be reduced and condensed, respectively, to successfully fit onto home computers, with text-only worlds and single-player adventures offered rather than richer experiences available at the time on machines with more memory. A workaround to these limitations involved using computer programs in a narrow sense: to aid in character design, dungeon layout, or the adjudication of combat. (Deeply influenced by such early fantasy games was "Lord British" Richard Garriott who, still a high school student in 1979, coded the role-playing videogame *Akalabeth* using Applesoft BASIC running on an Apple II, and then went on to create the *Ultima* series, also, at first, in BASIC.)

The centerpiece of *Write Your Own Fantasy Games* is *Dungeon of Doom*, a collection of three expandable BASIC programs written for the C64, the VIC-20, the BBC, the Electron, and the Spectrum (along with conversion lines for compatibility's sake). Listings for a dungeon generator, a character creator, and a game module were squeezed into the final third of the book. *Dungeon of Doom* spotlights the survivors of Crekkan, whose Magic Idol was buried in the bowels of the Castle Crekkan after sustaining a devastating attack by the evil sorcerer Klimm. The player was assigned the task of finding the lost Idol beneath the castle ruins. The included dungeon generator had users control a cursor to position graphical elements—like potions, monsters, and treasure chests—on a fifteen-by-fifteen grid; the program makes copious use of two-dimensional arrays. The character creator similarly afforded user flexibility: attributes, character types, and goods for sale were available. Finally, the game module served as the workhorse, interpreting the data generated from the dungeon generator and character creator by bringing the *Dungeon of Doom* world to life; essentially, the program housed the game engine, organized as a series of subroutines (e.g., implementing player moves like "get," "reveal," "attack," and "conjure," the last of which was the largest such routine in the game module).

The authors spill quite a bit of ink explaining how the three programs of *Dungeon of Doom* work their magic; flowcharts and diagrams populate page after page, revealing the inherent complexity of the routines along with the many variables that must be kept in check, the ways in which the code might be expanded, and the possible errors that could arise. Yet even typing in the BASIC lines exactly as they appeared in the text required great concentration, due to the compact variable naming scheme and the fact that there were multiple statements per line. Here is a representative example from the game module:

```
210 IF RH=C1 THEN LET X=NX:LET Y=NY:GOSUB570:LET NX=DX:LET NY=DY:LET
F(1)=F(1)-.03
```

In addition, even with the intermittent annotations, following the logic of the code was sometimes a tricky prospect. For example, again from the game module:

```
1060 IF SL=0 OR (O(17)=0 AND SL(5) OR (O(18)=0 AND SL>3) OR SL>6 THEN
GOTO1040
```

To top it off, the book offered narrative suggestions for budding fantasy storytellers, with the authors adding, "You could research a period in history or base a futuristic game on your favourite piece of science fiction." And if you couldn't find anyone to play the game with you, consider recruiting the support of a magazine via a "postal game," formally termed a play-by-mail (PBM) game: human competition was yours, albeit at a snail's pace, provided you pay an enrollment fee as well as a nominal payment for each round. Indeed, following the success of PBMs like *Diplomacy*, which arrived in the late 1950s, the early 1980s saw the release of *Crasimoff's World*, a play-by-mail RPG fantasy game designed by Kevin Cropper in the style of *D&D*. Advertised in the UK-based magazine *White Dwarf*, Cropper moderated in-game interactions between the many principals, effectively refereeing players' actions via snail mail; such correspondence cost players around £1.00 apiece.

Write Your Own Adventure Programs for Your Microcomputer offered much the same fare as *Write Your Own Fantasy Games*, with the difference that in an adventure game, "The player takes the leading role in the story, but he is not given a set of attributes as in role-playing games." Further, "[t]he player uses his own intelligence, cunning, and so on, not those of a character assigned to him at the beginning of the game."

Recall that the Usborne book *The Island of Secrets* dated the creation of computer adventure games to 1976, in the United States. *Write Your Own Adventure Programs* fleshes out this history: "The first adventure game was written in 1976 on a mainframe computer at Stanford University in the U.S.A. by William Crowther and Don Woods." That sentence oversimplifies matters, flattening a rich history. The text-based game was called *Colossal Cave*, sometimes referred to as *Colossal*, *Adventure*, or *Colossal Cave Adventure*, and ran on a PDP-10. It was programmed in FORTRAN—which "cannot handle words," in the authors' spare description—rather than BASIC. *Adventure*'s genesis came about as a result of the caving exploits of Will Crowther and, especially, his ex-wife Patricia within Mammoth Cave in Kentucky—specifically, as a means by Will to achieve closure after a difficult divorce. As described in the book *Broad Band: The Untold Story of the Women Who Made the Internet* by Claire L. Evans,

> The novelist Richard Powers once wrote that "software is the final victory of description over things." The painstaking specificity with which software describes reality approaches, and sometimes even touches, a deeper order. This is perhaps why Will Crowther felt compelled to make one last map. This one wasn't plotted from his wife's muddy notebooks but rather from his own memories. Translated into 700 lines of FORTRAN, they became *Colossal Cave Adventure*, one of the first computer games, modeled faithfully on the sections of Mammoth Cave he had explored with Patricia and mapped alongside her, on a computer [a Teletype terminal connected to a PDP-10 mainframe and 16-bit Honeywell 316 minicomputer "router," both owned by Will's employer, the Massachusetts-based Bolt, Beranek and Newman] that would form the backbone of the internet.

Though Crowther intended it to be played only by his daughters, the game was discovered by strangers across the vast electronic network that BBN helped construct: the

Advanced Research Projects Agency Network, or ARPANET. Don Woods was one of those strangers; at Stanford, Woods enhanced the subterranean world by including fantasy elements. Despite the changes, *Adventure*, with its second-person descriptions (e.g., "There are some keys on the ground here"), was still based on the topography of Mammoth Cave, even if Patricia didn't immediately recognize it at first.

Following *Adventure*, variations on the adventure genre sprouted up like weeds, with American programmer Scott Adams leading the way by writing some of the best known. After porting *Colossal Cave* to a microcomputer—TRS-80's *Adventure Land*—Adams created *Pirate Adventure, The Count, Mystery Funhouse*, and many more. These early adventure games didn't employ graphical elements; likewise, the coding approach in *Write Your Own Adventure Programs* was free of graphics routines, as the authors explain, "because graphics instructions vary so much from computer to computer."

By the Usborne authors' reckoning, an adventure program was really an interactive database, "a computer filing system which stores information and allows it to be called up in a variety of ways." Writing an adventure game involved more than just learning how to program a computer; that was arguably only the final step, since the computer language was used to translate some existing fantasy world into code—and that world, populated with creatures and the like, had to be created on paper, or at least in one's imagination, first. That meant deciding on themes—was a detective story to your liking? or a prehistoric conquest?—rules of engagement, characters, elements of magic, treasures. It also meant constructing maps of various sorts, specifying the layouts of gaming environments at both the macro and micro levels. Once these maps were sketched, transferring them to grid form—one numbered square on the grid per location in the imaginary world—facilitated the translation of fantasy into reality, at least in the form of BASIC lines. (Forgoing BASIC, and creating an adventure game as the professionals did back then, typically meant writing the program mostly or entirely in machine code. That way, not only could much more information be packed into the same amount of memory on cassette or disk—these were programs that juggled information-rich environments, after all—but the speed of execution was increased as well.) Plus, specifying precisely how players interacted with objects by employing imperative text commands like CLIMB, EXAMINE, LEAVE, STAKE, UNLOCK, USE, and GO NORTH (or any other cardinal direction) had to be planned out to the letter. Added complexity came in the form of creating puzzles for the player to solve.

A Microsoft BASIC-style program called *Haunted House*, set in a creepy gothic mansion where the richest man in the world lived out his final days, took center stage in *Write Your Own Adventure Programs*. In addition to the main program listing, the book also included the revisions necessary to coax the game into working properly on the ZX81 and Speccy, whose BASICs diverged significantly from Microsoft's.

Multiple arrays managed the action of *Haunted House*: the array D$ stored location descriptions, populated by READing in lines of DATA; likewise, the array R$, a parallel array of D$, held the route descriptions; and names of objects were housed in array O$. Other arrays referenced the locations of objects (array L), the objects the player was carrying (array C), and other assorted odds and ends. The array F contained *flags* (or markers), with each element assuming the value of zero or one; these elements tracked states of the many moving parts within the fantasy world and its environs. For example, a zero stored in a particular array element indicated a light was off, while a one stored in that same element denoted the light was on. If F(14) equaled 1, then the player had already climbed up the tree. Objects invisible at the game's start were each set to one; when these objects were discovered by the player, the ones switched to zeros. As the authors point out, flag registers in CPUs function in principle similarly to the flag array F, tracking states during program execution.

Inputs were restricted to two-word sentences, each parsed into a verb string (V$) and a word string (W$) and checked against the associated arrays that stored the possible verbs (also called V$) and words (also called W$). If matches were found, then *Haunted House* branched off to associated verb subroutines—such as the GO subroutine that navigated player movements, checking to ensure that walls and other obstacles weren't blocking the paths ahead.

The level of detail in *Write Your Own Adventure Programs* is extraordinary, with practically every important line of code in the *Haunted House* program explained and the reasoning behind every variable and array accounted for. By the time readers reach the section titled "Changing the program," they will be well versed in the ins and outs of the program logic. Suggestions were offered, such as adding a time limit, placing constraints on the number of objects that can be carried at one time, and employing sound effects (some machines generated sounds using the SOUND and/or PLAY statements, while others, like the Spectrum, had BEEP on offer; the VIC-20 needed to be POKEd before it made noise). The game's scoring system could be fiddled with as well. But users had to keep memory limitations in mind: before *Haunted House* even ran, it occupied 7K of RAM; once the action began, the game gobbled up another 4K of memory thanks to the arrays. *Haunted House* stretched any 16K micro to the max, leaving little opportunity to add much of anything to the program.

Once readers had consumed the BASIC beginner's books and pored their way through the intermediate volumes and the type-in "cookbooks," Usborne offered titles that brought other electronic hardware besides veritable microcomputers into play.

Straddling the fence between the BASIC-only books and the texts that used BASIC to power peripherals was *Practical Things to Do with a Microcomputer* (1983) by Judy Tatchell and Nick Cutler. After running through the basics of BASIC, as well as presenting relatively simple programs like a chatbot and what's termed a *quizmaster*, Tatchell and Cutler introduce programs that required additional equipment, interspersed with those that didn't. First up: printers—dot-matrix, teletype, and daisy-wheel—with word processing applications to match, along with copious use of the LPRINT (line printer) statement. Next, programs that calculate averages and sort data (bubble sort) serve as interstitials until more peripherals get the spotlight: namely, modems and acoustic couplers, along with a selection of programs on encrypting codes using ASCII as well as sending secret messages. Then came graphics: specifically, light pens for drawing on the screen. Of course, programs featuring graphics were among the least compatible between micros, in part because they drew upon machine-specific capabilities, which varied widely. For instance, to plot a point, some versions of BASIC utilized PLOT, while others employed PSET; to draw a line, DRAW, PLOT, or LINE might be used; to draw a circle or curve, CIRCLE, SIN, or COS might do the trick; to paint a closed shape, try PLOT, COLOUR, PAINT, or FILL; to change colors in the background or foreground, there was GCOL, INK/PAPER, or COLOR; to move the cursor, PLOT, CURMOV, CURSET, or MOVE; to change modes, MODE, HIRES, LORES, or PMODE; and to draw a line of symbols, PATTERN, DRAW, or PLOT.

A text-based game involving space aliens, two programs on inflation (an inflation calculator and a simulation featuring a graphical chocolate bar), a horoscope generator, and a random poetry creator precede the next set of peripherals examined: tapes and disk drives, which both offered the capability of saving programs. Computers directed cassette machines to store programs on tapes in *blocks*, featuring a hexadecimal (base 16, with digits 0 to 9 followed by A to F) *header* (label) for each block. Hence the reason for the dreaded BLOCK? and HEADER? error messages that sometimes appeared on-screen. Floppy disks, on the other hand, were made of *tracks* and *sections*, with at least several tracks designated for a directory (the list of programs on the disk). In order for a computer to properly use a disk, it required both hardware (a disk interface for the disk drive) and software (a Disk Operation System, or DOS, for instructions on how to store data).

Practical Things' filmsearch application is a program worth saving. "You can find the year you saw a particular film by typing in its name and code number, 1, which tells the computer to search for the year," write Tatchell and Cutler. "If you type ALL, and a year, it will list all the films you saw in that year." Take one look at the DATA, and you may—or may not—be comforted by the authors' taste in movies.

```
10 PRINT "FILMSEARCH"
20 DATA "SUPERMAN", 1977
21 DATA "THE BLACK HOLE", 1979
22 DATA "STAR WARS", 1980
23 DATA "MOONRAKER", 1980
24 DATA "CHARIOTS OF FIRE", 1981
25 DATA "THE EMPIRE STRIKES BACK", 1981
26 DATA "TRON", 1982
27 DATA "BLADE RUNNER", 1982
28 DATA "ET", 1983
29 DATA "NEVER SAY NEVER AGAIN", 1983
30 DATA "RETURN OF THE JEDI", 1983
100 DATA "END"
```

If issues arose with saving or loading the programs on cassette, a checklist of possible causes was offered, along with tips on cleaning the punch roller and spindle of the cassette player by using a cotton bud.

About halfway through *Practical Things*, the skill level ramps up, as readers are confronted with the section "Simple circuits to build"; these were circuits that connected to a computer using the input/output port or user port. (The BBC Micro and the Commodores came with user ports, unlike some other machines.) After listing the electronics needed—a micro switch, a single stand "hook-up" wire, a 1000-ohm (1K) resistor, a plug and lead (a flat ribbon cable) to fit the user port, and an optional small breadboard—instructions on how to connect the switch are proffered. Once assembled and plugged into the user port, a short BASIC program could reveal the workings of the computer's memory when the switch was pressed, albeit the program details depended on the hardware:

```
10 Set data direction register, if necessary
20 LET A=PEEK(Address of user port's memory location)
30 PRINT A
40 GOTO 20
```

The address of the user port was probably listed in the computer's manual, either in decimal or hexadecimal form (e.g., &FBF5, with the & prefix denoting hex). When the above program was run, typically the number zero was printed if the switch wasn't pressed, while some other number was output when the switch was pressed. But what was that number?

Signals the user port received were processed in binary. A user port had eight input pins, with each bit of a byte-sized binary number corresponding to one of these pins; the switch connected to one pin, which, when it received a voltage, was interpreted by the computer as 1. Pressing the switch would result in one of eight possible binary numbers, printed on-screen as the decimal 1, 2, 4, 8, 16, 32, 64, or 128. Suppose the switch was connected to the fourth pin; when the switch was pressed, the computer stored the binary digits 00010000, equivalent to $2^4 = 16$. If the switch was hooked up to the sixth pin instead, then pressing the switch stored the binary digits 00000100, equal to $2^2 = 4$.

So, you had a working switch that the computer recognized. Now what? Tatchell and Cutler offer some ideas. The switch could be fit under something private, like a diary, with a BASIC program monitoring if someone disturbed the space. If the diary was picked up, the switch would no longer be closed—and an alarm could be set to go off:

```
10 LET A=PEEK(Address)
20 IF A<>0 THEN GOTO 10
30 IF A=0 THEN (Alarm noise)
```

Hook up a reed switch, activated with a magnet, and you could trigger the alarm when a door was opened.

For those a little less paranoid, the computer could deliver an on-screen greeting to someone sitting down in front of it. Place a cushion on a chair, and position the switch underneath the cushion. When the cushion was depressed, the switch was triggered as well.

```
10 LET A=PEEK(Address)
20 IF A=0 THEN GOTO 10
30 IF A<>0 THEN PRINT "GREETINGS!"
```

From there, the projects got more complicated. Instructions on how to assemble a bitswitch keypad boasting eight switches, each connected to a separate bit in the user port, were offered. Pressing one switch at a time, or a combination of switches, would store binary numbers from 00000000 to 11111111 (in decimal, 0 to 255). And these numbers could then be converted into their associated ASCII characters using **CHR$** (or the equivalent BASIC command), turning the bitswitch keypad into a makeshift Microwriter, which was a six-button, handheld (designed for one hand) digital word-processor developed in the late 1970s and manufactured in the UK.

Instead of outputting characters, the authors suggest hooking up LEDs (light-emitting diodes) to display different patterns depending on the numbers typed on the keyboard. Like with the bitswitch keypad, a set of eight LEDs—one for each bit on the user port—could be connected by mounting them on a Veroboard. But additional equipment, like transistors and resistors, were required.

Practical Things culminates with detailed instructions on assembling a computer-controlled robot vehicle. Once built and hooked up properly, the vehicle could be maneuvered forward, backward, and through turns (any number of degrees) using a BASIC program. The functionality of this final project resembled a (physical) Logo turtle.

If you struggled with any of these book projects, whom could you turn to for help? There was no internet to speak of yet, after all. The authors of *Practical Things* offered several suggestions, including joining a local user group, contacting the computer manufacturer, writing to a home computer magazine, quizzing employees at a local computer dealer, or simply asking a teacher.

The book *How to Make Computer-Controlled Robots for C64, VIC 20, Spectrum & BBC* (1984) by Tony Potter upped the ante considerably for those interested in robots. Though positioned "for absolute beginners," most of the book's fifty pages guided readers through the scores of necessary steps to building a fully-fledged robot, replete with a robotic arm and gripper. About two-thirds the way into the book, BASIC programs appear: first, to test the robot, and second, to control it. In *Computer-Controlled Robots*, BASIC was a means to an end, rather than the star of the show.

In the same vein, and by the same author, consider *How to Make Computer Model Controllers for C64, VIC 20, Spectrum & BBC* (1984). In a nutshell: "This book shows you how to build simple electronic circuits so you can control model trains and cars." Like *Computer-Controlled Robots*, *Computer Model Controllers'* focus was not on BASIC—there were a handful of programs in the language, used to test and control the sensors and the models—but on the equipment and associated electronics. Though comprehensive and clearly illustrated, working through a book like this was far from simple, taking time and effort and requiring expertise and manual dexterity. Readers possessing the requisite BASIC skills (and the interest in programming) didn't necessarily overlap with those ready to get their hands dirty with electronics.

BASIC also mostly served as background noise in *Usborne Introduction to Keyboards & Computer Music* (1985) by Philip Hawthorn. A section of the book offered a BASIC program for synthesis and sequencing, along with a guide to program conversions for various microcomputers like the C64.

BASIC returned to center stage, at least for those with a scientific bent, in *Experiments with Your Computer* (1985) by Helen Davies. After presenting examples of how computers were used in science—for brain research, modeling the big bang, designing rockets, and solving crimes—Davies starts her readers off with a simple simulation, offering a BASIC type-in that flips a fair coin *n* times and reports back the count of heads and tails.

Next, physics equations were the star in a bouncing ball program. No graphics just yet—that would come near the end of the book—but there were options to replace the meters (or, as it's printed in the book, metres) in the code with feet. When run, the program asked the user to input an initial height, an initial direction (in degrees), an initial speed, a constant for acceleration due to gravity, and a value for "bounciness."

A health program, focusing on pulse rate experiments, followed. Then there was "Ethel's journey," with two pages of BASIC code, along with another four pages of instructions, to simulate trips by train or bus. "This program models the two routes, using random numbers to cope with variations from data to day," we learn in *Experiments*, although there is a warning posted: "The command which produces random numbers varies. In this program it is written RND." Indeed, some machines, like the VIC-20, the Beeb, the Oric-1, the TRS-80, and the Dragon, required an argument with RND, such as RND(1), while others, like the ZX81 and the Speccy, did not.

Economics was a science, too—even if it was dismal—and thus was featured in Davies's book in the form of a lengthy airline simulation program. After inputting values for macroeconomic variables, the inflation, interest, and exchange rates were monitored, all in an imaginary currency called Grotes (G).

Then, roughly halfway through the book, instructions on assembling a temperature sensor using a thermistor were proffered. These sensors only worked on machines with an "analogue port," reads the text, which included the C64, the VIC-20, the TRS-80, and the Beeb. Even with those machines, there were differences in what fit into the ports: the C64 and VIC-20 needed a D-type 8-way female (socket), the Beeb required a D-type 15-way male (plug), and the TRS-80 needed a 6-way DIN connector. Varying resistors were required as well. Multiple writing diagrams fill a page of *Experiments*, finally leading to a BASIC program designed to test the thermistor (albeit the program was tailored for the C64; BASIC conversions to other machines like the TRS-80 and BBC were found on later pages). After storing values for variables K1 (equal to 4000) and K2 (equal to 1), the three critical but abstruse lines of the program were:

```
1000 LET TR-1.84*PEEK(54297)
1010 LET R=1/(1/TR-1/1000)
1020 LET T=1/((LOG(R/K2))/K1+1/273)-273
```

Once the thermistor test program was run, R values, obtained from signals sent to the computer from the sensor, were output. Placing something hot next to the sensor, like a mug filled with steaming coffee, caused the values of R to increase. An easy way to convert the R values to degrees Celsius was to lodge the sensor inside a small bucket of ice and wait about ten minutes for the R values to decrease to a relatively constant amount (though they would still fluctuate slightly). Then, since you knew R at 0°C—a baseline—experiments with the sensor could begin. Your body temperature could be measured; the temperature changes in a room over the course of a day could be recorded; and so forth. In addition, *Experiments* offered code to direct the computer to draw time series graphs of the data, with variations in temperature displayed in graphical form.

If the thermistor was swapped out for a light-dependent resistor (LDR), then you'd have a functional light sensor. For the device to work properly, an ORP12 light-dependent resistor was necessary as well. After presenting detailed diagrams on the assembly process, Davies offers a light sensor program that outputs variations in light intensity. Possible applications included pointing the sensor at a television screen with a TV show playing, or aiming the sensor out a window to detect people walking by.

Since experiments generated lots of data, Davies spills some ink on ways to store information, such as by building a database application or coding utilities to obtain averages (mean, median, and mode) and correlations (measurements of the strength and direction of the linear relationship between pairs of variables). *Experiments* finishes off with a program introducing statistical tests of significance by simulating dice rolls and then determining the probability of obtaining the results by mere chance alone.

Undoubtedly, the most surprising entry of the 1980s Usborne series is called *Usborne Introduction to Machine Code for Beginners* (1983) by Lisa Watts and Mike Wharton. The book is arguably an adult-level general introduction to low-level programming disguised as a children's educational volume. It is worth taking the time to explore the concepts presented in this text not only because of their intimate connections to BASIC in particular and computer science in general, but also to help us have a softer landing next chapter when we peel back some of the low-level layers of GW-BASIC revealed by Microsoft's recent open-sourcing of the language.

In the "About this book" section opening *Introduction to Machine Code*, the authors position the content in relation to BASIC, explaining to readers that while machine code programs run faster and take up less memory than equivalently functioning BASIC programs, they also are more challenging to create and far more difficult to understand; plus, debugging them can be a nightmare.

Of course, BASIC programs had to be translated into machine code, one way or another, before they could be run. No microcomputer ran BASIC *natively*, executing it directly on the hardware; instead, BASIC source code had to be interpreted or compiled to execute, since any BASIC dialect was simply a specification of the language that was implemented as either an interpreter or a compiler.

The difficulty of writing in machine language resulted in the instructional goals of *Introduction to Machine Code* being modest, with the functionality of programs on its pages rather simple, such as flashing a message on-screen or adding two numbers. You certainly won't be learning how to write a compiler. What's more, since there were different machine codes, one for each *microprocessor* (which houses the central processing unit, or CPU, of the computer, acting like a conductor in an orchestra: directing the machine's actions and delegating responsibilities. The read-only memory, or ROM, contained software like BASIC that informed the behavior of the CPU), the book's authors restricted themselves to discussing only the Zilog Z80 and MOS Technology 6502 8-bit processors. The ZX81 and Spectrum were powered by the Z80 while the Atari, the Beeb, the Oric-1, and the VIC-20 ran using the 6502. The C64 employed the MOS

Technology 6510, but the Commodore could also interpret 6502 machine code. (The Dragon used the Motorola 6809, while the TI-99/4 used the TMS9900. However, the book didn't touch on either of these chips.)

Both the Z80 and the 6502 contained numerous *registers*, or places where data was stored and quickly transferred for use by the CPU; the Z80 had more registers than the 6502. The *accumulator*, a special kind of register, temporarily held the intermediate results of calculations made by the ALU, or arithmetic/logic unit, which was part of the CPU. (Unlike in the 6502, in the Z80, data for calculations with large numbers were stored in the HL register pair rather than the accumulator.) There were several other types of registers, including the flags register (in the Z80) or processor status register (in the 6502), the index registers, the general-purpose registers, the stack pointer, and the program counter. Pages 14 and 15 of *Introduction to Machine Code* enumerated the many similarities and differences between the two featured processors.

Machine code for the 6502 and Z80 represented instructions and pieces of data as binary numbers: strings of zeros and ones, or binary digits, also called bits; eight bits constituted one byte. Inside any microcomputer, a one was represented by a single pulse of electricity, while a zero was denoted by no pulse. Bytes, therefore, consisted of groups of eight pulses or no pulses; these bytes were messages of instructions and data that traveled along a *data bus*, or the "tracks" on printed circuit boards connecting together various components such as integrated circuits (i.e., chips).

Any decimal (base 10) number could be converted to binary (base 2), and vice versa. To convert from decimal to binary, the decimal number must be divided by two, and the remainder stored; then the previous quotient must be divided by two, and the remainder stored again; the process continues until there are no remainders left to obtain. Laying out the remainders in the reverse order they were calculated yielded the binary number.

Converting from binary to decimal is more straightforward, with successive powers of two multiplied and then summed. For instance:

$$10010111 \text{ in binary} = 1{\times}2^7+0{\times}2^6+0{\times}2^5+1{\times}2^4+0{\times}2^3+1{\times}2^2+1{\times}2^1+1{\times}2^0 = 151 \text{ in decimal}$$

When coding in machine language, the programmer had several options. Programs could consist entirely of zeros and ones. Or they could be written in hexadecimal (base 16). Hex, a sixteen-digit number system, offers the digits 0, 1, 2, 3, 4, 5, 6, 7, 8, 9, A, B, C, D, E, and F, where A corresponds to 10 in decimal, B pairs with 11, and so on. Hexadecimal has an intimate relationship with binary; bits grouped in sets of four can be converted directly to hex using the binary-to-decimal method detailed above, with each resulting decimal number turned into its hex equivalent digit. For instance:

1111 0111 →
1111 is 15 in decimal, and thus F in hex; 0111 is 7 in decimal, and thus also 7 in hex →
1111 0111 = F7 in hex

As book authors Watts and Wharton explained, "Machine code programs are written in hex rather than decimal numbers because binary numbers used in the computer's own code translate more neatly to hex than decimal." Yet most programmers wisely forwent coding directly in hex (or binary) in favor of using an assembly language, we also learn in *Introduction to Machine Code*. Moving up a level of abstraction—BASIC was perched atop the highest abstraction level in these microcomputers—assembly language stripped out most of the low-level binary or hex codes for *mnemonics*, which were short English abbreviations for the *opcodes*, or machine language instructions from the instruction set (the Z80 and 6502 had different instruction sets). Each machine language instruction typically contained an opcode and an *operand*. The operand was either an address (which was called *absolute addressing*), a piece of data (which was termed *immediate addressing*), or a register to be operated upon, while the opcode's hex code varied depending on the type of operand used.

There were instructions for loading a value into the accumulator, for adding a value to the contents of the accumulator, for storing the contents of the accumulator into a particular address, and for comparing the contents of the accumulator with some value, among many other operations available. For example, to load the hex number 08 into the accumulator, we typed either:

```
LD A &08      (for the Z80)
LDA #&08      (for the 6502, where the # symbol alerted the computer that &08 was data)
```

To convert the load instruction shown above to hexadecimal on the Z80, we would use 3E (for a data operand) or 3A (for an address operand) in place of mnemonic LD A; on the 6502, we would use A9 (for a data operand) or AD (for an address operand) instead of mnemonic LDA.

Instructions directing the accumulator had no obvious analogs in BASIC. However, like the **GOTO**s, the **IF/THEN**s, and the **GOSUB...RETURN**s of BASIC programs, machine language offered programmers branching possibilities in the form of unconditional jumps, conditional branches, and subroutines, respectively. To understand how these worked, first consider: the computer would defer to a *program counter*, or register containing the address of the next instruction, when traversing a machine language program. An unconditional jump in machine code, à la the **GOTO** statement, inserted the destination address for the jump into the program counter. A conditional jump, the equivalent of **IF/THEN**, tested a particular bit and, depending on that bit's value (zero or one), either branched or did not. And a jump to a subroutine in a machine language program required a return instruction, akin to **GOSUB...RETURN**. What's more, rather than jumping to specific addresses, *relative addressing* was possible, thus permitting forward or backward jumps by a *displacement* (also called an *offset*) amount; note that a backward displacement employed two's complement to represent negative notation in binary. (An assembler calculated the displacement amounts automatically.) Mnemonics for the aforementioned branching instructions varied between microprocessors: for example, JP or JMP for unconditional jumps, and CALL or JSR for subroutines.

An assembler made sense of the human-readable mnemonics of assembly code (also called the *source code*), translating the instructions into the microprocessor's native machine language (which resulted in the *object code*); similar to **REM** statements, comments, documenting the line-by-line instructions, could be used in assembly programs; BASIC-style variables were typically permitted in assembly code as well. Some microcomputers, like the Beeb, had assemblers built-in straight out of the box; other micros required the assemblers be loaded into memory via cassette or disk. Despite lacking an assembler, you could still write a program in assembly language and then laboriously hand-translate it into hexadecimal; even then, however, some machines needed a *hex loader* to understand the hexadecimal instructions.

Flip to page 24 of *Introduction to Machine Code* to find a hex loader written in BASIC. The BASIC program first queried the user: "ADDRESS WHERE THE MACHINE CODE IS TO BE STORED?" From there, pairs of hex digits were **READ**, one pair at a time, from **DATA** statements found near the end of the program, until the *sentinel value*—the string **END**—was encountered. (Any machine language program, and machine language subroutine for that matter, had to conclude with a return instruction, like RET or RTS, popping the final item off the stack—lest the machine would crash.) Sample **DATA** might look like the following:

```
160 DATA F7, E2, A8, END
```

The hex loader then took each valid one-byte pair of digits and converted the pair into a decimal number between 0 (00000000 in binary) and 255 (11111111 in binary); the process entailed transforming each individual hex digit into a numeric ASCII code using the **ASC** function and performing arithmetic to obtain the corresponding decimal value. Specifically, the decimal of the left-hand hex pair was multiplied by sixteen and then added to the decimal of the right-hand hex pair, resulting in a correct hexadecimal-to-decimal conversion. Let's work through an example:

F7 in hex →
F is the decimal number 15; multiply 15 by 16 to obtain 240 →
Then, add 7 to 240 to obtain 247 →
F7 = 247 in decimal

These decimal numbers, converted from the hex pairs, were **POKE**d one by one into successive memory locations—beginning at the initial address provided by the user at runtime—as shown in the line of code below.

```
130 POKE A+C, X
```

where **A** is the address of the first memory location, **C** is a counter variable (incremented for each stored hex pair), and **X** is the decimal value of the hex pair. Once loaded into memory, the machine language program could be run using a command, such as **CALL** or **PRINT USR**, along with the decimal address that stored the program's first byte.

Pore through *Introduction to Machine Code* and you'll notice that hex numbers were usually prefixed with ampersands (&), though computer manuals at the time might have denoted them with other symbols, such as hashes (#). Once armed with knowledge gained by reading the book, computer magazine listings of cryptic-looking *hex dumps*—machine code programs in which each line was prefixed by a hex address and followed by pairs of hex digits—became a little less mysterious.

Recall the memory map presented earlier. Ideally, a memory map contained the addresses marking the beginning of each area in the computer's memory:

Input/output *(&6000 / 24576)*
Screen memory (or "display file") *(&5C00 / 23552)*
Variable storage ---the border between variables and RAM varies, depending on the amount of storage needed for the variables---
User/free RAM *(&2E00 / 11776)*
Reserved for OS (or "monitor") use *(&2400 / 9216)*
BASIC *(&0400 / 1024)*
operating system or "monitor" *(&0000 / 0)*

Memory addresses, like &5C00 shown above—which is equal to 23552 in base 10, found by converting the hex value into decimal—each consumed two bytes of memory (the opcodes were typically one byte in length). Two bytes meant sixteen bits to play with; the largest 16-bit binary number possible was 11111111 11111111, which converted to FFFF in hex and 65535 in decimal. Thus, addresses could range from 00000 to 65535, allowing for a total of 65536 possible address locations. Each of these locations held one byte, and one kilobyte = 2^{10} = 1024 bytes, so, by dividing 65536 by 1024, we arrive at a familiar number: 64, as in 64K of combined ROM and RAM memory—the absolute maximum permitted on machines using a microprocessor of the 6502 or Z80 variety.

What's more, computer memory was split into *pages*, with one page housing 256 locations (the locations 0 to 255 were accorded the name "page zero"); consequently, four pages comprised one kilobyte. When decoding an address like &5C00, the leftmost pair of digits, called the *high-order byte*, denoted the page number—in this case, 5C in hex, equivalent to 92 in decimal—while the rightmost pair of digits, called the *low-order byte*, revealed the position on the page—here, 00 in hex, equivalent to 0 in decimal.

Next, let us reconsider the memory map. Dive deeper into the memory reserved for operating system use, and there were even more subdivisions, including areas to store user-defined graphics, systems variables, and buffers (which temporarily stored key-stroke data and the like), as well as three stacks: the calculator stack (which temporarily stored numbers for calculations), the machine/processor stack (which stored address-es), and the BASIC/**GOSUB** stack (which stored the line numbers utilized in **GOSUB** and **GOTO** statements). *Stacks* are data structures that stored data in RAM temporarily and operated exclusively on the most recently added item—a principle commonly known by the acronym LIFO, or last-in, first-out. Adding a new item to the stack was termed *pushing* the item, while removing the most recent item from the stack was called *popping* the item. In the CPU, the *stack pointer* held the address of the last item on the stack.

Programs written in BASIC were stored in user/free RAM without a second thought. But the memory layout had to be kept in mind when writing machine code, since it was the programmer's responsibility to find a place in RAM to safely store a program. On this point, *Introduction to Machine Code* is filled with warnings. Insert a ma-chine language program into RAM reserved for the OS, for instance, and you'd run the risk of crashing your computer.

Worse yet, if you stored a BASIC program along with a machine code program in RAM, there had to be an imaginary wall of memory—a so-called no-man's land—manually placed between them. Though machine code was typically stored at the top of the user/free RAM, also known as the RAMTOP (or HIMEM), that area might conflict with BASIC code, despite how little space a machine language program required (recall that each pair of hex digits consumed only a single byte of memory). By relocating the RAMTOP among the systems variables, the top of the user/free RAM could be low-ered, ensuring that the machine code was kept separate from the BASIC code—and thereby solving the problem. However, there were idiosyncratic ways to lower the top on these machines; once the address of RAMTOP was found, usually with the guidance of the computer's manual, a command to reserve an area of about one hundred bytes might look like this on one computer:

```
CLEAR ramtop address - 100
```

while appearing like this on another:

```
HIMEM ramtop address - 100
```

The authors devote several panels (on page 22) to instructing readers on how to lower the top of especially challenging micros, like the VIC-20 and the ZX81, as well as sug-gesting other locations in RAM for provisionally storing machine code (such as in areas designated for graphics).

Once a safe place to store the program was found, the machine code had to be **POKE**d into memory, one byte at a time—and, in many of these micros, those bytes had to be in decimal form (hence the BASIC hex loader discussed above, which converted one-byte pairs of hexadecimal digits into decimal before **POKE**ing). The programmer also had to be cognizant of data *produced* by machine language programs, such as the results of arithmetic calculations, since these *data bytes* had to be stored as well. Storing the data bytes ahead of the machine code, the authors suggested, offered the best results; that way, the data wouldn't interfere with the program. A `PRINT PEEK(decimal address)` command revealed a data byte value, albeit in decimal.

Introduction to Machine Code offered readers several short example programs, for both the Z80 and 6502, illustrating the differences between address modes—namely, immediate addressing, where the data was already part of the program, and absolute addressing, in which the programmer directed the computer to an address that stored the data. (There are a number of other types of addressing possible as well, such as *indirect addressing*, which uses registers to point to addresses.) Using an absolute addressing scheme, data had to be loaded into registers prior to any operations performed on the data, such as adding two numbers; during the process, the accumulator (A), a specialized register, took pride of place. Once a number was fetched from a faraway address, placed into the accumulator (A), and then transferred to another register (B), a second number, held in a different distant address, found its way into the accumulator (A). Next, an add instruction like `ADD A, B` summed the numbers in registers A and B, storing the result in the accumulator (A). Finally, a load instruction like `LD &AAAA, A` stored the sum of the two numbers into an address (AAAA).

If the sum of two numbers exceeded 255 in decimal (11111111 in binary), then the *carry flag* sprang into action: found in the flags register, the carry flag would be set to one, effectively functioning as a "ninth bit." Obtaining the value of the carry flag involved setting the accumulator to zero, adding zero by using the add with carry instruction (the `ADC` mnemonic on the Z80), and then checking the contents of the accumulator, which, when all was said and done, contained either a zero or a one.

Large numbers—base 10 numbers greater than 255—were stored in memory in two parts: as a high-order byte, accounting for the frequency of 256s in the number, and as a low-order byte, denoting the remainder. Suppose 12345 was the large number in question. To obtain the two bytes, first divide 12345 by 256, resulting in the whole number 48; then, find the remainder of the division, which is 57. Hence, storing the decimal 12345 required a high-order byte of 48 (in decimal) and a low-order byte of 57 (in decimal). Typically, when adding two large numbers, each number would be held in pairs of registers, with one byte of storage available in each register; for example, when programming using the Z80, one large number could be stored in the HL register pair, while the other might be stored in the BC register pair. *Introduction to Machine Code* presented the ins and outs of adding two large numbers in machine language, both for the Z80 and the 6502.

As the book neared its conclusion, careful readers were rewarded with two versions of a compact program, one for each featured microprocessor, that flashed text elements by using indirect addressing to rapidly swap the on-screen placement of two blocks of characters. The flashing program ran nearly as fast as the hardware allowed, and certainly much faster—and requiring less memory—than equivalent BASIC code could muster. Put simply, using high-level languages like BASIC to manipulate graphical elements or perform computationally-intensive tasks like sorting data was suboptimal; these were jobs better suited for dense machine language programs. That didn't mean throwing the BASIC out with the bathwater, however. As book authors Watts and Wharton point out, "One good way to use machine code is as a short subroutine to carry out a particular task in a BASIC program." Famously, the Dutch videogame designer Henk Rogers wrote *The Black Onyx*, a highly influential role-playing game in Japan, using a mix of BASIC and Z80 assembly code.

Introduction to Machine Code, the crown jewel in the Usborne book series, culminates with several helpful tables—of decimal to hex conversions, and of Z80/6502 mnemonics and hex codes—as well as a glossary of machine language terms.

Four decades later, we find that Usborne, like Great Britain herself, soldiers on. Since publishing their many 1980s BASIC-themed books, the company has moved forward, releasing volumes on languages like Python and Scratch, among a wide variety of educational works on computing for young readers already drowning in a sea of information abundance (most of it online). But in the type-in heyday, a time of information scarcity when one couldn't simply search the internet for instructional articles and videos on programming, the colorful, informative, entertaining, and uniformly high-quality Usborne books were both essential and unmatched.

CHAPTER 8

OPEN SOURCE
Of GW-BASIC and Pseudorandom Number Generators

How does GW-BASIC generate pseudorandom numbers?

And so it came to pass that BASIC became a mighty nation, and the saddlers, and the fishermen, and the *keepers* of the flocks, and the counters of the beans did populate its land and prosper thereof....

And so the people on the right hand of PDP, and of HP, and of Data General Nova, and of more, did leavest the cities and came to *dwell* among the villages of Apple II, and PET, and Commodore 64, and more.

And BASIC begat Tiny BASIC, and Altair BASIC, and BBC BASIC.

And Altair BASIC begat Micro-Soft BASIC, which begat MBASIC, which begat IBM Disk BASIC, *which* begat GW-BASIC.

—From the "History of BASIC, King James Edition" by John Browne

W‍ell known is the date of May 1, 1964, the supposed "birth" of BASIC—although Thomas Kurtz has called that birthdate a "pretty good myth." Until recently, however, the date February 10, 1983, had no meaning for the BASIC faithful. But on that day, the original source code for Microsoft GW-BASIC, one of the most widely distributed BASIC implementations of all time, was published—at least according to the header found on its forty assembly code source files, each of which begins as follows (in this assembly code, single-line comments start with a semicolon):

```
; [ This translation created 10-Feb-83 by Version 4.3 ]
```

In a nice touch of authenticity, the GW-BASIC files on GitHub show

Latest commit 09ad7bc on Feb 10, 1983

despite the GitHub service only coming into being in 2008. Of course, no pull requests were allowed, since Microsoft will not modify the code. However, shortly after its release in 2020, other programmers altered the GW-BASIC source code on their own GitHub pages with permission courtesy of the MIT (OSI) License.

As Rich Turner, the senior program manager at Microsoft who announced the open-sourcing of GW-BASIC in May 2020, wrote, "These sources, as clearly stated in the repo's [or repository, which is a central storage location] readme, are the 8088 assembly language sources from 10th Feb 1983, and are being open-sourced for historical reference and educational purposes." GW-BASIC was written entirely in assembly language in order to maximize the limited space available on early PCs, where "every single byte and every single instruction mattered," noted Turner. Thus, not a single line of C, Pascal, FORTRAN, PL/I, LISP, COBOL, or any other high-level language can be found in the GW-BASIC source files, because no matter how optimized and efficient the compiled code generated from these HLLs might have been, strict memory considerations on the early personal computers wouldn't have permitted the creation of a non-assembly (or non-machine language) GW-BASIC to pass muster. (Today, with space no longer an issue, it is not unusual to encounter BASICs implemented in HLLs like C or Python.)

The GW-BASIC 16-bit 8086 assembly code was generated from a master implementation; one observer who studied the code noted, "Comments left in the files are referring to LXI instruction or '[B,C]', '[D,E]' and '[H,L]' registers, therefore suggesting that the master could be 8080/8085 source code."

The software engineer Michal Necasek, though professing to be only "mildly curious" about GW-BASIC, also pored through the assembly files, and discovered they contained a treasure trove of information, yet were also missing critical elements. For instance, he questioned the February 10, 1983, birthdate, assuming it referred to the day a translator ran through the master BASIC source code in order to generate code for an 8086. Yet the source code was likely modified after that date, Necasek concluded, probably deep into 1983.

There are other mysteries that bugged Necasek. For one, Microsoft provided no documentation on how the source code was assembled: no batch file or build notes. So Necasek tried assembling the source code, one MASM (Microsoft Macro Assembler, an x86 assembler) version after another, until he stumbled upon one that finally worked—MASM 5.1—but only if he altered the line endings in a DOS style (CR/LF). After additional searching, and more trial and error, he struck gold: Microsoft Macro Assembler version 1.06 from 1982, which assembled all the source files with nary a change or syntax error in sight.

Necasek next turned his sleuthing skills to matching an extant GW-BASIC binary with the released GW-BASIC source. Eagle GWBASIC.EXE and BASICA.EXE for the Compaq Personal Computer turned out to be the closest matches, with both showing release dates several months past February 1983.

⇏

Regardless of the validity of the February 1983 birthdate, or how the source code was assembled, or which 8-bit microprocessor was used—the instruction set architecture (ISA) of the early personal computers was similar enough that ports of BASIC weren't all that different from the master implementation anyway, according to Rich Turner—the GW-BASIC source files unquestionably house a wealth of historical and technical information for the curious, even if we only permit ourselves to scan through the voluminous comments.

For example, the GWMAIN.ASM file begins as follows (note: the text reproduced below is enclosed in a multiline comment; the file extension .ASM is an abbreviation for assembly language source code, while the extension .MAC referenced below is a throwback to the DEC PDP-10's MACRO-10 assembly language, with which the first Microsoft BASIC was written by Gates et al.):

```
COMMENT *


--------- ---- -- ---- ----- --- ---- -----
COPYRIGHT 1975 BY BILL GATES AND PAUL ALLEN
--------- ---- -- ---- ----- --- ---- -----

ORIGINALLY WRITTEN ON THE PDP-10 FROM
FEBRUARY 9 TO  APRIL 9 1975

BILL GATES WROTE A LOT OF STUFF.
PAUL ALLEN WROTE A LOT OF OTHER STUFF AND FAST CODE.
MONTE DAVIDOFF WROTE THE MATH PACKAGE (F4I.MAC).


*
```

Which is similar but more specific than the equivalent assembly code comments establishing authorship of earlier Microsoft BASIC implementations, beginning with the original 4K Altair BASIC. Those first set of remarks (comments) were

```
PAUL ALLEN WROTE THE NON-RUNTIME STUFF.
BILL GATES WROTE THE RUNTIME STUFF.
MONTE DAVIDOFF WROTE THE MATH PACKAGE
```

Back then, as Bill Gates recalled for his *Byte* article "The 25th Birthday of BASIC," "Memory was so precious that we even replaced the **READY>** prompt [of Dartmouth BASIC] with **OK>** to save a few bytes." Memory constraints also partly led to their decision to forgo coding a compiler in favor of a single-representation interpreter, which stored a BASIC program's source code in a compact form. "But another factor was our fascination with interpreters, and the immediacy and ease of use they give to the programming art," Gates added. Everything had to be squeezed into 4K bytes of memory:

Using the lower values of a byte and the upper 128 ASCII values to tokenize BASIC keywords was an innovation in that interpreter. We also coined the short commands **TRON** and **TROFF** to turn on and off BASIC's earliest built-in debugging tool, a trace facility. Fitting the language's reserved words, error messages, and floating-point library to run programs in a 4K-byte machine required a lot of tricks—it's still my favorite piece of code because it is so refined.

Gates, Allen, and Davidoff wrote Altair BASIC, which employed a *lexer* to generate tokens from the user's BASIC code and a *parser* to interpret these tokens using a BASIC grammar, by effectively emulating the Altair on a PDP-10 computer at Harvard. In an editorial in the January/February 1977 issue of *Personal Computing*, Allen claimed that "[w]e chose BASIC originally, not because it seemed to be the best possible language that could be developed but because it was already in common use. Much literature was already available, and almost anyone could find some way to educate himself to the use of BASIC." Indeed, Gates and Allen had studied "dozens and dozens of BASICs," Gates claimed, and the result of their efforts, Altair BASIC, pleased the young Harvard dropout: "Actually, making a BASIC run in that little memory is a real feat.... Of all the programming I've done it's the thing I'm most proud of." Kemeny and Kurtz, though labeling Altair BASIC a "Street BASIC" and calling it "disastrous to the BASIC language," also admitted the early Microsoft effort was "a remarkable achievement."

The operating system hacker Michael Steil conducted a thorough analysis of the original 1978 Microsoft BASIC source code for the 8-bit MOS Technology 6502—the microprocessor that powered the earliest Apple, Atari, and Commodore home computers. "This is currently the oldest publicly available piece of source written by Bill Gates," Steil notes, and, like the earlier 8080 BASIC, the 6502 version was written using a MACRO-10 assembler running on a PDP-10. Paul Allen coaxed MACRO-10 to properly translate code into 6502 assembly by writing, unsurprisingly, a series of macros. For example, a MACRO-10 instruction like `LDAI 0` simulated the corresponding 6502 instruction `LDA #0`. Other macros included `SYNCHK (Q)`, which obtained the next character and ensured it was Q, otherwise it reported a syntax error; `LDWDI (WD)`, which loaded an intermediate constant into a register; and `PSHWD (WD)`, which pushed a 16-bit value from memory onto the stack. MACRO-10 would output one 36-bit PDP-10 word for each 6502 byte; thus, the binary for the 6502 could be built systematically by capturing one word at a time from the PDP-10.

But there were limitations with the translation that Allen had to work around. For one thing, MACRO-10 didn't support hexadecimal (base 16), so most of the numbers appearing in the 6502 source code were in decimal (base 10). For the floating-point code, though, octal (base 8) was utilized. When `RADIX` appeared in the translation, it denoted a switch between bases (`RADIX` artifacts populated the GW-BASIC source as well, a part of the implementation's significant inheritance from its Altair ancestor).

In his extensive analysis, Michael Steil also detailed the macros, compile-time configuration options, and targets—the type of computer system for which the binary code was generated. The constant `REALIO` was set to an integer value corresponding to the system: 0 for the PDP-10 simulating the 6502, 3 for the Commodore, 4 for the Apple; there were six versions in all. Steil posited that the numbering of the target values revealed the order in which Microsoft signed contracts with the companies, with Commodore preceding Apple, for instance.

These versions of Microsoft BASIC print **COPYRIGHT 1978 MICROSOFT** on-screen, with one notable exception: the Commodore. In that version, famously, there's an Easter egg: type **WAIT6502,1** into a Commodore PET running BASIC version 2, and the string **Microsoft!** will appear at the top-left corner of the screen. The string is hidden within the lines of assembly, deceptively encoded as ten bytes' worth of two floating-point octal values appended to coefficients used by the SIN trigonometric function—although, tellingly, the floating-point numbers commented are not the correct constants for sine. Interestingly, Steil noted, since the ten bytes were not conditionally assembled, some BASIC builds subsequent to the Commodore's also contained those same ten bytes, although the GW-BASIC source does not include them, as a quick glance through the file MATH1.ASM (which offers a host of math functions) confirms.

Microsoft was very possessive of BASIC. "What is interesting is that initially it was Microsoft adapting their source for the different computers, instead of giving source to the different vendors and having them adapt it," Steil wrote. "Features like file I/O and time support seem to have been specifically developed for Commodore, for example."

There are other bits of trivia you can discover by reading through the 6502 source code. For instance, the **NEW** command is referred to as SCRATCH in the comments and the labels. "[M]aybe other BASIC dialects called it that, and they decided to rename it to NEW later?" wondered Steil.

Here's more arcana. Recall that the 8080 source offered this comment:

```
PAUL ALLEN WROTE THE NON-RUNTIME STUFF
```

The 6502 source's comments expanded on the idea of "non-runtime stuff":

```
NON-RUNTIME STUFF
        THE CODE TO INPUT A LINE, CRUNCH IT, GIVE ERRORS,
        FIND A SPECIFIC LINE IN THE PROGRAM,
        PERFORM A "NEW", "CLEAR", AND "LIST" ARE
        ALL IN THIS AREA. [...]
```

So, non-runtime essentially meant anything and everything that supported the editing of a BASIC program. Thus it was Gates who wrote the code implementing BASIC statements, functions, and the like. Note, however, that a comment in the GW-BASIC source reads as

```
FIVEO 5.0 Features -WHILE/WEND, CALL, CHAIN, WRITE /P. Allen
```

implying that Allen wrote at least some of the "runtime stuff"—although it is far from clear just how much Allen or Gates was involved, if at all, with coding GW-BASIC. (Gates claimed to be "very involved in the creation of [IBM PC] BASIC," though, which only slightly predates GW-BASIC.)

The shy Monte Davidoff, mentioned in the BASIC comments along with Allen and Gates, was a Currier House dormmate of Gates's at Harvard University. Davidoff—who had programming experience dating back to high school, where he used a time-sharing system to code in BASIC, FOCAL, FORTRAN, ALGOL, and assembly language on a PDP-8 via Teletype and paper tape—first worked for the embryonic (and hyphenated) Micro-Soft in 1975.

While eating lunch at Currier one day, he overheard Gates and Allen, neither of whom he had yet met, say, "We need to find somebody who can write floating-point routines." Davidoff quickly spoke up, exclaiming across the lunch tables separating them, "I've written those!" That wasn't true, though he had disassembled FOCAL to learn how it evaluated expressions and implemented floating point. "I knew that I *could* write them," Davidoff told Randy Kindig, host of the Floppy Days retrocomputing podcast, in a recent interview. Gates, Allen, and Davidoff decided to meet later, in Gates's dorm room, to discuss the project. Without a contract, and without knowing how much he would be paid or many other details about the assignment, Davidoff agreed to write the floating-point routines.

While working at Micro-Soft, Davidoff programmed the Altair BASIC binary format floating-point routines as well as the mathematical functions (SIN, COS, LOG, the pseudorandom number generator, and more). It wasn't his first paid programming gig. The small manufacturing company Globe Union, based in Milwaukee, Wisconsin, from which Davidoff's high school rented PDP-8 computer time, had previously hired him to write a program that read data from a communications line and then wrote it to DECtape, the magnetic tape storage used by Digital Equipment Corporation computers; he successfully completed the assignment on a bare metal machine (i.e., one without an operating system).

Paul Allen had developed a simulator for the Intel 8008 that ran on the PDP-10; he rewrote the program so that it simulated the 8080's larger instruction set. Thus, Gates, Allen, and Davidoff were able to use development tools on the PDP-10, from which they rented time courtesy of the Albuquerque Public School, to write code for the Intel 8080, the microprocessor powering the Altair. For his part, Davidoff had never even heard of the Altair before Gates and Allen showed him the *Popular Electronics* cover story featuring the machine. Only one physical Altair unit was available to experiment with at the company.

Davidoff ended up writing two versions of the floating-point routines. In the first one, he modified the representation of the PDP-10's floating-point format, changing the word lengths, byte sizes, and field lengths to accommodate an 8-bit machine (as opposed to the 36 bits of the PDP-10). In the second version, Allen directed Davidoff to study and then modify floating-point code originally written at Intel for the 8008. "I used ideas from that [Intel] code and also took advantage of the additional 8080 instructions, and that ultimately became the floating point that was in Altair BASIC," Davidoff recalled.

"It was a lot of work but technically, it wasn't too challenging, because I knew what to do and, in some ways, the 8080, which is the microprocessor that ran the Altair 8800, its instruction set was more powerful than the PDP-8's—so in some ways it [Altair BASIC floating point] was easier to write than what" he had previously programmed on the DEC machine, Davidoff explained. His biggest challenge involved balance: how to successfully manage schoolwork despite spending so many hours—and sleepless nights—working on the project, which included testing all the code he wrote.

To program the mathematical functions, he studied the documentation for the PDP-10's FORTRAN scientific library, which included the polynomial approximations that computed the functions. "So, I used the same approximations and from their documentation wrote code to do that for the Altair," he said. But the documentation didn't include a pseudorandom number generator, "so I made something up for the Altair," Davidoff continued. "And, at that time, I had no idea how hard it was to write a good pseudorandom number generator.... Some of the things I did which I thought were making it more random were making it less random.... That was probably the biggest mistake I made."

Gates, Allen, and Davidoff would sometimes lay out BASIC listings on the floor and pore through the code, "com[ing] up with crazy ideas to save a byte here or a byte there." For example, if a subroutine was going to call another subroutine using a jump instruction, the three young programmers would instead reorder the code, placing one subroutine immediately after the other, thereby eliminating the need for a jump. Another space-saving trick involved using the LXI opcode in a clever way called a "look-see," shaving off one byte. Altair BASIC also gave users the option at startup of whether to load the transcendental functions: sine, cosine, square root, etc. If users opted not to load them, additional space would be freed up for their BASIC programs.

As for his boss, "Bill could get very loud. If he felt you weren't getting something, he would say the same thing, louder," Davidoff recalled elsewhere. Indeed, Gates has always exhibited a rather esoteric personality, evidenced by his sometimes-odd public behavior well into middle age and beyond. To take just one example, at a 2009 TED talk he delivered on malaria, Gates opened a transparent container filled with live mosquitoes, thereby releasing potentially dangerous insects into the crowd. "There's no reason only poor people should have the experience," the billionaire told the audience.

To continue at Microsoft as a permanent employee, Davidoff would have needed to drop out of Harvard—something that he, unlike Gates, couldn't afford to do. So, instead, Davidoff finished his studies, became a programmer, and ended up working at Honeywell on the Multics project.

Monte Davidoff's Altair floating-point routine, part of the "math package" referenced in BASIC source code comments, turned into Microsoft Binary Format (MBF), which appeared in later versions of BASIC, including GW-BASIC.

Let's now peel back the curtain to find out how some of the sausage was made. Open up GW-BASIC source files at random, and you're bound to learn something. Want to explore how the **WHILE...WEND** statement worked? Skim through the FIVEO.ASM file. Interested in how graphics routines like **PSET**, **LINE**, and **DRAW** were handled? Open up GENGRP.ASM to find out. There's even a detailed flowchart of keyboard operations, composed of comments, embedded in the GIOKYB.ASM file, shown on the top of the next page.

```
48   ; Keyboard Data-Flow/Control-Structure for GI086:
49   ;
50   ;    PLAY, LIST, NEWSTT                                          INCHRI
51   ;    ----------+----------                              (fixed length input)
52   ;         !                               INLIN                  !
53   ;         !                         (Screen Editor)     KYBSIN/CHGET
54   ;       CHKINT                            !            (Device Indep. input)
55   ;    +------------+                       !                      !
56   ;    !            !               +-----------------+
57   ;    !            !                       !
58   ;    !            !      INKEY$           KEYIN
59   ;    !          POLKEY    !                !
60   ;    !            !      +----------------+----+
61   ;    !        +-----+---------+-------+          !
62   ;    !        !   !     !     !       CHSNS (get 1 KEY {may be 2 bytes}
63   ;    !        ! CNTCCN KEYTRP PKEYQ         !     function key expansion)
64   ;    !        !   !                 -------+    !
65   ;    !        +----+            PUTQ ---> ! ! ! !--> CONIN (get 1 byte from queue)
66   ;    !            !                       -------+
67   ; POLLEV       KEYINP(OEM supplied)    (queue)
68   ;(OEM supp.)  (maps to MS Univ keyboard)
69   ;(test for trapable event)
```

"Many features that ended up in GW-BASIC (short for Gee Whiz)," Gates wrote in "The 25th Birthday of BASIC, "came from our experience writing interpreters for Japanese machines." In addition, "We [at Microsoft] developed the music and graphics-string macro languages that used the verbs **PLAY** and **DRAW**."

Next, consider this revealing comment block from MATH1.ASM, which described a particular process involving outputting a number's correct decimal location (only the first part of the detailed comment block is reproduced below):

```
;WHAT  IS  HAPPENING  HERE  IS  THAT  IF  WE  HAVE  MORE  DIGITS  THAN
REQUIRED
;WE MUST DIVIDE OUT THE EXCESS DIGITS SO THAT WE CAN ROUND AT THE
;CORRECT PRINT POSITION. ONCE WE HAVE PERFORMED THIS DIVISION WE
;WILL  NEED  TO  CALCULATE  THE  CORRECT  DECIMAL  POINT  POSITION  BY
ADDING
;THE DESIRED PRINT POSITIONS TO THE LEFT TO THE NUMBER OF POSITIONS
;WE SHIFTED OUT. THE REASON FOR THIS IS THAT REGARDLESS OF THE SIZE
;OF THE NUMBER WE GO TO $FOTCV WITH , A FIXED NUMBER OF DIGITS
;WILL BE PLACED IN THE OUTPUT BUFFER....
```

Going beyond the comments and parsing the code itself requires a fairly deep knowledge of 8080 assembly as well as the patience of a saint to disentangle the thousands of PUSHes and POPs and references to pointers and registers; you are reminded, as you become bleary-eyed scanning through countless lines (which are mostly in uppercase), that writing assembly is as much an art as a science, stamped with the unique stylistic cues and predilections of its coders. Even decoding precisely how the simplest of mathematical functions in GW-BASIC works is a pulling-your-hair-out exercise consisting of one part frustration and two parts self-flagellation.

Consider the absolute value function, for instance. In GW-BASIC's direct mode, if you type

?ABS(-2)

the output will be

2

because the absolute value of -2 equals the distance of the integer from zero on the number line, which is two units.

Open the MATH1.ASM source file to look under the hood of the **ABS** function, however, and you'll get more than you bargained for. The assembly code for ABSFN begins with a CALL to $GETYP. We learn that $GETYP—which a *label*, prefixed by a dollar sign, preceding an instruction or series of instructions that serves as an entry point from elsewhere in the assembly program—helps to decode the data type that **ABS** can handle, which could be of the integer, single precision, double precision, or string variety (the last of which, strangely, doesn't cause an error when serving as an argument for **ABS** but rather simply returns the string literal used as the argument). ABSFN then continues with:

```
JS      $IABS           ;IF INTEGER PROCEED
MOV     AL,BYTE PTR $FAC-1
OR      AL,AL           ;SEE IF CURRENTLY NEGATIVE
JS      $NEG            ;AND IF SO NEGATE
RET
```

But in order to understand what's above, we need to know the code that the $IABS label precedes:

```
$IABS:      MOV    AX,WORD PTR $FACLO        ;FETCH INTEGER
     OR     AX,AX           ;AND SEE IF ALREADY POS.
     JS     VN15
     RET                     ;RETURN IF POSITIVE
```

As well as the $NEG label:

```
$NEG:
     XOR    BYTE PTR $FAC-1,LOW 200  ;FLIP SIGN OF FAC
     RET
```

We could rattle off what each of the instructions is doing, line by line—for instance, MOV moves a byte of data from a source register to a destination register, JS is a conditional jump dependent on the value of a sign flag, XOR is a bitwise exclusive OR operator, and RET is an unconditional return (required at the conclusion of every subroutine)—but that might mistake the forest for the trees, and, at this point, it seems like we've missed the point(er).

Michal Necasek, who, recall, studied the GW-BASIC source code, lodged several complaints with its readability and structure. First, the fact that identifiers were restricted to only six characters in length made the code that much harder to comprehend.

Second, the code was unstructured, with JMP often (unnecessarily) being the preferred instruction rather than RET. "As a consequence, there are only minimal attempts to keep values in registers and almost all data is kept in memory," he explained, while lamenting the conspicuous absence of the PROC (procedure) instruction throughout the source code. And third, "The jumpy programming style also makes it impossible to use local variables on the stack," a consequence of the code being written to conform to the 8080—albeit these abuses, like the "mixing of code and data and jumping into the middle of an instruction," were corrected on the 8086.

Admittedly, it might give you a sense of self-satisfaction to know arcana like the number of cycles the 8080 needed for memory access in a variety of situations, or the manner in which the high bits or the low bits of a word were obtained, or how to efficiently align the stack to squeeze every last ounce of performance out of a particular microprocessor. That said, if you can't shake the assembly bug, here's a suggestion: Work your way through the code listing for an implementation of Tiny BASIC instead of GW-BASIC for a much more manageable exercise in reading lower-level code, since Tiny BASIC dialects—first written by such programmers as Dennis Allison, Tom Pittman, and Li-Chen Wang, and distributed in *Dr. Dobb's Journal of Computer Calisthenics & Orthodontia* a half century ago—were expressly designed to be functional albeit compact versions of BASIC that fit snugly into computers burdened with very little memory. As Allison explained it in Volume 1, Number 1, of *Dr. Dobb's*:

> The magic of a good language is the ease with which a particular idea may be expressed. The assembly language of most microcomputers is very complex, very powerful, and very hard to learn. The Tiny BASIC project at PCC [the People's Computer Company] represents our attempt to give the hobbyist a more human-oriented language or notation with which to encode his programs. This is done at some cost in space and/or time. As memory still is relatively expensive, we have chosen to trade features for space (and time for space) where we could.

Allison favored writing BASIC as an interpreter, rather than a compiler, because although "[c]ompiled code is a lot faster, [it] requires more space and some kind of mass storage device (tape or disk). Interpretive BASIC is the most common on small machines." A direct mode—or, as he put it, "Some kind of 'desk calculator' mode of operation"—was imperative so that BASIC program bugs could be stamped out more easily.

Tiny BASIC would feature integer arithmetic exclusively; twenty-six variables total (A to Z); arithmetic and relational operators; a subset of traditional BASIC statements (INPUT, PRINT, LET, GOTO, IF, GOSUB and RETURN); strings, but only as part of PRINT statements; a handful of functions, including RND; CLEAR, RUN, and LIST commands for execution control; and a maximum of 256 lines in a program. The BNF-style formal grammar of Tiny BASIC was printed in *Dr. Dobb's* for readers as well. For instance:

statement::= **PRINT** expr-list

...

expr-list::= (string | expression)(, (string | expression) *)

Allison spared no details when describing the functionality of Tiny BASIC in *Dr. Dobb's*. Each Tiny BASIC program would be stored in an array called PGM, in line number order; a pointer called PGP specified the first free area in the PGM array. And every line of source code would be read from the console and saved into a 72-byte array called LBUF (short for Line BUFfer), while another pointer, called CP, indicated the next available region in LBUF. But, because portability between microprocessors was a priority, the Tiny BASIC interpreter itself would *not* be written in a machine language or an assembly language:

> When you write a program in TINY BASIC there is an **abstract machine** which is necessary to execute it. If you had a compiler it would make in the machine language of your computer a program which emulates that abstract machine for your program. An **interpreter** implements the abstract machine for the entire language and rather than translating the program once to machine code it translates it dynamically as needed. Interpreters are programs and as such have theirs as abstract machines. One can find a better instruction set than that of any general-purpose computer for writing a particular interpreter. Then one can write an interpreter to interpret the instructions of the interpreter which is interpreting the TINY BASIC program. And if your machine is microprogrammed (like PACE), the machine which is interpreting the interpreter interpreting the interpreter interpreting BASIC is in fact interpreted. [emphasis in original]

He called this approach "multilayered, [and] onion-like."

The execution routine was written in the People Computer Company's Interpretive Language (IL) and required only around one hundred twenty lines to implement BASIC. After examining the code more than four decades later, author J. Alan Henning noted, "A common pattern in IL is to test for a keyword or token, then act on that information. Each test is an assertion as to what is next in the line buffer. If the assertion fails, control jumps to a subsequent label (usually looking for a new keyword or token)." That pattern is evident in the sample code below.

```
S1:   TST    S3,'GO'       ;GOTO OR GOSUB?
      TST    S2,'TO'       ;YES...TO, OR...SUB
      CALL   EXPR          ;GET LABEL
      DONE                 ;ERROR IF CR NOT NEXT
      XFER                 ;SET UP AND JUMP
```

The impetus for building and spreading Tiny BASIC came about partly as a reaction by members of the Homebrew Computer Club to the hefty price tag of Micro-Soft's Altair BASIC interpreter and Bill Gates's unwillingness to distribute it for free or at low cost (his famous 1976 "Open Letter to Hobbyists" decried the software piracy then running rampant; Tiny BASIC first appeared on the scene the previous year, however).

Dr. Dobb's Journal was a joint product of Dennis Allen and Bob Albrecht, both of whom were founders of the People's Computer Company. Interestingly, Albrecht is referenced in the 6502 Microsoft BASIC source code, next to an instruction checking to see if a bell character—represented by decimal number seven of the American Standard Code for Information Interchange—has been pressed on the keyboard:

```
CMPI    7                   ;IS IT BOB ALBRECHT RINGING THE BELL
                            ;FOR SCHOOL KIDS?
```

Presumably, the comment is meant as a nod to Albrecht's groundbreaking educational endeavors, which were detailed in the fifth chapter.

Regardless of how much you enjoy—or are pained by—examining lines of code at such a low level, let's mostly put such instructions aside for now, except when absolutely necessary, and instead return to sifting through descriptive comments in the GW-BASIC source code.

Finally having access to the guts of the language, of particular interest to explore is GW-BASIC's pseudorandom number generator (PRNG). If we type the following in direct mode:

```
FOR X=1 TO 5:PRINT RND:NEXT X
```

The output is:

```
.1213501
.651861
.8688611
.7297625
.798853
```

Type **SYSTEM** to close GW-BASIC, and then reopen the language and key in the line of code again—and watch as the same five decimal values, each between 0 (inclusive) and 1 (exclusive), appear. "**RND** generates the same sequence of numbers each time you run the program," explain Don Inman and Bob Albrecht in their definitive book *The GW-BASIC Reference* (1990). "These numbers are pseudorandom; if **RND** generated truly random numbers, the numbers produced would be unpredictable." Any "random" sequence is initialized with a *seed* value, which can be, to varying degrees, unpredictable (for example: the number of milliseconds since the computer was turned on). The programmer and former Novell Administrator Ted Muller, who devotes a section of his informative Ted's Computer World website to BASIC, notes sardonically, "randomness could be achieved by incorporating a seed based upon external input, such as the stereo set or static electricity from the household cat. Needless to say, that option has been deemed impractical."

Typically, the way to avoid repetition of output is to employ the **RANDOMIZE** statement, which can be used with or without an argument. Omit the argument, though, and you will be asked the following question during runtime:

Random number seed (-32768 to 32767)?

This is termed a *reseeding*, whereby an integer in the range of -2^{15} and $2^{15}-1$ must be entered, resulting in the generation of a specific *deterministic sequence*. (Computers are deterministic machines, because their next state is determined by their current state; likewise, a deterministic sequence is one whose next term is determined by the value of its current term.) Enter the same integer seed repeatedly, and you'll obtain the same sequence of numbers, much like a player piano keying its way through all the notes of a song over and over again. Reseeding is especially useful if you need to debug a program that employs **RND**: a particular seed X is guaranteed to result in program behavior Y, which can be replicated as many times as necessary.

The deterministic nature of these pseudorandom sequences offers a number of useful real-world applications. To take just one: automobile remotes. Each transmitter and associated receiver are seeded and synchronized with a 40-bit code obtained using a pseudorandom number generator. Press the remote button to unlock the car, and if the codes of the transmitter and receiver match up, entry into the vehicle is permitted—and the next "random" number is generated. Press the remote button too far away from the car, and the receiver and transmitter will no longer be synchronized. But the receiver will still recognize the remote the next time it is used near the vehicle, since the receiver searches not only for the "current" pseudorandom code but also for the next 256, or 2^8, valid codes. A problem only arises if the remote button is pressed more than 256 times in a row without it being sufficiently near the receiver: the transmitter must then be resynchronized with the receiver to work properly again.

Another way to use the **RANDOMIZE** statement is with **TIMER** as an argument, which seeds the sequence using a single-precision value generated by the computer's internal clock (specifically, the number of seconds elapsed since midnight or the system's last reset):

RANDOMIZE TIMER

The **RND** function, along with **RANDOMIZE TIMER**, is especially useful for creating simple probability simulations. For example, in the textbook *Workshop Statistics: Discovery with Data* by Alan Rossman and Beth Chance, the oddly titled "random babies experiment" is presented. Four newly born babies, the authors explain, have been handed back to their mothers, albeit in a random order. The babies have first names alliterative with their last names: Jerry Johnson, Marvin Miller, Sam Smith, and Willy Williams. A set of questions, including *What is the probability of Ms. Johnson receiving her correct baby?* and *How often does no mother get back her baby?*, are posed to the reader.

What follows is a program simulating the random babies' experiment, which can be run on GW-BASIC using an old PC (if you have a GW-BASIC executable file), GW-BASIC through the freely downloadable DOSBox x86 DOS emulator for a modern computer (again, if you have a GW-BASIC executable file), or PC-BASIC, a freely downloadable emulator of GW-BASIC designed for modern machines. (Speaking of DOSBox: early in the popular 2017 documentary *Perfect Bid: The Contestant Who Knew Too*

Much, we see *The Price is Right* superfan Ted Slauson, a middle school math teacher, running via DOSBox a *TPIS* GW-BASIC program that he wrote in the early 1990s—complete with the show's logo, theme song, and text-based pricing games. After keying in the names of the players, Slauson's program asks the user to enter a random number between 1 and 32,000 in order to randomize prices and prizes; thus, forgoing **RANDOMIZE TIMER**, he in effect coded a tailored version of **RANDOMIZE**. Later in the documentary, Slauson demos a Visual Basic version of *TPIS*, with significantly improved graphics, sound, and UI.)

```
5 RANDOMIZE TIMER
10 KEY OFF:COLOR 15,0:CLS
20 PRINT"THERE ARE FOUR MOTHERS: JOHNSON, MILLER, SMITH, AND WILLIAMS."
30 PRINT"THEY NEED TO GET BACK THEIR FOUR BABIES: JERRY, MARVIN, SAM, AND
   WILLY."
40 PRINT:INPUT"How many baby-back trials would you like to run";TRIAL
50 FOR LOOP=1 TO TRIAL
60 TOTAL=0
100 T=INT(1+4*RND(1))
110 IF T=1 THEN J=J+1:TOTAL=TOTAL+1
120 U=INT(1+4*RND(1))
130 IF U=T THEN 120
140 IF U=2 THEN M=M+1:TOTAL=TOTAL+1
150 V=INT(1+4*RND(1))
160 IF V=T OR V=U THEN 150
170 IF V=3 THEN S=S+1:TOTAL=TOTAL+1
180 W=INT(1+4*RND(1))
190 IF W=T OR W=U OR W=V THEN 180
200 IF W=4 THEN W=W+1:TOTAL=TOTAL+1
210 IF TOTAL=4 THEN CORRECT=CORRECT+1
211 IF TOTAL=3 THEN THREE=THREE+1
212 IF TOTAL=2 THEN TWO=TWO+1
213 IF TOTAL=1 THEN ONE=ONE+1
215 IF TOTAL=0 THEN WRONG=WRONG+1
216 PRINT"MATCHES:";TOTAL;".";
220 NEXT LOOP
240 PRINT
250 PRINT"TOTAL TIMES ALL MOTHERS GOT CORRECT BABY: ";CORRECT;"/";TRIAL
260 PRINT"TOTAL TIMES ONLY JOHNSON MOTHER GOT HER CORRECT BABY:
    ";J;"/";TRIAL
270 PRINT"TOTAL TIMES NO MOTHER GOT HER CORRECT BABY: ";WRONG;"/";TRIAL
280 PRINT"TOTAL TIMES OF THREE MATCHES: ";THREE;"/";TRIAL
290 PRINT"TOTAL TIMES OF TWO MATCHES: ";TWO;"/";TRIAL
300 PRINT"TOTAL TIMES OF ONE MATCH: ";ONE;"/";TRIAL
```

Of course, even when using **TIMER**, the numbers generated by GW-BASIC are not random since they can be replicated in sequence by employing the same seed value. In fact, even more patterns can be found in the generated numbers beyond merely the repetition of entire sequences. Like the **RANDOMIZE** statement, **RND** takes an argument as well—and a negative argument produces an interesting effect. First, consider the following direct mode statement and its associated output:

```
FOR X=1 TO 10:PRINT RND(-1*X):NEXT X
```

```
.65086
.65086
.90086
.65086
.27586
.90086
.52586
.65086
.46336
.27586
```

Clearly, there is a pattern: the values of counter variable **X** equaling 1, 2, 4, and 8 shown above are the same: `.65086`. If the argument is a power of two, and it is multiplied by negative one, the same number will be generated, as we see below.

```
FOR X=1 TO 10:PRINT RND(-1*2^X):NEXT X
```

```
.65086
.65086
.65086
.65086
.65086
.65086
.65086
.65086
.65086
.65086
```

The repetition is not restricted to simply multiplying the power of two by negative one; we can multiply by any negative number, including a decimal, and observe the same effect (albeit with a different decimal between 0 and 1 generated and then repeated). For instance,

```
FOR X=1 TO 10:PRINT RND(-5.3*2^X):NEXT X
```

results in `.7684625` printed ten times on-screen. But if you avoid powers of two, then the decimals generated will not repeat. Ted Muller observes that "duplication occurs for all numbers of the form $-k*2^n$, where **k** is any value and need not be an integer." He offers this prescription for selecting an argument of **RND**: "Note that when **x** is odd, there are no matching lower values. The only matches are at **2x**, **4x**, **8x**, etc. An odd number cannot be a double of any integer. So to be safe, simply: Use only odd-numbered negative primes for random seeds."

Rob Hagemans, a data scientist and theoretical physics Ph.D. based in the UK, developed PC-BASIC, the extremely accurate GW-BASIC emulator for modern operating systems that implements floating-point arithmetic in MBF (Microsoft Binary Format). PC-BASIC is a Python/NumPy emulation of the language that offers an extensive set of online documentation; for example, consider the description of the effect of using a negative argument for PC-BASIC's **RND** function:

> If x [the argument] is negative, x is converted to a single-precision floating-point value and the random number seed is set to the absolute value of its mantissa. The function then generates a new pseudorandom number with this seed. Since…only the mantissa of x is used, any two values whose ratio is a power of 2 will produce the same seed.

Likewise with GW-BASIC, which handled **RND** and its arguments in an ungainly fashion. But ultimate responsibility rests with early Dartmouth BASIC, since the compiler required a "dummy argument" to tag along with any instance of **RND** so that the syntax scanner wouldn't flag the numeric function. Thomas Kurtz freely acknowledged as much, blaming both Kemeny and himself for what the BASIC random number generator had become:

> **RND** provided a "random" number between 0 and 1, but was quaint in one way: no doubt we were merely being lazy when we required that **RND** have a dummy argument [in Dartmouth BASIC]. Although in later versions we quickly removed this unfortunate syntax, the damage had been done, and our bad choice later resurfaced in several ugly forms.

Kurtz was certainly, at least in part, referencing Microsoft BASIC and its many iterations when he penned that acerbic criticism for the ACM SIGPLAN History of Programming Languages Conference in June 1978.

Although pseudorandom number generators for computers are relatively new, the need for random numbers is not. Over the past few centuries, various physical methods were leveraged to obtain these numbers: rolls of dice, flips of coins, draws of balls from overused urns. Sometimes existing data sets, such as those obtained from a population census, were selectively culled to provide the requisite "random" digits.

Last century, prior to the advent of electronic computers, mechanical devices were built to generate tables of random numbers. Notably, M. G. Kendall and B. Babington Smith used this technique to produce a table of 100,000 digits. In "Randomness and Random Sampling Numbers" (1938), published in the *Journal of the Royal Statistical Society*, they described the ontological foundations of randomness, carefully laying out a definition of the concept through the lens of probability and statistics; next, they detailed methods of selecting digits randomly; and then they discussed several ways to test the randomness of data, the most intuitive of which was the *frequency test*: "all the digits shall occur an approximately equal number of times."

In building their table of digits, Kendall and Smith commented on the questionable technique of using census data:

> So far as we are aware, the only tables of random numbers at present in existence are those due to L. H. C. Tippett, who compiled them by taking digits "at random" from census reports. This amounts to an abandonment of the mechanical method in favour

of one which may reasonably be supposed to be free from bias. The reliability of such numbers must, however, depend on the results which they give, and it is stated (in the introduction to these tables) that Tippett's numbers have been found by experiment to give results in accordance with expectation.

In other words, perhaps Tippett's numbers are respectable, but tread carefully. Kendall and Smith described their "randomizing machine," which

consists of a disc divided into ten equal sections, on which the digits 0 to 9 are inscribed. The disc rotates rapidly at a speed which can, if necessary, be made constant to a high degree of approximation by means of a tuning-fork. The experiment is conducted in a dark room, and the disc is illuminated from time to time by an electric spark or by a flash of a neon lamp, which is of such short duration that the disc appears to be at rest. At each flash a number is chosen from the apparently stationary disc by means of a pointer fixed in space.

From this machine derives their table of 100,000 digits. The authors then subjected tests of randomness to both their data and Tippett's census data, unsurprisingly finding the latter wanting.

By the early 1950s, computers were being put to work generating random digits. The general-purpose Ferranti Mark 1, produced by Ferranti Ltd. after the company was commissioned by Manchester University to build a commercial version of the Manchester "Baby" electronic stored program computer, offered an "enhanced order code" containing the /W instruction, which populated random bits in the accumulator's twenty least significant digits by employing a resistance noise generator. (Recall that an accumulator is a special register that stores the intermediate results of operations.) In the second edition of the *Programmers' Handbook for the Manchester Electronic Computer Mark II* (1952), preeminent mathematician and computing pioneer Alan Turing described a problem suitable for modeling using the /W instruction:

A man in New York starts walking from a street intersection, and at each street intersection decides in which direction to walk by twice tossing a coin (each of the four directions is chosen equally often). It is required to find the probability that before walking twenty blocks he will have succeeded in returning to his starting point. For this purpose New York is to be assumed to be an infinite rectangular lattice of streets and avenues.

Then, in 1955, the RAND Corporation published a four-hundred-page book titled *A Million Random Digits with 100,000 Normal Deviates*. These random digits were generated as a corrective to the table of Kendall and Smith. "One distinguishing feature of the digit table is its size," the book's Introduction reads. "On numerous RAND problems the largest existing table of Kendall and Smith, 1939, would have had to be used many times over, with the consequent dangers of introducing unwanted correlations." A physical process, powered by electricity, generated the digits.

The random digits in this book were produced by rerandomization of a basic table generated by an electronic roulette wheel. Briefly, a random frequency pulse source, providing on the average about 100,000 pulses per second, was gated about once per second by a constant frequency pulse. Pulse standardization circuits passed the pulses through a 5-place binary counter. In principle the machine was a 32-place roulette wheel which made, on the average, about 3000 revolutions per trial and produced one number per second. A binary-to-decimal converter was used which converted 20 of the 32 numbers (the other twelve were discarded) and retained only the final digit of two-digit numbers; this final digit was fed into an IBM punch to produce finally a punched card table of random digits.

But RAND's table, like the Ferranti Mark 1's, relied on hardware for randomization. Might software alone be capable of generating random numbers? Although tables of pre-formulated numbers could in theory be loaded into memory, the limitations of memory as well as the time required for such input made the practice infeasible in the earliest days of electromechanical and electronic computing.

In the mid-1940s, Kemeny's fellow Hungarian-American mathematician John von Neumann developed a strictly arithmetic means of pseudorandom number generation called the *middle-square method*, after he and scientist Stanislaw Ulam found Monte Carlo methods of producing tables of random digits too unwieldly. (The modern form of Monte Carlo simulation originates courtesy of Ulam. While recovering from an illness, Ulam, busying himself by playing solitaire, formulated probabilistic questions about the card game. Finding it too difficult to answer these questions using traditional combinatorial methods, he instead thought of using computers to simulate many random plays of the game and then counting the number of successful trials to arrive at a probability. Ulam described the idea to von Neumann, and in short order they put the Monte Carlo method into practice in the realm of mathematical physics.) Von Neumann's idea for generating pseudorandom digits was as follows: starting with an n-digit seed, take the square of the seed and then extract the middle n digits. Next, take those middle n digits and square that number, resulting in a new output in which the middle n digits are again extracted. And so on.

Several years later, von Neumann weighed in on the ontology of randomness by noting that "[a]nyone who considers arithmetical methods of producing random digits is, of course, in a state of sin." Indeed, his middle-square method proved to be a remarkably poor way to generate strings of convincingly random numbers, with sequences often getting stuck in cul-de-sacs of short repeating cycles.

A better way, called the *linear congruential method*, was developed by the American mathematician Derrick Henry (D. H.) Lehmer, who introduced it in a 1948 paper presented at a conference. As Shu Tezuka writes in his book *Uniform Random Numbers: Theory and Practice* (1995), "The linear congruential method is the most popular algorithm for random number generation in the field of computer simulations." Variants of the algorithm are used to generate pseudorandom numbers for scientific calculators, personal computers, and the C programming language.

While writing the books *Not Ok* and *Endless Loop* years ago, I did my best to ascertain GW-BASIC's method of pseudorandom number generation; unfortunately, Inman and Albrecht provided no clues in *The GW-BASIC Reference*, despite the text running to nearly eight hundred pages. And an article I discovered, published in a 1993 issue of the academic journal *Behavior Research Methods, Instruments, & Computers*, offered few insights:

> The Advanced BASIC (IBM, 1986), GW-BASIC (Microsoft, 1987), and QBASIC (Microsoft, 1991) programming languages provide the function **RND**, which is initialized by the **RANDOMIZE** command together with a number between -2^{15} and $2^{15}-1$, and which returns a pseudorandom single-precision number between 0 and 1.... [T]he generating algorithm is undocumented in the manual. Our letters to Microsoft Inc. about the algorithm remain unanswered.

A search for pseudorandom generation on Microsoft's website was more helpful, revealing that "Microsoft Basic uses the linear-congruential method," presumably referring to Visual Basic. Yes, a linear congruential generator (LCG) was also probably used in GW-BASIC, but, unable to find the smoking gun, in *Endless Loop* I sadly concluded, "Thus, the mystery of GW-BASIC random number generation will likely remain just that—a mystery."

But now, the open-sourced GW-BASIC was ready to reveal its secrets. Buried deep in the MATH2.ASM file is the following line:

```
SUBTTL      $RND   PSEUDO-RANDOM NUMBER GENERATOR
```

And, underneath that, we find a series of comments documenting the PRNG:

```
;       $RND    GENERATE THE NEXT RANDOM NUMBER IN THE
;               SEQUENCE.
;
;       CALLING SEQUENCE:        CALL     $RND
;               WITH THE PREVIOUS RANDOM NUMBER IN $RNDX
;               AND DATA ITEMS $RNDA AND $RNDC SET PROPERLY
;       METHOD: LINEAR CONGRUENTIAL FROM VOL. 2 CHAPTER 3 OF
;               KNUTH - THE ART OF COMPUTER PROGRAMMING.
;               M=16,777,216 OR 2^24; [ A MOD 8 ]=5 AND
;               [ C MOD 8 ]=3
;               RND(N+1)=(RND(N)*A+C)MOD M
;
;               THE DATA ITEMS A AND C CORRESPOND TO $RNDA
;               AND $RNDC RESPECTIVELY AND WERE CAREFULLY
;               CHOSEN TO MEET THE RECIPE IN KNUTH.
```

A fair number of GW-BASIC source code comments reference computer scientist Donald Knuth, including the one above, which tells us to consult Knuth's multi-volume collection *The Art of Computer Programming* for more information. In volume 2, chapter 3, section 2, part 1, he details the linear congruential method. First, four "magic integers" (Knuth's words) must be chosen:

- A positive value for *m*, the *modulus*, which is the remainder when one number is divided by another;

- A value greater than zero for a, the *multiplier*, which cannot be larger than the modulus;
- A value greater than zero for c, the *increment*, which also cannot be larger than the modulus; and
- A *starting value* for the sequence of pseudorandom numbers, denoted by X_0, which must be between zero and the modulus.

Then, the linear congruential sequence of pseudorandom numbers was obtained using the following formula, where n, the term number, is greater than or equal to zero:

$$X_{n+1} = (aX_n + c) \bmod m$$

The "mod" refers to modular arithmetic: we divide $aX_n + c$ by m and report back only the remainder of the operation. For instance, if $a = 1$, $X_0 = 2$ (the seed), $c = 3$, and $m = 2$, then we find the remainder to be:

$$(1 \cdot 2 + 3) \bmod 2$$
$$5 \bmod 2$$
$$1$$

So far, we have calculated only one term of our linear congruential sequence: 1. To obtain the next term, we use 1 as the new X_n value:

$$(1 \cdot 1 + 3) \bmod 2$$
$$4 \bmod 2$$
$$0$$

The sequence is now two terms in length: 1, 0. Plugging in 0 as our new X_n value, we find the following:

$$(1 \cdot 0 + 3) \bmod 2$$
$$3 \bmod 2$$
$$1$$

Now the sequence is 1, 0, 1. Continuing, we discover the linear congruential sequence to be as follows: 1, 0, 1, 0, 1, 0, …. These congruential sequences, without exception, repeat in cycles classified as *periods*. The period of our sequence above is a paltry two integers in length. Certainly this periodicity, evident after only several terms, leads to one inescapable conclusion: Using $a = 1$, $X_0 = 2$, $c = 3$, and $m = 2$ results in a deterministic sequence that wouldn't even fool a toddler into believing the values produced by it were random.

As Knuth observes, "A useful sequence will of course have a relatively long period." Thus, we need to choose integers for a, X_0, c, and m that facilitate a long enough period to convincingly simulate randomness deterministically in a finite-state machine. Note that the bigger the value of m, the larger the number of unique integer values possible for the sequence. In our couldn't-fool-a-toddler example above, m was 2, meaning there were only two possible integer values generated: 0 and 1. That's because when dividing integers by 2, there are only two possible remainders: 0 if the integer is even, and 1 if the integer is odd. Increase m to, say, 10, and then there are ten possible values for a sequence: the digits 0 to 9. In general, there are $m - 1$ possible values for a given linear congruential sequence. Knuth offers an obvious suggestion when setting the value of m: "We want m to be rather large, since the period cannot have more than m elements." But the magnitude of m must be tempered with another consideration: picking a value such that the computation of the modulus is speedy.

The GW-BASIC comments reveal that 16,777,216, or 2^{24}, was chosen as the m (modulus) value. Although that number may at first seem to be arbitrarily large, in fact 16,777,216 converted to binary is 100000000000000000000000. Why this particular number? Unlike addition or subtraction, division is a "comparatively slow operation," Knuth explains, so "it can be avoided if we take m to be a value that is especially convenient, such as the *word size* of our computer"; call this word size w, which is equal to 2^e on a binary computer with e bits of memory. We can get around employing the (relatively) slow operation of division if we *shift* the binary number stored in the accumulator to the left—meaning quite literally shifting the bits of the operand to the left by x bits, which is the effective equivalent of multiplying the decimal representation of the number by 2^x. (This is a simplification of bit shifts. Note that there are some bit shifts that preserve the sign of the original number, and others that don't, but to account for this would have us wading through the trickier territory of sign bits. Instead, we have simplified matters for clarity's sake.) Here is the upshot: "The result of an addition operation is usually given in modulo w [the word size]…and multiplication mod w is also quite simple, since the desired result is the lower half of the product," writes Knuth.

Hence, by using an m value equal to the word size w of the computer, we can shortcut the expensive operations of multiplication and division by employing the speedier and simpler addition, subtraction, and shifting operations. (An alternative to setting m equal to w: find the largest prime number less than w and make that m.) There are further considerations—namely, the periodicities (and thus random-looking behavior) of the low- and high-order bits—that must be factored into the decision as well.

Unlike with m, the vaunted GW-BASIC programmers were cagey when it came to the values they selected for a and c, writing in the comments that the numbers were "carefully chosen to meet the recipe in Knuth." But what was this recipe?

Knuth floats the idea of using a value of zero for c to speed up the generation of numbers; however, the tradeoff is that the period length decreases concomitantly. According to Shu Tezuka in *Uniform Random Numbers*,

> In the 1960's, the most popular choice of parameters was $c = 0$ and $M = 2^w$, $w \geq 4$; in this case $a = 3$ or 5 (mod 8) is the necessary and sufficient condition for the maximal period. (For example, RANDU, [the] IBM scientific library subroutine widely used all over the world in the 1960s, used the parameters $a = 65539$, $c = 0$, and $M = 231$.) However, it is now known that this choice is problematic because of the non-randomness of the low-order bits of X_n. To be precise, the least significant l bits of X_n,

$n = 1, 2, ...$, have a period of at most 2^l. Recently, therefore, a common choice has been to take M as prime and a as a primitive root modulo M.

GW-BASIC must use a positive number for c, not zero, since the source code comments reveal that $c \bmod 8 = 3$, whereas 0 mod *any* positive integer yields zero. In addition, m is not prime since it is greater than two and equal to a power of two.

The comments also reveal that $a \bmod 8 = 5$. Knuth suggests choosing a value for a that maximizes the period length—hopefully resulting in a period longer than necessary for any conceivable application (otherwise the repetition of the sequence will puncture the carefully crafted illusion of randomness). Ideally, the length of the period should equal the value of m, but that is only possible if all the following conditions are met:

1. c is *relatively prime* (also called *coprime*) to m, meaning that no integer greater than 1 evenly divides into both c and m.
2. $b = a - 1$ is a multiple of p, for every prime p that divides into m.
3. b is a multiple of 4, but only if m is a multiple of 4.

Page upon page of additional mathematical details, including theorems and proofs, fill up the remainder of Knuth's chapter. Rather than continue the mathematics lesson, all we really want to know is this: What were the values of a and c chosen for GW-BASIC?

Look at the comment prefacing the PRNG again:

```
;                THE DATA ITEMS A AND C CORRESPOND TO $RNDA
;                AND $RNDC RESPECTIVELY AND WERE CAREFULLY
;                CHOSEN TO MEET THE RECIPE IN KNUTH.
```

Indeed, in the assembly code, there are calls to $RNDA and $RNDC, in lines such as

```
MOV    DX,WORD PTR $RNDC        ;FETCH LOW 16 OF C
```

and

```
MOV    AL,BYTE PTR $RNDA+2      ;FETCH UPPER 8 BITS OF A
```

The MOV mnemonic copies the data stored in the location denoted by the second operand (following the comma) into the location denoted by the first operand (preceding the comma); thus, in the generalized instruction MOV A, B, the A is the destination and the B is the source.

To find the values of a and c, then, we need to search the source code for where $RNDA and $RNDC are defined. But we don't have to look far: the values we seek are in the MATH1.ASM file, though they come with a warning:

```
;CONSTANTS FOR THE RANDOM NUMBER GENERATOR FOLLOW
;DO NOT CHANGE THESE WITHOUT CONSULTING KNUTH VOL 2
;CHAPTER 3 FIRST
```

Then the values appear:

```
$RNDA:      DB    375       ;214013
            DB    103
            DB    003
$RNDC:      DB    303       ;2531011
            DB    236
            DB    046
```

The DB statement above, meaning "define bytes," allocates bytes in memory. The comments reveal the value of *a* as 214,013, and the value of *c* as 2,531,011. Notice that *c* and *m* are relatively prime (easily checked; write a program or search on the internet for an online tool to do your bidding), as we would expect (recall that part of the recipe to maximize the period length was to ensure that the two values were coprime, meaning their greatest common divisor is 1). Thus, by knowing the values of *m*, *a*, and *c*, we can calculate a maximal recurrence of period of *m* which is, in this case, 2^{24}—"meaning that after less than 17 million calls RND will wrap around and start running through the exact same series of numbers all over again. RND should not be used for cryptography, scientific simulations or anything else remotely serious," warns Rob Hagemans in the PC-BASIC documentation, tongue firmly in cheek.

If we wanted to do something more than "remotely serious" with random number generation, though, we'd need to consider employing a process like "external entropy collection." As relayed in the book *10 PRINT CHR$(205.5+RND(1)); : GOTO 10*:

> In some cases the computer has to turn to a human to become more random, recording data from users mashing the keys on their keyboard or wiggling their mouse around to generate a random key or password. Even more unguessable are inputs from physical systems of sufficient complexity—anything from video of a lava lamp to atmospheric radio distortions can be used to create random numbers for computation.

When an LCG is run on a computer, typically the numbers generated are not integers but are instead normalized over a uniform interval from 0 to 1. Put in BASIC terms, when we **PRINT RND**, a decimal, not an integer, is the result. (To obtain an integer, several manipulations need to be performed: e.g., **PRINT INT(1+15*RND(1))** outputs an integer between 1 and 15.) To obtain decimals over a uniform interval, we perform the following calculation:

$$U_n = \frac{x_n}{m} \text{ for } n = 1, 2, 3, \ldots$$

A program in GW-BASIC that simulates GW-BASIC's LCG might look like this:

```
5 REM LINEAR CONGRUENTIAL GENERATOR
10 CLS
20 X#=0
30 N#=0
35 R#=0
40 A!=214013!
50 C!=2531011!
60 M#=16777216#
```

```
70 INPUT "Enter Seed:";X
80 FOR J=0 TO 9
90 N#=(A!*X#+C!)MOD M#
100 R#=N#/M#
110 PRINT "integer: ";N#;TAB(10);"uniform interval value";R#
120 X#=N#
130 NEXT J
```

But there's a problem. Despite the use of double-precision variables, when the program is executed, the output is

```
Enter Seed:? 0
Overflow in 90
Ok
```

The numbers involved in the calculation are simply much too big for GW-BASIC to handle outright.

Let's try running (effectively) the same program in Java instead.

```
//linear congruential generator

import java.util.Scanner;

public class Main {

    public static void main(String[] args)  {

        Scanner input = new Scanner(System.in);
            long x = 0;          //the initial value (seed)
            long n = 0;          //the pseudorandom integer
            long a = 214013;     //the multiplier
            long c = 2531011;    //the increment
            long m = 16777216;   //the modulus, 2^24
            double r = 0.0;      //will equal n/r, setting random number
                                 //over uniform interval [0,1)

        System.out.print("Enter seed: ");
        x = input.nextInt();

        for(int j = 0; j < 10; j++){

            n = (a * x + c) % m;        //calculates pseudorandom integer
            r = (double)n / (double)m;  //turns n integer value into uniform
                                        //value over [0,1)

            System.out.println("integer: " + n + "  \t\t" + "uniform interval
            value: "+ r);

            x = n;

            }
        }

    }
```

Now the program works as intended. What follows is a sample run showing a replicable set of decimals over a uniform interval.

```
Enter seed: 0
integer: 2531011            uniform interval value: 0.1508600115776062
integer: 2592378            uniform interval value: 0.1545177698135376
integer: 16145237           uniform interval value: 0.9623311161994934
integer: 8724676            uniform interval value: 0.520031213760376
integer: 9915511            uniform interval value: 0.5910105109214783
integer: 1398110            uniform interval value: 0.08333384990692139
integer: 11376297           uniform interval value: 0.678080141544342
integer: 1949384            uniform interval value: 0.11619234085083008
integer: 13795947           uniform interval value: 0.822302520275116
integer: 9732994            uniform interval value: 0.5801316499710083
```

By the way, Rob Hagemans not only used an LCG for PC-BASIC, which arrived on the scene years before the open-sourcing of GW-BASIC; he also correctly ascertained the values of *m*, *a*, and *c*. Look at the PC-BASIC documentation for proof: "PC-BASIC's **RND** function generates pseudo-random numbers through a linear congruential generator with modulo 224, multiplier 214013 and increment 2531011. This exactly reproduces the random numbers of GW-BASIC's **RND**."

Despite Microsoft's decades-long effort at shrouding the source code in secrecy, perhaps GW-BASIC's method of pseudorandom number generation wasn't that much of a mystery after all.

CHAPTER 9

CALISTHENICS & ORTHODONTIA REDUX
Building Your Own BASIC...In BASIC

Can a BASIC interpreter be written using a BASIC interpreter?

No shortage of BASIC compilers and interpreters have been written in languages other than machine or assembly. PC-BASIC, written in Python, is a prototypical example, but there are many others.

Unusual is the BASIC compiler or interpreter written in BASIC (True BASIC's compiler was coded in True BASIC, for example). Rare, however, is the BASIC compiler or interpreter written in a form of unstructured, line-numbered BASIC. Rarer still is one that doesn't make use of **PEEK**, **POKE**, or machine language routines.

Why attempt to code such an implementation? Certainly not for utility's sake. Writing a program in unstructured BASIC already shackles the modern user with a number of onerous limitations; the lack of an explicit control statement like **END IF** in most line-numbered BASICs of old tests one's patience even when coding modest programs, with **GOTO**s and **GOSUB...RETURN**s picking up the slack while simultaneously making program readability a nightmare. (At trying times like these, one can almost come to agree with Dijkstra's conviction that BASIC mutilates the mind "beyond hope of regeneration.") But writing a working *programming language* using unstructured BASIC? Well, to classify the task as nontrivial is an understatement. We'll be challenging ourselves by tying both hands behind our backs—but why make things easy?

Following an unsuccessful attempt to scale Mt. Everest, George Mallory was asked why he still wished to climb the world's tallest mountain. "Because it's there," he famously replied. Why build a version of BASIC using BASIC? Because we (definitely, maybe) can.

We'll make use of GW-BASIC in the attempt; many of the old microcomputer BASICs could be used, and the interpreter we construct in this chapter can be converted to a host of other line-numbered BASIC dialects with a few changes here and there. True, once you pause to consider the significant limitations imposed on such an effort, the color may drain from your face. GW-BASIC is an interpreted language; the BASIC we construct will be interpreted as well—by GW-BASIC in real time. As a double-interpreted language, it will be perforce slow and ponderous, so let's call our implementation LBASIC, the L fittingly standing for *Limited*. Perhaps the L could also refer to *Limited Edition*, if we're feeling in a more optimistic mood. (Writing an interpreter using an interpreter isn't unusual; for example, Python interpreters have been implemented using Python. For that matter, even double-interpreted BASIC is not an unprecedented phenomenon. As we saw last chapter, Dennis Allison, when describing the design of Tiny BASIC, noted that "if your machine is micro-programmed [like PACE], the machine which is interpreting the interpreter interpreting the interpreter interpreting BASIC is in fact interpreted." And TI BASIC, designed for the 16-bit TI-99/4 home computer, was an interpreted dialect that had to be interpreted using GPL, an 8-bit virtual machine in ROM.)

LBASIC will be a proof of concept and, as such, have what might charitably be viewed as draconian limitations on its use. Like Allison's description of Tiny BASIC, our interpreter will also be multilayered and onion-like—in that as we peel back each layer, we'll cry.

Let us briefly list the features—as well as the attendant limitations—of our double-interpreted language.

- Programs can be saved as sequential data files (with the file extension *.TXT*) and later loaded back into memory.
- Only one statement per line is permitted (à la Dartmouth BASIC).
- A maximum of one hundred lines are available for a program, numbered from **1** to **100**.
- Twenty-six variables are set aside for use, labeled **A** to **Z**, but arrays are not available.
- A **PRINT** statement can output either a single string literal or the value stored in a single variable, but not both; added to that, concatenation of strings and numeric data—either as arguments for **PRINT** statements or in variable assignment statements—is not possible, nor can the values of expressions be calculated directly using **PRINT**.
- The **LET** statement offers programmers numerous options for using mathematical expressions, albeit those options are highly circumscribed.
  - A variable can be assigned the value of a numeric literal; examples include:
    - `LET A = 10`
    - `LET P = 3.14`
  - A variable can be assigned the value of a linear combination of another variable, in the form $a \times Variable + b$; examples include:
    - `LET B = 1 * C + 0`
    - `LET F = 1 * F + 1`
    - `LET G = 1 * G + -2`
    - `LET M = 3 * N + -6`

Though inelegant, more complex expressions can be woven together by employing multiple **LET**s with the linear combination option; for instance, consider these three successive lines in a sample program:

```
LET A = 1 * A + 1
LET B = 2 * A + 5
LET C = 0.33333 * B + -9
```

Additional composite **LET** statements can be constructed using the remaining **LET** options, which are as follows:

- A variable can be assigned the value of a randomly generated integer from 0 to *n*; examples include:
  - **LET T = RND(5)**
  - **LET X = RND(40)**
- A variable can be assigned the square root of the value stored in another variable; for example:
  ```
  LET W = 9
  LET V = SQR(W)
  ```
- A variable can be assigned to the sum of two variables, as in:
  - **LET J = K + L**
- A variable can be assigned to the exponentiation of two variables; consider:
  - **LET J = Q ^ R**
- A variable can be assigned to the result of a modular arithmetic expression; for instance:
  - **LET E = F MOD G**

These handful of **LET** permutations were chosen to account for as wide a variety as possible of LBASIC programming needs. More permutations can be added as needed.

- The **INPUT** statement accepts numeric data only.
- The **FOR/TO/STEP** and **NEXT** statements work as expected, subject to the following limitations: the **STEP** must be greater than zero, and only one loop is permitted in a program.
- The **IF/THEN** statement (**ELSE** is unavailable) compares the value of one variable with the value of another, jumping to a program line if the comparison is evaluated as true; possible comparisons include equal, not equal, greater than, and greater than or equal to. The jumps take the form of either **GOTO** or **GOSUB**. For example:
  - **IF A>=B THEN GOTO 10**
  - **IF R<>T THEN GOSUB 70**

Note: **GOSUB** can only be utilized within an **IF/THEN** statement; the programmer must remember to include an associated **RETURN** statement in the code.

- The **GOTO** statement, employed for unconditional jumps, works without any restrictions.
- The **END** statement, which terminates the execution of a program, works without any restrictions.

- The **REM** statement, used for single-line comments, works without any restrictions.
- Pressing the <Escape> key terminates an LBASIC program during execution.
- Since arrays cannot be used or defined (there is no **DIM** statement), the **READ** and **DATA** statements are unavailable as well.
- Defining single-line functions using the **DEF** statement is not available.
- Grouping symbols (e.g., parentheses) for calculations are not explicitly available.
- With the exception of **RND**, **SQR**, and **MOD**, mathematical functions (e.g., **ABS**, **SIN**, **COS**, **TAN**, and **LOG**) are not available.
- The error-checking facilities are primitive, to say the least.

To help the programmer conform to these significant coding constraints, a command line editor is dispensed with in favor of a simple text-based prompt-driven system. (A command line editor would require a tokenizer and a lexer—code to convert the characters of a user-entered string into meaningful tokens that could then be handed off to a parser to build the LBASIC program—concepts we will return to later in this chapter.) Bearing a faint resemblance to Sinclair BASIC, an 8-bit dialect that employed a keyword-entry system of keystroke sequences, the LBASIC interface permits programmers to write a programming statement, delete a line, clear an entire program from memory, list a program, load a program, save a program, or quit to the operating system (which, for LBASIC, is GW-BASIC)—using only several keystrokes.

Sure, a simple "Hello World" program can be coded and executed in LBASIC with no issues:

```
10 PRINT "HELLO WORLD"
20 GOTO 10
```

A screenshot of LBASIC, a BASIC interpreter running in GW-BASIC (that's running in PC-BASIC).

Perhaps we want a printout of the sum of the integers from 1 to 100. Also easily accomplished in LBASIC:

```
10 LET S = 0
20 FOR A = 1 TO 100 STEP 1
30 LET S = S + A
40 NEXT A
50 PRINT "THE SUM OF THE NUMBERS FROM 1 TO 100 IS"
60 PRINT S
70 END
```

But can a small, albeit more robust, program—perhaps even a simple game—be coded in the language?

Suppose we wish to write a simple guessing game in LBASIC, one in which the computer picks a random integer between 0 and 100. The user is prompted to place a guess for the number. Then, depending on the input, the computer responds with one of three statements: the guess is too high, the guess is too low, or the guess is correct. If the guess is correct, the computer relays how many attempts were needed to guess the number. Finally, the user is offered a choice to play the game again or exit.

Such a guessing game, similar to the program *Number* found in Bob Albrecht's book *What to Do After You Hit Return*, could be coded in LBASIC as follows:

```
5 REM GUESS.TXT
7 PRINT "THE GUESSING GAME"
8 LET C = 0
9 LET E = 1
10 LET B = RND(100)
15 PRINT "The computer picked a random integer between 0 and 100."
16 PRINT "What number did the computer pick?"
20 INPUT A
22 LET C = 1 * C + 1
25 IF A>B THEN GOTO 50
30 IF B>A THEN GOTO 60
40 IF A=B THEN GOTO 70
50 PRINT "Your guess is too big. Try again!"
55 GOTO 16
60 PRINT "Your guess is too small. Try again!"
65 GOTO 16
70 PRINT "You guessed correctly!"
75 PRINT "It took you this many tries..."
77 PRINT C
80 PRINT "Type 1 to play again or any other number to quit"
82 INPUT D
85 IF D=E THEN GOTO 5
90 PRINT "Goodbye!"
95 END
```

Though GUESS.TXT is certainly underwhelming, the program works as expected—exactly as it would on a generic version of BASIC—successfully executing on a BASIC interpreter, written in BASIC, which runs using a different BASIC interpreter. If LBASIC is run on PC-BASIC, then LBASIC technically becomes a *triple*-interpreted language, since Python, the language PC-BASIC was built in, is interpreted. It's interpreters all the way down.

The key to LBASIC's functionality rests with its arrays—lots and lots of arrays, almost all of which contain one hundred elements, indexed from 1 to 100 and thus corresponding to lines 1 to 100 of an LBASIC program. (Set the size of these many arrays any larger, and GW-BASIC won't run LBASIC due to memory constraints. Hence the hundred-line limitation of LBASIC programs.) Sometimes, values stored in the arrays are employed as flags—such as in the **LIN** array, which stores 1 in an index if the LBASIC program line contains a statement or 0 otherwise. Other times, the values stored in arrays correspond to the type of statement used in a program line; for instance, the **LET0** array relays the type of **LET** statement—assignment of a numeric literal, assignment of a linear combination, and so forth—present on the line. Still other arrays store values of variables or string literals, such as the **VAR2** and **PRI$** arrays, respectively.

What follows are declarations for the arrays as well as the initializations of several other variables found on lines **0** to **48** of **LBASIC.BAS**.

```
0 REM LBASIC.BAS
5 KEY OFF:SCREEN 9:SCREEN 0:COLOR 14,0:CLS:RANDOMIZE
  TIMER:PROG$="PROGRAM.TXT"
6 PRINT"***'LIMITED' BASIC (LBASIC) - A BASIC INTERPRETER RUNNING IN GW-
  BASIC***":PRINT:COLOR 15
7 REM SET UP ARRAYS
10 DIM LIN(100)       'A VALUE OF 1 = LINE IN USE; A VALUE OF 0 = LINE NOT
   IN USE
12 DIM REMARK$(100)  'ALL REMARKS ARE STRINGS, STORED IN THIS ARRAY BY
   LINE
13 DIM EN(100)        'TRIGGERS AN END STATEMENT, STORED IN THIS ARRAY BY
   LINE
14 DIM INPU(100)      'TRIGGERS AN INPUT DURING RUNTIME FOR THE VARIABLE
   STORED IN THIS ARRAY
15 DIM IFTHEN1(100)  'STORES VARIABLE1 FOR COMPARISON
16 DIM IFTHEN2(100)  'STORES VARIABLE2 FOR COMPARISON
17 DIM IFTHEN3(100)  'STORES TYPE OF COMPARISON (EQUAL TO, NOT EQUAL TO,
   GREATER THAN, OR GT/EQUAL TO)
18 DIM IFTHEN4(100)  'STORES LINE NUMBER TO JUMP TO IF COMPARISON IS TRUE
19 DIM IFTHEN5(100)  'STORES VALUE INDICATING WHETHER IF/THEN = GOTO (1)
   OR GOSUB (2)
20 DIM PRI$(100)      'ALL PRINT ARGUMENTS ARE STRINGS, STORED IN THIS
   ARRAY BY LINE
21 DIM PRI(100)       'ALL PRINT ARGUMENTS ARE VARIABLE NUMBERS (FROM 1 TO
   26, FOR A TO Z), STORED IN THIS ARRAY BY LINE
```

```
22 DIM FORNEXT1(100)    'STORES LOOPING VARIABLE FOR FOR/NEXT LOOP, INDEXED
   BY LINE NUMBER OF 'FOR'
23 DIM FORNEXT2(100)    'STORES THE INITIAL VALUE OF FOR LOOP, INDEXED BY
   LINE NUMBER OF 'FOR'
24 DIM FORNEXT3(100)    'STORES THE FINAL VALUE OF FOR LOOP, INDEXED BY
   LINE NUMBER OF 'FOR'
25 DIM FORNEXT4(100)    'STORES THE STEP AMOUNT OF FOR LOOP, INDEXED BY
   LINE NUMBER OF 'FOR'
26 DIM FORNEXT5(100)    'STORES THE LINE CONTAINING THE FOR LOOP, INDEXED
   BY LINE NUMBER OF 'NEXT'
27 DIM FORNEXT6(100)    'STORES THE LINE CONTAINING THE NEXT STATEMENT,
   INDEXED BY LINE NUMBER OF 'FOR'
28 LOOPS=0                'ONLY ONE FOR LOOP PER PROGRAM ALLOWED
29 DIM RESTORENEXT(100)'STORES THE LINE CONTAINING THE FOR LOOP INDEXED BY
   'NEXT'...WHEN THE NEXT IS DELETED AFTER LOOP RUNS
30 DIM GOT(100)          'ALL VALUES FOR GOTO ARGUMENTS ARE NUMERICAL,
   STORED IN THIS ARRAY BY LINE
31 DIM VAR1(26):DIM VAR2(26)   'ARRAYS FOR VARIABLES--FIRST ARRAY IS 0 OR
   1, DEPENDING IF VARIABLE IS INITIALIZED; FIRST ARRAY CONTAINS VALUES OF
   VARIABLES; ONLY 26 VARIABLES AVAILABLE (A TO Z)
32 DIM LET0(100) 'INDICATES A LET STATEMENT--IF EQUAL TO 1, THEN A LET
   VARIABLE = VALUE; IF EQUAL TO 2, THEN A LET VARIABLE = OTHER VARIABLE
   (LINEAR COMBINATION); ETC.
33 DIM LET1(100)  'VARIABLE, FROM 1 TO 26, PRESENT ON LEFT SIDE OF EQUALS
   SIGN OF LET STATEMENT
34 DIM LET2(100)  'IF OPTION 2 OF LET (VARIABLE = OTHER VARIABLE...) THEN
   INDICATES WHICH OTHER VARIABLE (1 TO 26)
35 DIM LET3(100)  'IF OPTION 2 OF LET (VARIABLE = OTHER VARIABLE...) THEN
   INDICATES THE MULTIPLIER OF OTHER VARIABLE: a*OTHERVARIABLE+b
36 DIM LET4(100)  'IF OPTION 2 OF LET (VARIABLE = OTHER VARIABLE...) THEN
   INDICATES THE ADDITIVE PORTION OF OTHER VARIABLE: a*OTHERVARIABLE+b
37 DIM LET5(100)  'STORES VALUE OF A VARIABLE IN A SIMPLE LET STATEMENT
   (LET VARIABLE = VALUE)
38 DIM LET6(100)  'SINGLE VALUE THAT VARIABLE ON LEFT SIDE OF STATEMENT IS
   EQUAL TO--OPTION 3 OF LET STATEMENT ONLY (OPTION 3 = RND)
39 DIM LET7(100)   'MAX INTEGER VALUE OF RND; RND BETWEEN 0 AND THIS VALUE
40 DIM LET8(100)   'VARIABLE TO TAKE THE SQUARE ROOT OF (IF OPTION 4)
41 DIM LET9(100)   'VARIABLE TO TAKE VARIABLE + OTHERVARIABLE--OPTION 5 OF
   LET STATEMENT
42 DIM LET10(100) 'VARIABLE TO TAKE VARIABLE + OTHERVARIABLE--OPTION 5 OF
   LET STATEMENT
43 DIM LET11(100) 'VARIABLE TO BE THE BASE, IN BASE ^ EXPONENT--OPTION 6
   OF LET STATEMENT
44 DIM LET12(100) 'VARIABLE TO BE THE EXPONENT, IN BASE ^ EXPONENT--OPTION
   6 OF LET STATEMENT
45 DIM LET13(100) 'VARIABLE TO BE THE FIRST VARIABLE, IN VARIABLE MOD
   OTHERVARIABLE--OPTION 7 OF LET STATEMENT
46 DIM LET14(100) 'VARIABLE TO BE THE SECOND VARIABLE, IN VARIABLE MOD
   OTHERVARIABLE--OPTION 7 OF LET STATEMENT
47 DIM GOS(100)  'STORES A VALUE OF 1 = LINE IN USE FOR A 'RETURN'
   STATEMENT
```

```
48 RETURNLINE=0    'VARIABLE WHICH STORES THE LINE NUMBER + 1 OF THE MOST
   RECENT 'GOSUB' ENCOUNTERED DURING RUNTIME
```

Only two of the lines listed above—lines **5** and **6**—use any GW-BASIC-specific statements. Let's work through examples illustrating how the arrays are used in LBASIC before continuing with the code listing.

Each line in an LBASIC program takes the following form:

<Line Number> <Keyword> <Parameters>

where the parameters are associated with the BASIC keyword on the line. No line can have more than one BASIC keyword, with one exception: the **IF/THEN** statement offers the option of **GOTO** or **GOSUB**. The line numbers serve as labels for **GOTO** and **GOSUB** as well as a means to sort the LBASIC statements in ascending order.

Suppose we code the following line in an LBASIC program:

```
5 REM GUESS.TXT
```

The presence of an LBASIC statement on line **5** is recorded with **LIN(5)=1**. Then, the **REMARK$** array stores the comment: **REMARK$(5)="GUESS.TXT"**. Later, when RUNing, LISTing, LOADing, or SAVE-ing the LBASIC program, these values stored in the **LIN** and **REMARK$** arrays are interpreted, output, read into memory, or stored by GW-BASIC.

Consider this line:

```
7 PRINT "THE GUESSING GAME"
```

As with a remark, two arrays are used. First, **LIN(7)=1**. Then, **PRI$(7)="THE GUESSING GAME"**.

Once variables are introduced in a program, the complexity increases, albeit slightly. Take a look at the following:

```
8 LET C = 0
```

When an LBASIC program using variables is run—but not before—two arrays manage any work with the variables: **VAR1** and **VAR2**, both of which have indices spanning from 1 to 26. Of course, since variables in LBASIC are restricted to a single letter, 1 represents variable **A**, 2 represents variable **B**, and so on. At runtime, the **VAR1** array stores either 0, indicating the variable is not in use, or 1, indicating the variable is in use, for all twenty-six elements. The **VAR2** array stores the numeric values of the single-letter variables at runtime. Thus, once the interpreter reaches line **8** shown above, the assignments **VAR1(3)=1** and **VAR2(3)=0** are explicitly made. Note that it is not possible to use elements of **VAR2** as flags indicating whether particular variables are in use, since variables can be initialized to 0, like in line **8** above; therefore, both the **VAR1** and **VAR2** arrays are necessary.

With respect to the **LET** statement in line **8**, though, several array assignments are required outside of runtime. First, **LIN(8)=1**. Then, **LET1(8)=3**, denoting that the variable **C** is present on the left side of the equals sign. Next, since LBASIC's **LET** offers a number of (highly circumscribed) permutations for mathematical expressions, we need to indicate which of these permutations is in use; **LET0(8)=1**—representing the simplest **LET** statement, where a single numeric value is stored in a variable—does the trick. Finally, the value on the right side of the equals sign must be stored; **LET5(8)=0** accomplishes this task. Note that the index used for all these arrays is 8, the line number of the statement.

An LBASIC program line such as

```
22 LET C = 1 * C + 1
```

requires populating the **LIN** array for the line-number-in-use flag, the **LET0** array in order to indicate **LET** option 2—a linear combination in the form $a \times Variable + b$—as well as the arrays **LET1**, **LET2**, **LET3**, and **LET4** for the associated variables and constants. The remaining **LET** arrays handle generating random numbers and computing sums, exponentiations, and modular arithmetic problems, none of which apply to line **22** above.

What about user input? Consider the line:

```
20 INPUT A
```

First, **LIN(20)=1**. Then, **INPU(20)=1**, where the **1** represents variable **A**—the location in which to store the numeric input from the user. (Notice we couldn't call the array **INPUT**, since **INPUT** is a reserved word in GW-BASIC.)

Next, consider **PRINT** statements that output the values stored in variables, such as:

```
77 PRINT C
```

After setting **LIN(77)=1**, we need **PRI(77)=3**, indicating the variable value to be output.

A line like

```
55 GOTO 16
```

also only requires populating two arrays: **LIN(55)=1** and **GOT(55)=16**.

And the line

```
95 END
```

uses two arrays as well: **LIN(95)=1** and **EN(95)=1**.

Now, let us unpack the following:

```
25 IF A>B THEN GOTO 50
```

In LBASIC, **IF/THEN** statements come in several varieties. Here, we first need to employ the array **LIN(25)=1**. Then, we must store values for all five **IFTHEN** arrays: **IFTHEN1(25)=1**, which stores the first variable for comparison (variable **A**); **IFTHEN2(25)=2**, which stores the second variable for comparison (variable **B**); **IFTHEN3(25)=3**, which stores the type of comparison (1 = equal to; 2 = not equal to; 3 = greater than; 4 = greater than or equal to. There is no need for the less than and less than or equal to inequalities, since the two variables can swap positions in the statement); **IFTHEN4(25)=50**, which stores the line number to jump to if the comparison is true; and **IFTHEN5(25)=1**, which stores the type of jump: **GOTO** (option 1) or **GOSUB** (option 2). Whenever a **GOSUB** is encountered by LBASIC during runtime, the line number + 1 of the **GOSUB** is stored in the variable **RETURNLINE**. Of course, use of **GOSUB** necessitates including a **RETURN** statement; any line with a **RETURN** is denoted in LBASIC using the **GOS** array. When encountered by the interpreter, the **RETURN** statement passes program control to the statement immediately following the **GOSUB**, the line number of which is stored in **RETURNLINE**.

The most complex statements are **FOR/TO/STEP** and **NEXT**. Even without them, loops are still possible in LBASIC by employing a counter variable using **LET** and an **IF/THEN** statement to transfer program control when the counter variable reaches a certain value, as demonstrated in the LBASIC snippet below.

```
10 LET A = 0
15 LET B = 10
20 LET A = 1 * A + 1
30 PRINT A
40 IF A=B THEN GOTO 60
50 GOT0 20
60 PRINT "DONE"
70 END
```

When run, the integers **1** through **10** are output, followed by the string **DONE**. An equivalent **FOR** loop approach in LBASIC is as follows.

```
10 FOR A = 1 TO 10 STEP 1
20 PRINT A
30 NEXT A
40 PRINT "DONE"
```

To store an LBASIC **FOR** loop into memory, first we need **LIN(10)=1**. But we also need **LIN(30)=1** to indicate the presence of the **NEXT** statement. Then, **FORNEXT1(10)=1**, which stores the loop variable; **FORNEXT2(10)=1**, which stores the initial value of the loop variable; **FORNEXT3(10)=10**, which stores the final value of the loop variable; **FORNEXT4(10)=1**, which stores the **STEP** increment (the increment must be a positive number); **FORNEXT5(30)=10**, which stores the line number of the **FOR/TO/STEP** statement, indexed by the line number of the **NEXT** statement;

and FORNEXT6(10)=30, which stores the line number of the NEXT statement, indexed by the line number of the FOR/TO/STEP statement.

During runtime, the RESTORENEXT array stores the line number containing the FOR/TO/STEP statement, indexed by the line number of the NEXT statement; once a FOR loop runs to completion, the NEXT statement is "deleted," but the record of it remains in RESTORENEXT. The variable LOOPS ensures that no more than one FOR loop appears in an LBASIC program. Rewriting LBASIC.BAS to permit more than one FOR loop is certainly possible, but the complexity of the source code greatly increases when we consider that loops could be nested as well.

But what of the user interface? How are budding LBASIC programmers to enter in lines of code? A text-based prompt-driven system, which is awkward to use at first, becomes second nature after some practice. Take a look at output from part of a sample run of LBASIC.BAS:

```
Type line (1 to 100), 0 to LIST, -1 to RUN, -2 for NEW, -3 to EXIT, -4 to
LOAD, or -5 to SAVE:? 10
Type the number for the statement for line 10:
0.REM 1.PRINT 2.GOTO 3.LET 4.INPUT 5.FOR/NEXT 6.IF/THEN
7.RETURN 8.END 9.DELETE LINE
->? 3
Choose among the following options for LET:
1.LET VARIABLE = NUMERIC LITERAL
2.LET VARIABLE = OTHER VARIABLE VALUE (LINEAR COMBINATION)
3.LET VARIABLE = RND(INTEGER)
4.LET VARIABLE = SQR(SOME VARIABLE)
5.LET VARIABLE = SOME VARIABLE + SOME VARIABLE (SUM)
6.LET VARIABLE = SOME VARIABLE ^ SOME VARIABLE (EXPONENTIATION)
7.LET VARIABLE = SOME VARIABLE MOD SOME VARIABLE (MODULAR ARITHMETIC)
Which option? 2
What variable (type a letter from capital A to Z)? D
Consider the right side of the LET statement: LET VARIABLE =
a*OTHERVARIABLE+b
What is the OTHER VARIABLE (type a letter from capital A to Z)? D
What is the scalar 'a' to multiply OTHERVARIABLE by? 1
What is the scalar 'b' to add to a*OTHERVARIABLE? 2
Type line (1 to 100), 0 to LIST, -1 to RUN, -2 for NEW, -3 to EXIT, -4 to
LOAD, or -5 to SAVE:? 0
PROGRAM.TXT
 10 LET D = 1 * D + 2
Type line (1 to 100), 0 to LIST, -1 to RUN, -2 for NEW, -3 to EXIT, -4 to
LOAD, or -5 to SAVE:?
```

What follows is the LBASIC.BAS code listing that permits users to create an LBASIC program.

```
49 COLOR 15:PRINT"Type line (1 to 100), 0 to LIST, -1 to RUN, -2 for NEW,
   -3 to EXIT,"
50 PRINT"-4 to LOAD, or -5 to SAVE:";
55 INPUT PROMPT
60 IF PROMPT=-3 THEN END
70 IF PROMPT=0 THEN GOTO 2000
80 IF PROMPT=-1 THEN GOTO 1000
90 IF PROMPT=-2 THEN GOTO 6100
97 IF PROMPT=-5 THEN GOTO 7000
98 IF PROMPT=-4 THEN GOTO 7500
100 LIN(PROMPT)=1
110 PRINT"Type the number for the statement for line ";PROMPT;": "
111 PRINT"0.REM 1.PRINT 2.GOTO 3.LET 4.INPUT 5.FOR/NEXT 6.IF/THEN
112 PRINT"7.RETURN 8.END 9.DELETE LINE"
115 INPUT"->";STATEMENT
120 IF STATEMENT=1 THEN 200
125 IF STATEMENT=2 THEN 300
130 IF STATEMENT=3 THEN 400
135 IF STATEMENT=0 THEN 500
140 IF STATEMENT=4 THEN 550
145 IF STATEMENT=5 THEN 700
150 IF STATEMENT=6 THEN 630
153 IF STATEMENT=7 THEN 950
155 IF STATEMENT=8 THEN 600
160 IF STATEMENT=9 THEN 800
190 GOTO 115
200 REM PRINT STATEMENT
202 INPUT"Type 1 for PRINTing a STRING, or 2 for PRINTing a VARIABLE";OPT
203 IF OPT=1 THEN 210
205 IF OPT=2 THEN 230
209 GOTO 202
210 INPUT"What is the string to PRINT";S$
215 PRI$(PROMPT)=S$
220 GOTO 49
230 INPUT"What is the variable to PRINT (type a letter from capital A to
    Z)";NUM$
231 NUM=ASC(NUM$)-64
235 IF NUM<1 OR NUM>26 THEN 230
240 PRI(PROMPT)=NUM
250 GOTO 49
300 REM GOTO STATEMENT
310 INPUT"What is the line number to GOTO";G
320 GOT(PROMPT)=G
330 GOTO 49
400 REM LET STATEMENT
405 PRINT"Choose among the following options for LET:"
410 PRINT"1.LET VARIABLE = NUMERIC LITERAL"
415 PRINT"2.LET VARIABLE = OTHER VARIABLE VALUE (LINEAR COMBINATION)"
420 PRINT"3.LET VARIABLE = RND(INTEGER)"
421 PRINT"4.LET VARIABLE = SQR(SOME VARIABLE)
422 PRINT"5.LET VARIABLE = SOME VARIABLE + SOME VARIABLE (SUM)"
423 PRINT"6.LET VARIABLE = SOME VARIABLE ^ SOME VARIABLE (EXPONENTIATION)"
```

```
424 PRINT"7.LET VARIABLE = SOME VARIABLE MOD SOME VARIABLE (MODULAR ARITHM
    ETIC)"
425 INPUT"Which option";OPT
430 IF OPT=1 THEN 450
435 IF OPT=2 THEN 470
436 IF OPT=3 THEN 490
438 IF OPT=4 THEN 484
439 IF OPT=5 THEN 7700
440 IF OPT=6 THEN 7770
441 IF OPT=7 THEN 7900
445 GOTO 425
450 INPUT"What variable (type a letter from capital A to Z)";NUM$
451 NUM=ASC(NUM$)-64
452 IF NUM<1 OR NUM>26 THEN 450
455 INPUT"Assign what numeric value to variable in the LET state-
    ment";VALUE
462 LET0(PROMPT)=1       'SETS LINE NUMBER TO LET STATEMENT, OPTION 1
463 LET1(PROMPT)=NUM     'INDICATES THE VARIABLE IN LET STATEMENT, OPTION 1
464 LET5(PROMPT)=VALUE   'INDICATES THE VALUE OF VARIABLE OF LEFT SIDE OF
    LET STATEMENT
469 GOTO 49
470 INPUT"What variable (type a letter from capital A to Z)";NUM$
471 NUM=ASC(NUM$)-64:IF NUM<1 OR NUM>26 THEN 470
472 PRINT"Consider the right side of the LET statement: LET VARIABLE =
    a*OTHERVARIABLE+b"
473 INPUT"What is the OTHER VARIABLE (type a letter from capital A to
    Z)";OVAR$
474 OVAR=ASC(OVAR$)-64:IF OVAR<1 OR OVAR>26 THEN 473
475 INPUT"What is the scalar 'a' to multiply OTHERVARIABLE by";SCALA
476 INPUT"What is the scalar 'b' to add to a*OTHERVARIABLE";SCALB
478 LET0(PROMPT)=2       'SETS LINE NUMBER TO LET STATEMENT, OPTION 2
479 LET1(PROMPT)=NUM     'INDICATES THE VARIABLE OF LEFT SIDE OF LET
    STATEMENT
480 LET2(PROMPT)=OVAR    'INDICATES THE "OTHER VARIABLE" ON RIGHT SIDE OF
    LET STATEMENT
481 LET3(PROMPT)=SCALA   'INDICATES VALUE OF THE SCALAR A
482 LET4(PROMPT)=SCALB   'INDICATES VALUE OF THE SCALAR B
483 GOTO 49
484 INPUT"What variable to assign SQR (type a letter from capital A to
    Z)";NUM$
485 NUM=ASC(NUM$)-64:IF NUM<1 OR NUM>26 THEN 484
486 INPUT"Calculate SQR of variable (type a letter from capital A to
    Z)";V$
487 V=ASC(V$)-64:IF V<1 OR V>26 THEN 486
488 LET0(PROMPT)=4:LET1(PROMPT)=NUM  'SETS LINE NUMBER TO LET, OPTION
    4/INDICATES VARIABLE
489 LET8(PROMPT)=V:GOTO 49   'INDICATES THE VARIABLE TO TAKE THE SQUARE
    ROOT OF
490 INPUT"What variable to assign RND (type a letter from capital A to
    Z)";NUM$
491 NUM=ASC(NUM$)-64:IF NUM<1 OR NUM>26 THEN 490
492 INPUT"RND generates integer between 0 and what integer";MAX
```

```
493 LET0(PROMPT)=3       'SETS LINE NUMBER TO LET STATEMENT, OPTION 3
494 LET1(PROMPT)=NUM     'INDICATES THE VARIABLE OF LEFT SIDE OF LET
    STATEMENT
495 LET6(PROMPT)=1       'INDICATES THE VARIABLE OF LEFT SIDE OF LET
    STATEMENT HAS AN RND ASSOCIATED WITH IT
496 LET7(PROMPT)=MAX     'RANDOM INT GENERATED BETWEEN 0 AND MAX
499 GOTO 49
500 REM REM STATEMENT
510 LINE INPUT"Type your REMark here: REM ";R$
520 REMARK$(PROMPT)=R$
530 GOTO 49
550 REM INPUT STATEMENT
560 INPUT"What variable for INPUT (type a letter from capital A to
    Z)";NUM$
561 NUM=ASC(NUM$)-64
565 IF NUM<1 OR NUM>26 THEN 560
570 INPU(PROMPT)=NUM
580 GOTO 49
600 REM END STATEMENT
610 PRINT"END statement inserted"
620 EN(PROMPT)=1
625 GOTO 49
630 REM IF/THEN STATEMENT
635 INPUT"What is first variable for comparison (type a letter from capi
    tal A to Z)";NUM1$
636 NUM1=ASC(NUM1$)-64
637 IF NUM1<1 OR NUM1>26 THEN 635
640 INPUT"What is second variable for comparison (type a letter from capi
    tal A to Z)";NUM2$
641 NUM2=ASC(NUM2$)-64
642 IF NUM2<1 OR NUM2>26 THEN 640
645 INPUT"What type of comparison (1 = equals; 2 = not equal; 3 = greater
    than; 4 = greater than/equal)";SYM
650 INPUT"Jump to what line if comparison is true";JMP
651 INPUT"Is the jump a GOTO or a GOSUB (type 1 for GOTO, 2 for GOSUB)";GG
652 IF GG=1 THEN GOTO 655
653 IF GG=2 THEN PRINT"Don't forget to insert a RETURN statement in the
    program, too":GOTO 655
654 GOTO 651
655 IFTHEN1(PROMPT)=NUM1
660 IFTHEN2(PROMPT)=NUM2
665 IFTHEN3(PROMPT)=SYM
670 IFTHEN4(PROMPT)=JMP
680 IFTHEN5(PROMPT)=GG
690 GOTO 49
700 REM FOR/NEXT STATEMENT - ONLY ONE PERMITTED PER PROGRAM
701 PRINT"Only one FOR/NEXT loop permitted in a program"
705 IF LOOPS=1 THEN LIN(PROMPT)=0:GOTO 49
710 INPUT"What is the variable for the FOR loop (type a letter from capi
    tal A to Z)";NUM$
711 NUM=ASC(NUM$)-64
715 IF NUM<1 OR NUM>26 THEN 710
```

```
720 INPUT"What is the initial variable value for the FOR loop";INITIAL
730 INPUT"What is the final variable value (must be >= initial value)";
    FINAL
735 IF FINAL < INITIAL THEN 730
740 INPUT"What is the STEP for the loop (step amount must be > 0)";STP
745 IF STP <=0 THEN 740
750 PRINT"What is the line number for the NEXT statement (must be after
    line ";PROMPT;"): ";
755 INPUT NXT
757 IF NXT <= PROMPT THEN 750
760 FORNEXT1(PROMPT)=NUM         'SIGNIFIES VARIABLE OF FOR LOOP
765 FORNEXT2(PROMPT)=INITIAL     'INITIAL VALUE OF FOR LOOP
770 FORNEXT3(PROMPT)=FINAL       'FINAL VALUE OF FOR LOOP
775 FORNEXT4(PROMPT)=STP         'STEP AMOUNT
780 FORNEXT5(NXT)=PROMPT         'STORES LINE WITH FOR LOOP IN LINE WITH NEXT
782 FORNEXT6(PROMPT)=NXT         'STORES THE LINE WITH 'NEXT' STATEMENT IN
    LINE WITH FOR
785 LIN(NXT)=1                   'INDICATES LINE IN USE (WITH 'NEXT'
    STATEMENT)
787 LOOPS=1
790 GOTO 49
800 REM DELETE A SINGLE LINE
810 'FIRST, CLEAR OUT ALL ARRAYS EXCEPT VAR1 AND VAR2 (NOT NECESSARY TO
    CLEAR) AND FORNEXT
820 LIN(PROMPT)=0
825 EN(PROMPT)=0
830 INPU(PROMPT)=0
835 IFTHEN1(PROMPT)=0:IFTHEN2(PROMPT)=0:IFTHEN3(PROMPT)=0:IFTHEN4(PROMPT)
    =0:IFTHEN5(PROMPT)=0
840 PRI(PROMPT)=0
845 GOT(PROMPT)=0
850 LET0(PROMPT)=0:LET1(PROMPT)=0:LET2(PROMPT)=0:LET3(PROMPT)=0:LET4(PROM
    PT)=0:LET5(PROMPT)=0
852 LET6(PROMPT)=0:LET7(PROMPT)=0:LET8(PROMPT)=0:LET9(PROMPT)=0:LET10(PRO
    MPT)=0:LET11(PROMPT)=0
853 LET12(PROMPT)=0:LET13(PROMPT)=0:LET14(PROMPT)=0
855 REMARK$(PROMPT)=""
860 PRI$(PROMPT)=""
862 IF GOS(PROMPT)=1 THEN GOS(PROMPT)=0    'DELETE RETURN (IF IT EXISTS ON
    THE LINE)
865 'NOW DEAL WITH FORNEXT ARRAYS
870 'IF THE LINE IS A 'NEXT' LINE, THEN THAT LINE AND THE FOR LOOP LINE
    MUST BE DELETED
880 IF FORNEXT5(PROMPT)<>0 THEN 900
890 IF FORNEXT1(PROMPT)<>0 THEN 920
895 GOTO 49
900 LOOPS=0:TEMP=FORNEXT5(PROMPT):LIN(TEMP)=0:FORNEXT5(PROMPT)=0
905 FORNEXT1(TEMP)=0:FORNEXT2(TEMP)=0:FORNEXT3(TEMP)=0:FORNEXT4(TEMP)=0:
    TEMP=0
910 GOTO 49
920 LOOPS=0:FORNEXT1(PROMPT)=0:FORNEXT2(PROMPT)=0:FORNEXT3(PROMPT)=0:FOR
    NEXT4(PROMPT)=0
```

```
930 LIN(FORNEXT6(PROMPT))=0:FORNEXT5(FORNEXT6(PROMPT))=0:FORNEXT6(PROMPT)
    =0
940 GOTO 49
950 REM RETURN
955 GOS(PROMPT)=1         'INDICATES A 'RETURN' ON THE LINE
956 PRINT "RETURN statement inserted"
960 GOTO 49
...
7700 'LET STATEMENT - OPTION 5 (FIND THE SUM OF VARIABLE + OTHERVARIABLE)
7710 INPUT"What variable on the left side of = (type a letter from capital
     A to Z)";NUM$
7720 NUM=ASC(NUM$)-64:IF NUM<1 OR NUM>26 THEN 7710
7725 LET0(PROMPT)=5      'SETS LINE NUMBER TO LET STATEMENT, OPTION 5
7730 LET1(PROMPT)=NUM    'INDICATES THE VARIABLE OF LEFT SIDE OF LET
     STATEMENT
7732 PRINT"Consider the right side of the LET statement: LET VARIABLE =
     VARIABLE1 + VARIABLE2"
7735 INPUT"What first variable to add (type a letter from capital A to
     Z)";NUM$
7740 NUM=ASC(NUM$)-64:IF NUM<1 OR NUM>26 THEN 7735
7745 LET9(PROMPT)=NUM    'INDICATES THE FIRST VARIABLE TO ADD
7750 INPUT"What second variable to add (type a letter from capital A to
     Z)";NUM$
7755 NUM=ASC(NUM$)-64:IF NUM<1 OR NUM>26 THEN 7735
7760 LET10(PROMPT)=NUM    'INDICATES THE SECOND VARIABLE TO ADD
7765 GOTO 49
7770 'LET STATEMENT - OPTION 6 (EXPONENTIATION: BASE ^ EXPONENT)
7775 INPUT"What variable on the left side of = (type a letter from capital
     A to Z)";NUM$
7780 NUM=ASC(NUM$)-64:IF NUM<1 OR NUM>26 THEN 7710
7785 LET0(PROMPT)=6       'SETS LINE NUMBER TO LET STATEMENT, OPTION 6
7790 LET1(PROMPT)=NUM    'INDICATES THE VARIABLE OF LEFT SIDE OF LET
     STATEMENT
7795 PRINT"Consider the right side of the LET statement: LET VARIABLE =
     BASE ^ EXPONENT"
7800 INPUT"What variable is the BASE (type a letter from capital A to
     Z)";NUM$
7805 NUM=ASC(NUM$)-64:IF NUM<1 OR NUM>26 THEN 7800
7810 LET11(PROMPT)=NUM    'INDICATES THE BASE
7815 INPUT"What variable is the EXPONENT (type a letter from capital A to
     Z)";NUM$
7820 NUM=ASC(NUM$)-64:IF NUM<1 OR NUM>26 THEN 7815
7825 LET12(PROMPT)=NUM    'INDICATES THE EXPONENT
7830 GOTO 49
7900 'LET STATEMENT - OPTION 7 (MODULAR ARITHMETIC: VARIABLE MOD
     OTHERVARIABLE)
7905 INPUT"What variable on the left side of = (type a letter from capital
     A to Z)";NUM$
7910 NUM=ASC(NUM$)-64:IF NUM<1 OR NUM>26 THEN 7775
7915 LET0(PROMPT)=7   'SETS LINE NUMBER TO LET STATEMENT, OPTION 7
7920 LET1(PROMPT)=NUM    'INDICATES THE VARIABLE OF LEFT SIDE OF LET
     STATEMENT
```

```
7925 PRINT"Consider the right side of the LET statement: LET VARIABLE =
     VARIABLE1 MOD VARIABLE2"
7930 INPUT"What variable is the first variable (type a letter from capital
     A to Z)";NUM$
7935 NUM=ASC(NUM$)-64:IF NUM<1 OR NUM>26 THEN 7930
7940 LET13(PROMPT)=NUM    'INDICATES THE FIRST VARIABLE
7945 INPUT"What variable is the second variable (type a letter from capi-
     tal A to Z)";NUM$
7950 NUM=ASC(NUM$)-64:IF NUM<1 OR NUM>26 THEN 7945
7955 LET14(PROMPT)=NUM    'INDICATES THE SECOND VARIABLE
7960 GOTO 49
```

There are several sections of the above code worth highlighting. First, look at lines **230** to **240**. Though the user is prompted to enter in a capital letter as a variable name, the letter is transformed into a number, from 1 to 26, by converting the input character to numeric data using the **ASC** function—which finds the ASCII code of the character—and then subtracting 64. (Uppercase A corresponds to decimal 65 in ASCII, and $65 - 64 = 1$, the integer representation for the **A** variable in LBASIC.) In addition, by using a conditional statement, **LBASIC.BAS** ensures that the user is only able to type a letter from **A** to **Z**. Each time an LBASIC programmer has to type in a variable, these lines (with some modifications) repeat.

Second, lines **800** to **940** are designed to delete a single line of code in an LBASIC program. Note how many factors must be considered when deleting a line, especially since some LBASIC statements may have precedents or dependents (e.g., **FOR/TO/STEP** and **NEXT**). Erasing an entire LBASIC program from memory, however, is more straightforward, as shown in the code listing below.

```
6100 REM ********NEW COMMAND********
6105 INPUT"Are you sure you want to delete your program? Type 1 for Yes, 2
     for No";NE
6106 IF NE=1 THEN 6110 ELSE 49
6110 'FIRST, CLEAR OUT ALL VARIABLE VALUES AND VARIABLE INITIALIZATIONS
6115 PROG$="PROGRAM.TXT"
6120 FOR AA=1 TO 26:VAR1(AA)=0:VAR2(AA)=0:NEXT AA
6130 'THEN, CLEAR OUT ALL NUMERIC ARRAYS
6140 FOR AA=1 TO 100
6150 LIN(AA)=0
6155 EN(AA)=0
6160 INPU(AA)=0
6165 IFTHEN1(AA)=0:IFTHEN2(AA)=0:IFTHEN3(AA)=0:IFTHEN4(AA)=0:IFTHEN5(AA)=0
6170 PRI(AA)=0
6175 FORNEXT1(AA)=0:FORNEXT2(AA)=0:FORNEXT3(AA)=0:FORNEXT4(AA)=0:FORNEXT5
     (AA)=0:FORNEXT6(AA)=0
6180 RESTORENEXT(AA)=0:LOOPS=0
6185 GOS(AA)=0
6190 GOT(AA)=0
6200 LET0(AA)=0:LET1(AA)=0:LET2(AA)=0:LET3(AA)=0:LET4(AA)=0:LET5(AA)=0:
     LET6(AA)=0:LET7(AA)=0
6205 LET8(AA)=0:LET9(AA)=0:LET10(AA)=0:LET11(AA)=0
6207 LET12(AA)=0:LET13(AA)=0:LET14(AA)=0
```

```
6210 NEXT AA
6215 RETURNLINE=0
6220 'FINALLY, CLEAR OUT ALL STRING ARRAYS
6230 FOR AA=1 TO 100
6240 REMARK$(AA)=""
6250 PRI$(AA)=""
6260 NEXT AA
6270 IF LOD=1 THEN 7504
6300 GOTO 49
```

With the values in all arrays cleared out, and several other variable values reset, an LBASIC programmer can begin coding anew.

Which leaves **LBASIC.BAS** code for four remaining LBASIC commands: **LIST**, **RUN**, **SAVE**, and **LOAD**. Let's begin with **LIST**, which must translate the many values stored in the arrays into human-readable LBASIC source code. Notice in the lines below that variables stored as integers between 1 and 26 must be converted back into their respective alphabetic representations.

```
2000 REM ********LIST PROGRAM********
2005 COLOR 12:PRINT PROG$
2010 FOR X=1 TO 100
2020 IF LIN(X)=1 THEN PRINT X;" ";
2025 IF REMARK$(X)<>"" THEN PRINT "REM ";REMARK$(X)
2030 IF PRI$(X)<>"" THEN PRINT"PRINT ";CHR$(34);PRI$(X);CHR$(34)
2035 IF PRI(X)<>0 THEN PRINT"PRINT ";CHR$(PRI(X)+64)
2040 IF GOT(X)<>0 THEN PRINT"GOTO ";GOT(X)
2050 IF LET0(X)=1 THEN PRINT "LET ";CHR$(LET1(X)+64);" = ";LET5(X)
2060 IF LET0(X)=2 THEN PRINT "LET ";CHR$(LET1(X)+64);" = ";LET3(X);" *
     ";CHR$(LET2(X)+64);" + ";LET4(X)
2070 IF LET0(X)=3 THEN PRINT "LET ";CHR$(LET1(X)+64);" = RND(";LET7(X);")"
2075 IF LET0(X)=4 THEN PRINT "LET ";CHR$(LET1(X)+64);" = SQR(";CHR$
     (LET8(X)+64);")"
2076 IF LET0(X)=5 THEN PRINT "LET ";CHR$(LET1(X)+64);" = ";CHR$(LET9(X)
     +64);" + ";CHR$(LET10(X)+64)
2077 IF LET0(X)=6 THEN PRINT "LET ";CHR$(LET1(X)+64);" = ";CHR$(LET11(X)
     +64);" ^ ";CHR$(LET12(X)+64)
2078 IF LET0(X)=7 THEN PRINT "LET ";CHR$(LET1(X)+64);" = ";CHR$(LET13(X)
     +64);" MOD ";CHR$(LET14(X)+64)
2080 IF INPU(X)<>0 THEN PRINT "INPUT ";CHR$(INPU(X)+64)
2085 IF EN(X)=1 THEN PRINT "END"
2087 IF GOS(X)=1 THEN PRINT "RETURN"
2090 IF IFTHEN1(X)<>0 THEN GOSUB 5500
2100 IF FORNEXT5(X)>0 THEN PRINT "NEXT ";CHR$(FORNEXT1(FORNEXT5(X))+64)
2110 IF FORNEXT4(X)<>0 THEN PRINT "FOR ";CHR$(FORNEXT1(X)+64);" =";
     FORNEXT2(X);" TO ";FORNEXT3(X);" STEP ";FORNEXT4(X)
2299 NEXT X
2300 GOTO 49
...
5500 REM OUTPUT OF THE IF/THEN STATEMENT
5505 IF IFTHEN5(X)=1 THEN TYPE$=" GOTO " ELSE TYPE$=" GOSUB "
```

```
5510 IF IFTHEN3(X)=1 THEN PRINT"IF ";CHR$(IFTHEN1(X)+64);"=";CHR$(IFTHEN2
     (X)+64);" THEN";TYPE$;IFTHEN4(X):RETURN
5515 IF IFTHEN3(X)=2 THEN PRINT"IF ";CHR$(IFTHEN1(X)+64);"<>";CHR$(IFTHEN2
     (X)+64);" THEN";TYPE$;IFTHEN4(X):RETURN
5520 IF IFTHEN3(X)=3 THEN PRINT"IF ";CHR$(IFTHEN1(X)+64);">";CHR$(IFTHEN2
     (X)+64);" THEN";TYPE$;IFTHEN4(X):RETURN
5525 IF IFTHEN3(X)=4 THEN PRINT"IF ";CHR$(IFTHEN1(X)+64);">=";CHR$(IFTHEN2
     (X)+64);" THEN";TYPE$;IFTHEN4(X):RETURN
5530 RETURN
```

What follows in the code listing for RUNning a program.

```
1000 REM ********RUN PROGRAM********
1001 'FIRST, CLEAR OUT ALL VARIABLE VALUES AND VARIABLE INITIALIZATIONS
1002 FOR AA=1 TO 26:VAR1(AA)=0:VAR2(AA)=0:RESTORENEXT(AA)=0:NEXT AA
1005 'THEN, SEARCH THROUGH PROGRAM FIRST TO SET UP INITIAL VALUES OF
     FOR/NEXT LOOP VARIABLES ONLY
1006 FOR SEARCH=1 TO 100
1007 IF FORNEXT1(SEARCH)<>0 THEN
     VAR1(FORNEXT1(SEARCH))=1:VAR2(FORNEXT1(SEARCH))=FORNEXT2(SEARCH)
1008 NEXT SEARCH
1009 COLOR 14:PRINT"Press <ESC> key to BREAK ";PROG$:COLOR 11
1010 L=1          'INITIAL LINE NUMBER = INDEX FOR ARRAYS
1020 IF LIN(L)=1 THEN 1030 ELSE 1100
1030 IF PRI$(L)<>"" THEN PRINT PRI$(L)
1035 IF PRI(L)<>0 THEN PRINT VAR2(PRI(L))
1040 IF GOT(L)<>0 THEN L=GOT(L):GOTO 1910          'ENCOUNTERS GOTO
     STATEMENT
1050 IF GOS(L)=1 THEN L=RETURNLINE:GOTO 1910          'ENCOUNTERS RETURN
     STATEMENT
1100 IF LET0(L)=1 THEN GOSUB 3000     'LET STATEMENT, OPTION 1
1110 IF LET0(L)=2 THEN GOSUB 3100     'LET STATEMENT, OPTION 2
1120 IF LET0(L)=3 THEN GOSUB 3200     'LET STATEMENT, OPTION 3
1125 IF LET0(L)=4 THEN GOSUB 3300     'LET STATEMENT, OPTION 4
1126 IF LET0(L)=5 THEN GOSUB 3330     'LET STATEMENT, OPTION 5
1127 IF LET0(L)=6 THEN GOSUB 3360     'LET STATEMENT, OPTION 6
1128 IF LET0(L)=7 THEN GOSUB 3382     'LET STATEMENT, OPTION 7
1130 IF INPU(L)<>0 THEN GOSUB 4000   'CAPTURE INPUT DURING RUNTIME
1140 IF EN(L)=1 THEN 49               'END PROGRAM
1150 IF IFTHEN3(L)=1 AND VAR2(IFTHEN1(L))=VAR2(IFTHEN2(L)) THEN GOSUB
     1190:GOTO 1910
1160 IF IFTHEN3(L)=2 AND VAR2(IFTHEN1(L))<>VAR2(IFTHEN2(L)) THEN GOSUB
     1190:GOTO 1910
1170 IF IFTHEN3(L)=3 AND VAR2(IFTHEN1(L))>VAR2(IFTHEN2(L)) THEN GOSUB
     1190:GOTO 1910
1180 IF IFTHEN3(L)=4 AND VAR2(IFTHEN1(L))>=VAR2(IFTHEN2(L)) THEN GOSUB
     1190:GOTO 1910
1185 GOTO 1200    'SKIPS PAST IF/THEN IF NOT FOUND, AND CONTINUES BY
     CHECKING FOR/NEXT
1190 'CHECK TO SEE IF THE IF/THEN IS A GOSUB OR NOT; SET THE APPROPRIATE
     LINE NUMBER FOR JUMP
```

```
1191 IF IFTHEN5(L)=2 THEN RETURNLINE=L+1     'IF GOSUB, THEN RETURNLINE IS
     ONE LINE PAST THE GOSUB
1192 L=IFTHEN4(L)     'INDICATES NEW LINE TO JUMP TO
1194 RETURN
1200 IF FORNEXT5(L)>0 THEN GOSUB 6000:GOTO 1910     'SUBROUTINE TRIGGERED
     WITH 'NEXT' STATEMENT
1900 L=L+1
1905 IF INKEY$=CHR$(27) THEN GOSUB 6060:GOTO 49
1910 IF L<=100 THEN GOTO 1020 ELSE GOSUB 6060:GOTO 49
...
3000 REM LET STATEMENT, OPTION 1
3010 VAR1(LET1(L))=1:VAR2(LET1(L))=LET5(L)
3020 RETURN
3100 REM LET STATEMENT, OPTION 2
3110 VAR1(LET1(L))=1:VAR2(LET1(L))=LET3(L)*VAR2(LET2(L))+LET4(L)
3120 RETURN
3200 REM LET STATEMENT, OPTION 3
3210 VAR1(LET1(L))=1:VAR2(LET1(L))=INT(1+(LET7(L)+1)*RND(1))-1
3220 RETURN
3300 REM LET STATEMENT, OPTION 4
3310 VAR1(LET1(L))=1:VAR2(LET1(L))=SQR(VAR2(LET8(L)))
3320 RETURN
3330 REM LET STATEMENT, OPTION 5
3340 VAR1(LET1(L))=1:VAR2(LET1(L))=VAR2(LET9(L))+VAR2(LET10(L))
3350 RETURN
3360 REM LET STATEMENT, OPTION 6
3370 VAR1(LET1(L))=1:VAR2(LET1(L))=VAR2(LET11(L))^VAR2(LET12(L))
3380 RETURN
3382 REM LET STATEMENT, OPTION 7
3384 VAR1(LET1(L))=1:VAR2(LET1(L))=VAR2(LET13(L)) MOD VAR2(LET14(L))
3386 RETURN
4000 REM INPUT STATEMENT
4010 INPUT I
4020 VAR1(INPU(L))=1:VAR2(INPU(L))=I
4030 RETURN
...
6000 REM RUNNING FOR/NEXT LOOP
6010 VAR2(FORNEXT1(FORNEXT5(L)))=VAR2(FORNEXT1(FORNEXT5(L)))+FORNEXT4
     (FORNEXT5(L))  'INCREMENT LOOPING VARIABLE BY STEP
6020 'Now we need to 'delete' the NEXT statement if the next value of
     looping variable equals/exceeds the final value of FOR statement:
6030 IF (VAR2(FORNEXT1(FORNEXT5(L)))+FORNEXT4(FORNEXT5(L)))>FORNEXT3(
     FORNEXT5(L)) THEN RESTORENEXT(L)=FORNEXT5(L):FORNEXT5(L)=0
6040 L=FORNEXT5(L)+1   'NEW LINE NUMBER TO JUMP TO = ONE LINE AFTER THE
     FOR LOOP
6050 RETURN
6060 REM RESTORE NEXTs WHEN PROGRAM TERMINATED
6070 FOR T=1 TO 100
6075 IF RESTORENEXT(T)<>0 THEN FORNEXT5(T)=RESTORENEXT(T)
6080 NEXT T
6090 RETURN
```

Next, we will create a sequential data file, storing all the values of each array, line by LBASIC line—even if those values happen to be equal to zero or empty strings (although any empty strings will be converted to **"0"**'s first before writing them to the data file; in addition, the values of all array elements, regardless of data type, are stored in the data file as strings). Commas neatly separate array values stored on each line.

```
7000 REM ********SAVE PROGRAM********
7010 PRINT"A program name is needed in order to SAVE it. Make sure you"
7015 PRINT"use the file extension TXT with the name: for example,
     PROGRAM.TXT"
7020 INPUT"What is the name of the program";PROG$
7025 OPEN "O",#1,PROG$
7030 FOR AA=1 TO 100
7035 PRINT #1,STR$(LIN(AA));",";
7040 PRINT #1,STR$(EN(AA));",";
7045 PRINT #1,STR$(INPU(AA));",";
7050 PRINT #1,STR$(IFTHEN1(AA));",";
7055 PRINT #1,STR$(IFTHEN2(AA));",";
7060 PRINT #1,STR$(IFTHEN3(AA));",";
7065 PRINT #1,STR$(IFTHEN4(AA));",";
7070 PRINT #1,STR$(IFTHEN5(AA));",";
7075 PRINT #1,STR$(PRI(AA));",";
7080 PRINT #1,STR$(FORNEXT1(AA));",";
7082 PRINT #1,STR$(FORNEXT2(AA));",";
7084 PRINT #1,STR$(FORNEXT3(AA));",";
7086 PRINT #1,STR$(FORNEXT4(AA));",";
7088 PRINT #1,STR$(FORNEXT5(AA));",";
7090 PRINT #1,STR$(FORNEXT6(AA));",";
7092 PRINT #1,STR$(GOS(AA));",";
7094 PRINT #1,STR$(GOT(AA));",";
7100 PRINT #1,STR$(LET0(AA));",";
7102 PRINT #1,STR$(LET1(AA));",";
7104 PRINT #1,STR$(LET2(AA));",";
7106 PRINT #1,STR$(LET3(AA));",";
7108 PRINT #1,STR$(LET4(AA));",";
7110 PRINT #1,STR$(LET5(AA));",";
7112 PRINT #1,STR$(LET6(AA));",";
7114 PRINT #1,STR$(LET7(AA));",";
7115 PRINT #1,STR$(LET8(AA));",";
7116 PRINT #1,STR$(LET9(AA));",";
7117 PRINT #1,STR$(LET10(AA));",";
7118 PRINT #1,STR$(LET11(AA));",";
7119 PRINT #1,STR$(LET12(AA));",";
7120 PRINT #1,STR$(LET13(AA));",";
7121 PRINT #1,STR$(LET14(AA));",";
7122 IF REMARK$(AA)="" THEN PRINT #1,"0";","; ELSE PRINT #1,REMARK$(AA);
     ",";
7123 IF PRI$(AA)="" THEN PRINT #1,"0" ELSE PRINT #1,PRI$(AA)
7124 NEXT AA
7125 CLOSE #1
7130 PRINT "Program saved...as a text file called ";PROG$
```

```
7140 GOTO 49
```

When the LBASIC guessing game is saved, and the resultant text file GUESS.TXT is opened and inspected in a text editor, most of the one hundred lines of characters appear as follows—since the majority of lines from **1** to **100** are unused in the LBASIC program:

```
0, 0, 0, 0, 0, 0, 0, 0, 0, 0, 0, 0, 0, 0, 0, 0, 0, 0, 0, 0, 0,
0, 0, 0, 0, 0, 0, 0, 0, 0, 0,0,0
```

But, of course, not every line is awash with only zeros. What follows is the complete source code of the guessing game and, underneath each line, the corresponding saved format from the GUESS.TXT file.

```
5 REM GUESS.TXT
1, 0, 0, 0, 0, 0, 0, 0, 0, 0, 0, 0, 0, 0, 0, 0, 0, 0, 0, 0, 0,
0, 0, 0, 0, 0, 0, 0, 0, 0, 0,GUESS.TXT,0
7 PRINT "THE GUESSING GAME"
1, 0, 0, 0, 0, 0, 0, 0, 0, 0, 0, 0, 0, 0, 0, 0, 0, 0, 0, 0, 0,
0, 0, 0, 0, 0, 0, 0, 0, 0, 0,0,THE GUESSING GAME
8 LET C = 0
1, 0, 0, 0, 0, 0, 0, 0, 0, 0, 0, 0, 0, 0, 0, 0, 0, 1, 3, 0, 0, 0,
0, 0, 0, 0, 0, 0, 0, 0, 0, 0,0,0
9 LET E = 1
1, 0, 0, 0, 0, 0, 0, 0, 0, 0, 0, 0, 0, 0, 0, 0, 0, 1, 5, 0, 0, 0,
1, 0, 0, 0, 0, 0, 0, 0, 0, 0,0,0
10 LET B = RND(100)
1, 0, 0, 0, 0, 0, 0, 0, 0, 0, 0, 0, 0, 0, 0, 0, 3, 2, 0, 0, 0,
0, 1, 100, 0, 0, 0, 0, 0, 0, 0,0,0
15 PRINT "The computer picked a random integer between 0 and 100."
1, 0, 0, 0, 0, 0, 0, 0, 0, 0, 0, 0, 0, 0, 0, 0, 0, 0, 0, 0, 0,
0, 0, 0, 0, 0, 0, 0, 0, 0, 0,0,The computer picked a number between
0 and 100
16 PRINT "What number did the computer pick?"
1, 0, 0, 0, 0, 0, 0, 0, 0, 0, 0, 0, 0, 0, 0, 0, 0, 0, 0, 0, 0,
0, 0, 0, 0, 0, 0, 0, 0, 0, 0,0,What number did the computer pick?
20 INPUT A
1, 0, 1, 0, 0, 0, 0, 0, 0, 0, 0, 0, 0, 0, 0, 0, 0, 0, 0, 0, 0,
0, 0, 0, 0, 0, 0, 0, 0, 0, 0,0,0
22 LET C = 1 * C + 1
1, 0, 0, 0, 0, 0, 0, 0, 0, 0, 0, 0, 0, 0, 0, 0, 2, 3, 3, 1, 1,
0, 0, 0, 0, 0, 0, 0, 0, 0, 0,0,0
25 IF A>B THEN GOTO 50
1, 0, 0, 1, 2, 3, 50, 1, 0, 0, 0, 0, 0, 0, 0, 0, 0, 0, 0, 0, 0, 0,
0, 0, 0, 0, 0, 0, 0, 0, 0, 0,0,0
30 IF B>A THEN GOTO 60
1, 0, 0, 2, 1, 3, 60, 1, 0, 0, 0, 0, 0, 0, 0, 0, 0, 0, 0, 0, 0, 0,
0, 0, 0, 0, 0, 0, 0, 0, 0, 0,0,0
40 IF A=B THEN GOTO 70
1, 0, 0, 1, 2, 1, 70, 1, 0, 0, 0, 0, 0, 0, 0, 0, 0, 0, 0, 0, 0, 0,
0, 0, 0, 0, 0, 0, 0, 0, 0, 0,0,0
```

```
50 PRINT "Your guess is too big. Try again!"
1, 0, 0, 0, 0, 0, 0, 0, 0, 0, 0, 0, 0, 0, 0, 0, 0, 0, 0, 0, 0, 0,
0, 0, 0, 0, 0, 0, 0, 0, 0, 0,0,Your guess is too big. Try again!
55 GOTO 16
1, 0, 0, 0, 0, 0, 0, 0, 0, 0, 0, 0, 0, 0, 0, 0, 16, 0, 0, 0, 0, 0,
0, 0, 0, 0, 0, 0, 0, 0, 0, 0,0,0
60 PRINT "Your guess is too small. Try again!"
1, 0, 0, 0, 0, 0, 0, 0, 0, 0, 0, 0, 0, 0, 0, 0, 0, 0, 0, 0, 0, 0,
0, 0, 0, 0, 0, 0, 0, 0, 0, 0,0,Your guess is too small. Try again!"
65 GOTO 16
1, 0, 0, 0, 0, 0, 0, 0, 0, 0, 0, 0, 0, 0, 0, 0, 16, 0, 0, 0, 0, 0,
0, 0, 0, 0, 0, 0, 0, 0, 0, 0,0,0
70 PRINT "You guessed correctly!"
1, 0, 0, 0, 0, 0, 0, 0, 0, 0, 0, 0, 0, 0, 0, 0, 0, 0, 0, 0, 0, 0,
0, 0, 0, 0, 0, 0, 0, 0, 0, 0,0,You guessed correctly!
75 PRINT "It took you this many tries..."
1, 0, 0, 0, 0, 0, 0, 0, 0, 0, 0, 0, 0, 0, 0, 0, 0, 0, 0, 0, 0, 0,
0, 0, 0, 0, 0, 0, 0, 0, 0, 0,0,It took you this many tries
77 PRINT C
1, 0, 0, 0, 0, 0, 0, 0, 3, 0, 0, 0, 0, 0, 0, 0, 0, 0, 0, 0, 0, 0,
0, 0, 0, 0, 0, 0, 0, 0, 0, 0,0,0
80 PRINT "Type 1 to play again or any other number to quit"
1, 0, 0, 0, 0, 0, 0, 0, 0, 0, 0, 0, 0, 0, 0, 0, 0, 0, 0, 0, 0, 0,
0, 0, 0, 0, 0, 0, 0, 0, 0, 0,0,Type 1 to play again and any other
number to quit
82 INPUT D
1, 0, 4, 0, 0, 0, 0, 0, 0, 0, 0, 0, 0, 0, 0, 0, 0, 0, 0, 0, 0, 0,
0, 0, 0, 0, 0, 0, 0, 0, 0, 0,0,0
85 IF D=E THEN GOTO 5
1, 0, 0, 5, 4, 1, 5, 1, 0, 0, 0, 0, 0, 0, 0, 0, 0, 0, 0, 0, 0, 0,
0, 0, 0, 0, 0, 0, 0, 0, 0, 0,0,0
90 PRINT "Goodbye!"
1, 0, 0, 0, 0, 0, 0, 0, 0, 0, 0, 0, 0, 0, 0, 0, 0, 0, 0, 0, 0, 0,
0, 0, 0, 0, 0, 0, 0, 0, 0, 0,0,Goodbye!
95 END
1, 1, 0, 0, 0, 0, 0, 0, 0, 0, 0, 0, 0, 0, 0, 0, 0, 0, 0, 0, 0, 0,
0, 0, 0, 0, 0, 0, 0, 0, 0, 0,0,0
```

All that remains of the **LBASIC.BAS** program listing is code for **LOAD**ing a program, which is as follows:

```
7500 REM ********LOAD PROGRAM********
7501 'Must clear out any program already stored first, which means NEWing
     the code
7502 LOD=1
7503 GOTO 6110
7504 LOD=0
7507 FILES     'Show all files in current directory
7510 INPUT"What is the name of the program to load (use the .TXT extension
     )";PROG$
7515 OPEN "I",#1,PROG$
7520 FOR AA=1 TO 100
7525 INPUT #1,LIN(AA)
```

```
7530 INPUT #1,EN(AA)
7535 INPUT #1,INPU(AA)
7540 INPUT #1,IFTHEN1(AA)
7545 INPUT #1,IFTHEN2(AA)
7550 INPUT #1,IFTHEN3(AA)
7555 INPUT #1,IFTHEN4(AA)
7560 INPUT #1,IFTHEN5(AA)
7565 INPUT #1,PRI(AA)
7570 INPUT #1,FORNEXT1(AA)
7572 INPUT #1,FORNEXT2(AA)
7574 INPUT #1,FORNEXT3(AA)
7576 INPUT #1,FORNEXT4(AA)
7578 INPUT #1,FORNEXT5(AA)
7580 INPUT #1,FORNEXT6(AA)
7582 INPUT #1,GOS(AA)
7584 INPUT #1,GOT(AA)
7590 INPUT #1,LET0(AA)
7592 INPUT #1,LET1(AA)
7594 INPUT #1,LET2(AA)
7596 INPUT #1,LET3(AA)
7598 INPUT #1,LET4(AA)
7610 INPUT #1,LET5(AA)
7612 INPUT #1,LET6(AA)
7614 INPUT #1,LET7(AA)
7616 INPUT #1,LET8(AA)
7617 INPUT #1,LET9(AA)
7618 INPUT #1,LET10(AA)
7619 INPUT #1,LET11(AA)
7620 INPUT #1,LET12(AA)
7621 INPUT #1,LET13(AA)
7622 INPUT #1,LET14(AA)
7624 INPUT #1,REMARK$(AA)
7625 IF REMARK$(AA)="0" THEN REMARK$(AA)=""
7630 INPUT #1,PRI$(AA)
7635 IF PRI$(AA)="0" THEN PRI$(AA)=""
7640 NEXT AA
7650 PRINT"Program ";PROG$;" loaded."
7655 GOTO 49
```

Thanks to the commas separating data items on each line of the text files, the **INPUT #1** statements are able to fill the arrays appropriately. The comma acts as an explicit *delimiter*—a character that separates fields in the data—which opens up avenues for further exploration. (Note that double quotation marks also serve as delimiters for string and numeric expressions in GW-BASIC; thus, any strings included in remarks and **PRINT** statements of LBASIC programs must be saved to sequential disk files without double quotes.)

As promised, we have developed a working BASIC interpreter coded using a BASIC interpreter, albeit with a host of limitations (the structure and statements) and compromises (the UI). Although it successfully runs BASIC-type code, programming in

LBASIC doesn't quite *feel* like programming in a generic form of line-numbered BASIC. Can we do anything to address these shortcomings?

While a command line interface for LBASIC, rather than a prompt-based one as detailed in the LBASIC program listing in this chapter, would be preferred—since such an interface conforms to how people have programmed in most BASIC dialects for decades, after all—two complications arise.

First, the suffocating restrictions of the LBASIC language would require programmers to be "perfect" when typing in lines, although that much is true with BASICs of old regardless. Second, we would need to program a tokenizer in GW-BASIC, which could strip away comments, whitespace, and the like of each LBASIC line of code, leaving only the tokens; then, obtain the lexical information from the tokens (e.g., classifying the tokens as keywords, operators, variables, expressions, and so forth); and finally, build a parser in order to construct an abstract syntax tree (AST) from the tokens—essentially, interpreting the tokens utilizing a grammar rule—that can then be interpreted in order to generate machine code on the fly.

Programming a tokenizer, lexer, and parser in GW-BASIC presents manifold issues, not least of which involves the speed of execution of LBASIC interpreted programs. Essentially, even if we *could* successfully code versions of all three, an LBASIC program might consequently run slower than molasses in January.

Nonetheless, let us take a moment to explore the attendant difficulties with tokenizing an input string in GW-BASIC. Suppose we wanted to build a simple calculator, one that could accept user input in the form

<operand> <operator> <operand>

where both operands are numerical constants while the arithmetic operator is +, −, *, or /, and then output the result of the calculation. Consider this sample run:

```
->56+6
62
->5-10
-5
->12.2*3
36.6
->15/2
7.5
->EXIT
Ok
```

Here is one possible approach:

```
0 REM CALC.BAS
10 LINE INPUT"->";PROMPT$
15 C$=""
20 X=1
```

```
25 IF PROMPT$="EXIT" OR PROMPT$="exit" THEN 200
30 WHILE C$<>"+" AND C$<>"-" AND C$<>"*" AND C$<>"/"
40   C$=MID$(PROMPT$,X,1)
50   X=X+1
60 WEND
70 NUMBER1=VAL(MID$(PROMPT$,1,X-2))
80 LENGTH=LEN(PROMPT$)
90 NUMBER2=VAL(MID$(PROMPT$,X,LENGTH-X+1))
100 OPERATION$=C$
110 IF OPERATION$="+" THEN RESULT=NUMBER1+NUMBER2
120 IF OPERATION$="-" THEN RESULT=NUMBER1-NUMBER2
130 IF OPERATION$="*" THEN RESULT=NUMBER1*NUMBER2
140 IF OPERATION$="/" THEN RESULT=NUMBER1/NUMBER2
150 PRINT RESULT
190 GOTO 10
```

The program informally "tokenizes" the input string by delimiting it using the arithmetic operator symbols (+, −, *, or /), searching the string one character at time with the **MID$** function. The resulting first number of the expression is stored into the variable **NUMBER1**. When a delimiter is encountered, program control is transferred out of the **WHILE** loop, at which point the operator and the second number are stored. From there, it is only a matter of performing the correct arithmetic operation and outputting the result.

But tokenizing *any* line of LBASIC in this manner, with its many permutations of possible strings, while perhaps technically possible, would be a monumentally complex undertaking rife with countless inefficiencies.

Another approach lies with using one of GW-BASIC's built-in delimiters: the comma (**,**). Consider the following program:

```
5 REM COMMA.BAS
10 PRINT"TRY A COMMA WITH YOUR INPUT--IT WILL SAY 'REDO FROM START'"
20 INPUT T$
30 PRINT"NOW, THERE'S AN INPUT WITH TWO STRING INPUTS--TRY A COMMA WITH"
40 PRINT"YOUR LINE, LIKE 'HELLO,THERE'--AND YOU'LL SEE IT SPLITS IT INTO"
50 PRINT"TWO STRINGS, MEANING THE COMMA IS THE DEFAULT DELIMITER"
60 INPUT A$,B$
70 PRINT "FIRST WORD:";A$
80 PRINT "SECOND WORD:";B$
```

When run, including a comma in string input for variable **T$** is not permitted. But inserting a single comma between two words—let's say, **HELLO,THERE**—for the **INPUT** statement on line **60** results in the user input automatically being delimited by the comma and thereby split into two tokens and stored into two different variables, **A$** and **B$**.

Certainly, it would be awkward to always have to type LBASIC lines with commas separating every token, like this:

```
10,FOR,A,=,0,TO,16,STEP,2
```

However, we can now conceive of a means to tokenize at the time of input. Consider the GW-BASIC program shown below. A sample run follows.

```
5 REM FIVEC.BAS
10 DIM I$(5)
20 PRINT "TYPE A LINE OF CODE, SEPARATING FIVE TOKENS WITH COMMAS:"
30 INPUT I$(1),I$(2),I$(3),I$(4),I$(5)
40 FOR X=1 TO 5
50 PRINT "TOKEN:";I$(X)
60 NEXT X

TYPE A LINE OF CODE, SEPARATING FIVE TOKENS WITH COMMAS:
10,LET,A,=,1
TOKEN:10
TOKEN:LET
TOKEN:A
TOKEN:=
TOKEN:1
```

From there, we could easily store the line number in LBASIC and deal with the **LET** statement via existing **LBASIC.BAS** code.

But the approach has several disadvantages. First, the user is stuck typing in five tokens—no more, no less—otherwise GW-BASIC queries for input again. Second, including commas between every token is an unnatural way to interact with an interpreter, not to mention it being very un-BASIC-like.

If commas could somehow be inserted in place of whitespace (excepting whitespace in string literals) of user-entered strings, and tokenized from there, then perhaps we've hit upon a provisional solution to our LBASIC user-interface dilemma.

First, we will insert the commas by reconstructing the user-entered string, character by character; each whitespace character will be replaced with a comma—save for whitespace in user-defined string literals. Then, the reconstructed string will be written to a text file, immediately thereafter loaded up; with the comma delimiting, a string array will capture token after token from the one-line text file, thereby successfully chopping up the original string into tokens. Here is the resulting GW-BASIC program:

```
10 REM FILETOK.BAS
14 COUNT=0        'COUNT OF THE TOKENS
15 C$=""          'USED TO CHECK A CHARACTER OF THE STRING
17 SENT$=""       'USED TO BUILD A NEW STRING, WITH THE COMMAS
18 DIM TOK$(20)   'USED TO STORE THE RESULTANT TOKENS
19 QUOTE=0        'USED TO CHECK IF A QUOTATION MARK WAS ENCOUNTERED
20 PRINT"TYPE A  'LINE' OF CODE WITH NO COMMAS"
30 INPUT PROMPT$
40 LENGTH=LEN(PROMPT$)
50 FOR X=1 TO LENGTH
60 C$=MID$(PROMPT$,X,1)
65 IF C$=CHR$(34) THEN QUOTE=1    'CHECKS FOR QUOTATION MARK
69 'ONLY INSERT A COMMA IN PLACE OF WHITESPACE IF NOT INSIDE A STRING
   LITERAL:
```

```
70 IF C$=" " AND QUOTE=0 THEN C$=",":COUNT=COUNT+1
75 SENT$=SENT$+C$     'BUILD THE NEW STRING, WITH THE COMMAS
80 NEXT X
90 PRINT SENT$
95 'SEND THE STRING TO A TEMPORARY FILE:
100 OPEN "O",#1,"TEMP.TXT"
110 PRINT #1,SENT$
120 CLOSE #1
130 'OPEN THE STRING FROM THE TEMPORARY FILE:
140 OPEN "I",#1,"TEMP.TXT"
145 FOR X=1 TO COUNT+1
150 INPUT #1,TOK$(X)
160 NEXT X
170 FOR Y=1 TO COUNT+1
180 PRINT "TOKEN:";TOK$(Y)
190 NEXT Y
```

Output from a sample run might appear as follows.

```
TYPE A 'LINE' OF CODE WITH NO COMMAS
? 10 PRINT "HELLO WORLD"
10,PRINT,"HELLO WORLD"
TOKEN:10
TOKEN:PRINT
TOKEN:HELLO WORLD
```

Consider how the program might be integrated into **LBASIC.BAS**. We could store the first token—i.e., the line number—into the **LIN** array, making sure to convert the string to numeric data: **LIN(VAL(TOK$(1)))=1**. Next, we need to decode the second element of the array, **TOK$(2)**, which stores the LBASIC statement on the line. From there, once the statement is properly decoded—a tedious but far from impossible task—the same techniques we used earlier to store the data into the associated **LBASIC.BAS** arrays can be implemented. With that completed, an LBASIC command line interface is no longer a pipe dream. Implementation details are left to the reader.

Consider other improvements that could be made on the road toward greater LBASIC robustness. For one thing, LBASIC lines that force users to employ *magic numbers*—or the hardcoding of numerical constants, rather than variables, in statements—such as

```
10 LET B = RND(100)
```

and

```
20 FOR A = 1 TO 100 STEP 1
```

underscore the fact that the LBASIC programmer is, to understate matters again, not permitted a great deal of flexibility. Offering additional options for these lines, with LBASIC at least being able to parse

```
10 LET B = RND(C)
```

and

```
20 FOR A = 1 TO X STEP 1
```

and

```
20 FOR A = Z TO X STEP Y
```

unfortunately requires keying in yet more explicit permutations in the source code: more arrays, more conditional statements, more subroutines. By keeping things "simple" initially, and sidestepping building an AST, we have ultimately made things much more complex.

Welcome to the life of a BASIC programmer.

COMMUNING WITH THE PAST

Declining the guided tour was the right decision. After spending an exhausting but intellectually invigorating day at the BASIC Museum, you can skip the gift shop because you'll be leaving with the best possible souvenir: answers to those ten pressing questions.

You now understand why BASIC was born at Dartmouth; after all, the college had the perfect combination of ingredients for the programming language stew. Carefully tracing the moments leading up to the birth of BASIC and the DTSS shed new light on Kemeny and Kurtz's design decisions. Sister Mary Kenneth Keller, though a computing pioneer in her own right, most likely had nothing to do with the creation of Dartmouth BASIC. The formal standardization of BASIC failed largely because events overtook the well-intentioned process, which was interminable. Though Microsoft landed a contract with Texas Instruments to develop a BASIC implementation for the company, the TI BASIC found on TI-99/4 and TI-99/4A microcomputers was probably an in-house effort. BASIC never quite conformed to the emerging "computer literacy" initiatives, which hastened the language's demise, especially in schools. In response to fears of being left behind, in the 1980s the British government helped put a computer with BASIC into every school. An abundance of UK home-grown micros, along with a few imports, led to the publication of a series of educational Usborne books, which taught BASIC to a generation of intrepid children. With its source code laid bare, many secrets of GW-BASIC were exposed, including its method of generating pseudorandom numbers. And yes, a BASIC interpreter like GW-BASIC could be used to program a BASIC interpreter, but the results left much to be desired.

While discovering these elusive answers, you explored how BASIC influenced a generation of videogame designers around the world; learned about the poetry and prose of BASIC; uncovered why BASIC code was transmitted over the airwaves; investigated programming languages like COMAL, FOCAL, Logo, Pascal, and Python, in addition to VPLs and microcontrollers, that tried to replace BASIC in the educational arena; examined how BASIC impacted pop culture; recounted the programming pranks that Dartmouth undergraduates played on unsuspecting time-sharing users; reviewed BASIC contests from the past and present; debated what might best earn the title of a "modern BASIC"; and much, much more.

When you arrive back at your hotel in Hanover, you finally feel at peace. You lay down on the bed, slip under the covers, and switch off the light. Drifting into that liminal state between wakefulness and sleep, however, a question bubbles up from the dark recesses of your mind—a new question about BASIC. Your eyes snap open. "I guess I don't have to get home right away," you think. "Maybe I'll stop by the museum again tomorrow."

The timelessness of BASIC, whatever dialect is preferred, will now and forever remain fixed, proverbially etched in stone, a port of safety and familiar amidst the everchanging, ever-evolving, violently-stormy computing seas. In the final analysis, that is why communing with computing's past inescapably draws us into the orbit of the Beginner's All-purpose Symbolic Instruction Code: It is something we can hang our hat on tonight, secure in the knowledge it will still be there come morning.

RESOURCES

What follows is a list of the key resources that were used for researching and writing this book. For online materials, in addition to associated websites, the authors, dates, and source publications are provided (if available).

Books

Ahl, David. (1978). *BASIC Computer Games: Microcomputer Edition.* New York: Creative Computing.

——. (1986). *BASIC Computer Adventures.* Redmond, Washington: Microsoft Press.

Albers, Donald, and Alexanderson, Gerald. (1985). *Mathematical People: Profiles and Interviews.* Cambridge, Massachusetts: Birkhäuser Boston.

Alberts, Gerard (ed.), and Oldenziel, Ruth (ed.). (2014). *Hacking Europe: From Computer Cultures to Demoscenes.* London: Springer-Verlag.

Albrecht, Bob. (1972). *My Computer Likes Me When I Speak in BASIC.* Menlo Park, California: Dymax.

——. (1975). *What to Do After You Hit Return.* Menlo Park, California: People's Computer Company.

Alcock, Donald. (1978). *Illustrating BASIC.* Cambridge, England: Cambridge University Press.

Benson, John, et al. (1995). *Algebra 2 and Trigonometry,* Evanston, Illinois: McDougal Littell/Houghton Mifflin.

Bergin, Thomas (ed.), and Gibson, Richard (ed.). (1996). *History of Programming Languages II.* Boston, Massachusetts: Addison-Wesley Professional.

Beyer, Kurt. (2009). *Grace Hopper and the Invention of the Information Age.* Cambridge, Massachusetts: MIT Press.

Biancuzzi, Federico. (2009). *Masterminds of Programming: Conversations with the Creators of Major Programming Languages.* Sebastopol, California: O'Reilly Media.

Cisek, Günter. (2021). *The Triumph of Artificial Intelligence: How Artificial Intelligence is Changing the Way We Live Together.* New York: Springer.

Cox, Donna, et al. (2018). *New Media Futures: The Rise of Women in the Digital Arts.* Urbana, Illinois: Board of Trustees of the University of Illinois.

Dicker, Terence. (1984). *Computer Programs for the Kitchen.* Blue Ridge Summit, Pennsylvania: Tab Books.

Eco, Umberto. (1989). *Foucault's Pendulum* (translated by Weaver, William). Orlando, Florida: Harcourt.

Evans, Claire. (2020). *Broad Band: The Untold Story of the Women Who Made the Internet.* New York: Penguin.

Gay, Martin. (2000). *Recent Advances and Issues in Computers.* Phoenix, Arizona: The Oryx Press.

Gold, Matthew. (2012). *Debates in the Digital Humanities.* Minneapolis, Minnesota: University of Minnesota Press.

Good, Dan. (2020). *The Microsoft Story: How the Giant Rebooted Its Culture, Upgraded Its Strategy, and Found Success in the Cloud.* New York: HarperCollins.

Greenberger, Martin (ed.). (1962). *Computers and the World of the Future.* Cambridge, Massachusetts: Massachusetts Institute of Technology.

Hague, James. (1997). *Halcyon Days: Interviews with Classic Computer and Video Game Programmers.* Self-published.

Hamming, Richard. (1997). *The Art of Doing Science and Engineering: Learning to Learn.* Australia: Taylor & Francis.

Harris, Sam. (2004). *The End of Faith: Religion, Terror, and the Future of Reason.* New York: W. W. Norton & Company.

Inman, Don, and Albrecht, Bob. (1990). *The GW-BASIC Reference.* Berkeley, California: Osborne McGraw-Hill.

Isaacson, Walter. (2011). *Steve Jobs.* New York: Simon & Schuster.

——. (2014). *The Innovators: How a Group of Hackers, Geniuses, and Geeks Created the Digital Revolution.* New York: Simon & Shuster.

Kelly-Bootle, Stan. (1995). *The Computer Contradictionary, Second Edition.* Cambridge, Massachusetts: MIT Press.

Kemeny, John. (1972). *Man and the Computer.* New York: Scribner.

Kemeny, John, and Kurtz, Tom. (1985). *Back to BASIC: The History, Corruption, and Future of the Language.* Reading, Pennsylvania: Addison-Wesley.

Kemeny, John, and Snell, J. Laurie. (1960). *Finite Markov Chains.* New York: Springer-Verlag.

Kidder, Tracy. (1981). *The Soul of a New Machine.* Boston, Massachusetts: Little, Brown and Company.

Kim, Dorothy, and Koh, Adeline. (2021). *Alternative Historiographies of the Digital Humanities.* Santa Barbara, California: Punctum Books.

Knuth, Donald. (1998). *The Art of Computer Programming (3rd ed., vol. 2).* Reading, Massachusetts: Addison-Wesley.

Levy, Steven. (2010). *Hackers: Heroes of the Computer Revolution.* Sebastopol, California: O'Reilly.

Lien, David. (1978). *The BASIC Handbook: An Encyclopedia of the BASIC Computer Language.* San Diego, California: CompuSoft.

Lohr, Steve. (2001). *Go To: The Story of the Math Majors, Bridge Players, Engineers, Chess Wizards, Maverick Scientists, and Iconoclasts—the Programmers Who Created the Software Revolution.* New York: Basic Books.

——. (2015). *Data-ism: Inside the Big Data Revolution.* London: Oneworld Publications.

Lorenzo, Mark. (2017). *Endless Loop: The History of the BASIC Programming Language (Beginner's All-purpose Symbolic Instruction Code).* Philadelphia, Pennsylvania: SE Books.

——. (2018). *Adventures of a Statistician: The Biography of John W. Tukey.* Philadelphia, Pennsylvania: SE Books.

——. (2019). *Abstracting Away the Machine: The History of the FORTRAN Programming Language (FORmula TRANslation).* Philadelphia, Pennsylvania: SE Books.

——. (2021). *Everlasting Code: The Education of Grace Hopper and the History of COBOL (COmmon Business-Oriented Language)*. Philadelphia, Pennsylvania: SE Books.

Manes, Stephen, and Andrews, Paul. (1994). *Gates: How Microsoft's Mogul Reinvented an Industry—and Made Himself the Richest Man in America*. Seattle, Washington: Cadwallader & Stern.

Metropolis, Nicholas. (1980). *A History of Computing in the Twentieth Century*. Orlando, Florida: Academic Press.

Meyers, Robert. (2001). *Encyclopedia of Physical Science and Technology (3rd ed.)*. Cambridge, Massachusetts: Academic Press.

Montfort, Nick, et al. (2012). *10 PRINT CHR$(205.5+RND(1)); : GOTO 10*. Cambridge, Massachusetts: MIT Press.

Paltrowitz, Stuart, and Paltrowitz, Donna. (1983). *The Science Fiction Computer Storybook*. New York: Tribeca Communications.

Papert, Seymour. (1980). *Mindstorms: Children, Computers, and Powerful Ideas*. New York: Basic Books.

Petzold, Charles. (2000). *Code: The Hidden Language of Computer Hardware and Software*. Redmond, Washington: Microsoft Press.

Rankin, Joy. (2018). *A People's History of Computing in the United States*. Cambridge, Massachusetts: Harvard University Press.

Rossman, Allan, et al. (2001). *Workshop Statistics: Discovery with Data and the Graphing Calculator, 2nd Edition*. Hoboken, New Jersey: Wiley.

Savetz, Kevin. (2012). *Terrible Nerd*. Portland, Oregon: Savetz Publishing.

Sayers, Jentery (ed.). (2018). *The Routledge Companion to Media Studies and Digital Humanities*. New York: Routledge.

Schuman, Michael. (2008). *Bill Gates: Computer Mogul and Philanthropist*. New York: Enslow Publishing.

Seibel, Peter (2009). *Coders at Work: Reflections on the Craft of Programming*. New York: Apress.

Shetterly, Margot. (2016). *Hidden Figures: The American Dream and the Untold Story of the Black Women Mathematicians Who Helped Win the Space Race*. New York: William Morrow.

Smith, Alexander. (2019). *They Create Worlds: The Story of the People and Companies That Shaped the Video Game Industry, Vol. I: 1971-1982*. Boca Raton, Florida: CRC Press.

Švelch, Jaroslav. (2018). *Gaming the Iron Curtain: How Teenagers and Amateurs in Communist Czechoslovakia Claimed the Medium of Computer Games*. Cambridge, Massachusetts: MIT Press.

Tezuka, Shu. (1995). *Uniform Random Numbers: Theory and Practice*. New York: Springer Science+Business Media.

Vee, Annette. (2017). *Coding Literacy: How Computer Programming is Changing Writing*. Cambridge, Massachusetts: Massachusetts Institute of Technology.

Wexelblat, Richard. (1981). *History of Programming Languages (ACM Monograph Series)*. New York: Academic Press.

The Usborne Series

Davies, Helen. (1985). *Experiments with Your Computer*. London: Usborne Publishing.

Hawthorn, Philip. (1985). *Usborne Introduction to Keyboards & Computer Music*. London: Usborne Publishing.

Howarth, Les, and Evans, Cheryl. (1984). *Write Your Own Fantasy Games for Your Microcomputer*. London: Usborne Publishing.

Isaaman, Daniel and Tyler, Jenny. (1982). *Computer Battlegames*. London: Usborne Publishing.

——. (1982). *Computer Spacegames*. London: Usborne Publishing.

Oxlade, Chris, and Tatchell, Judy. (1984). *The Mystery of Silver Mountain*. London: Usborne Publishing.

Potter, Tony. (1984). *How to Make Computer Model Controllers for C64, VIC 20, Spectrum & BBC*. London: Usborne Publishing.

——. (1984). *How to Make Computer-Controlled Robots for C64, VIC 20, Spectrum & BBC*. London: Usborne Publishing.

Smith, Brian. (1982). *Introduction to Computer Programming: BASIC for Beginners*. London: Usborne Publishing.

Smith, Brian, and Watts, Lisa. (1983). *Usborne Guide to Better BASIC: A Beginner's Guide to Writing Programs*. London: Usborne Publishing.

Tatchell, Judy, and Cutler, Nick. (1983). *Practical Things to Do with a Microcomputer*. London: Usborne Publishing.

Tyler, Jenny (ed.) (1983). *Creepy Computer Games*. London: Usborne Publishing.

Tyler, Jenny, and Howarth, Les. (1983). *Write Your Own Adventure Programs for Your Microcomputer*. London: Usborne Publishing.

——. (1984). *The Island of Secrets*. London: Usborne Publishing.

Tyler, Jenny, and Oxlade, Chris. (1984). *Computer Spy Games*. London: Usborne Publishing.

——. (1984). *Weird Computer Games*. London: Usborne Publishing.

Waters, Gaby. (1984). *First Computer Library: Computer Fun*. London: Usborne Publishing.

——. (1984). *First Computer Library: Simple BASIC*. London: Usborne Publishing.

Waters, Gaby, and Cutler, Nick. (1983). *Practise Your BASIC: Puzzles, Tests and Problems to Improve Your Skills*. London: Usborne Publishing.

Watts, Lisa, and Wharton, Mike. (1983). *Usborne Introduction to Machine Code for Beginners*. London: Usborne Publishing.

Chapter 1: When BASIC Ruled Campus

"Royal Precision LGP-30 Advertisement" for the Computer History Museum

https://www.computerhistory.org/revolution/early-computer-companies/5/116/1889?position=0

"LGP-30 – A Drum Computer of Significance" (2019) by Norbert Landsteiner for mass:werk

https://www.masswerk.at/nowgobang/2019/lgp-30

"LGP-30" (2021) by Ed Thelen

http://ed-thelen.org/comp-hist/lgp-30.html

"Royal Precision Electronic Computer LGP-30 Programming Manual" (1957) by the Royal McBee Corporation

http://ed-thelen.org/comp-hist/lgp-30-man.html

"LGP-30: Your Greatest Computer Value on the Market…" (1960) advertisement in *Datamation*, Vol. 6, No. 5

https://ia803101.us.archive.org/23/items/bitsavers_datamation_12088101/196009-10.pdf

"History of Computers – Software" (1995), a talk by Richard Hamming

https://youtu.be/2e5_Z6oZ0rM

"A BASIC History of BASIC" (2012) by John Szczepaniak for *Game Developer*

https://www.gamedeveloper.com/business/a-basic-history-of-basic-on-its-50th-birthday

"Basic History of BASIC – Dr Kurtz, David Ahl, John Lutz, Steve Wozniak [Additional Quotations and Materials]" (2012) by John Szczepaniak

http://blog.hardcoregaming101.net/2012/09/basic-history-of-basic-dr-kurtz-david.html

"Tracking Down DOPE, the First Computer Language for Normal Humans" by Sean Haas for *Vice*

https://www.vice.com/en/article/5dpq48/tracking-down-dope-the-first-computer-language-for-normal-humans

"The Two Cultures" – The Rede Lecture (1959) by C. P. Snow

http://s-f-walker.org.uk/pubsebooks/2cultures/Rede-lecture-2-cultures.pdf

"A Time Sharing Operator Program for Our Projected IBM 709" Memorandum (1959) by John McCarthy for Philip M. Morse

https://archive.computerhistory.org/resources/access/text/2016/06/102724637-05-01-acc.pdf

"Dartmouth Time-Sharing" (1968) by John Kemeny and Thomas Kurtz for *Science*

http://dtss.dartmouth.edu/sciencearticle/index.html

"Dartmouth Timeshare System: Transcripts of 1974 National Computer Conference Pioneer Day Session" (1974) for the American Federation of Information Processing Societies History of Computing Project

http://dtss.dartmouth.edu/transcript.php

"BASIC Necessities: How GE Helped Launch the Computing Language That Changed the World" (2019) by Liz Wishaw and Tomas Kellner for General Electric

https://www.ge.com/news/reports/basic-necessities-how-ge-helped-launch-the-computing-language-that-changed-the-world

"GOTO 1964" (2014) by Stefan Holtgen for *Telepolis* (original text in German; English translations used)

https://www.heise.de/tp/features/GOTO-1964-3364759.html

Birth of BASIC (2014), a documentary for Dartmouth College

https://youtu.be/WYPNjSoDrqw

"The 25th Birthday of BASIC" (1989) by Bill Gates for *Byte*

https://vintageapple.org/byte/pdf/198910_Byte_Magazine_Vol_14-10_Mac_Portable.pdf

First Dartmouth BASIC Manual (1964)

http://www.bitsavers.org/pdf/dartmouth/BASIC_Oct64.pdf

"The Kiewit Computation Center & The Dartmouth Time-Sharing System" (1966) by John Kemeny for Dartmouth College

http://dtss.dartmouth.edu/brochure/pages/page01.html

"*John Kemeny Speaking: Selected Addresses, Talks and Interviews*" (1999) edited by A. Alexander Fanelli for Dartmouth College

https://math.dartmouth.edu/news-resources/history/kemeny-history/kemeny.lectures.pdf

"NH Historical Markers Aren't Geeky Enough and We're Going to Fix that, Starting with BASIC" (2018) by David Brooks for the *Concord Monitor*

https://granitegeek.concordmonitor.com/2018/08/16/nh-historical-markers-arent-geeky-enough-and-were-going-to-fix-that-starting-with-basic/

"Who Needs a Primary When We're First in the Nation for Computer Programming History?" (2019) by David Brooks for the *Concord Monitor*

https://www.concordmonitor.com/BASIC-Dartmouth-Kemeny-time-sharing-historical-26164409

"New IEEE Plaque at Collis Center Marks the Birth of BASIC" (2021) by William Platt for the Dartmouth website

https://home.dartmouth.edu/news/2021/02/new-ieee-plaque-collis-center-marks-birth-basic

"50 Years of BASIC Computer Language" (2014) for National Public Radio (NPR)

https://www.npr.org/transcripts/309006785?storyId=309006785?storyId=309006785

"The History of Language Processor Technology in IBM" (1981) by Frances Allen for the *IBM Journal of Research and Development*

https://web.archive.org/web/20060106193227/http://www.research.ibm.com/journal/rd/255/ibmrd2505Q.pdf

"Dartmouth Professor Jon Appleton – Biography" by Jon Appleton

http://www.appletonjon.com/biography.htm

"The Commercial Launch of GE Time-sharing Services" by John R. Zinchak

https://www.ammannato.it/geis-alumni/documents/launch_1965.pdf

"Multics" on the MIT website

https://web.mit.edu/multics-history/

"Programming Systems and Languages 1965-75" (1972) by Saul Rosen for *Communications of the ACM*

https://dl.acm.org/doi/10.1145/361454.361482

"Harold W. Lawson – Award Recipient" (2021) for the Institute of Electrical and Electronics Engineers (IEEE)

https://www.computer.org/profiles/harold-lawson

"The Early Years of Academic Computing: A Memoir by William Y. Arms" (2014) for the Cornell University Library eCommons

https://ecommons.cornell.edu/handle/1813/36926

"The Many Roles of Computing on the Campus" (1969) by Thomas Kurtz for the AFIPS Spring Joint Computer Conference, held on May 14-16, 1969

https://dl.acm.org/doi/abs/10.1145/1476793.1476903

Mathematics Genealogy Project – Thomas E. Kurtz

https://www.genealogy.math.ndsu.nodak.edu/id.php?id=35248

"'Thinking, Judging, Noticing, Feeling': John W. Tukey Against the Mechanization of Inferential Knowledge" (2021) by Alexander Campolo for *KNOW: A Journal on the Formation of Knowledge*

https://www.journals.uchicago.edu/doi/pdf/10.1086/713021

"Citation Needed [Zero-Versus-One-Indexing]" (2013) by Mike Hoye for *blarg?*

http://exple.tive.org/blarg/2013/10/22/citation-needed/

"EWD 831: Why Numbering Should Start at Zero" (1982) by Edsger W. Dijkstra

https://www.cs.utexas.edu/users/EWD/transcriptions/EWD08xx/EWD831.html

"Go To Statement Considered Harmful" (1968) by Edsger W. Dijkstra for *Communications of the ACM*

http://www.u.arizona.edu/~rubinson/copyright_violations/Go_To_Considered_Harmful.html

"EWD 498: How Do We Tell Truths That Might Hurt?" (1982) by Edsger W. Dijkstra for *Selected Writings on Computing: A Personal Perspective*

https://www.cs.utexas.edu/users/EWD/ewd04xx/EWD498.PDF

"GOTO" *xkcd* comic strip by Randall Munroe

https://xkcd.com/292/

Dilbert comic strip by Scott Adams (1994)

https://dilbert.com/strip/1994-06-10

"A Linguistic Contribution of GOTO-less Programming" (1973) by R. Lawrence Clark for *Datamation*

http://neil.franklin.ch/Jokes_and_Fun/Goto-less_Programming.html

"The INTERCAL Programming Language Reference Manual" (1973) by Donald R. Woods and James M. Lyon

https://archive.org/details/intercal-ref/mode/2up

"Very Early Days of Matrix Computations" (2003) by Beresford Parlett for *SIAM News*

http://homepages.neiu.edu/~zzeng/304/Fall12/Notes/EarlyMatrixComputation.pdf

"Ode To A Computer – 'G.E. 235 We Sing Thy Praises'" (1966) for *The Dartmouth*

https://8bitworkshop.com/blog/platforms/basic/

"Computers in Higher Education: Report of the President's Science Advisory Committee" (1967)

https://books.google.com/books?id=laSImxaLAnQC

"History at the Texas A&M University, Department of Computer Science & Engineering" (2022)

https://engineering.tamu.edu/cse/about/history.html

"Programming Languages: History and Future" (1972) by Jean Sammet for *Communications of the ACM*

https://dl.acm.org/doi/10.1145/361454.361485

"An Apple on Every Desk" (1985) by Fred Pfaff for *Dartmouth Alumni Magazine*

https://archive.dartmouthalumnimagazine.com/article/1985/6/1/an-apple-on-every-desk

Chapter 2: BASIC Sainthood

BASIC Wikipedia Page, English-language Website

https://en.wikipedia.org/wiki/BASIC

BASIC Wikipedia Page, English-language Website, from June 5, 2018

https://web.archive.org/web/20180605162309/https://en.wikipedia.org/wiki/BASIC

BASIC Wikipedia Page, German-language Website

https://de.wikipedia.org/wiki/BASIC

Mary Kenneth Keller Wikipedia Page, English-language Website

https://en.wikipedia.org/wiki/Mary_Kenneth_Keller

"UW-Madison Computer Science Ph.D.s Awarded, May 1965 – August 1970" for the University of Wisconsin-Madison website

https://research.cs.wisc.edu/includes/textfiles/phds.65-70.txt

"Sister Mary Kenneth Keller" (2018) by Amy Ballor for the Acton Institute

https://acton.org/religion-liberty/volume-28-number-3/sister-mary-kenneth-keller

"Sister Mary Kenneth Keller, BVM: A Pioneer in Computer Science" (2018) by Jennifer Head for the Catholic Archives

https://catholicarchives.bc.edu/2018/05/sister-mary-kenneth-keller-bvm-a-pioneer-in-computer-science/

"The First Woman to Earn a Doctorate in Computer Science was a Nun" (2017) by Angelo Stagnaro for *The National Catholic Register*

http://www.ncregister.com/blog/astagnaro/the-first-woman-to-earn-a-doctorate-in-computer-science-was-a-nun

"Pioneering Women in Computer Science" (1995) by Denise Gürer for *Communications of the ACM*

https://doi.org/10.1145/204865.204875

"Pioneering Women in Computer Science" (2002) by Denise Gürer for *ACM SIGCSE Bulletin*

https://doi.org/10.1145/543812.543853

"Pioneering Women in Computer Science" (1995) count of citations in Google Scholar

https://scholar.google.com/scholar?cluster=16114418131603415042&hl=en&as_sdt=5,39&sciodt=0,39

"Who Earned First Computer Science Ph.D.?" by Ralph L. London for *Communications of the ACM*

https://cacm.acm.org/blogs/blog-cacm/159591-who-earned-first-computer-science-ph-d/fulltext

"Sister Mary Kenneth Keller (PhD, 1965): The First PhD in Computer Science in the US" (2019) by Maeve Ryan for the University of Madison-Wisconsin website

https://www.cs.wisc.edu/2019/03/18/2759/

"Inductive Inference on Computer Generated Patterns" (1965), a doctoral dissertation by Mary Kenneth Keller

https://www.proquest.com/openview/38f138c544c0e79cc42d6502abd71467/1?pq-origsite=gscholar&cbl=18750&diss=y

https://books.google.com/books?id=1gedAAAAMAAJ&q=Inductive+Inference+on+Computer+Generated+Patterns&dq=Inductive+Inference+on+Computer+Generated+Patterns&hl=en&sa=X&ved=2ahUKEwiCiraMvo_kAhUHrlkKHbgKB48Q6AEwAHoECAAQAg

"Andrei Petrovich Ershov" (1995) by J.A.N. Lee for the IEEE Computer Society

https://history.computer.org/pioneers/perlis.html

"Veiled Figures: Pioneering Women Religious in the Sciences" (2018) by Jennifer Head for *Studies: An Irish Quarterly Review*

https://www.jstor.org/stable/10.2307/90024682

Tweets about Keller by software developer Brenda Romero

https://twitter.com/br/status/1102211551111598080

Tweet about Keller by MIT professor Nick Montfort

https://twitter.com/nickmofo/status/1208059144911163392

"Religious Scientists: Sr. Mary Kenneth Keller B.V.M. (1913-1985) – Computer Science" (2019) by Robert Macke for the "Religious Scientists of the Catholic Church" series of the Vatican Observatory website

https://www.vaticanobservatory.org/sacred-space-astronomy/religious-scientists-sr-mary-kenneth-keller-b-v-m-1913-1985-computer-science/

"Half a Century of Computer Science" (2015) from *Clarke: The Magazine of Clarke University*

https://issuu.com/clarkeuniversity/docs/magazine_spring2015_forweb

"List of Members in the Iowa Section of the MAA [Mathematical Association of America] as of March 2, 1964"

http://sections.maa.org/iowa/history/scannedDocs/OldFilesToJune1967/OldFilesMembersIowaSection1964.pdf

"MAA Members in the Iowa Section as of March 4, 1966"

http://sections.maa.org/iowa/history/scannedDocs/1967/1967MembersMarch1966.pdf

"Oral History Interview: Seymour Parter" (2004) conducted by Joyce Coleman for the University of Wisconsin-Madison

https://minds.wisconsin.edu/handle/1793/72132

"Women at Dartmouth: A History Filled with Controversy" (1995) by Siobhan Gorman for *The Dartmouth*

http://www.thedartmouth.com/article/1995/02/women-at-dartmouth-a-history-filled-with-controversy

"ITS Tools" Timeline (2018) for the Dartmouth Website

https://www.dartmouth.edu/its-tools/archive/history/timeline/1960s.html

"Dartmouth Computing Pioneers Reunite" (2007) by Rebecca Bailey for *VOX of Dartmouth*

http://www.dartmouth.edu/~vox/0708/0625/sysprogs.html

"Sharing the Computer: How the Dartmouth Time-Sharing System Made Computing (More) Accessible" (2022) for the Dartmouth website

https://www.dartmouth.edu/library/rauner/exhibits/sharing-the-computer.html

"Dartmouth Timeshare System: Transcripts of 1974 National Computer Conference Pioneer Day Session" (1974) for the American Federation of Information Processing Societies History of Computing Project

http://dtss.dartmouth.edu/transcript.php

"The Computer and the Campus: An Interview with John Kemeny" (1991)

https://www.youtube.com/watch?v=HHi3VFOL-AI

Mary Kenneth Keller Obituary in the *Annals of the History of Computing* (Volume 8, Number 2, April 1986)

https://ieeexplore.ieee.org/stamp/stamp.jsp?arnumber=4640410

Tweets about Keller by Ana Campón

https://twitter.com/AnaCamponA/status/1359783162428207105

"Kathleen Booth" for the Centre for Computing History

http://www.computinghistory.org.uk/det/32489/Kathleen-Booth/

"If Discrimination, Then Branch: Ann Hardy's Contributions to Computing" (2018) by David C. Brock for the Computer History Museum

https://computerhistory.org/blog/if-discrimination-then-branch-ann-hardy-s-contributions-to-computing/

"Dr. Joy Lisi Rankin – About"

http://joyrankin.com/about

"Tech-Bro Culture Was Written in the Code" (2018) by Joy L. Rankin for *Slate*

https://slate.com/technology/2018/11/dartmouth-basic-computer-programmers-tech-bros.html

"Kiewit Comments" for the Dartmouth Library (Archives & Manuscripts)

https://archives-manuscripts.dartmouth.edu/repositories/2/archival_objects/185891

"Multiple Terminals Under User Program Control in a Time-Sharing Environment" (1973) by John S. McGeachie for *Communications of the ACM*

https://dl.acm.org/doi/10.1145/362375.362376

"Tabular Form in Decision Logic" (1961) by Burton Grad for *Datamation*

http://www.bitsavers.org/magazines/Datamation/196107.pdf

"Just like 'Planning a Dinner'? The Feminization of Computer Programming" (2021) by Alana Staiti for the National Museum of American History

https://americanhistory.si.edu/blog/feminization-computer-programming

"Built to Last" (2020) by Mar Hicks for *Logic*

https://logicmag.io/care/built-to-last/

"Computer Hookup to Home Foreseen" (1966) by Stuart H. Loory for the *New York Times*

https://www.nytimes.com/1966/12/05/archives/computer-hookup-to-home-foreseen-dartmouth-professor-holds-that-by.html

"Joy Lisi Rankin: 'A People's History of Computing in the United States' | Talks at Google" (2018)

https://www.youtube.com/watch?v=zXhT7Xc_-xk&t=950s

"When Women Stopped Coding" (2014) by Steve Henn for National Public Radio (NPR)

https://www.npr.org/sections/money/2014/10/21/357629765/when-women-stopped-coding

"Basic to BASIC: Dartmouth Celebrates 50th Anniversary of a Groundbreaking Computer Language" by Tom Blinkhorn for the *Valley News*

https://www.vnews.com/Archives/2014/05/basic-vn-050314

"John Kemeny and Tecmo's BASIC FTBALL Granddaddy" (2017) by Keith Good

https://tecmobowlers.com/2017/10/17/kemenys-basic-ftball-tecmos-granddaddy/

The BASIC program listing of *Dartmouth Championship Football* (1965)

http://www.vintage-basic.net/bcg/ftball.bas

"Final Report: Time-Sharing Computer Applications in Undergraduate Anthropology at Dartmouth College" (1968) for the Dartmouth Department of Anthropology

https://files.eric.ed.gov/fulltext/ED078767.pdf

Mary Kenneth Keller Wikipedia Page, French-language Website

https://fr.wikipedia.org/wiki/Mary_Kenneth_Keller

"Shelby Steele and America's 'Poetic Truth'" (2020) by Mark Judge for *Law & Liberty*

https://lawliberty.org/shelby-steele-and-americas-poetic-truths/

"Where Citations Come From" *xkcd* comic strip by Randall Munroe

https://m.xkcd.com/978/

"Programming in America in the 1950s – Some Personal Impressions" (2022), a talk delivered by John Backus in 1976 at the International Research Conference on the History of Computing in Los Alamos, New Mexico

https://youtu.be/EylBknGtkqA

Chapter 3: Fiddling While BASIC Burned

"Prolog Dialects: A *Deja Vu* of BASICs" (1987) by Raymond Sosnowski for *ACM SIGPLAN Notices*

https://dl.acm.org/doi/10.1145/24900.24903

"On the Way to Standard BASIC" (1982) by Thomas Kurtz for *Byte*

https://www.tech-insider.org/personal-computers/research/acrobat/8206.pdf

"The Case Against...BASIC" (1971) by Jerry Ogdin for *Datamation*

http://www.bitsavers.org/magazines/Datamation/19710901.pdf

"When Children Learn Programming: Antecedents, Concepts and Outcomes" (1985) by Ben Shneiderman for *Computing Teacher*

https://eric.ed.gov/?id=EJ314171

"The Educational Programming Language Elan"

http://www.cs.ru.nl/elan/about.html

"COMAL's Challenge to BASIC" (1981) for *Your Computer*

https://archive.org/details/your-computer-magazine-1981-11/page/n39/mode/2up

"Toward Standardization of BASIC" (1971) by Thomas Kurtz and Stephen Garland for *ACM SIGCUE Outlook*

https://dl.acm.org/doi/abs/10.1145/965880.965883

"Interdialect Translatability of the Basic Programming Language" (1972) by Gerald Isaacs for the American College Testing Program

https://eric.ed.gov/?id=ED083819

"Minicomputers" for the Computer History Museum

https://www.computerhistory.org/revolution/minicomputers/11
https://www.computerhistory.org/brochures/minicomputers/

"The Minicomputers of the 70s" (2001) by Georg Wittenburg as part of the lecture "History of Computing" by Raoul Rojas at The Institute of Computer Sciences – Freie Universität Berlin

http://www.inf.fu-berlin.de/lehre/SS01/hc/minicomp/

"PDP-11: Variations on a Theme" (1977), a Digital Equipment Corporation Brochure

http://s3data.computerhistory.org/brochures/dec.pdp-11.1977.102646131.pdf

"From 1977: Trying to Pythonize BASIC" (2019) for the Adafruit blog

https://blog.adafruit.com/2019/04/24/from-1977-trying-to-pythonize-basic-programming-languages-basic-python/

"Let's Improve BASIC" (1977) by Russ Walter for *Personal Computing*

https://archive.org/details/PersonalComputing19770102/page/n63/mode/2up

"The Formal Definition of the BASIC Language" (1972) by J.A.N. Lee for *The Computer Journal*

https://www.researchgate.net/publication/220458301_The_formal_definition_of_the_BASIC_language

"The Impact of Computing on the Teaching of Mathematics" (1972) by Walter Koetke for the Proceedings of the Spring Joint Computer Conference of the American Federation of Information Processing Societies (AFIPS)

https://dl.acm.org/doi/abs/10.1145/1478873.1479011

"A Comparative Evaluation of Versions of BASIC" (1976) by Bennet P. Lientz for *Communications of the ACM*

https://dl.acm.org/doi/abs/10.1145/360032.360038

"The Proposed Standard for BASIC" (1983) by James Harle for *ACM SIGPLAN Notices*

https://dl.acm.org/doi/10.1145/948249.948252

"ANSI BASIC – The Proposed Standard" (1982), a Panel Session held at ACM '82: Proceedings of the ACM '82 Conference

https://dl.acm.org/doi/abs/10.1145/800174.809806

"Standard ECMA-55: Minimal BASIC" (1978) by the European Computer Manufacturers Association

https://www.ecma-international.org/wp-content/uploads/ECMA-55_1st_edition_january_1978.pdf

"Why 0.1 Does Not Exist in Floating-Point" (2012) by Rick Regan for ExploringBinary.com

https://www.exploringbinary.com/why-0-point-1-does-not-exist-in-floating-point/

"Algorithm 605: PBASIC: A Verifier Program for American National Standard Minimal BASIC" (1983) by T. R. Hopkins for *ACM Transactions on Mathematical Software*

https://dl.acm.org/doi/10.1145/356056.356057

"The New ANSI BASIC Standard" (1983) by Kurt Guntheroth for *ACM SIGPLAN Notices*

https://dl.acm.org/doi/10.1145/988216.988221

"*BASIC Programming*: Atari Game Program Instructions" (1979)

https://ia601903.us.archive.org/17/items/Basic_Programming_1979_Atari_US_a/Basic_Programming_1979_Atari_US_a.pdf

"*BASIC Programming*" for *Atari Mania*

http://www.atarimania.com/game-atari-2600-vcs-basic-programming_18124.html

"*Astro BASIC*" (2020) by J. Alan Henning for *Troy Press*

https://troypress.com/astro-basic/

"*Bally BASIC/Astro BASIC* Manual" (1981)

https://ballyalley.com/basic/Astro_BASIC_Manual_(instructions)(astrocade)(a1)(color)(300%20dpi).pdf

"SC-3000" for *Sega Retro*

https://segaretro.org/SC-3000

"SC-3000 *BASIC Level II* Manual" (1983)

https://segaretro.org/images/a/ae/Basic_Level_II_SC3000_JP_Manual.pdf

"The BASIC Programming Language and How It Ended Up on the Sega Saturn" (2020) by Modern Vintage Gamer

https://youtu.be/O_QU8eaMymo

"Nintendo Famicom *Family Basic*" (2021) by Usagi Electric

https://youtu.be/3K_1GRTab4U

"Nintendo *Family BASIC* Manual" (1984)

https://famicomworld.com/Personal/uglyjoe/FamilyBasicManual.pdf

"*Kagirinaki Tatakai*" (2012) by John Sczepaniak for Hardcore Gaming 101

http://www.hardcoregaming101.net/kagirinaki-tatakai/

"*Catrap*" (2012) by John Sczepaniak for Hardcore Gaming 101

http://www.hardcoregaming101.net/catrap/catrap.htm

"The History of BASICODE" for Stichting Hobbyfonds Scoop

https://hobbyscoop.nl/the-history-of-basicode/

"The *Hobbyscoop* Newspaper" for Stichting Hobbyfonds Scoop

http://hobbyscoop.nl/de-hobbyscoop-krant/

"Programme Index – The Chip Shop" for the BBC

https://genome.ch.bbc.co.uk/58aae80bd5844a729097ca16998c6c02

"BASICODE: the 8-bit Programming API that Crossed the Berlin Wall" (2020), presented by Rob Hagemans for FOSDEM 2020

https://youtu.be/U1vCpm1-9Yc

"Retro: Computer Broadcasts in the 1980s" (2021) for 8Bit-Museum.de

https://8bit-museum.de/retro-computersendungen-in-den-1980er/

"Hard-Bit-Rock at Computer Club: That is a *True* Classic!" by Andre Jay Meissner

http://klick-ass.com/awesomeness/computer-club-2-an-epic-blast-from-the-past/

"BASICODE Repository" by Rob Hagemans

https://github.com/robhagemans/basicode

True BASIC – About

https://www.truebasic.com/about

"Stephen J. Garland – Biography" by Stephen Garland

https://people.csail.mit.edu/garland/Biography.html

"MITS Altair BASIC Reference Manual" (1975)

https://archive.org/details/h42_MITS_ALTAIR_BASIC_REFERENCE_MANUAL/page/n1/mode/2up

"What is the Oldest Reference to PEEK, POKE, and USR?" (2020) featuring research by Jeffrey Henning on Stack Exchange

https://retrocomputing.stackexchange.com/questions/15872/what-is-the-oldest-reference-to-peek-poke-and-usr

"Digital Equipment Corporation DECsystem-10 Monitor Calls" (1971 – First Printing)

http://bitsavers.informatik.uni-stuttgart.de/www.computer.museum.uq.edu.au/pdf/DEC-10-OMCMA-B-DN1%20DECsystem10%20Monitor%20Calls.pdf

"RSTS/E System Manager's Guide" (1974 – First Printing)

http://www.bitsavers.org/pdf/dec/pdp11/rsts/V05/DEC-11-ORSMC-A-D_sMgr_Mar75.pdf

Chapter 4: Lone Star Mystery

"The Coming Crisis in Home Computers" (1983) by Andrew Pollack for the *New York Times*

https://www.nytimes.com/1983/06/19/business/the-coming-crisis-in-home-computers.html?pagewanted=all

"The Texas Instruments 99/4: The World's First 16-Bit Home Computer" (2017) by Walden Rhines for *IEEE Spectrum*

https://spectrum.ieee.org/the-texas-instruments-994-worlds-first-16bit-computer

"A Successful Failure: The TI-99/4A Turns 40" (2021) by Ben Edwards for How-To Geek

https://www.howtogeek.com/731558/a-successful-failure-the-ti-994a-turns-40/

"Texas Instruments 99/4 Home Computer" (1980) by Steve North for *Creative Computing*

https://archive.org/details/creativecomputing-1980-03/page/n21/mode/2up

"Texas Instruments" (1984) by David Ahl for *Creative Computing*

https://www.atarimagazines.com/creative/v10n3/30_Texas_Instruments.php

"990 Computer Family Systems Handbook" (1975) by Texas Instruments

http://www.bitsavers.org/pdf/ti/990/945250-9701_990_Computer_Family_Systems_Handbook_3ed_May76.pdf

"TI-99/4A BASIC Reference Manual" (1984) by Carol Casciato and Donald Horsfall

https://archive.org/details/tibook_ti994a-basic-reference-manual/page/n9/mode/2up

"Let's Talk About TI BASIC on the TI-99/4A" (2021) by PixelPedant

https://youtu.be/ls-PxqRQ35Q

"TI-99/4A BASIC Performance, Games and Comparison to Other 8 Bit Systems" (2020) by Noel's Retro Lab

https://youtu.be/H05hM_Guoqk

"TI 99/4 Personal Computer System Software Design Specification" (1980) by the Texas Instruments Personal Computer Division

http://www.99er.net/files/docs/TI99_Software_Design_Spec.pdf

"GPL: Graphic Programming Language" (1999) by Thierry Nouspikel

http://www.unige.ch/medecine/nouspikel/ti99/gpl.htm

"TI-99 Infospot"

http://www.ti99.eu/?page_id=2&lang=en

"Specification of a TI Standard for the BASIC Language" (1978) by Texas Instruments

https://atariage.com/forums/applications/core/interface/file/attachment.php?id=701320
https://atariage.com/forums/topic/301568-ti-basic-interpreter-documentation/

"TI BASIC Interpreter System Documentation" (1978) by Robert Greenberg

https://atariage.com/forums/applications/core/interface/file/attachment.php?id=703684
https://atariage.com/forums/topic/301568-ti-basic-interpreter-documentation/

"Microsoft's Odd Couple" (2011) by Paul Allen for *Vanity Fair*

http://www.vanityfair.com/news/2011/05/paul-allen-201105

"Bill Gates & Paul Allen Talk" (1995), an interview conducted by *Fortune*

https://archive.fortune.com/magazines/fortune/fortune_archive/1995/10/02/206528/index.htm

"Historical Interviews with TI employees" (2019) on AtariAge.com

https://atariage.com/forums/topic/295223-historical-interviews-with-ti-employees/

"Floppy Days Episode 113 – Monte Davidoff, Developer of Altair BASIC Floating Point" (2022), an interview conducted by Randy Kindig

https://floppydays.libsyn.com/floppy-days-113-monte-davidoff-developer-of-altair-basic-floating-point

"Mini Memory Solid State Software Command Module Manual" (1982) by Texas Instruments

https://www.digitpress.com/library/manuals/ti994a/mini%20memory.pdf

"Who created TI-99 BASIC, TI or MS?" (2019) on AtariAge.com

https://atariage.com/forums/topic/295214-who-created-ti-99-basic-ti-or-ms/

"The Personal Computer Division White Papers" (2020) on AtariAge.com

https://atariage.com/forums/topic/301039-the-personal-computer-division-white-papers/

"TI Basic Interpreter Documentation" (2020) on AtariAge.com

https://atariage.com/forums/topic/301568-ti-basic-interpreter-documentation/

"Product 359 documents (Extended Basic)" (2021) on AtariAge.com

https://atariage.com/forums/topic/322715-product-359-documents-extended-basic/

Chapter 5: Computer Literacy and Its Discontents

"Literate Programming" (1984) by Donald E. Knuth for *The Computer Journal*, **Vol. 27, Issue 2**

http://www.literateprogramming.com/knuthweb.pdf

"Coding Values" by Annette Vee for *enculturation*

http://enculturation.net/node/5268

"Alan J. Perlis" (2019) by David Nofre for the ACM A.M. Turning Award

https://amturing.acm.org/award_winners/perlis_0132439.cfm

"Alan J. Perlis" (1995) by J.A.N. Lee for the IEEE Computer Society

https://history.computer.org/pioneers/perlis.html

"GAT" for the Online Historical Encyclopaedia of Programming Languages

https://hopl.info/showlanguage.prx?exp=409

"Epigrams on Programming" (1982) by Alan Perlis

https://dl.acm.org/doi/10.1145/947955.1083808

"Selected Papers on Computer Languages" by Donald Knuth

https://www-cs-faculty.stanford.edu/~knuth/cl.html

"The Early Development of Programming Languages" (1976) by Donald Knuth and Luis Trabb Pardo for the Stanford University Computer Science Department

https://ia801301.us.archive.org/14/items/DTIC_ADA032123/DTIC_ADA032123.pdf

"The Case for Computer Literacy" (1983) by John Kemeny for *Daedalus*, **Vol. 112, No. 2**

https://www.jstor.org/stable/20024860

"As We May Think" (1945) by Vannevar Bush for *The Atlantic*

https://www.theatlantic.com/magazine/archive/1945/07/as-we-may-think/303881/

"EWD 858: Trip report E. W. Dijkstra, USA, 10 June – 3 July 1983" (1973) by Edsger W. Dijkstra

https://www.cs.utexas.edu/users/EWD/transcriptions/EWD08xx/EWD858.html

"How You Wound Up Playing *The Oregon Trail* in Computer Class" (2016) by Matt Jancer for *Smithsonian Magazine*

https://www.smithsonianmag.com/innovation/how-you-wound-playing-em-oregon-trailem-computer-class-180959851/

"He Created *The Oregon Trail*" (2021) by Robert Whitaker for *Slate*

https://slate.com/news-and-politics/2021/11/oregon-trail-game-history-inventor-don-rawitsch.html

"The Book That Incited a Worldwide Fear of Overpopulation" (2018) by Charles C. Mann for *Smithsonian Magazine*

https://www.smithsonianmag.com/innovation/book-incited-worldwide-fear-overpopulation-180967499/

The Jargon File – The Jargon Lexicon (version 4.4.7)

http://catb.org/jargon/html/index.html

"Robert Uiterwyk's BASIC" (2015) by Michael Holley, based on an interview with Uiterwyk conducted by the author in 2005

https://deramp.com/swtpc/BASIC_2/Uiterwyk.htm

Southwest Technical Products Corporation Advertisement in the December 1976 issue of *Byte*

https://deramp.com/swtpc/BYTE/Dec1976/Byte_Dec_1976cov2.jpg

"Dave Tells Ahl – The History of *Creative Computing*" (1984) by John J. Anderson for *Creative Computing*

https://www.atarimagazines.com/creative/v10n11/66_Dave_tells_Ahl__the_hist.php

"FOCAL Programming Manual" (1968) for the Digital Equipment Corporation

http://www.bitsavers.org/www.computer.museum.uq.edu.au/pdf/DEC-08-AJAB-D%20PDP-8-I%20FOCAL%20Programming%20Manual.pdf

"ANTIC Interview 280 – David and Betsy Ahl, *Creative Computing* Magazine" (2017) conducted by Kevin "Kay" Savetz

https://ataripodcast.libsyn.com/antic-interview-280-david-and-betsy-ahl-creative-computing-magazine

"*Star Trek*: The Original Computer Game" (2013) by Tony Smith for *The Register*

https://www.theregister.com/2013/05/03/antique_code_show_star_trek/

The BASIC program listing of *STTR1: Star Trek* (1972) by Mike Mayfield

https://github.com/darkoverlordofdata/retro-trek/blob/master/app/bas/hp2k/STTR1.bas

"A Personal Computer for Children of All Ages" (1972) by Alan C. Kay for the Xerox Palo Alto Research Center

https://www.mprove.de/visionreality/media/Kay72a.pdf

"Seymour Papert: Father of Educational Computing" (2016) by Gary S. Stager for *Nature*

https://www.nature.com/articles/537308a

"Logo History" (2015) for the Logo Foundation

https://el.media.mit.edu/logo-foundation/what_is_logo/history.html

"Professor Emeritus Seymour Papert, Pioneer of Constructionist Learning, Dies at 88" (2016) by the MIT Media Lab for MIT News

https://news.mit.edu/2016/seymour-papert-pioneer-of-constructionist-learning-dies-0801

"Computer Geometry – Mr. Wizard's New Frontiers"

https://youtu.be/4EkTwzMjcfk

"Turn Your Computer Into A Stopwatch (Mr. Wizard)"

https://www.youtube.com/watch?v=xRnznr2kioo

"A History of Visual Programming: From Basic to Bubble" (2020) by Vivienne Chen for bubble.io

https://bubble.io/blog/visual-programming/

"Visual History of Visual Programming Languages" (2018) presentation by Emily Nakashima for Coding Tech

https://youtu.be/mdYfFDJCDHc

"The RAND Tablet: iPad Predecessor" (2018) for the *RAND Review*

https://www.rand.org/blog/rand-review/2018/09/the-rand-tablet-ipad-predecessor.html

"Chapter 1: Pygmalion: An Executable Electronic Blackboard" (1993) by David Canfield Smith from the book *Watch What I Do: Programming by Demonstration* edited by Allen Cypher

http://acypher.com/wwid/Chapters/01Pygmalion.html

"Chapter 2: Pygmalion: An Executable Electronic Blackboard" (1993) by David Canfield Smith from the book *Watch What I Do: Programming by Demonstration* edited by Allen Cypher

http://acypher.com/wwid/Chapters/02Tinker.html

"Logo, Papert and Constructionist Learning" by Cynthia Solomon

https://web.archive.org/web/20111207111525/http://logothings.wikispaces.com/

"Logo Memo 1: A Computer Laboratory for Elementary Schools" (1971) by Seymour Papert

http://web.sonoma.edu/users/l/luvisi/logo/logo.memos.html

"LOGO Manual" (1974) by Hal Abelson, Nat Goodman, and Lee Rudolph for the MIT Artificial Intelligence Laboratory

https://dspace.mit.edu/handle/1721.1/6226

"FLEX – A Flexible Extendable Language" (1968) by Alan Kay for the University of Utah

https://www.semanticscholar.org/paper/FLEX-A-Flexible-Extendable-Language-Kay/cafc3af149b80430d98b5467ca579ec3fdcd324d

"The Early History of Smalltalk" (1993) by Alan Kay for *ACM SIGPLAN Notices*

https://dl.acm.org/doi/10.1145/155360.155364

"ACM A.M. Turing Award: Edsger Wybe Dijkstra" (2019)

https://amturing.acm.org/award_winners/dijkstra_1053701.cfm

"Oral History of Captain Grace Hopper" (1980) conducted by Angeline Pantages for the Computer History Museum

https://archive.computerhistory.org/resources/access/text/2015/06/102702026-05-01-acc.pdf

"Extended BASIC User's Manual" (1978) for the Data General Nova

https://archive.org/details/bitsavers_dgsoftwarendedBASICJan78_8088942/mode/2up

"Taking a Second Look at the Learn-to-Code Craze" (2017) by Kate M. Miltner for *The Conversation*

https://theconversation.com/taking-a-second-look-at-the-learn-to-code-craze-86597

A Nation at Risk: The Imperative for Educational Reform (1983) by the U.S. Department of Education

https://www2.ed.gov/pubs/NatAtRisk/index.html

"How Steve Jobs Brought the Apple II to the Classroom" (2015) by Audrey Watters for *Hack Education*

http://hackeducation.com/2015/02/25/kids-cant-wait-apple

"Why Johnny Can't Code" (2006) by David Brin for *Salon*

https://www.salon.com/2006/09/14/basic_2/

"Johnny…Janie and Jamal Still Can't Code…Though Ivan Can" (2019) by David Brin for the Contrary Brin blog

http://davidbrin.blogspot.com/2019/05/johnny-janie-and-jamal-still-cant-code.html

"TRS-80 – Books" (2022) by Ira Goldklang for the TRS-80 Revived Site

https://www.trs-80.com/wordpress/books/#pocketcomputer

"TI BASIC One-Liners" (1983) by Michael A. Covington for *Compute!*

https://www.atarimagazines.com/compute/issue36/108_TI_BASIC_One-Liners.php

"The Automatic Proofreader: For VIC 64, And Atari" (1984) by Charles Brannon for *Compute!*

https://www.atarimagazines.com/compute/issue47/135_1_The_Automatic_Proofreader.php

"First encounter: *COMPUTE!* Magazine and Its Glorious, Tedious Type-in Code" (2018) by Nate Anderson for *Ars Technica*

https://arstechnica.com/staff/2018/11/first-encounter-compute-magazine-and-its-glorious-tedious-type-in-code/

"BASIC 10 Liner Contest Rules"

https://gkanold.wixsite.com/homeputerium

"BASIC 10 Liner Contest History"

https://gkanold.wixsite.com/homeputerium/kopie-von-2020

"Show 007 – Contests" (2022) for the Next Without For podcast hosted by Earl Evans and Randy Kindig

http://www.nextwithoutfor.org/2022/03/show-007-contests.html

"Show 008 – 64 Bites" (2022) for the Next Without For podcast hosted by Earl Evans and Randy Kindig

http://www.nextwithoutfor.org/2022/06/show-008-64-bites.html

"A Different BASIC Contest for the ZX Spectrum Can Land You a ZX-Uno!" (2022) by Paulo Garcia for Vintage is the New Old

https://www.vintageisthenewold.com/a-different-basic-contest-for-the-zx-spectrum-can-land-you-a-zx-uno

"*First Screening: Computer Poems* by bpNichol" by Jim Andrews et al.

https://vispo.com/bp/

"*Endemic Battle Collage* & Other 1987 Apple Basic Poems by Geof Huth" by Jim Andrews et al.

https://vispo.com/huth/

"Speaking in Code" (2015) for the Rhizome Blog

https://rhizome55.rssing.com/chan-5190884/all_p34.html

"The First Digital Poetry" (2019) by Jeremy Norman for HistoryOfInformation.com

https://historyofinformation.com/detail.php?entryid=3805

"A Platform Poetics: Computational Art, Material and Formal Specificities, and 101 BASIC Poems (2013–)" (2021) by Nick Montfort for *The Digital Review*

https://thedigitalreview.com/issue01/montfort-a-platform-practice/index.html

"*Using Electricity* Series" (2022) for Counterpath Press

http://counterpathpress.org/using-electricity

All issues of *Taper* magazine, published by Bad Quarto

https://taper.badquar.to/

Bad Quarto website

https://badquar.to/

"Python is the new BASIC" (2015), a discussion board on Hacker News

https://news.ycombinator.com/item?id=9981440

"The 'Wildcat' Episode, or, Did Broadway Love Lucy?" (2020) by Darin Strauss for the *New York Times*

https://www.nytimes.com/2020/07/31/theater/lucille-ball-wildcat.html

"Learning the BASICs," a Command Line Heroes podcast (season 3, episode 2)

https://www.redhat.com/en/command-line-heroes/season-3/learning-the-basics

"Post: Endless Loop – The History of the BASIC Programming Language" (2021) by Ilya Tulvio

https://tulv.io/stories/endless-loop/

"End User Programming – Real Computer Literacy" (2021) by Carl Gundel for the BASIC Programming blog

https://basicprogramming.blogspot.com/

"What's a Microcontroller? Student Guide for Experiments #1 through #6" (version 1.9 for the BASIC Stamp) (1999)

https://legacy.arts.ufl.edu/composition/downloads/MicroV1_9.pdf

"Colour Maximite 2" for Geoff's Projects by Geoff Graham

https://geoffg.net/maximite.html

"MMBasic Homepage" for mmbasic.com

https://mmbasic.com/

"TinyBASIC for Raspberry Pi" (2012) for Raspberry Pi News

https://www.raspberrypi.com/news/tinybasic-for-raspberry-pi/

"BBC micro:bit—A Free Single-Board PC for Every Year 7 Kid in the UK" (2015) by Sebastian Anthony for _Ars Technica_

https://arstechnica.com/gadgets/2015/07/bbc-microbit-a-free-single-board-pc-for-every-year-7-kid-in-the-uk/

"The BBC micro:bit" for the BBC

https://www.bbc.co.uk/programmes/articles/4hVG2Br1W1LKCmw8nSm9WnQ/the-bbc-micro-bit

"BASIC for micro:bit" for Coridium

https://www.coridium.us/coridium/blog/basic-for-microbit

"Small Basic: How to Use micro:bit" (2015) for Microsoft _TechNet_

https://social.technet.microsoft.com/wiki/contents/articles/40340.small-basic-how-to-use-micro-bit.aspx#h1

"The Lost World of Soviet PCs" (2015) by Benj Edwards for _PC Magazine_

https://www.pcmag.com/news/the-lost-world-of-soviet-pcs

Tweet about _Make Friends With Me, Computer!_ by Cryptkeeper D. Long (Хранитель Склепа Лонг)

https://mobile.twitter.com/octonion/status/1427844414605508622/photo/1

"5 BASIC Statements on Computational Literacy" by Mark Sample for _enculturation_

http://enculturation.net/node/5269

"Introduction: What was the Dartmouth Seminar?" (2020) by Annette Vee for the WAC Clearinghouse

https://wac.colostate.edu/resources/research/dartmouth/introduction-what-was-the-dartmouth-seminar/

"Reflection from Annette Vee and Megan McIntyre – Annette Vee" (2021) by Annette Vee for the WAC Clearinghouse

https://wac.colostate.edu/resources/research/dartmouth/critical-reflections/vee-and-mcintyre/

Chapter 6: The UK Connection, Part I

"*Stranger Things* BASIC" (2018) by Martin Müller for martin-m.org

https://martin-m.org/2018/11/28/stranger-things-basic/

"Does Bob from *Stranger Things* Know How to Program in BASIC?" (2018) by The Retro Coder

https://youtu.be/kq68kQ3b00k

"*Stranger Things* Basic Code rewritten in Python," a Reddit thread on r/geek

https://www.reddit.com/r/geek/comments/79pxs5/stranger_things_basic_code_rewritten_in_python/

"The Basics of BASIC, the Programming Language of the 1980s" (2017) by The 8-Bit Guy

https://youtu.be/seM9SqTsRG4

"Information on *Abenteuer in BASIC*" for spectrumcomputing.co.uk

https://spectrumcomputing.co.uk/entry/2000774/Book/Abenteuer_in_BASIC

"Associated Titles for Rüdeger Baumann" for spectrumcomputing.co.uk

https://spectrumcomputing.co.uk/list?label_id=12668

Look Around You: Season 1 Pilot – "Calcium"

https://youtu.be/FBaVwwuErmU

"*Look Around You:* The Programmes" for the BBC

http://www.bbc.co.uk/comedy/lookaroundyou/

BBC Micro Ignites Memories of Revolution (2008) by Hermann Hauser, Steve Furber, Sophie Wilson and John Radcliffe for BBC News

http://news.bbc.co.uk/2/hi/technology/7307636.stm

"This Mysterious Computer Could Prove Time Travel Exists" (2021) by the Nostalgia Nerd

https://youtu.be/nEDgG5MKndo

"Ghost in the Machine" (2010) for Mercurius Politicus

https://mercuriuspoliticus.wordpress.com/about/

The BBC Computer Literacy Project: 1980 to 1989

http://34.242.82.140/

"The Computer Programme" (1982)

https://www.youtube.com/watch?v=5dIcOXx3Exc&list=PLOtimvwAoYtnCtLiLspq_Gnng1XusYwPU

"The Legacy of the BBC Micro: Effecting Change in the UK's Cultures of Computing" (2012) by Tilly Blyth for the London Science Museum

https://media.nesta.org.uk/documents/the_legacy_of_bbc_micro.pdf

"How the BBC Micro Started a Computing Revolution" (2012) by Charles Arthur for the *Guardian*

https://www.theguardian.com/education/2012/jan/10/bbc-micro-school-computer-revolution

"Codes that Changed the World: BASIC" (2015) by Aleks Krotoski for *BBC Sounds*

https://www.bbc.co.uk/sounds/play/b05pnvmh

"Codecademy vs. The BBC Micro" (2019) for *Two Bit History*

https://twobithistory.org/2019/03/31/bbc-micro.html

"COMAL's Challenge to BASIC" (1981) for *Your Computer*

https://archive.org/details/your-computer-magazine-1981-11/page/n39/mode/2up

"Towards Computer Literacy: The BBC Computer Literacy Project 1979-1983" (1983) by John Radcliffe

http://34.242.82.140/media/BBC-CLP-Towards-Computer-Literacy.pdf

"Acorn's Would-be ZX Spectrum Killer, the Electron, is 30" (2013) by Tony Smith for *The Register*

https://www.theregister.com/2013/08/23/acorn_electron_history_at_30/?page=1

"Phantom Flan Flinger: The Story of the Elan Enterprise 128" (2013) by Tony Smith for *The Register*

https://www.theregister.com/2013/10/24/elan_flan_enterprise_micro_is_30_years_old?page=1

"Microcomputing, British Style" (1983) by Gregg Williams for *Byte*

https://archive.org/details/byte-magazine-1983-01/page/n41/mode/2up?view=theater

Chapter 7: The UK Connection, Part II

"Usborne 1980s Computer Books" (2021)

https://usborne.com/us/books/computer-and-coding-books

"Crasimoff's World" for RPGGeek.com

https://rpggeek.com/rpg/53405/crasimoffs-world

"Comparing BASIC Capabilities of Different Systems"

https://ldx.ca/notes/basic-capabilities.html

"Ultima and Lord British – Origins" for *The Dot Eaters*

https://web.archive.org/web/20160305021330/http://thedoteaters.com/?bitstory=ultima-and-lord-british

Chapter 8: Open Source

"History of BASIC, King James Edition" (2013) by John Browne for mobilize.net

https://www.mobilize.net/blog/history-of-basic-king-james-edition

"Microsoft Open-Sources GW-BASIC" (2020) by Rich Turner for Microsoft

https://devblogs.microsoft.com/commandline/microsoft-open-sources-gw-basic/

Open-Sourced GW-BASIC Files on GitHub

https://github.com/microsoft/GW-BASIC

"Microsoft Just Open Sourced GWBASIC!" by EEVblog2

https://youtu.be/41gK3lYejgE

"Alter Egos" (2000) by Mark Leibovich for the *Washington Post*

https://web.archive.org/web/20161225224631/https://www.washingtonpost.com/archive/politics/2000/12/31/alter-egos/91b267b0-858c-4d4e-a4bd-48f22e015f70/

"Software Column" (1977) by Paul Allen for *Personal Computing*

https://archive.org/details/PersonalComputing19770102/page/n67/mode/2up

***Perfect Bid: The Contestant Who Knew Too Much* (2017)**

https://youtu.be/HdFKZtZop7A

"Beware of GW-BASIC's Random Number Generator" by Ted Muller for *Ted's Computer World*

https://tedmuller.us/Computer/BewareBasicsRandomNumberGenerator.htm

"A Theoretical and Empirical Comparison of Mainframe, Microcomputer, and Pocket Calculator Pseudorandom Number Generators" (1993) by Patrick Onghena for *Behavior Research Methods, Instruments, & Computers*

https://link.springer.com/article/10.3758/BF03204529

"Randomness and Random Sampling Numbers" (1938) by M. G. Kendall and B. Babington Smith for the *Journal of the Royal Statistical Society*, Vol. 101, No. 1

https://www.jstor.org/stable/2980655?seq=1

"Ferranti Ltd." for the Computer History Museum

https://www.computerhistory.org/brochures/d-f/ferranti-ltd/

"Programmers' Handbook for the Manchester Electronic Computer Mark II (2nd ed.)" (1952) by Alan Turing and revised by R. A. Brooker

http://curation.cs.manchester.ac.uk/computer50/www.computer50.org/kgill/mark1/progman.html

"A Million Random Digits with 100,000 Normal Deviates" (1955) by the RAND Corporation

https://www.rand.org/pubs/monograph_reports/MR1418.html

"How Does java.util.Random Work and How Good is It?" for Javamex.com

https://www.javamex.com/tutorials/random_numbers/java_util_random_algorithm.shtml

"PC-BASIC Documentation" (2018) by Rob Hagemans

https://robhagemans.github.io/pcbasic/doc/1.2/

"BASIC Commands" (2014) by Thomas Kurtz for Dartmouth's BASIC at 50 website

https://www.dartmouth.edu/basicfifty/commands.html

"How Remote Entry Works" (2001) by Marshall Brain for HowStuffWorks.com

https://auto.howstuffworks.com/remote-entry2.htm

"Microsoft BASIC for 6502 Original Source Code [1978]" (2015) by Michael Steil for pagetable.com

https://www.pagetable.com/?p=774

"GW-BASIC Source Notes" (2020) by Michal Necasek for the OS/2 Museum

https://www.os2museum.com/wp/gw-basic-source-notes/

"Trying to Recompile the 1983 BASIC Interpreter" (Four Parts) (2020) by GynvaelEN

https://youtu.be/2QHxtcfKqgM
https://youtu.be/mVI-GL6aWMw
https://youtu.be/dI0AraZIozQ
https://youtu.be/ogaXkL7y6co

Dr. Dobb's Journal of Computer Calisthenics & Orthodontia, Volume One (1976)

https://archive.org/details/dr_dobbs_journal_vol_01/mode/2up

"The Tiny BASIC Interpretive Language IL – and Onions" (2017) by J. Alan Henning for *Troy Press*

https://troypress.com/the-tiny-basic-interpretive-language-il-and-onions/

Modified GW-BASIC Source Code on GitHub

https://github.com/tkchia/GW-BASIC

"Floppy Days Episode 113 – Monte Davidoff, Developer of Altair BASIC Floating Point" (2022), an interview conducted by Randy Kindig

https://floppydays.libsyn.com/floppy-days-113-monte-davidoff-developer-of-altair-basic-floating-point

"Bill Gates Once Released a Swarm of Mosquitoes on a Crowd to Make a Point about Malaria" (2017) by Yoni Blumberg for CNBC.com

https://www.cnbc.com/2017/11/28/bill-gates-released-swarming-mosquitoes-to-make-a-point-about-malaria.html

ACKNOWLEDGMENTS

First and foremost, I would like to thank Thomas Kurtz, who graciously took the time to answer several critical BASIC history questions I posed to him.

Second, I'd like to thank my readers, especially those who pored through *Endless Loop* and then publicly commented on the book. Their unsolicited suggestions—such as to offer more description of the 1980s home computer scene in the United Kingdom; recount the history of the language on minicomputers; write more on the development of certain BASIC dialects on microcomputers, especially the TI-99/4; present a more robust examination of why, precisely, early language-design decisions were made; devote more space to the multifarious factors that caused the language's decline; include a discussion of BASIC on microcontrollers; provide more technical details overall; and incorporate additional BASIC anecdotes—led to several chapters, and numerous portions of other chapters, in GOSUB WITHOUT RETURN.

Third, I must give heartfelt thanks to the retro coders around the globe, the countless people in the retrocomputing community who keep old hardware and software alive. You understand a key fact about technology: just because something is newer doesn't always mean it's better. While rejecting "chronological snobbery," which is, as C. S. Lewis put it, "the uncritical acceptance of the intellectual climate of our own age and the assumption that whatever has gone out of date is on that count discredited," you also believe to your core that BASIC is most definitely not a "childish thing"—and so it *never* needs to be put away.

My method of writing a book like this one is aligned with historian Studs Terkel's process: "Some days are more sunny than others, some hours less astonishing than I'd hoped for…but it is, for better or worse, in my hands. I'd like to believe I'm the old-time cobbler, making the whole shoe." Nevertheless, it hasn't escaped my notice that, at times, my reach has exceeded my grasp, and since my work is in the public sphere, it cannot be exempt from criticism. As the novelist David Mitchell writes in *Black Swan Green*, "If you show someone something you've written, you give them a sharpened stake, lie down in your coffin, and say, 'When you're ready.'" Any book, when set loose to find an audience and thus sink or swim, no longer belongs to the author but to its readers—to do with it what they may, whether that be to enjoy it, learn from it, tear it apart, or, indeed, ignore the very fact of its existence.

With all that said, any errors and omissions in the text are completely unintentional, but entirely my fault.

ABOUT THE AUTHOR

Mark Jones Lorenzo, a teacher of mathematics and computer programming, is the author of *Endless Loop: The History of the BASIC Programming Language* as well as a number of other books. He lives in Pennsylvania with his dogs.

Printed in Great Britain
by Amazon

26084608R00205